Neurosis
and
Civilization

MICHAEL SCHNEIDER

NEUROSIS AND CIVILIZATION

A Marxist/Freudian Synthesis

translated by Michael Roloff

A Continuum Book
THE SEABURY PRESS • NEW YORK

The Seabury Press
815 Second Avenue
New York, N.Y. 10017

English translation © 1975 by The Seabury Press
Designed by Carol Basen
Printed in the United States of America

Library of Congress Cataloging in Publication Data

Schneider, Michael, 1943-
   Neurosis and civilization: a Marxist-Freudian synthesis

   (A Continuum book)
   1. Psychoanalysis.   2. Communism and society.
I. Title.
BF173.S37313   335.43'8'1501952   75-12987
ISBN 0-8164-9230-1

Contents

Introduction

The controversy between Marxism and psychoanalysis is as old as psychoanalysis itself. It reached its historical apogee at the end of the twenties when an irreparable break occurred between orthodox Marxists (that is, Stalinists) on the one hand and socialist Freudians (the "Freudo-Marxists") and the Frankfurt School on the other. During the Stalinist era in the East and the National Socialist dictatorship in the West the discussion between Marxism and psychoanalysis was put on ice for several decades. It did not become topical again until the re-awakening of the European class struggle in Italy, France, the Federal Republic of Germany, and the United States in the sixties.

Psychoanalysis played an important role in the emancipation of the middle-class intellectuals during the anti-authoritarian phase of the student-protest movement, particularly in France. Yet to a certain degree the students' conflict with the internal authorities and with their own sexually circumscribed situation was also a manifestation of class privilege. Only middle-class youth could afford to indulge in extensive preoccupation with the subjective aspect of their existence. That is because they had not directly experienced the domination of capital in the factory or in the office but only at secondhand, in their family, their schools, and their universities. On the other hand, the extremely long period of material dependence of middle-class youth on families and parents, and their entrance into the socially productive process only after a protracted educational period, has succeeded in creating a set of unique psychological problems towards which psychoanalysis made, or at least promised to make, a contribution. However, for obvious reasons it played almost no role at all in the emancipation of proletarian youth. For their psychology has largely been determined in a milieu where the social and pathogenetic side-effects are self-enclosed and thus not generally accessible to psychoanalytical observation. The nature of the various psychological problems of middle-class intellectuals, however, namely, those who are pursuing some sort of emancipation, was related not only to their specific class but also to their specific generation. Moreover, the young postwar generation has had to deal to a particularly high degree with an authoritarian and, in Germany, Nazi-fascistic older generation; and this factor lent additional significance to its conflict with psychoanalysis and with various types of "authoritarian personality" with which it has been confronted.

During the later, more "organized" phase of the student-protest movement, any coming-to-terms with psychoanalysis was once again blocked, this time by the splinter parties of the young Left. The convulsive attempt of the organized socialist movement to link up with a traditional line, whether Bolshevik or Stalinist, had a number of consequences, one being the revival of Bolshevik as well as Stalinist aversion to psychoanalysis. Any kind of preoccupation with the "subjective factor" was from then on regarded as *"petit bourgeois,"* "spontaneistic," "anarchistic," and so on. Today's situation, in the meantime, resembles that of the twenties: the "economistic" allies of W. Pieck and the psychological allies of W. Reich again confront one another irreconcilably because each side opposes in the other what it itself lacks. The present organized condemnation of psychoanalysis by neo-Stalinism, revisionism, and Maoism reproduces unchanged all of the anti-Freudian prejudices of the thirties.

Instead of conducting a Stalinist show trial of psychoanalysis all over again, however, it is rather time for the prosecution to submit itself to a genuine, that is to say, dialectical-materialist "trial." And for this purpose it is necessary to revive the Stalinist show trial once more—but critically. It is necessary, for one thing, because almost all of the topical arguments which the anti-Freudian Left marshals against psychoanalysis have been borrowed from the catechism of the Stalinist inquisition of the twenties and thirties. And it is necessary because, on the other hand, the pro-Freudian Left (inasmuch as it is influenced by the Frankfurt School and by German Freudo-Marxism) is strapped with the bourgeois ideology of "Freudicism," an ideology which is justifiably condemned by Stalinist criticism even now. While the Stalinists have generally wished to dismiss psychoanalysis altogether, seeking to liquidate its subversive together with its bourgeois side, the pro-Freudian Left generally has had no idea where to draw the line between the subversive investigator of sexuality and the conservative critic of culture and neurosis. While the former approach runs the danger of running aground in undialectical negation, the latter founders on an undialectical affirmation.

The present work, on the contrary, has its starting point in the "combinative character" of Freud's work. It seeks to retain the ambivalence between the psychological-materialistic empiricism and bourgeois ideology, between the subversive, psychoanalytical knowledge and bourgeois anthropology, which runs through Freud's work—so as to overcome the false alternatives between "pure" Left-bourgeois pro-Freudians on the one hand and "pure" orthodox-Marxist anti-Freudians on the other. One can do justice to the combinative character of Freud's work neither with a simple "pro" nor with a simple "contra." For Marxists today it is a question of "negating" [*aufheben*] in the threefold Hegelian sense: to "retain," to "destroy," and to "raise to a higher level." The three parts of this book correspond to these three stages of Hegelian negation. The thrust of the first part—"With Freud Against a Vulgarized Marxism"—is to "retain" the dialectical-materialistically subversive, social-ideologically critical side of Freud's work and to defend it against its Stalinist and neo-Stalinist inquisitors. In Part Two—"With Marx Against the Bourgeois Ideology of Psychoanalysis"—the point is to lay bare and "destroy" the bourgeois-idealistic anthropology of Freud, which has surreptitiously entered almost all psychoanalytical categories and which has also largely escaped the notice of the German Freudo-Marxists and the Frankfurt School. In Part Three—"The Utilization of Capital and Psychic Impoverishment, or Society as Illness"—I have sought to historicize and materialize the heart of Freud's theory, his dichotomous psychology of the ego and id in general and his theory of neurosis (and psychoanalysis) in particular; that is, I have sought to derive Freud's phenomenological description of the structure of the "bourgeois psyche" from the very laws of the economic movement of bourgeois society.

In imperialistic metropolises the contradiction between increasing material well-being and affluence (of which the capitalist class of course enjoys the lion's share) on the one hand and the increasing psychological destitution and illness on the other is becoming drastically marked. This contradiction is new in its historical acuteness and therefore requires a new political interpretation which can draw the connection between the utilization of capital and psychic impoverishment, which can grasp it propagandizingly; but it also requires a new political solution which must contain a growing "therapeutic" dimension.

The question is whether and to what extent psychoanalysis can make a contribution in this respect. In my opinion, it can do so under two conditions: firstly, if it faces up to the critique of political economy, so that the secret ideological and historical dimension, which has surreptitiously entered its categories, can be made manifest; secondly, if it is willing to make the effort to find new materialistic causes for the neurosis that it has described. Instead of totally rejecting Freud's psychoanalytic theories of neurosis, we must begin to "stand them on their feet." While classical psychoanalysis has limited itself to treating the patient *within* society, it has now become the task of a materialistically emancipatory psychoanalysis to treat society itself as an illness. Whereas classical psychoanalysis saw its therapeutic task as adjusting the allegedly "ill" to an allegedly "healthy" society, the therapeutic objective of an emancipatory psychoanalysis must be to translate the element of unconscious subversion and passive resistance that expresses itself in this illness into a conscious *political* subversion and into active political resistance to an "ill" society.

Berlin, December 1972

part one
With Freud
Against Vulgar
Marxism

The truth is the totality.

HEGEL

1. The Stalinist Show Trial of Psychoanalysis

The Methodological Difficulties of Psychoanalysis

How did the Stalinist prosecution propose to prove its case in its trial of psychoanalysis? What criteria and premises did it use as its point of departure? What picture did it have of psychoanalysis?

The Stalinist plaintiffs, employing every means at their disposal, especially Pavlov's theory of reflexes, sought to convict Freud's psychology of idealism. According to Jurinec, "Today psychoanalysis . . . idealism clothed in the latest fashion, is infiltrating the Marxist camp . . . Freud as well as the Freudians do not even acknowledge the psycho-physical parallelism. On the contrary, they consider it one of Freud's greatest achievements that he looks for the causes of nervous disorders not in physiological but in purely mental origins, in contrast to the early psycho-neurologists."[1] The very concepts of psyche and psychic energy were a provocation to vulgarized Russian materialism which stood completely under the sway of Pavlov's discoveries. This materialism, which regarded human beings as utterly determined by physical and chemical processes, had not developed beyond its eighteenth and nineteenth-century infancy and had already been severely criticized by Marx and Engels. Even today psychoanalysis is still being criticized in the name of a mechanical materialism for which every independent psychological law is a Platonic phantom. For example, K. Wells remarks, "The idealistic orientation of psychoanalysis manifests itself in different ways, the first and most important of which being Freud's treatment of human consciousness. Although Freud paid lip service to the proposition that the mind is a function of the brain, he develops a purely spiritual psychology and psychotherapy without reference to the functioning of the brain. [. . .] He treats the immaterial spirit as an entity with its own 'psychic energy.'"[2]

Freud's psychology of instincts in reality is as equally well armed against the mechanical-materialistic materialism of someone like Vogt ("thought is the secretion of the brain") as it is against the Platonic idealism of traditional philosophy and psychology ("the spirit creates the body"). Freud observes, for example: "By an instinct is provisionally to be understood the psychical representation of an endosomatic, continuously flowing source of stimulation as contrasted with a 'stimulus' which is set up by single excitations coming from without. The concept of instinct is thus one of those lying on the frontier between the mental and the physical. [. . .] The source of an instinct is a process of excitation occurring in an organ and the immediate aim of the instinct lies in the removal of this organic stimulus."[3] Although Freud's attention focussed particularly on an investigation of the psychological side of instinctual activity, he never lost sight of the somatic side, the "inner-somatic source of excitation," the organic source of the instinct. Time and again he expressed the hope that psychoanalysis would one day be put on an organic footing; and it was with the concept of "sexual chemistry," which played a large role in his theory of the libido, that he set his sights on that "psychic parallelism" which orthodox Marxist criticism has accused him of having suppressed.

Modern, psychoanalytically oriented animal psychology has reached the conclusion in the meantime that Pavlov, the classic witness of Russian orthodoxy, and his teaching of the "simple" and "conditioned reflex" confirm psychoanalysis precisely when its physiological gap appeared at its widest. The Russian Marxists have always triumphantly accused the Freudians of the fact that they could not even verify the "economic-dynamic laws" of the instincts with the generally acknowledged Pavlovian theory of conditioned reflexes; but modern animal psychology has shown that no basic contradiction exists between the Pavlovian theory and Freud's theory of instincts. According to Brun, Freud's concept of the super-ego is to be understood in Pavlov's sense as "a conditioned mental reflex to conform to social behavior"; just as Freud's distinction between "primary instincts" bound to the id and "secondary instincts" attached to the ego, that is, super-ego, is equivalent to Pavlov's distinction between "simple conditioned" and "conditioned" reflexes. Brun continues: "The basic dynamic-economic laws of the instincts under normal and pathological conditions—which Freud discovered, of all places, in the most complicated of test objects, the human being with disturbed instincts—were confirmed by modern animal psychology in every respect: (a) the mechanism of direct discharge of energy of a dammed-up instinct in the form of anxious restlessness (anxiety neurosis); (b) regression, that is, the return of the instincts to an earlier stage of individual or phylo-behavior (ontogenetic or phylogenetic regression or atavism); (c) the displacement compensation, that is, compensatory gratification for the withdrawal of an instinctual object during the phase when an instinct attained self-realization; (d) transference of an instinct to a surrogate object; (e) the—usually pathological—reaction-formation against the repressed instinct with over-emphasis on the repressing authority."[4]

If this "psychic parallelism" can be proved, this equivalence between Freud's theory of instincts and Pavlov's theory of reflexes, that does not mean, however, that every mental phenomenon is the immediate product of the reflexive and physiological processes that underlie it—just as little as Marx claimed that ideological phenomena are unmediated secretions of the factory. Psychic phenomena are indeed immediately bound to definite biological and physiological functions and changes; but within this biologically determined complex they obey their own independent organically and physiologically determined laws. A neurotic symptom such as the nervous twitch of an eye, although obviously manifesting itself physically, nevertheless is not caused by a physical disturbance, say of the facial muscles. Rather its cause is to be sought in the disturbance of the psycho-social process. That is why Freud's concept of instincts is not some mechanistic-idealistic construct which allows one to "conduct a Janus-like politics in relation to materialism and idealism," as Jurinec charged.[5] Instead it is the expression of the "qualitative leap" between the biological-physiological and the psychological level.

To vulgar Russian Marxism (and its heirs today) every independent physiological law represented a Platonic illusion. Thus Jurinec criticized the laws of "ego-defense" (projection, for example) which psychoanalysis had discovered as "idealistic prejudice." The fact that the ego is intent on "removing" an embarrassing emotion or a concept unacceptable to consciousness by projecting one or the other onto another person seemed to vulgar Marxist rationalism a reversion to mysticism. "By this means," according to Jurinec, "the individual's psychic world transforms itself into the outer world; the upper membrane of the brain becomes the knot where mystical projection occurs [. . .] Absolute subjectivism, stylized into a sumptuous dress of physiology [. . .]"[6] Meanwhile this "absolute subjectivism" became a "material force" in the form, for example, of anti-Semitism, in which millions of people projected their repressed anti-Semitic and sexual resentments onto the "filthy-money Jews." The Marxist criticism is justifiable only where—instead of attacking the clinical facts of projection—it takes aim at Freud's "projective" relationship to history (also compare pp. 64f), according to which the patriarchal state and the patriarchal God are nothing but institutionalized projections of the Oedipus complex. Here Jurinec is right when he says that "individual psychic content transforms itself into the outer world."

Vulgar Marxist critique also called Freud an "idealist" and "Platonist" where—as in his ego and neurosis physiology—he proved the relative independence of the mental and psycho-physiological processes from the physiological and organic functions. On the other hand, they attacked him as a "mechanical materialist" when he sought to represent his discoveries —especially in the realm of the unconscious—by employing auxiliary concepts from physics, thermo-dynamics, and other scientific areas (doing so perhaps in order to buttress psychoanalysis as a natural science). Thus Jurinec goes on to say: "As with Herbart, these atomic realities contain dynamic qualities. They transmit impulses to each other and inhibit each other during transition into consciousness, etc. [. . .] Mental phenomenon in a certain sense is thus made the equivalent of a box full of atoms in the manner of the kinetic theory of gases."[7] When Freud employed the language of physics to give metaphorical expression to the unconscious, vulgar Marxism insisted on the qualitative difference between physical and psychological reality; but when Freud accounted for this qualitative difference with his own nomenclature ("libido," "id," and so forth) the Marxist critics accused him of failing to express psychological reality in the precise language of the natural sciences. Stoljarov, for instance, discredited the psychoanalytical method of self-observation and free association as "an extremely subjective form of onesidedness" because it totally ignored one of the principles of Marxist psychology: "Self-observation under control of objective methods."[8]

This charge against the psychoanalytic method, which some Marxists still make today, derives from a positivistic, that is, scientistic conception of science whose sole criterion is quantification. However, in contrast to the exact sciences, psychoanalysis (like biology) has to do with highly complex phylo-specific living organisms, which is why it cannot quantify and mathematicize either in its research or in its results. Thus L. Rosenkötter remarks: "In physics, for example, the measured size and the measuring instruments must be as unequal as possible so that the former is not altered by the measuring process. This prerequisite, however, does not hold true for the mental processes. We grasp the mental processes of others with something of the same kind, that is, with our own mental processes which seek to empathize with the events in other psyches by identifying with them. That means that the act of perception is a different one from the rational and objective process of the exact sciences."[9]

The methodological difficulties of psychoanalysis are comparable to those of atomic physics which Heisenberg defined in his famous "uncertainty principle," namely, that the method of investigating an object alters it. Just as little as we can measure the authentic speed of an elementary particle—because the measuring process itself provides it with energy, that is, alters its speed—can psychoanalysis observe the unconscious *in statu nascendi*, because the investigative process, that is, the making conscious, eliminates its quality of being unconscious. The methodological paradox of psychoanalysis consists in articulating the speechlessness of the unconscious in the language of consciousness, for—according to Freud—the unconscious is that aspect which has not been socialized through language: "[. . .] the real difference between the unconscious and preconscious idea (thought) consists in this: that the former is carried by some material which remains unknown, whereas the latter (the preconscious) is in addition brought into connection with word presentations."[10] Just as higher mathematics had to solve the paradox of expressing the world of imaginary numbers in the medium of real numbers, so Freud was confronted with the paradoxical task of reconstructing the speechless world of neurosis in the medium of language.

Freud could scarcely have overcome his methodological difficulties with a "borrowed language" which he derived from the field of atomic physics, biology, the philosophy of his time, and even from mythology ("eros," "Oedipus complex," "narcissism," and the like). Freud had to be, as Althusser says, "his own father, and construct the theoretical framework for his discoveries with his own hands. With strings taken from every side, he had to construct the net with which he was supposed to catch, in the depth of blind experience, the great fish of the unconscious which mankind calls mute because it speaks when they sleep."[11] This "borrowed language" was for Russian orthodoxy proof of the "eclecticism" and "aestheticism" (Jurinec) of Freud's theory. The fact that Freud had adopted Nietzsche's concept of the "id" was sufficient reason to dismiss the entire theory of the unconscious as a new psychological version of *Lebensphilosophie* and German Romantic philosophy. According to Jurinec, "Freud misused this concept [of the 'id'] and it finally becomes the *asylum ignorantiae* which is supposed to help its author through every difficulty in the conscious and hyperconscious processes. With the concept of the 'id' we enter a region where all cats are gray. The origin of the 'id' is obvious. It is a pale reflection of German Romantic philosophy, the modernized 'absolute' of Schelling. As nature and spirit, reality and idea are secretions of the womb of the absolute in Schelling, the 'ego' and 'super-ego' are products of the 'id' in Freud."[12] In fact, however, even though Freud's theory of instinct and culture did manifest a certain proximity to German *Lebensphilosophie* (compare also pp. 67f), it did not consider the "id" as an absolute principle, but rather as a methodological auxiliary concept for the purpose of distinguishing the uniqueness of the conscious processes as "secondary processes." The "id" is no *asylum ignorantiae* but a kind of metaphor for a psychic new-found-land ruled by other forces than the world of consciousness, which had been the object of traditional psychological and philosophical efforts just as the atomic micro-world was a physical new-found-land ruled by forces other than the mechanical Newtonian universe. Atomic and inner-atomic events could no more be interpreted with the concepts and formulas of classical mechanics than could the unconscious world and the "archaic logic" that governed it be interpreted by means of traditional "Aristotelian" logic. The vulgar Marxist accusation that can still be heard today, namely, that Freud never provided an exact definition of the "id," the "unconscious," is therefore just as irrelevant as the analogous accusation on the part of classical mechanics that atomic physics has never provided an unequivocal model of the atom. Just as atomic physics has developed apparently contradictory models of the atom, such as the wave model and the corpuscle model, each of which is capable of explaining certain aspects of the atomic world, so Freud has developed different models of the psychic apparatus—such as the dynamic (unconscious, preconscious, conscious), the topological (id, ego, super-ego), and the energetic (libido) model, each of which is capable of explaining a particular aspect of psychic activity, though primarily the unconscious.

Therefore it is simple-minded for vulgar Marxist criticism, now as then, to play these different models off against each other and thereby demonstrate their "discrepancies." Jurinec says, for example: "And the 'id' plays different roles. Once it appears in a certain form as absolutely undifferentiated [. . .] soon it assumes the function of the unconscious and transforms itself into the expression of the pleasure principle [. . .] soon it is a useful means for explaining to us the source of our feelings."[13] How difficult a task it would be for vulgarized Marxism to have to imagine the atom simultaneously as a wave process and as a material corpuscle as atomic physics asks it to do, if it still cannot get the hang of the three functions of the "id" metaphor—the unconscious, the pleasure principle, and the source, that is, the refuge of feelings.

Freud's Psychology of Conflict and Dialectical Logic

What the anger of the vulgar Marxists really amounts to is that Freud discovered a world that could not be contained in the categories of political economy. These schoolmasters had reached the end of their wisdom when confronted with the world of the unconscious, with its "archaic" laws of "compression," "compensation," and "inversion" (compare also Freud's *The Interpretation of Dreams*[14]). That is why they tried, whenever possible, to prove that Freud was breaking the laws of dialectical materialism.

According to the Stalinist critics, the dynamic model of the mental apparatus was particularly lacking in credibility, as Jurinec sought to prove by citing Freud's work on humor: "Freud offers us a peculiar theory of dialectics in his work 'The Joke and Its Relationship to the Unconscious' [. . .] A characteristic of the joke is its transition from contradiction to contradiction, its 'refined' derision of logic. These leaps are an expression of the psyche's inborn tendency to nonsense and reflect the a-logical nature of the unconscious [. . .] But dialectic is what is nonsense for Freud: it appears in the joke but the whole activity of the unconscious is intent on removing the senselessness."[15] Thus from the fact that Freud had in the joke tracked down the unconscious sense in seeming nonsense, Jurinec was able to conclude that dialectic for Freud was nonsense. But it was particularly in his work on the joke that Freud brilliantly demonstrated the dialectic of conscious and unconscious; for, as he showed, it is in humor that socially unacceptable aggressive and sexual wishes, which have been repressed into the unconscious, come into open conflict with the dominant consciousness. The joke has its liberating effect because the psychic energy deployed for the repression and displacement of the socially despised instinctual impulses is temporarily negated and "liberated" in laughter.

Where the Stalinist critics did in fact register an "absence of dialectics" they sought to make the psychoanalytic method responsible for this "absence" instead of its object. J. Gabel, taking the example of schizophrenia, has demonstrated how the psycho-pathological world of consciousness is characterized by "failure," that is, stoppage of dialectical movement.[16] From the clinically provable fact that pathological consciousness liquidates its own contradictions by "displacing" or "projecting" one part of the contradiction, the vulgar Russian Marxists have concluded that Freud's concept of consciousness was undialectical. That is because Freud's theory of "ambivalence of feelings" was, in their opinion, irreconcilable with the picture of dialectic leaps of consciousness from step to step as Hegel had provided in *The Phenomenology of the Spirit.*[17] They did not comprehend that the pathological consciousness with which Freud was dealing can no longer react dialectically to reality but internalizes its contradictions as an "ambivalence of feelings." According to Foucault: "The conflict produced by the neurotic compromise is not simply an external contradiction of the objective situation, but is an immanent contradiction whose parts mingle in such a way that the compromise, instead of producing a solution, finally only deepens the conflict [. . .] The pathological contradiction is not the same as the normal conflict; the latter enters the subject's affective life from the outside; it produces contradictory forms of behavior in the subject, makes it waver [. . .] Where the normal individual experiences a contradiction the ill individual has a contradictory experience [. . .] Normal conflict or ambiguity of the situation; pathological conflict or ambivalence of experience."[18]

However, what the vulgar Russian Marxists considered the worst offense against dialectical materialism was Freud's concept of "repetition compulsion" [*Wiederholungszwang*]. They declared that the law of repetition compulsion disputed the laws of dialectical development of nature and society. Rather, like Nietzsche's concept of the "eternal return," it was an expression of a cyclical conception of history. Again these schoolmasters made Freud responsible for having discovered a phenomenon that did not seem to fit into their "healthy" world-view of vulgar Marxism, namely, psychosexual developmental disturbances and inhibitions which manifest themselves clinically as the "compulsion to repeat." Freud had proved that every instinctual repression throws the libido back to an earlier (oral, anal, phallic) stage and that the repressed element "returns" in dreams, slips of the tongue, and (neurotic or psychotic) symptoms. Repetition compulsion as a clinical fact can no more be denied than the physical fact of gravitation. "And upon close inspection," it becomes apparent, as W. Reich has shown, "that Freud's concept of repetition turns out to be dialectical in every respect. For what is repeated is invariably the old as well as something altogether new: the old in a new garb or as a new function."[19]

Reich demonstrated the reconcilability of repetition compulsion with the principles of dialectical logic while using the process of symptom formation: "What, then," he asked, "does the dialectical nature of symptom formation consist in? On the one hand, there are the demands of instinct, and on the other hand, there is reality which prohibits or punishes its gratification; this contradictory situation calls for a solution. The ego is too weak to resist reality, but also too weak to control the urge. [. . .] It [this conflict] is now dealt with in such a way that the ego, ostensibly serving the dictates of society, but really acting in order not to be punished or destroyed, [. . .] represses the urge. Thus repression is the consequence of a contradiction which cannot be resolved under conditions of consciousness. The becoming unconscious of the urge is a temporary, albeit pathological, solution of the conflict. Second phase: after the repression of the wish, which has been both denied and affirmed by the ego, the ego itself is now changed; its consciousness is poorer by one component (instinct) and richer by another (temporary peace). The instinct, however, can no more relinquish its urge for gratification when it is suppressed than when it is conscious—if anything, less, because it is no longer subject to the controls of consciousness. Repression posits its own destruction, since as a result of repression, instinctual energy is powerfully dammed up until it finally breaks through the repression. The new process of breaking through the repression is a result of the contradiction between suppression and the increased strength of the dammed-up instinct; just as repression itself was a result of the contradiction between the instinctual wish and its denial by the outside world (given the condition that the ego is weak). Thus there is no such thing as a tendency toward symptom formation; we have seen how the development arises from the contradictions of psychological conflict. As soon as there is repression there are also the conditions for its breakthrough on account of the increased energy of the dammed-up unsatisfied instinct. Does the breakthrough of the repression in the second phase restore the initial situation? Yes and no. Yes, insofar as the instinct once again dominates the ego; no, insofar as it reappears in the conscious as a symptom, that is to say, in changed or disguised form. The symptom contains the old element—the instinct—but also, at the same time, its opposite, the resistance of the ego. In the second phase (symptom) the original contradictions are therefore united in the same phenomenon. That phenomenon itself is a negation (breakthrough) of a negation (repression)."[20]

The Marxist critique of recurrence compulsion is only justified where Freud stylized this clinical fact into a metaphysical principle and postulates, as in *Beyond the Pleasure Principle,* a generally applicable "nirvana principle"—a general human trait, the instinct for "repetition," for a return to "primitive, primordial conditions," a "death instinct." Indeed, as Stalinist criticism has emphasized, Freud's theory of instincts with its nirvana principle "inadvertently entered the harbor of Schopenhauer's philosophy, for whom death was the actual 'result of life,' and thus the purpose of life, but the sexual instinct the embodiment of the will to life."[21] By having raised Haeckel's "basic biogenetic law" that ontogenesis *repeats* phylogenesis to a metaphysical principle, Freud transformed his political conservatism into an anthropological confession of faith. That is, like decadent bourgeois philosophers he mistook the "death instinct" of a murderous and suicidal class, the imperialist bourgeoisie, for the "instinctive nature of man *as such.*"

The theory of repetition compulsion earned for psychoanalysis the accusation that its entire anthropology was ruled by a psychological determinism irreconcilable with dialectical materialism. This charge has recently been levelled again by Wells: "The manner in which the child gets through the various infantile phases and its individual variations determines the consciousness of the adult. Character qualities and the 'choice' of neurosis are determined from childhood on [. . .] The determination of consciousness through racial inheritance and repressed infantile memories only admits of quantitative changes [. . .] The only thing that develops is what was there from the very beginning: the inborn destiny, the determined complex and complexes, and their consequences [. . .] Since he [Freud] derives transformations from a purely predetermined and quantitative letting-itself-unfold, he confesses to a static rather than to a changeable order of things."[22] Freud's discovery that the mature consciousness is determined, not only by its economic existence, but also its (of course, economically mediated) childhood existence, the so-called infantile instinctual destiny, was such a provocation for the vulgar Marxist mind that even today it abhors this supposition as part of a fatalistic and predeterminist philosophy.

The Marxist charge of predeterminism against psychoanalysis is justified insofar as it is largely blind to the economic and social determinants of personality development. (Compare also pp. 107f.) But Marxist anthropology in turn must admit to the accusation that it has criminally neglected the psychosexual determinants of personality formation which Freud has discovered. Thus I. Caruso is correct when he remarks, in the same vein as Sartre, that "Marxist anthropology has neglected the child from the very beginning. And, therefore, the adult too has been shortchanged in some respects [. . .] 'Official Marxism,' on the other hand, has treated the human being as a member of a concrete society but to a certain degree as an *abstract* member of the same. Despite several attempts in the right direction, Marxism is still waiting for a personal psychology which treats this member as a concrete human being in a concrete society."[23] There is no doubt that the psychoanalytical theory of personality—despite its inherent bourgeois ideology and its neglect of various socio-economic determinants in the development of instinct and character—has provided the most important contribution to the "personal psychology" of the bourgeois era to date. The charge of psychological determinism itself usually is guilty of an economic determinism which cannot comprehend "personal psychology" except as an "abstract" result of a socio-economic system of vectors.

For a long time Freud's "monistic" ("libido") and, later, "dualistic" ("eros" and "thanatos," "libido" and "aggression") formulation of the concept of instinct prevented Marxism from seeing that the lasting operative principle in the psychoanalytical theory of personality is the principle of dialectical negation. For example, the object-libido arises from the narcissistic-libido and can be changed back into the latter at any time. So the process of identification replaces the original object-cathexis: by identifying with the educators the child negates them (that is, in its relationship to them in the outside world), but at the same time it affirms them by internalizing them (that is, by accepting them in altered form in its ego-ideal). The process of identification simultaneously initiates the formation of the super-ego: what originally was fear of punishment ("actual fear") becomes moral inhibition (conscience). The contradiction between instinct-ego and outerworld thus produces the new contradiction between instinct-ego and super-ego. Freud also conceived of neurosis and perversion as dialectically coupled contraries: neurosis is the "negative of perversion" because the perversion lives out the forbidden instinctual impulses which the neurotic opposes, that is, represses. In the psychoanalytic theory of character, "defense mechanisms" (reaction formations) are understood as the negation of "primary" instinctual impulses. Thus, for example, a cruel child can become the most empathetic person, although a thorough analysis might be able to demonstrate the old cruelties within the empathy. A child that likes filth can later become obsessed with cleanliness; a curious and sensual child can later become a painfully discrete and ascetic person; and so forth.

The psychoanalytical interpretation of dreams, too, is largely determined by the dialectical principles of "dialectical negation" and "unity of opposites." As Freud says: "Among the most surprising findings is the way in which the dream-work treats contraries that occur in the latent dream [. . .] Well, contraries are treated in the same way as conformities, and that is with a special preference for expressing them by the same manifest element. Thus an element in the manifest dream which is capable of having a contrary may equally well be expressing itself or its contrary or both together."[24] Especially does Freud's interpretation of dreams refute the vulgar Marxist charge that psychoanalysis only creates a formal symbolic link between individual objects and events (something that Jurinec called "aestheticism") instead of mirroring their true internal connection. Reuben Osborn too has pointed out that the dream-life frequently provides a truer, more accurate, that is, more materialistic reflection of the true internal connection between individual objects and events than the waking consciousness which the vulgar Marxists tout so highly. "In the waking condition [. . .] thought is generalized; ideas are formed through abstractions of the concrete. The concrete is perceived in abstract concepts while in the dream abstract ideas ['dream thoughts'—author] are presented in concrete form. [. . .] The habit of abstracting general qualities from experience suggests a tendency to turn into concrete form what is actually in a state of flux. On the other hand, the dream-life represents its content in a form of highly dramatic actions. In the waking condition the objects are observed as isolated and separate from one another. Dream-life, on the other hand, appears to reflect in a more precise, if also stranger, manner the connection between things, for it is prepared to use a thing to symbolize another which appears to have no connection with it when regarded in a state of wakefulness."[25] It is precisely Freud's analysis of dreams which uncovers the frequently abnormal and yet real connection between individual things and events, connections of which the vulgar Marxists in their waking consciousness normally would not even dare to "dream."

The third principle of dialectical logic, that of the "leap of quantity into quality," also plays a remarkable role in Freud's psychology. Freud assigned great significance to the quality-quantity relationship in the conflicting energies of the psychic apparatus: "You will no doubt have observed that in these last discussions I have introduced a fresh factor into the structure of the aetiological chain—namely the quantity, the magnitude of the energies concerned. We have still to take this factor into account everywhere. A pure qualitative analysis of the aetiological determinants is not enough [. . .] We must tell ourselves that the conflict between two trends does not break out till certain intensities of cathexis have been reached. [. . .] The quantitative factor is no less decisive as regards capacity to resist neurotic illness. It is a matter of *what quota* of unemployed libido a person is able to hold in suspension and of *how large a fraction* of his libido he is able to divert from sexual to sublimated aims."[26] Freud here states quite explicitly that the law of the leap of quantity into quality takes effect during the creation of neuroses; that the libido makes "qualitative" leaps—for example, in the form of symptoms —only during a certain quantity, that is, degree of intensity, of repression.

The long-standing controversy between Marxist orthodoxy and socialist Freudians whether psychoanalysis is a dialectical psychology cannot be answered with an unequivocal yes or no. Psychoanalysis, inasmuch as it functions as a psychology of conflict—as in its model of psychosexual development and in its analysis of dreams, slips, and neuroses—is based, if not explicitly, on dialectical principles. However, it keeps losing the dialectic wherever it anthropologizes the insights it has won from its experience in a certain culture- and class-bound "clinic" and replaces historical dialectic between social forms of production and behavior and the corresponding forms of instinctual and ego development (compare also p. 123) with a biological conception of the instinctual nature of mankind. Dialectic, so to speak, governs only the inner-political relationships of psychoanalysis, that is, wherever it seeks to grasp the intrapsychic conflict-dynamic of the bourgeois individual. In its "foreign-policy" relationships, however, that is, wherever it becomes a question of the dialectic of socio-economic and instinctual structure, it is blind. Here the crudest kind of idealism, biologism, and psychologism is dominant.

The Unconscious Subversion of Reified Consciousness

Marxists have completely misunderstood Freud's two central discoveries, that of the unconscious and of "infantile sexuality." August Thalheimer, for example, saw them as proof of the reactionary character of psychoanalysis. In 1926 he directed the following tirade against Freud: "Two elements have made Freud the prophet of a particular state of bourgeois degeneration. The first of these is his descent from the world of lucid consciousness into the underworld of the 'dark unconscious' and its dark drives—and simultaneously its justification, the rehabilitation of what appears when you scratch the average philistine. Secondly, he made sexuality the axis of the world. Especially in this respect, Freud was the prophet of a slovenly Viennese philistinism."[27] Orthodox Marxism was incapable of distinguishing between the revolutionary discoveries of the unconscious and infantile sexuality on the one hand and Freud's decadent bourgeois cultural philosophy on the other. What it regarded as an especially pornographic provocation was the naturalistic "inner-political" principle of psychoanalysis, that is, its attempt to seek the origin of all so-called "higher values" of bourgeois society, such as love ethics or religion, in the very manifestations of "lower" values, in other words in manifestations and perversions of the primary "sexual instinct." Since the sexual instinct occupied a "low" place in the bourgeois scale of values, psychoanalysis was bound to strike bourgeois as well as Marxist consciousness as an attempt to understand everything exclusively in sexual terms. The narcissistic insult which Freud administered to bourgeois and vulgar Marxist consciousness, namely, that the "ego" is no longer ruler of its own house but is largely dominated by unconscious instinctual forces, garnered for it the broad accusation of being "pan-sexual." However, psychoanalysis turned into pan-sexualism only when it tried to play the high role of theory of history and reduced the history of class struggle to an anthropological conflict between the instincts, to the "eternal conflict between Eros and Thanatos." (See also p. 65.) Psychoanalysis's inner-analytical principle, to track down the hidden unconscious drives behind conscious utterances and to demonstrate the origin of "high" moral, ethical, philosophical, and artistic values in a "low" psychosexual basis, remains just as unscathed by an accusation of pan-sexualism as Marxism by the analogous charge of pan-economism.

Marxism did not even recognize the subversive element of the psychology of the unconscious, whereby the conscious ego is decentralized and exposed as a fraud and clown. Freud thus observes: "The ego is [. . .] playing the ludicrous part of the clown in a circus who by his gestures tries to convince the audience that every change in the circus ring is being carried out under his orders. But only the youngest of the spectators are deceived by him."[28] The psychological decentralization of the bourgeois ego was simultaneously an expression of the disintegration and crisis of the bourgeois ego-identity whose societal prerequisites for its social reproduction were no longer assured. (See also p. 159.) In the last analysis this means the expression of the social and political decentralization of a class which in fact was no longer the ruler of its own house because the proletarian revolution had stood at the door of the highly developed European countries since the beginning of the twentieth century. The vulgar Marxists did not understand the "asociality and irrationality of the unconscious" (Freud) as an unconscious rebellion against the "direction of the general colonialist reason" (Foucault), that is, against the rationality of capital whose destructive dynamics had become obvious in the age of imperialism.

Orthodox Marxism saw particular proof of the a-historical character of Freud's theory in the "archaic" view of the unconscious. It entirely missed the social element of this archaism, namely, that unconscious wishes are "archaic" and "timeless" only because they run counter to "contemporary" behavior, which is determined by the calculating rationale of capitalism, and therefore have to be shunted aside. (See also **pp. 141f.**) This "archaic" and "timeless" quality is, so to speak, the deadened social element, the petrification of social needs which have remained unfulfilled. "What is true in Freud's view of the archaic," says Adorno, "if not the timelessness of the unconscious, is the following: concrete social situations and motivations do not enter that realm unchanged, only 'reduced.' The non-contemporaneity of the unconscious and conscious is itself a stigma of a contradictory social development. Whatever remains unsatisfied, what has to pay the bill for progress and enlightenment, sediments itself in the unconscious. Underdevelopment becomes timeless."[29]

The universal Marxist accusation that psychoanalysis's grasp of the unconscious is a-historical therefore succeeds in making things quite easy on itself. In his early writings Freud repeatedly pointed to the connection between social censorship, which those in power exercise so as to support the existing order, and individualistic self-censorship. In *The Interpretation of Dreams* he made the explicit comparison between political censorship and "dream censorship": the "latent" dream ideas are primarily suppressed into the unconscious because they are "unfit for society," that is, scandalous to the ruling consciousness. Unconsciousness appears here as a psychic dark room into which socially unacceptable subversive wishes and needs are relegated. Not until his later writings did Freud again withdraw this social interpretation of the unconscious as a psychic sediment of the socially forbidden; the unconscious at that point in his life represented only the biological side of personality, the so-called "archaic inheritance" in which the natural history of mankind has sedimented itself. The original subversive social element disappears in the larger biological view of the unconscious. And here we must support the criticism of Russian orthodoxy that Freud's view of personality, primarily in its unconscious dimension, is biologically obtuse. Its archaic biological understanding of the unconscious prevented psychoanalysis from perceiving the historical changeability of the unconscious's experiential content. Only Reich has reminded us of that again: "What demonstrates the fact that the unconscious also changes with time is the interesting clinical fact that with the development of new technology the unconscious also acquires new symptoms. Thus during the hubbub about dirigibles many patients dreamed of airships as representations of the male sex organ."[30]

The orthodox Marxist approach to psychoanalysis in many respects resembles its attitude to surrealism. The arguments which it supplies against both are in many cases identical, for it regards surrealism as another abomination of bourgeois decadence, as an "extreme case of bourgeois art,'' as the attempt by the ruling class to find an escape from its bad conscience in irrationalism. Vulgar Marxism altogether missed the point that surrealism—despite its inherently bourgeois ideology—was also a protest movement against the ruling logic of the imperialist bourgeoisie. But vulgar Marxism rejected surrealism's subversion just as it rejected the psychoanalytical subversion of reified consciousness.

Marxist orthodoxy treated Freud's libido theory in much the same way as it had his theory of the unconscious. It denounced it as a grandiose regression into the neo-hedonism, neo-Platonism, and neo-vitalism of the nineteenth century. According to Jurinec, Freud's view of the world was something as follows: ''Infinite rivers of mental energy flow from the unconscious depths of our ego; or it is an elementary, always active, blind lava which seeks 'to overflow all bounds.' This mental energy (libido) is the stream of life that wants to embrace everything, wants to drag everything into its vortex. But in the depths of this stream, which Freud—like Plato—often calls Eros, there arises a second, opposing, principle: the reality principle.''[31] Even if Freud's concept of the libido manifests idealistic and Platonic traits—especially in its later universal expansion where almost all social and cultural productions are understood as ''libidinous productions'' (see also p. 64)—the actual subversive center of the concept consists in having truly revolutionized the bourgeois conception of sexuality. By investigating the psycho-sexual history of the child (which had been socialized within bourgeois society), and by showing how the individual (oral, anal, and phallic) ''partial instincts,'' which strive primarily for their own pleasure, are finally integrated under the ''primacy of genitality,'' Freud broadened—through the ''rehabilitation of the partial instincts''[32]—the concept of sexuality beyond that of pure genitality. Freud's concept of libido—not as a psychological or philosophical concept but as a technical-developmental psychological one—resists all positivistic and reified interpretations of pleasure, happiness, and love which are formed according to the model of bourgeois genitality, the principle of repressive genitality. By holding fast to the specific quality of childhood wishes and to the specific erogenous nature of the partial instincts and zones he stands in antagonistic relationship to the ''reality principle.'' As long as this principle, be it of Stalinist or capitalist origin, limits infantile sexuality and delimits the partial instincts through the creation of a repressive genital principle, Freud's concept of the libido will retain its subversive quality.

Orthodox Marxism was just as blind to the subversive element of Freud's theory of neurosis, which also broke through all reified conceptions of mental illness and deviance. In order to show Freud's accomplishment in its proper historical setting it is necessary to review briefly the pre-Freudian conception of mental pathology.

Antique slave and medieval feudal society still interpreted psychic deviance in immediate social terms, yet in a mythologically, that is, in a religiously embellished way. Madness, delirium, and fits were thought to be a "misfortune" imposed by the gods as punishment for a conscious or unconscious crime. In antiquity, the Erinyes, the goddesses of revenge, were made responsible for madness and delusions; the Middle Ages regarded madmen and hysterics as "possessed by the devil." All this changed during the Enlightenment, which sought to provide its concept of psychology with a scientific foundation. Consequently the Enlightenment threw out the mythologically and religiously embellished concept of madness of antiquity and the Middle Ages. Yet it distanced itself further than ever before from any social interpretation of mental illness. The enlightened mind no longer regarded mental deviance as a "judgment" of the gods or of God but as a "variation" in the sense of being un- or anti-natural. The madman or hysteric was regarded as someone who had been neglected or deprived not by society—but by nature. This naturalistic concept of mental illness thus mirrors the reification of consciousness that accompanied the development of capitalism. Bourgeois psychiatry then constructed this concept into a "scientific system," that is, into a system of "psychiatric nomenclature" (Laing) whose only sense consisted in delivering the patient (that is, mental deviant) into the hands of the state apparatus and to administer him in total institutions. (See also p. 195.)

Freud confronted this biological and naturalistic concept of mental illness of bourgeois psychiatry and psychology and medicine with a genetic concept of illness acquired through the study of hysteria. He derived the causes of mental illness, hysterical symptoms for example, from early childhood traumas and psycho-sexual misdevelopment. Bernfeld, too, repeatedly emphasizes the genetic character of Freud's psychology: "Psychoanalysis differs from official psychology by its genetic standpoint [. . .] It is the most consistent among the genetic psychological schools, the only one with a historical point of view [. . .] A phenomenon is regarded as 'understood' in psychoanalysis if its determinants have been discovered in the pre-history of the phenomenon (that is, in the history of the individual, if necessary in the history of humanity or the living)."[33] This genetic concept of illness was *subversive* since Freud saw an element of revolt against the "reality principle" both in neurosis and in psychosis. "Neurosis and psychosis are both expressive," he wrote, "of the rebellion of the id against the outer world, of its displeasure, or if you want its inability to adjust to general distress."[34]

It was indeed a revolutionary scientific achievement to have shattered the reified concept of pathology of the bourgeoisie. Just as little as the "enlightened" citizen—before Marx—had been able to perceive in money a "relationship concealed under a reified mask" had the sane citizen—before Freud—been able to perceive under the "reified mask of the symptoms of neurosis or madness" a disturbed psycho-social relationship. As incapable as he was of perceiving social sense in the chaos of supply and demand, so was he unable to recognize the social sense (the "sense of the symptoms"—Freud) in psychic chaos. If it was to the credit of the critique of political economy to have rediscovered the "extra-economic existence of the use value" (Lukács) and to have liberated it from its reified relationships, likewise it was to the credit of psychoanalysis to have rediscovered in mental crises, that is, illnesses, or in other words beneath the reified surface of the symptoms of neurosis or madness, the use form of the libido, that is, of repressed childhood wishes. (See also p. 141.) This achievement of Freud was totally ignored by orthodox Marxists.

The Sociological Substance of Psychoanalysis

The only validity which Russian party Communism granted psychoanalysis was as individual psychology. Every attempt to apply psychoanalytical methods to social or ideological areas was rejected either as an "encroachment" into the realm of historical materialism or as an act "exceeding its competence." So as to make psychoanalysis at least somewhat more acceptable to Marxism, Reich sought to throttle its wild sociological excursions. Thus he wrote: "The actual object of psychoanalysis is the mental life of the socialized human being. The mental life of the masses interests it only insofar as individual phenomena make an appearance in the masses (as in the problem of the leader); and also insofar as manifestations of the 'mass psyche' such as fear, obedience, panic, etc., can be explained in terms of the individual. But it looks as if the phenomenon of class consciousness is scarcely accessible to psychoanalysis and as though problems like mass movements, of politics, of strikes which belong to the realm of social theory, could not be the object of its methods. Thus psychoanalysis cannot replace social theory nor can it develop a social theory of its own. However, it can assist social theory, for example as social psychology."[35] With such formulations did Reich seek to put an end to the wild sociological speculations of Roheim, Ferenczi, Laforgue, and the like. For the psychoanalytical misinterpretations of social and economic matters had assumed grotesque forms in the 1920's. Laforgue, for example, derived the institution of police from sadism, that is, people's need for punishment.[36] Ferenczi's derivation of capital accumulation from anal eroticism[37] was proof of that idealistic overvaluation of the autonomous power of the internal instincts which, however, was already inherent in Freud's concept of the instinct. (See also p. 64.) Extrapolation from the psychology of the id led to a misinterpretation of social institutions, which were perceived as emanations, as solidified "projections," of an ontological unconscious; and this frequently combined with a crude psychoanalytical anti-communism which seemed even to justify the Stalinist prejudice against psychoanalysis. For example, Kolnai described the proletarian revolution as collective parricide and Bolshevik "anarcho-communism" as a regression into the womb.[38] Socialist Freudians such as Reich, Fromm, Fenichel, and Bernfeld, among others, strongly opposed such psychoanalytical misinterpretations of social and political phenomena which threatened to alienate psychoanalysis from Marxism once and for all. Nor did they exclude Freud's own sociological writings from this "cleansing operation." Stalinist prosecutors thought that the original "sociological sin" of psychoanalysis was Freud's "Mass Psychology and Ego Analysis." Jurinec was justified in attacking the "formalism" of Freud's concept of the masses which posited the same common denominator for the regressive and irrational psychology of fascism and the emancipatory psychology of the communist mass movement.[39] Reich's rigorous delimitation of psychoanalysis from the social sciences was supposed to check the former's bent for psychological and historical interpretation, which had been abetted by Freud's hybrid slogan "sociology as applied psychology."

On the other hand, the reduction of psychoanalysis to the clinical realm of individual psychology, which had been performed with a polemical intent, did not do justice to psychoanalysis. That is why Bernfeld wrote in opposition to Reich: "The Reichian formula that psychoanalysis is appropriate for individual psychological, and Marxism for sociological, matters does not provide a correct assessment of the relationship between psychoanalysis and (communist) Marxism. Rather Freud's conception of psychoanalysis had always counted among the objects of its investigations a significant group of phenomena which, according to the division of science of that time, were also the object of sociology and, in particular, of the social psychology which Sapir had described. Psychoanalysis and sociology therefore are in no way mutually exclusive or simply stand side by side."[40] In fact, the demand made frequently even today that psychoanalysis's place is in clinical individual psychology is still part and parcel of the division of labor of the bourgeois sciences. Just as little as historical materialism fit into the traditional scheme of the sciences, since it tore down the fences between philosophy and the religious, historical, and economic sciences, letting each of these individual sciences circle around the axis of political economy, can one subsume psychoanalysis under one single traditional scientific discipline. Bernfeld observes: "If one approaches psychoanalysis with the demands customarily made of the psychology of consciousness one finds that it has overemphasized the unconscious, or that it biologizes; if one measures it against physiology, it becomes easy to accuse it of being insufficiently materialistic; if one regards it as an individual psychology, it looks monotonous and abstract; if one wants to use it as social psychology, one finds that it makes 'unusually' great allowances for individual and unique qualities."[41]

The Marxists are only lending bourgeois science objective assistance when they seek to reduce psychoanalysis—as they are trying to do again today—to a clinical psychology of the individual. For they have never forgiven psychoanalysis the fact that it transgresses its "actual realm," individual psycho-pathology. The expansion of psychoanalysis beyond this domain is, however, justified in principle by the subversive substance of its discoveries, even if this expansion frequently led to wrong and grotesque generalizations, analogies, and hypotheses. As genetic psychology and as psychology of the unconscious, psychoanalysis still represents a healthy provocation for bourgeois intellectual and social sciences. Therefore, if Marxists seek to confine psychoanalysis to its individual psychological domain, they simultaneously liquidate its contribution to the struggle against bourgeois ideology: against, namely, the idealistic and positivist concept of consciousness of bourgeois philosophy and psychology, against the biologistic and naturalist concept of the pathology of bourgeois psychiatry and medicine, against the reactionary concept of the morality of bourgeois pedagogy, and so on. As long as the socialist movement stands in an ideological struggle against the bourgeois sciences it should thus avail itself of the subversive findings of psychoanalysis, although not without simultaneously attacking psychoanalysis's own bourgeois ideology.

Moreover, nothing is to be gained by a relegation of psychoanalysis to the realm of individual psychology. Its bourgeois idealism and anthropology—as we will show later—is part not only of its social psychology, that is, its sociology, but also of its individual psychological categories. However, the "latent" ideological dimension which has entered, for instance, the category of individual psychology, as well as in psychoanalysis's concept of the ego, becomes "manifest" (and therefore annoying) only in its sociological extrapolation. To want to reduce psychoanalysis to individual psychology therefore would only mean to alter its ideological aggregate, that is, push back its ideological content from a manifest to a latent condition.

Psychoanalysis's actual sociological, that is, socio-critical substance is not to be found where it thinks of itself as "applied psychology" in the sense of Freud's concept of sociology, but rather where it only appears to be individual psychology. Orthodox Marxism, however, has been so disgusted by psychoanalysis's sociological confusions and presumptions that it has remained completely unaware of this aspect. For the radical individualism of psychoanalytical categories expresses a serious social state of affairs: that the social and "private" existences of the bourgeois individual have completely split, because the bourgeois can afford "psychology" only outside the market and productive system, in the so-called "private" sphere. Adorno thus remarks: "Freud was right precisely where he was wrong: the power of his theories derives from his blindness to the separation of psychology and sociology which, however, is the result of those social processes which some revisionists, using the language of the German philosophical tradition, call the self-alienation of mankind. Even if these revisionists have let themselves be seduced by critical insight into the destructive aspects of this separation into pretending that the antagonism between private and social being could be cured through psychotherapy, Freud adequately described through his psychological atomism a reality where men are in fact atomized and separated from each other by an 'unbridgeable gulf.'"[42] Freud's monadological categories, for example his monadological ego concept (see also p. 75), derive their analytical strength not from the general validity of their anthropological content—that precisely constitutes the "scientistic misunderstanding" of psychoanalysis (Habermas)[43]—but from their blind historical and sociological content. Freud's "psychologistic atomization" reflects the psychology of bourgeois individuals who have become isolated and indifferent to each other through the principle of exchange and competition. To quote Marx: "The further we go back in history the more the individual and, therefore, also the producing individual, appears as unself-sufficient, as belonging to a greater whole [. . .] Only in the eighteenth century, in bourgeois society, do the different forms of social interrelatedness appear to the individual as means designed purely and simply for his private use, as outer necessity. But the era which produced this viewpoint, of the individuated individual, is precisely the one which manifests the most highly developed social [. . .] relationships up to that point."[44] Freud's individualistic and atomistic psychology belies the blind anthropological concept behind the individuated individual of the bourgeois era. It therefore should be regarded not as a general scientific psychology but—as Reich desired—as a scientific reflex of the psychology of the bourgeois individual, of the individuated individual. What constitutes its sociological substance, something of which orthodox Marxism remained completely unaware, is its individualistic obtuseness.

Marxism recognized psychoanalysis as a clinical individual psychology only because it was itself under the suasion of a bourgeois concept of "health." Irreconcilable with its "healthy" view of the world was any possibility that the psychology of the bourgeois individual should appear tendentiously only as a psychology of "disturbance," as a dysfunction between ego and id, as a "pathic gap" (compare also p. 136) between an abstractly calculating "ratio" (of the capitalist market) and its "irrational," that is, incalculable "passions." But precisely because the "clinical" exception has become the rule and bourgeois society has socialized psychic dysfunction and neurosis, psychoanalysis has always been and is in principle also social and mass psychology. Thus Adorno says: "The fact that psychology became illness expresses not only society's false consciousness of itself but simultaneously what really became of human beings in this society [. . .] the allegedly social concretization—each individual the other's opponent—has his identity solely determined by something thing-like, an abstract act' of exchange which has become totally separated from his specific determination."[45] Freud's psychology, that is, psycho-pathology, does not have much to say about capitalist society, but a great deal about what "really has become of human beings in it."

The Critical Substance of Psychoanalysis

Soviet Marxism and the communist parties under its sway were incapable of comprehending the "combinative character" of Freud's work, namely, that its conservative affirmation of the economic foundations of bourgeois society went hand in hand with a subversive critique of its moral foundations. Even though Freud himself assumed a sceptical attitude towards the class struggle, proletarian revolution, and socialist construction in the Soviet Union, he nonetheless opened up a new theoretical and practical front against the ideology of bourgeois society. The subversive kernel of his discoveries—that the demands of the individual's instincts are irreconcilable with the cultural norms of society—was politically so explosive that it frequently endangered the legality of psychoanalysis. As long as Freud held fast to the subversiveness of repressed and suppressed instinctual demands, he found himself in irreconcilable conflict with bourgeois society. Accordingly he stated: "Society will be in no hurry to grant us authority. It is bound to offer us resistance, for we adopt a critical attitude towards it. We point out to it that it itself plays a great part in causing neurosis. Just as we make an individual our enemy by uncovering what is repressed in him, so society cannot respond with sympathy to a relentless exposure of its injurious effects and deficiencies. Because we destroy illusions we are accused of endangering ideals."[46]

Freud's discovery and rehabilitation of infantile sexuality was a massive attack on the ideology and morality of bourgeois society. His theory of neurosis, which had been developed on the basis of an investigation of infantile sexuality, was simultaneously a critique of the bourgeois educational system that was at least as biting as the Marxist one. "Education must inhibit, prohibit, and suppress," Freud wrote, "and has always done so to a large measure. But analysis has taught us that this repression of the instincts produces the danger of neurotic illnesses."[47] Freud described the bourgeois educational principle as a "social breaking in" by which society assumes control over childhood. "Experience must no doubt have taught educators that the task of making the sexual will of the new generation tractable could only be carried out if they began to exercise their influence very early, if they did not wait for the storm of puberty but intervened already in the sexual life of children which is preparatory to it. For this reason almost all infantile sexual activities were forbidden to children and frowned upon; an ideal was set up of making the life of children asexual!"[48] And in "The Sexual Enlightenment of Children" he unrelentingly analyzed the social function of sexual repression, which was seen to be the outcome of religious threats meant "to stifle human beings' capacity for autonomous thinking so as to make 'obedient' and 'decent' children of them!"[49] In his investigation of female sexuality Freud interpreted the widespread intellectual underdevelopment of women "as a result of the prohibition to occupy oneself, even in one's thoughts, with sexuality."[50] This and other sexual prohibitions imposed on young girls is thus one of the reasons for their subsequent mental inhibition, for their "intellectual inferiority complex," which is the psychological pillar of patriarchal culture. By describing the bourgeois educational enterprise as a producer of neuroses, as a "breaking in" of sexually and intellectually inhibited, that is, pliable human beings, Freud was actually like "a Leftist radical with respect to his view of the instincts" (J. M. Brohm), even though with respect to his political views he should be regarded as a *petit-bourgeois* liberal. Thus he could write: "We can present society with a blunt calculation that what it describes as morality calls for a bigger sacrifice than it is worth, and that its proceedings are not based on honesty and do not display wisdom."[51]

The Marxists missed Freud's social and ideological-critical dimension primarily because, as Jurinec wrote, "it is far removed from any thought of the class structure of society. This fact by itself consigns Freud's investigation to complete fruitlessness."[52] But even if Freud never developed an explicit class psychology, and although his psychology of the ego has to be historically relativized as a scientific self-interpretation of the liberal bourgeoisie (see also p. 74), he nonetheless thought about the relationship between class structure and sexuality. In *The Future of An Illusion* Freud maintained the thesis that culture is based both on the compulsion to work and the relinquishment of instinctual gratification and that it "inevitably provokes opposition among those who are subjected to these demands."[53] And Freud differentiated quite consciously between an instinctual repression to which all civilized human beings are subjected, such as the incest wish, and repression which applies only to certain classes, groups, and individuals. "If a culture has not got beyond the point," he wrote, "at which satisfaction of any portion of its participants depends upon the suppression of another and perhaps larger, portion—and this is the case in all present-day cultures—it is understandable that the suppressed people should develop an intense hostility towards a culture whose existence they make possible by their work but in whose wealth they have too small a share. [. . .] It goes without saying that a civilization which leaves so large a number of its participants unsatisfied and drives them into revolt neither has nor deserves the prospect of a lasting existence."[54]

Although Freud regarded Marxism sceptically all his life, many of his cultural-critical formulations brought him into the vicinity of a materialistic conception of history. He seemed perfectly aware that the history of class struggle had also left its mark on sexuality. For example, he wrote: "The tendency on the part of civilization to restrict sexual life is no less clear than its other tendency to expand the cultural unit. Its first, totemic, phase already brings with it the prohibition against an incestuous choice of object, and this is perhaps the most drastic mutilation which man's erotic life has in all time experienced. Taboos, laws and customs impose further restrictions [. . .] Not all cultures go equally far in this; and the economic structure of society also influences the amount of sexual freedom that remains. Here, as we already know, civilization is obeying the laws of economic necessity, since a large amount of the psychical energy which it uses for its own purposes has to be withdrawn from sexuality. In this respect civilization behaves towards sexuality as a people or stratum of its population does which has subjected another to exploitation. Fear of a revolt by the suppressed elements drives it to strict precautionary measures. A high point in such development has been reached in our Western European civilisation."[55]

In *The Future of An Illusion* Freud demonstrated more precisely how the "economic structure" of society also influences what remains of sexual freedom. For here he developed the idea that the degree of instinctual and need gratification which a culture can afford its members is dependent not only on the degree of its control over nature, that is, the developmental state of its productive forces, but also on social "institutions," that is, the social organization of the means of production, the relationships that result from production. As he observed: "Human civilisation [. . .] presents as we know two aspects to the observer. It includes on the one hand all the knowledge and capacity that men have acquired in order to control the forces of nature and extract its wealth for the satisfaction of human needs, and, on the other hand, all the regulation necessary in order to adjust the relation of men to one another and especially the distribution of available wealth [*sic*!]. The two trends of civilisation are not independent of each other; firstly because the mutual relations of men are profoundly influenced by the amount of instinctual satisfaction which the existing wealth makes possible; secondly, because an individual man can himself come to function as wealth in relation to other men in so far as the other person makes use of his capacity for work, or chooses him as a sexual object [. . .]."[56] At this point Freud's argument is more Marxist than that of many of his Marxist critics: by relating the sexual ownership of another as sexual object to the material possession of the other as exploitable labor he points to the fundamental connection between relationships within capitalist production and the sexual-object relationships that correspond to them. F. Gantheret remarks: "Freud here contributes a fundamental insight: the fact of functioning as a sexual object for another consigns the individual into the same position as a material commodity for another; it is the same as functioning as labor power."[57]

Soviet Marxists did not allow psychoanalysis any social relevance because it lacked a class concept, and they denounced its attempts to be critical of ideology with the argument that it overvalued the "idealistic forces" in the historical process. However, such self-confident Marxist criticism usually failed to admit that the classics of scientific socialism, Engels for instance, accorded an important place in human life to idealistic forces:

"The will is determined by passion or thought. But the levers which directly determine passion or thought are of a very different kind. In part they may be outside circumstances, in part idealistic motivation, ambition, 'enthusiasm for truth and justice,' personal hatred or purely individual quirks of all kinds. But on the other hand, we have seen that the many individual wills that act in the historical process frequently produce entirely different results—sometimes the opposite ones—from those desired, so that their motives can only be regarded as of subordinate significance to the final result. On the other hand, one must continue to inquire what driving forces stand behind these motives, what historical causes transform themselves into motivation in the minds of those who act."[58]

Engels expressly states that there is no such thing as a simple reflex relationship between being and consciousness, as the vulgar Marxists usually impute, but that the mediations between the many "individual wills that act in history and their historical result" is generally very complicated and contradictory.[59] The psychoanalytical contribution to the enlightenment of the dialectic between being and consciousness consists in having genetically grasped the idealistic motivations ("ambition, 'enthusiasm for truth and justice,' personal hatred or, also, purely personal quirks") which enter the historical process, and which the Marxist classics, for lack of a genetic psychology, could generally only describe phenomenologically. If, according to Engels, "it is unavoidable that everything which motivates human beings first has to go through their head," then psychoanalysis is the science which investigates in the individual how this "movement through the head," through the ego of the individuated individual, actually occurs, and how it forms itself into a will.

At the same time Engels' sentence also shows the objective limits of the psychological (psychoanalytical) comprehension of ideological phenomena: "that its motivations are in any case of subordinate importance for the total result." So psychoanalysis should be accused not of applying its method to ideological phenomena but of not taking sufficient account of the "subordinate" importance of individual motivation for the historical process. In this respect one must admit the relevance of Russian orthodoxy, say of Sapir's criticism: "The element of individual psychology plays methodologically a subordinate role in social-psychological processes, which in their turn are subordinated to other more powerful (economic) forces of historical development, and thus stand with these latter in a—so to speak—subordinate relationship to the second power."[60] Although Freud never denied the significance of social and economic forces in the formation of ideology, he frequently denigrated it unjustly in his ignorance of political economy. To admit to this "lacuna," that is, "source of errors," in the psychoanalytical method does not mean, however, as Stalinist criticism decreed, that psychoanalysis is useless in the sphere of ideological criticism. This is especially true when it is a question of bourgeois ideology, "cultural sexual morality," and religion among others.

Such Marxist rigorism suppresses the fact that the Marxist and Freudian methods of derivation and "reduction" of ideological phenomena coincide at a certain point. According to Max Eastman: "The word 'ideology' is for Marx simply a substantive which serves to name the malformations in social and political thinking which have been produced by repressed social motivation. This word reproduces the idea rather accurately that the Freudians have in mind when they speak of rationalization, surrogate, transference, displacement, and sublimation."[61] And it is remarkable that Engels described the process of the formation of ideology in a thoroughly Freudian sense: "Ideology is a process which occurs in the consciousness of what is called thinking, but in the false consciousness. What actually motivates it, it remains unaware of; otherwise it would not be an ideological process. It imagines itself as false, that is, as illusory motivation."[62] The social and economic forces which have determined their ideologies usually remain unknown to most people, as "unconscious" as the psychosexual forces which determine their individual rationalizations.

What Marxist criticism of Freud has overlooked altogether until now is the astonishing parallelism, not to say congeniality, of Freud's and Marx's methodological procedures. In other words it has failed to detect the hidden economic, that is, sexual driving forces behind social ideologies on the one hand and individual rationalizations on the other. In the one, with respect to their producer, they have made themselves autonomous in the form of commodities and in the other in the form of neuroses. (See also pp. 153f.) Bernfeld too has already pointed to the parallelism between this methodological procedure of tracing "high," apparently irreducible "values," to occurrences of a lower degree of value. "For example," he has written, "Marx will declare that wartime patriotism is the ideological superstructure of the imperialist class interest, whereas Freud will detect an element of sadism in the enthusiasm of the individual wartime volunteer. In any event, neither of them will respectfully protect patriotism as a value independent from scientific analytical reduction."[63]

For vulgar Marxism ideological phenomena such as religion, art, morality, philosophy, and so on are exclusively determined by their economic and social basis, that is, through the respective relationships within production and property of the period. Although economic and social relationships as a whole determine the form and content of the religious, artistic, moral, and philosophical production of a particular period, and are so to speak its mean determinants, no particular work of art, philosophical system, moral custom, or religious cult is exhaustively determined by the social conditions or economic class position of its creator or adherent. Above and beyond that one has to make allowances for sexual-psychological determinants which psychoanalysis has investigated, although these with respect to socio-economic conditions should be regarded as less important ideological phenomena—subdeterminants, so to speak, as they are called in mathematics. In this respect Sartre rightly has observed that if we had psychoanalytical "case histories" from the seventeenth and early eighteenth centuries we would have much better information today about the social revolution of that era, that is, about the decline of feudal nobility and the rise of the bourgeoisie.

A genetic interpretation of monotheistic religions, which in a certain sense is a sexual-psychological supplement to the Marxist criticism of religion, shows the contribution which psychoanalysis can in fact make to a differentiated enlightenment, especially of phenomena relating to the bourgeois superstructure. Thus Lenin has explained religious ideology in the following manner: "The impotence of the exploited classes in their fight against the exploiters just as inevitably produces a belief in a better life in the hereafter as the impotence of aboriginal man in his fight with nature produces a belief in gods, devils, miracles, and the like. Someone who works all his life and suffers all his life is taught humility and patience in the here and now by religion which consoles him with the hope for heavenly recompense [. . .]." According to Lenin, religion is therefore nothing but a "phantastic mirror image in the mind of those outer forces which govern their everyday lives, a reflection in which the earthly powers assume the form of supernatural ones." He concludes: "As long as people in today's bourgeois society are determined by the means of production, which they have produced themselves, as by an alien power [. . .] the foundation for a religious reflex will continue to exist as well."[64]

Thus did Lenin analyze—in the tradition of Marx's critique of religion in the Introduction to the *Critique of Hegel's Philosophy of Law*—the outward, "social genesis" of the religious reflex as a result of the process of production, a reflex which then becomes autonomous. However, he says nothing about the inner, "psychological genesis" of the religious reflex and the particular determinants of the patriarchal-monotheistic complex. Here the psychoanalytic interpretation can help. According to Freud, the "basic religious feeling" is produced by the father and Oedipus complex, that is, by childhood fears and the need for protection which are "projected" onto the "all-mighty" God-father *imago.*

"The [religious] doctrine is that the universe was created by a being resembling a man, but man magnified in every respect, in power, wisdom and strength of his passions—an idealized superman [. . .] It is an interesting fact that this creator is always only a single being even when there are believed to be many gods. It is interesting, too, that the creator is usually a man, though there is far from being a lack of indication of female deities, and some mythologies actually make the creation begin with a male god getting rid of a female deity, who is degraded into being a monster. [. . .] Our further path is made easier to recognize, for this god-creator is undisguisedly called 'father.' Psychoanalysis infers that he really is the father, with all the magnificence in which he once appeared to the small child. A religious man pictures the creation of the universe just as he pictures his own origin [. . .] For the same person to whom the child owed his existence, the father [. . .] also protected and watched over him in his feeble and helpless state, exposed as he was to all dangers lying in wait in the external world; under his father's protection he felt safe. When a human being has himself grown up, he knows, to be sure, that he is in possession of greater strength, but his insight into the perils of life has also grown greatly and he rightly concludes that fundamentally he still remains just as helpless and unprotected as he was in childhood, that faced by the world he is still a child. [. . .] But he has long since recognized, too, that his father is a being of narrower, restricted power, and not equipped with every excellence. He thus resorts to the mnemonic image of the father whom in his childhood he so greatly overvalued. He exalts the image into a deity and makes it into something contemporary and real. The effective strength of this mnemonic image and the persistence of his need for protection jointly sustain his belief in God."[65]

This comparison of the Marxist and psychoanalytic critiques of religion would seem to show that psychoanalysis, despite its lack of political and economic enlightenment and its ideological implications, can make an important contribution to the "differentiation of the superstructural schema" (Sandkühler). Especially as a genetic psychology and as a psychology of the unconscious is it able to illumine the "latent" content behind the "manifest" ideological surface, that is, the "unconscious" basis of the ideological phenomena of consciousness. That is why Sandkühler's suggestion to "document the existing marriage between an historico-materialistically comprehensible dialectic of being and consciousness and being and unconsciousness, which psychoanalysis has brought to light," should also be taken seriously by Marxists.[66]

2. Stalinism and Freudo-Marxism

Stalinist Resistance to Psychoanalysis

We have seen why Bolshevik and Stalinist theoreticians were incapable of comprehending the "combinative character" of Freud's work. One question that remains to be answered is why they—and in their wake almost the entire communist world movement—were also incapable of a *critical-dialectical* approach to Freud's work. The reactionary degeneration of certain "psychoanalytical" schools which invoked Freud certainly played a role in this connection: the *Reichsdeutsche* society which propagated a kind of Nordic hero psychology, the English school of Jones with its Victorian prudishness, the American schools run by pseudo-scientific luxury-class doctors—these and other vulgar scientific and revisionist deformations of Freud's school have made its understanding by the worker movement that much more difficult. Another reason for communist incomprehension lies—according to Dahmer—in the deficient reception of psychoanalysis: "One looks vainly for traces of an acquaintance with Freud's theory in the work of Lenin, Bukharin, Luxemburg, Lukács, and Korsch. Among the Bolshevik leaders Trotsky is the exception that proves the rule."[67] But this still does not explain *why* the reception of Freud among Bolshevik theoreticians was so deficient. This fact has far-reaching political, social, and ideological reasons which are to be found in the history of the Russian revolution and the Second International.

The official Stalinist verdict on psychoanalysis was grounded primarily in a quite incidental and amateurish private opinion that Lenin voiced about Freud. In his conversations with Clara Zetkin he dismissed psychoanalysis as a "bourgeois fad." He went on to say: "Freud's hypothesis looks 'cultured,' yes even scientific, but is nothing but amateurishness. Freud's theory is just another fashion. I am suspicious of these sexual theories published in articles, pamphlets, etc.: in short, I am against the theories of a specific literature which luxuriates on the hot-beds of bourgeois society. I am mistrustful of those who focus on the sexual question the way an Indian saint stares at his navel." In view of the burning "social question" it made sense that Lenin neglected the "sexual question." As a revolutionary and political strategist he eval-uated scientific theories primarily according to their practical usefulness in the class struggle. Since he had not yet had to deal with a proletariat that had adopted *petit-bourgeois* values, neither the "sexual question" nor the problem of "neurotic mass suffering" were relevant for him. That is probably also why Lenin never thoroughly occupied himself with psychoanalysis or he probably would not have been so ignorant as to mistake psychoanalysis with bourgeois pornography. Even though Lenin frequently discussed "free love" with his womanfriend F. Armand he himself stuck to rather a rigid model of "proletarian marriage." Extra-marital intercourse, birth control, and abortion did not seem to him appropriate for the proletarian woman and family.[68] The degree to which Lenin's puritanism concerning the "sexual question" had largely subjec-tive roots, that is, as J. M. Brohm claims, was itself a product of "cultural sexual morality," is idle speculation. It is much more important to reflect on the objective economic, political, and cultural forces which have produced Bolshevik rigorism in questions of sexual morality and psy-choanalysis.

The official Stalinist condemnation of psychoanalysis as a "product of bourgeois decadence" should be regarded in light of the general restora-tional tendency of the Stalinist era. As a consequence of the rigid centrali-zation in the party and the state, which was preceded by liquidations within the party and in Soviet democracy (even during Lenin's lifetime), psychoanalysis too, as a theory which tended "to take the side of the individual, at least of his instinctual demands" (P. Brückner[69]), had to be liquidated. Thus Stoljarov decreed: "The psychology of Freud is 'anti-social' in the sense of its ultra-individualistic character."[70] Every political and psychological theory of spontaneity, no matter whether it supported the self-organization of work or the "self-organization of sexual needs" (Reich), was perceived as an "anarchist threat" by the hypercentralized Stalinist party and state apparatus. Political restoration in the Stalinist era therefore found its consistent sexual-political comple-ment in the reintroduction of bourgeois legislation relating to the family, education, marriage, and sexuality. All reactionary sexual-political para-graphs that had been eliminated after the October Revolution, such as those concerning abortion, homosexuality, the prohibition of divorce and birth control, were reintroduced in the wake of Stalinization.[71] The "co-educational schools" which had been established everywhere after the revolution were also eliminated.

Thereupon psychoanalytical theory, which had laid bare the role of sexual repression in the family, marriage, and education as the basis of the "authoritarian personality," also automatically entered the index of the Stalinist inquisition. The "bureaucratically deformed worker's state" —so Lenin in 1924—could do as little without the structural fabric of the "authoritarian personality" as the bourgeois state. "The 'Thermidor' of the worker and Soviet democracy necessarily also becomes the 'Thermidor' of the family hearth" (Trotsky). "The authoritarian motive for today's cult of the family doubtless is the need of bureaucracy for a stable hierarchy of social relationships and for the discipline of youth by means of 40 million strong points of authority and power" (Trotsky[72]). The bureaucratization of all areas of life, public and private, under the dictatorship of the Stalinist party and state apparatus also had to be psychologically secured: the re-establishment of the patriarchal nuclear family became the psychological transmission belt of bureaucratic centralism and of the Stalinist cult of personality. Stalinism, therefore, had to fear psychoanalysis that much more since the latter put every form of cult, monotheistic or Stalinist, into question and showed its origin in the patriarchal family structure, in the father and Oedipus complex. And psychoanalysis (this constitutes its "blind spot") yet ignored the economic and political conditions that made such a situation possible. "Stalinism and the cult of personality"according to Sandkühler," "recurring father fixation as a surrogate formation of libidinous needs and increased repression, the official verdicts on liberation and sexuality, all were questioned as to motive. Psychoanalysis thus explained the censorship that was its fate without arguing against the historical necessity of the dictatorship of the proletariat."[73] The fact that psychoanalysis "refused to remain silent against proletarian rule" (Sandkühler) was one of the main reasons for its condemnation.

Political restoration was immediately followed by cultural restoration. The primacy of Stalinist economic policy, aimed at catching up with the productive level of the capitalist countries (even at the price of a partial reintroduction of bourgeois competitive and profit mechanisms,[74] of "material incentives" and "premiums" as "economic levers"), also corresponded to the primacy of Stalinist cultural and educational policy, namely, to catch up with the bourgeois level. But adjusting and fixing the post-revolutionary workers' movement according to bourgeois cultural and educational standards—and the moral rigidity resulting therefrom— was not strictly the end-result only of a Stalinist educational policy. As P. Brückner has pointed out, this situation has a longer history than that: "One should remember that the workers' movement of the nineteenth century (and far into our own) quite intentionally desired to place the worker on a 'higher moral plane' and perform a piece of educational work on the cultural level of bourgeois society. The 'Report on Negotiations of the First Congress of the German Workers League' (Frankfurt 1836), for example, says that the contemporary worker 'was not only immature, ignorant, and awkward,' but also lacked 'industriousness' and a sense of 'the higher values of life,' of 'simplicity and purity of manners, for good behavior and character [. . .]' I want to add that bourgeois culture also had to be taken over in its narrower sense of art, of 'higher education,' in accordance with the 'dialectic of inheritance,' in all its schoolmaster purity. Even in Rosa Luxemburg and Karl Liebknecht bourgeois culture is affirmed in the sense of a conservative overtaking from the Left, an almost perverse formula.''[75]

Such a "conservative overtaking," already inherent in the educational concept of nineteenth-century German Social Democracy and made programmatic by Stalinist and revisionist cultural policy, had to be perceived by Stalinist cultural criticism as having a dangerous braking effect on the surge to the "heights of bourgeois culture." Freud's cultural criticism particularly, which traced "the higher values of life, simplicity and purity of manners, good behavior and character" to the "lower" psychosexual mechanism at its basis, especially to repression and the renunciation of instincts; which, that is, manifested the repressive element behind the moral and cultural forces at work in the bourgeoisie—such a criticism had to be almost as much feared by Stalinist cultural policies as by bourgeois. Renunciation of instinctual gratification, at which price the working human being could reach "a higher moral plane," was not rendered problematical by the reformist and revisionist workers' movement. Simple affirmation of bourgeois culture and educational standards also meant affirmation of the mental price the individual had to pay for them. Since psychoanalytical cultural criticism presented a threat to the new socialist *"petit-bourgeois"* manner and the restored superstructure of the "bureaucratically deformed" workers' state, it had to be "fought off" at any price. This, among others, is the reason why particularly the anti-bourgeois side of psychoanalysis, the "critique of cultural sexual morality," was dismissed with such Stalinist pejoratives as "bourgeois," "decadent," and "counter-revolutionary."

On the other hand, Stalinist opposition to psychoanalysis also had its sound, historically legitimate reasons. For the Stalinist "reality principle" of "primary socialist accumulation" was indeed irreconcilable with the hedonistic "pleasure principle" of psychoanalysis. "Primary accumulation" in an underdeveloped country such as the Soviet Union could be accomplished only through immense material and moral deprivations. With this as a historical background, Stoljarov's polemic against the Freudians becomes at least comprehensible: "The anti-proletarian character of the ideology of Freudianism [. . .] manifested itself in an overvaluation of the importance of the pleasure principle and of eroticism as well as of narcissism and individualism.''[76]

Indeed, the rigid socialist work-morality, which imposed an extraordinary renunciation of consumption and instinctual gratification on the Russian workers and farmers, was historically unavoidable in a country which was "constructing socialism" and actually threatened by the capitalist world. This "socialist workers' morality," which was created under conditions of the most extreme internal economic necessities (and which found its most extreme expression in the Stachanov workers), was also the basis of an equally rigid "sexual morality." The economic prerequisites of an increased labor productivity had corresponding psychosexual prerequisites as a consequence: primarily the training and disciplining of the body into an instrument which—in the phase of primary capital accumulation (see also p. 135)—would be achieved at the price of repression of "polymorphous perverse sexuality" (Freud) and the limitation of sexual freedom. Sandkühler remarks: "The hideous economic situation in the Soviet Union, which had been bled by the burdens of war and defense against counter-revolutionary intervention, demanded the renunciation of instincts and needs. This necessarily forced the political rulers to an ideology and apology of the work principle, to the Leninist definition of freedom as 'insight into the necessity of temporary unfreedom' [. . .]."[77]

However, the bourgeois as well as socialist Freudians were far removed from this insight. In "Über eine Weltanschauung" Freud accused Soviet Marxism of having "developed into a religion which has erected an edict against thinking just as unrelenting as that of religion in its time [. . .] Doubting its [Marxist] theory is an activity as persecuted as blasphemy once was by the Catholic Church. The works of Marx and Engels as sources of revelation have replaced the Bible and the Koran."[78] Since Freud was not very enlightened about economic and socialist developmental conditions, his criticism of Stalinism moved very much in the wake of bourgeois ideology. His *petit-bourgeois* class situation made it impossible for him to criticize Stalinism except in terms of "bourgeois unfreedom," of freedom to think and speak. His only explanation for Stalinist "totalitarianism" was "Machiavellism." Freud's bourgeois anti-Stalinism and his misunderstanding of Marxism as an economic philosophy which grievously neglected its psychological factors was one further reason for Russian orthodoxy to put his psychoanalytical theories on its index. Thus it escaped the vulgar Marxists that, although the *petit-bourgeois* Freud was subjectively their enemy, his subversive criticism of sexuality and ideology made him objectively their ally in the struggle against bourgeois ideology.

Stalinist orthodoxy distanced itself not only from bourgeois but also from socialist Freudianism, especially from the German Freudo-Marxists W. Reich, Fromm, Fenichel, and Bernfeld among others. Although these men were justified in defending themselves against the global Stalinist verdict on psychoanalysis, which was the outcome primarily of power-political considerations, and although Reich trenchantly analyzed the connection between political and sexual restoration in the U.S.S.R., his criticism of Stalinist cultural and sexual reaction emanated in many respects from idealistic, even sexual-anarchist wish-fulfillment. Nor did Reich have a proper concept of the economic and political necessity which blocked the way of the "sexual revolution" in the U.S.S.R. What he and the German Freudo-Marxists should have kept in mind was that a satisfactory sexual life was possible only on the basis of a "democratic work" society; and that even in the "democratic work" phase of the Russian revolution, when the worker, farmer, and soldier Soviets were still the true political organs of decision and action in the dictatorship of the proletariat, work was and had to be in good part "forced labor" in the sense of "alienated labor," and that even the brutal Stalinist labor laws were historically necessary to a certain degree.

In that respect their thinking was certainly not Marxist when they ignored Marx's insight that it is only "large industry, in the decisive role it assigns to women, younger persons, and children of both sexes in the socially organized production process outside their mere existence in the home, which creates a new economic foundation for a higher form of the family and of relationships between the sexes."[79] But this "new economic foundation" did not yet exist in the Soviet Union; it first of all had to be created. Nor were the socialist Freudians all that "Freudian" when they ignored the fact that Freud's general claims for culture also had to pertain to Stalinist culture: in other words, that culture has to "channel the energies of sexual activities into the demands of work,"[80] as long as *Ananke,* the necessities of life, that is, the low developmental level of production, demands as much.

Economistic Reduction in the Stalinist Concept of Ideology

The animosity towards psychology that marked the Stalinist era and determines the communist reception of Freud to this day is based primarily on the Marxist concept of the "character mask." The Leftist "anti-psychologism" of neo-Stalinist and Maoist groups in Germany and elsewhere also seeks to condemn psychoanalysis time and again with the argument that Marx's concept of the "character mask" has superseded psychology once and for all. Such a vulgar anti-psychologism, however, mistakes the polemical nature of the concept. Marx used it primarily to attack bourgeois psychologism which sublimated the principle of *"homo homini lupus est"* into an eternal verity of human nature. Marx's criticism is justified to the extent to which psychoanalysis is indebted to Social Darwinist ideology, which raises bourgeois laws of competition to an anthropological constant. (See also pp. 63f.)

Marx also used the concept of "character mask" to oppose bourgeois social psychologism which, though it admitted the influence of the social milieu on the psychology and behavior of people, finally became mired in a reformist ideology. Leftist anti-psychologism also mistook the instrumental nature of this concept. In his Preface to *Capital*, Marx expressly says that he is speaking of persons only insofar as they "are the personifications of economic categories, bearers of certain class relationships and interests."[81] The concept of "character mask" posits the priority of economic processes which occur independently of the will and consciousness of the subject; but simultaneously it points up the "blind spot" of his theory, one which Marx himself was aware of, namely, the psychological, that is, psychosexual "character" of the subject inasmuch as it is not subsumed under the "character mask" in the commodity form of his identity; the consciousness of the subject inasmuch as it is not identical with its being; the life history of the subject inasmuch as it is not identical with the history of its species.

This psychological "blind spot" in Marx's theory (which nonetheless does have its psychological dimension, as we will show later) should therefore not be regarded as a "no confidence" vote on psychology as such but as an expression of priorities. As long as it is a matter of naked survival and existence every preoccupation with the "subjective factor" had to look like the cynicism of bourgeois science. The fact that Marx's interest was not focussed on an investigation of this psychological difference between "sexual character" and "character mask," between subjective consciousness and economic being, does not mean, however, that this difference is irrelevant for the historical process as such. The theoreticians and practitioners of historical materialism could neglect it only as long as it was insignificant with respect to the social and economic driving forces of history. As long as the average consciousness adequately reflected economic existence, that is, class conditions, as was by and large the case in the workers' movement of the nineteenth century, every psychological difference in Marx's concept of ideology was irrelevant. However, the convergence between being and consciousness claimed by the Marxist theory of reflection fell apart at the very latest with the fascist mass movements in Italy and Germany. The German Communist party found itself at a complete loss when confronted by the fact that not only the middle class, politically ambivalent in any event, but some of the workers, even those previously communist, turned fascist. Faced by the fact that—as Reich said—a "gap" opened up between being and consciousness and that individuals within a class no longer behaved in accordance with their class interest but contrary to it, Soviet Marxism in its downplay of the psychological dimension had come to a dead end. Now vulgar Marxist arrogance had its come-uppance, especially with regard to the facility with which psychology had been historically extirpated from Marx's concept of "character mask" and from the Marxist concept of ideology.

This extirpation found its purest expression in the Stalinist "theory of reflection" which liquidated the subject together with its psychology. Stalin thus declared: "Marxism conceives of the laws of science—no matter whether it is a question of the laws of natural science or laws of political economy—as a reflection of objective processes that exist independently of the will of men. Men can discover these laws, recognize them, investigate them, give them consideration, use them for the sake of society, but they can neither change nor eliminate these laws. And of course they are even less able to create or establish new scientific laws [. . .] The same must be said of the laws of political economy—no matter whether it is a question of the period of capitalism or socialism."[82] Such an objectivist understanding of course allows no room for the subject and its psychology. At best the subject can passively imitate what it cannot itself determine. The Stalinist "theory of reflection" which Rubinstein later canonized for psychology, and thereby for psychological science in the Stalinist era, no longer had anything to do, however, with Marx's view that "circumstances form men just as much as men create their circumstances."[83] The Stalinist theory is particularly obtuse, moreover, when it comes to finding the qualitative difference between the historical role of the subject in capitalist and in socialist society.

The Stalinist theory of reflection and the attendant animosity towards psychology perhaps have found their most intelligent expression in Lukács' *History and Class Consciousness,* which even today performs a yeoman's service as a theoretical legitimation for the concept of a party and class consciousness devoid of all psychology. For Lukács "class consciousness [is] not the psychological awareness of the individual proletarian or the [mass psychological] consciousness of their totality [. . .] but the sense of their historical situation of the class of which they have become conscious."[85] Lukács' objectivist concept of class consciousness consciously abstracts from the subjective driving forces, that is, from the barriers of class consciousness, for "the nature of scientific Marxism thus consists in the recognition of the independence of the actual driving forces of history from the [psychological] consciousness of man about them."[86] Although Lukács admits that "the proletariat is forced to seize power in a state of mind and at a time when it still perceives the bourgeois social order as the natural actual and legal one,"[87] and that it "remains caught in many ways in the forms of thought and feeling of capitalism,"[88] yet instead of taking account of these subjective factors of the "bourgeoisefication" of the proletariat and the psychological mechanism of its "emotional ties" to the bourgeois social order for the inhibition of class consciousness—of which Reich at least began to take account—he flees into a mechanistic mythology of party and history: into the party as the "bearer of proletarian class consciousness."[89] The consciousness of the individual proletarian may be totally deformed, but that remains inconsequential with respect to the party as the "bearer of the class consciousness of the proletarians, the conscience of its historical mission."[90] Since class consciousness is "neither the sum nor the average of what single individuals who constitute the class think, perceive, and feel,"[91] it has so to speak to be delegated to the party as an incarnation of the "objective [proletarian] spirit" even if non-proletarian elements such as the intellectuals wield decisive influence in party policies.

This mystical trust in the realization of the "objective spirit" through the party presupposes, however, that the "subjective side functions rationally, that it is the correct consciousness in the sense of the historically achieved average level of development of rationality. Ideologies differ from mass psychoses through the excess of social and the relative insignificance of psychic determinants of the false consciousness: reality in the consciousness of mentally healthy individuals appears in these ideologies for social reasons as an 'inverted world.' "[92] But what Lukács overlooked (as well as the German Communist Party), and what Reich vainly sought to call to their attention, was the historically new degree of the "deformation of the subjective spirit" which fascism knew how to amass and exploit. Horn has noted: "When the spirit—as in German fascism—becomes psychologically entwined, and so personalizes the laws of capitalist society as to reduce them to the alleged anthropology of the Jews, instead of seeing through reified conditions and unmasking the capitalists in turn as 'personifications,' as 'character masks,' then consciousness is not only ideological but also pathological!"[93] This not merely ideological but also "pathological" consciousness, which fascism knew how to mobilze so successfully, could be only insufficiently grasped by the categories of political economy and not at all by those which the vulgar Marxists had delimited. That was why the Stalinist definition of fascism as the rule of the most extreme reactionary, militaristic, and chauvinistic faction of finance capital was blind to the "subjective conditons of objective irrationality" (Adorno), that is, to the mental and psycho-pathological reservoir from which National Socialism was drawing its strength.

Official Stalinist party communism was incapable of grasping the qualitatively different average consciousness in highly developed capitalist countries because it based its evaluation on its experience of the Russian revolution, that is, of a revolution in an industrially underdeveloped agrarian country whose consciousness was still, so to speak, a "*tabula rasa,*" an ideological consciousness of by and large "mentally healthy individuals." In Russia the proletarian revolution was successful without it having been necessary to investigate the "deformations of the subjective spirit and reckoning with them politically. Here the class whose irrational reservoir German fascism had known how to tap so successfully had neither much political nor strategic weight. And this middle class sought to compensate for what had been expropriated from it, and for the subsequent proletarization as a result of the concentration of capital and the world economic crisis of 1929, by means of corresponding ideological and psycho-pathological reaction formations (anti-Semitism, heroism, chauvinism, Arianism, and the like), which Reich brilliantly has described in *The Mass Psychology of Fascism.*[94]

The only exception was the Trotskyite analysis of fascism. It was because of his practical experience in the psychology and politics of the revisionist worker and fascist popular movement that Trotsky arrived at a far more differentiated understanding of the role of the "subjective factor" in history than did the Stalinists who despised him. Among Stalinists he was also the only Bolshevik leader who was relatively familiar with psychoanalysis. In his book *Literature and Revolution* Trotsky minutely detailed the determining influence of the social milieu of many Russian revolutionaries and writers on their feelings, characterological and ideological structures, and forms of expressions; and in his autobiography *My Life* he brilliantly analyzed the social and psychological bases of revisionism in the workers' movements, and noted the striking contradiction between the revolutionary thinking and the philistine-conservative sense of life of the Austro-Marxists which prevented them from developing a truly revolutionary practice.[95] Trotsky also very early recognized the psychological side of fascism, the anti-Semitism and chauvinist resentment which finally turned into a "material force"; and he also suggested the proper tactical and strategic response.[96]

Although Trotskyite politics and theory did greater justice to the meaning of the "subjective factor" in history than did the purely anti-psychological allergy of the Stalinist comintern and the KPD (German Communist Party), his political psychology failed when it came down to his own situation, namely, the relationship of Trotskyite politics and theory to Stalinism. Trotsky's belief in the "missionary consciousness of the working class," especially the Russian, which one day would cast out "Thermidor"—in other words his voluntaristic conception of "permanent revolution"—underestimated the psychological and political lassitude that the Russian working class put up against its being further revolutionized. Trotsky projected not only his very personal disgust onto Stalinism but also his very personal willingness to fight and his "revolutionary virtue"[97] onto the Russian working class as a whole. He therefore made the same mistake with respect to the Russian proletariat that the Stalinist comintern leadership and the KPD, which was at the mercy of this mistake, made with respect to the German working class when it slipped into a Romantic psychologism which in a certain sense was the other side of the coin of Stalinist economism. Just as the Stalinist KPD idealized the German proletariat, so Trotsky idealized the Russian one. Stalin and the Stalinist KPD were just as reluctant to admit that sections of the German proletariat sympathized with fascism, thereby objectively betraying their own class interest, as Trotsky was reluctant to admit that a large part of the Russian proletariat supported Stalin's anti-Trotskyite terror, thereby also betraying its class interest for a long time to come.

Trotsky's belief in materialistic rationality, the victory of historical reason, which finally would also win out over Stalin, was just as blind to the demoralizing effect of the Stalinist terror and Stalinist ideology as the Stalinist KPD was blind, until 1933, to the immense mobilizing success of Nazi ideology and demagogy. Trotsky had just as little understanding of the increasingly autonomous and irrational dynamic of Stalinist bureaucracy, which literally sought to exterminate the Trotskyite opposition, as Stalin and the Stalinist comintern had of the irrational reservoirs that fed the fascist movement. Compared to the paranoiac crusades of the GPU, from which Trotsky was not safe even in his Mexican exile in Cocoyan, Trotskyite rationality appears quite feckless. In H. Lange's "Trotzki in Cocoyan" Rühle makes this reply to Trotsky's bodyguard who refuses in the name of materialistic reason to have seen a vampire in front of Trotsky's house: "Why always so much rationalism, comrade Rosmer? Think about it, the mysticism of the GPU has been knocking against this door for three years!"[98]

The same paranoiac spirit that governed the anti-Trotskyite crusades of the Stalinist GPU also determined the infights among the Trotskyite factions. The endless bifurcations of the Trotskyite splinter groups could scarcely have been motiviated by political reason: "For example, one can ask oneself whether certain splits which befell Trotskyism in the darkest hours of Stalinist persecution did not arise from a certain guilt feeling, whether in fact they were not a form of hara-kiri. When the bureaucracy and its methods seem to be proved right every day, when this bureaucracy keeps reiterating that it is infallible, when a puny opposition is faced with the gravest misery day in and day out, then it becomes difficult not to experience eventually what one of us has called 'a crisis of loneliness in an unfriendly world.' . . . This then can lead to a person's feeling responsible for the crimes of which he is accused, considering himself a traitor to the working class, and giving himself up to self-destructive thoughts."[99]

Stalin's anti-Trotskyite campaign of destruction and the anti-Stalinist self-destruction of the Trotskyite splinter groups, to which large parts of the Russian intelligentsia fell victim, were as incomprehensible in purely economic categories as the anti-Semitic extermination campaign of the Nazis (even if both are not on the same level, that is, cannot be simply equated as bourgeois totalitarianism theory does). For from a purely economic standpoint, the extermination of a highly qualified Jewish labor force—particularly during a period of acute labor shortage caused by increased war production—was just as irrational as the extermination of a large part of a highly qualified (and not only Trotskyite) intelligentsia. Both phenomena were signs that ideology had become autonomous with respect to its basis, the false and primarily "pathological" consciousness with respect to economic existence. This did not so much point up the inexactitude of Marx's phrase "being determines consciousness," but only its "blind spot," namely, how (class) psychological mechanisms are translated into class consciousness by means of social and economic contradictions—and what is much more important, how this blind spot could be eliminated.

For no matter the difference between the political and ideological motivation behind the Nazis' mad system of anti-Semitism and the Stalinists' anti-Trotskyite madness, both had one mass-psychological function in common: to divert attention from their inner social contradictions—in Nazi Germany from that between capitalists and the working class; in the U.S.S.R. from that between Stalinist bureaucracy and the masses of the people—by projecting them on an external enemy. It was the fundamental weakness of Trotsky's policy towards Stalinism, as well as of Stalinist policy towards the Nazis, that neither, for lack of a political psychology, foresaw these individual and collective "defense formations" of class consciousness, nor grasped their mechanisms. Both "parties" were devoid of any notion of the psychic mechanisms that come into play during the destruction of class consciousness. That the "defense mechanisms of the ego" (Anna Freud[100]), among them projection, introjection, repression, and denial, also stand in the service of the rejection of class consciousness, and that social contradictions, for example, can be banned from the collective consciousness for decades (as through paranoiac projection onto the Jews or onto the Trotskyites), seemed just as incomprehensible to the Stalinists as to the Trotskyites. Both of them acted "idealistically" when they—Trotsky to the Russian, the Stalinist KPD to the German proletariat—imputed a rational consciousness, that is, political acting and thinking that just so happened to be subjectively identical with their objective class interests for the workers. Both of them therefore underestimated the idealist-bourgeois elements in the consciousness of the proletariat, its susceptibility to irrational ideologies and feelings inimical to its class.

Reich's Revolutionary Question: The "Split" Between Being and Consciousness

The mechanistic economism of the Stalinist comintern and its dependent KPD found its clearest expression in its theory of "revolutionary uplift." Even though the economic destitution and social insecurity caused by the crisis of 1929 produced an ideological movement to the Right of wide worker and *petit-bourgeois* strata, the Stalinists managed to read the consequences of the sharpening of this crisis as a general Left-ward drift. The unconscious reverse side of this mechanistic economism was a Romantic psychologism in which the KPD projected its own revolutionary position and feelings onto the working class as a whole, thus ignoring the decisive question to which W. Reich—here in the words of one of his followers—had tried to call attention: "That human beings who are hungry become rebellious does not surprise us, but that [. . .] human beings let themselves be oppressed for a wage which is too large to die and too small to live on is a fact worth contemplating. Moreover, when proletarian masses vote for a fascist party that is manifestly in the pay of the capitalists or push through the *Anschluss* of the Saar region to Thyssen and Röchling's Hitler Germany, in short, actually act in their own disinterest, then we are faced with a fact before which our entire Marxist knowledge collapses [. . .] No wonder, because these questions are of a psychological nature and we do not have a useful Marxist psychology."[101]

The fact that the working masses already followed the nationalist slogans in 1914; that their majority did not support the Spartacus movement during the November revolution but went over to the bourgeois parties; that, finally, in 1933, they succumbed by and large to fascist propaganda—all these indeed are not simply "questions of a psychological nature," and neither are they questions which could be solved solely by resorting to political economy. Yet there were Marxist answers to them: the power of bourgeois ideology and manipulation, the privileged position of certain segments of the working class and the corruption of the workers' bureaucracy, the absence of a truly revolutionary *avant-garde*, and so on. But these answers do not explain the blind loyalty with which the workers remained attached to organizations which had led them, in 1933, into defeat without their ever putting up a fight.

Reich's *The Mass Psychology of Fascism* provided, so to speak, the psychological complement to Lenin's exclusively politically and economically founded "theory of the worker aristocracy" which meant to explain the absence of revolution in highly developed imperialist countries, especially Germany. According to Lenin, imperialism had created a vertical line of division between a workers' aristocracy, which participated in the colonial surplus profits of the imperialist bourgeoisie and had been politically corrupted by the Social Democrats, and the class-conscious aspect of the workers. In Reich's view, however, there existed not only a vertical but also a horizontal line of division in the psychic structure and in the consciousness of the individual worker himself. "Men, human beings, succumb to the conditions of being in two ways: directly through the immediate effect of their economic and social conditions, and indirectly, as mediated by the ideological structure of their society [. . .] The worker is exposed to his class situation as well as to the general ideology of bourgeois society."[102] From this Reich concluded that the average worker is neither unequivocally revolutionary nor unequivocally reactionary, but carries within himself a contradiction between a revolutionary stance (on the basis of his class situation) and bourgeois inhibitions (on the basis of his ideological indoctrination).

But for the KPD there existed only the vertical dividing line and that is why it drew that fatal "vertical" line of separation—because of its theory of social fascism which it had taken over from the comintern—between the Social Democratic party of the workers, who were designated "social fascists," and the allegedly revolutionary party of the workers. But that was what sabotaged the united front between the Social Democratic and communist workers once and for all and the downfall of the German workers was sealed. The National Socialists in their political propaganda took into consideration the horizontal line of separation in the consciousness of the average worker by appealing, with their anti-capitalist "social rhetoric," to a murky "revolutionary attitude," while simultaneously using their nationalistic and *völkisch* ideology to augment their "bourgeois inhibitions," that is, their identification with the "Führer state." Of course, the victory of the National Socialists and the defeat of the communist movement cannot be explained solely by means of the "mass psychological" success of Nazi propaganda; rather it was the historical sum of a whole era of class struggles which were being kept at low pitch on the one hand by the leadership of a corrupt and opportunistic Social Democracy and by a bureaucratically petrified comintern on the other; and this era was almost bound to conclude with the victory of fascist reaction. Yet the Nazis also owed their victory on the ideological front to the fact that they took into account the psychological and political ambivalence of the average worker's consciousness instead of setting out from a materialistic-Manichean view of "bad" social fascists and "good" revolutionary communists.

Since the KPD completely subscribed to the Stalinist verdict against psychoanalysis, it also rejected Reich's social-psychological declaration and delineation of "bourgeois inhibitions" in the consciousness of a wide strata of *petit bourgeoisie* and workers. Since Stalinist economics remained completely caught up in the bourgeois conception of sexuality it remained blind to the psychosexual foundations of the "authority-bound" character (Fromm) and the latter's reactionary ideologies. Since Stalinism itself was a victim of "cultural sexual morality" it did not consider sex a primary need. For the simple communist understanding counted only hunger and thirst among the primary needs—what Freud called "the instincts for self-preservation"—and as part of the "basis." Sexuality pure and simple was consigned to the area of consumption. Thus W. Pieck rejected Reich's concept with the argument that "he was setting out from the sphere of consumption and not of production."[103] It was to no avail that Reich repeatedly emphasized the productive or destructive role of sexuality, that is, of bourgeois sexual morality for the character and ideology of the human being.

E. Fromm had already pointed out the need for an "analytical social psychology,"[104] whose basis was to be Freud's dualist theory of instinct, that is, the psychoanalytical differentiation between "instincts" (hunger, thirst) which press rigidly for immediate gratification, and "sexual drives" which are to a high degree replaceable, repressible, and modifiable, that is, which are transformed into pathological symptoms upon non-gratification and look for surrogates in the form of pathological symptom-, character-, and ideology-formations. According to Fromm and Reich these replaceable, repressible, and modifiable "sexual drives," which official Marxism shunted "to the Right," constituted the psychological and psycho-pathological potential which fascist and imperialist ideologies utilize. In his *Mass Psychology of Fascism* Reich showed how an ideology which is inimical to sexuality and pleasure, an ideology to which the proletariat had also been subjected, makes one fearful, shy, authority- and God-fearing, obedient, manageable in the bourgeois sense because every rebellious, class-struggle-like impulse is laden with heavy neurotic fear. He likewise showed how the prohibition of sexual thought finally has as a consequence a general inability to think and be critical and how this condition leads to blind loyalty to family, religious and state authorities, and authoritarian political organizations; in short, how an ideology which opposes sexuality ahd pleasure creates a long-suffering citizen in family, school, and church, someone who is adjusted to a patriarchal private-economical order despite material need and humiliation.

The KPD rejected this psychoanalytical interpretation of any such "bourgeois inhibitions" in the mental structure of the average worker, that is, the average member of the *petit bourgeoisie,* with the argument among others that the categories underlying it had been developed from case histories of bourgeois patients and therefore were irrelevant for the psychology of the proletariat. From the fact that psychoanalysis had primarily investigated individuals of the bourgeoisie, that is, of the decadent class, orthodox Marxism drew the short-circuit conclusion that psychoanalysis itself was a decadent science. Marxism did not understand that psychoanalysis as a science of the pseudo-nature of the bourgeois human being could play an important role in the emancipation of the proletariat insofar as the proletariat itself was bourgeois. Indeed, psychoanalysis was unsuited to grasp the psychology of the proletariat, which is determined by the capitalist production process, because it did not reflect upon—this was one of its blind spots—the effect of wage labor on consciousness, behavior, and the structure of the instincts. (See also

p. 70.) Yet it was in a position genetically to analyze those elements in the psychology and ideology of the proletariat which were assimilated products from *(petit) bourgeois* ideology; and to such products belonged primarily that complex of moral conceptions which were the immediate product not of the class situation but of the bourgeois family structure of the proletariat. That is why Reich and Fromm focussed their attention chiefly on the patriarchal-monogamous family as the "structure factory" of the complexes of feelings and ideology which opposed the formation of class consciousness: for example, sado-masochistic submission to patriarchal authority as the basis of the "bond to the Führer"; incestuous mother and family fixations as the subjective basis of nationalist "home-land feeling" and a *völkisch* blood-and-soil ideology; moral over-compensation as a defense mechanism against homo- and heterosexuality in the form of "feelings about honor," "heroism," "racial purity"; and so on.

Particularly Reich showed that the bourgeois process of socialization, which specifically deforms the sexual drives and to which the proletariat is more or less subjected, can become the psychological turntable between being and consciousness, so that the individual consequently no longer conforms to what is his class interest but to what is contrary to it. This "split" could not be explained by the orthodox "theory of reflection" because it either ignored "social-psychological links" (Fromm), that is, the specific socializing mediation between being and consciousness, or considered them irrelevant. With its mechanistic concept of ideology orthodox party communism was incapable of explaining the genesis and resistance of *petit-bourgeois* feelings and moral concepts in the ranks of the worker movement, not to mention of its inability to give a political account of them. For that would have required the despised psychoanalytical theory of socialization which could have made an important contribution towards explaining the "cultural lag" between being and consciousness.

According to Freud, the outer forces and the norms of society are interiorized through mediation of the super-ego; the transformation of the outer social forces into inner "moral" compulsion occurs in the process of socialization through identification of the child with failing educators and the enthronement of parental pre- and proscriptions. The conservative character of super-ego ideologies becomes evident from the fact that parents and educators in their educational procedures hold to the rules of their super-egos. The ego, that is, the super-ego of the child is therefore not actually modeled on the parents themselves, but on the parental super-ego: "it [the super-ego of the child] is filled with the same content, it becomes the carrier of the tradition, of all timeless values which have been handed on over the generations."[105] The super-ego becomes the psychic guarantor of all traditional conceptions of value and morality which oppose social progress. It has the same "shackling effect" in the psychic economy as relationships within production have towards the productive forces in capitalist economy. Just as—according to Marx —the social-productive powers are transformed into destructive powers under pressure of relationships within production, so the instinctual powers are transformed into destructive powers under pressure of the super-ego. This means that a portion of instinctual energy is mobilized by the suppressors and led into a class struggle on the side of the suppressors, particularly that portion utilized for the acceptance and appropriation of "sexually inimical bourgeois morality" (Reich). In a certain sense the super-ego thus becomes the "Trojan horse of a class society in each and every individual, structurally reproducing that society in the mind [. . .] If everyone functions as his own policeman, as his own secret police, not only towards himself but primarily against all others, such is the ideal super-ego of bourgeois society [. . .] The super-ego consequently represents the root of the counter-revolution at the deepest level of the instinctual nature of the individual."[106]

The relatively determinative character of childhood experiences and the relative "fixation" of pre- and proscriptions interiorized during childhood are the reasons for the effectiveness of certain characterological and ideological structures which often retain that effectiveness far beyond their actual social need. The psychic structure in a certain sense functions as a balance wheel that maintains its pendulum movement even if the motor stops. At this point Freud's critique of the idea of historical materialism was completely justified: "It seems likely that what are known as materialistic views of history sin in underestimating this factor. They brush it aside with the remark that human ideologies are nothing other than the product and superstructures of their contemporary economic conditions. That is true, but very probably not the whole truth. Mankind never lives entirely in the present. The past, the tradition of the race and of the people, lives on in the ideologies of the super-ego and yields only slowly to the influences of the present and to new changes; and so long as it works through the super-ego it plays a powerful part in human life, independent of the economic conditions."[107]

The relative independence of super-ego ideologies, acquired in childhood, towards the actual development of economic and social conditions can, under certain conditions, become a mighty ideological brake on a pre- or post-revolutionary period. P. Brückner has pointed out that, "As Lenin writes, it is not only the 'small property-owners' who surround, drench, and demoralize the proletariat after the revolution. Lenin also mentions, in connection with the 'millions upon millions of small-scale owners' who restore the power of the bourgeoisie through their imperceptible, intangible desiccation, the 'habits' of human beings as 'the most horrible power,' and worried that the revolutionaries would so to speak be sucked up by the habits of the masses."[108] Since Marxism-Leninism ignored Freud's insight into the genesis and resistance of such an atrophied ideology of the super-ego, it necessarily underestimated their practical contribution to the "Thermidor" of the revolution. The backward development of the Russian revolution provided ample proof that the psychological and ideological petrification of this "second nature" on the level of consciousness would allow restoration of such things as the production of commodities on the level of existence. And the German workers' movement in 1933 provided proof that these petrified ideologies of the super-ego, these relationships determined by production, cannot be revolutionized without a pre-, that is, cultural-revolutionary, alteration of that "second nature"—despite the objective ripeness of the historical situation. The degree to which the "ideology of the super-ego, the past, the tradition of the race and the people, continued to persist" (Freud) was proved by the ease with which the Nazis were able to inculcate their *völkisch,* racist, and revanchist ideology ultimately even in the workers' movement.

It was to Reich's credit that he applied the Marxist law of "non-simultaneity of development" to the relationship between being and consciousness by introducing Freud's theory of socialization into the Marxist concept of ideology. However, we should note that Reich and the German Freudo-Marxists tended to overestimate the importance of the "subjective (inhibiting) factor" because they lacked insight into the *objective* reasons for the defeat of the German workers' movement.Thus nowhere does one find in Reich, Bernfeld, Fromm, Fenichel, and others an exhaustive analysis of the historical and political background of the defeat of the German workers' movement: namely, in the corruption of the Social Democrats which already began with the "elective party" in the eighties and nineties of the nineteenth century, and which is intimately connected with the revisionist degeneration of the II International; also in the policies of the Stalinist comintern which since the III World Congress wanted to undercut any revolutionary strategy of the European worker movement because Stalin's Russian policy of "socialism in one country" depended on the cooperation of the European bourgeoisie and the consequent cessation of activities of the European workers' movement; in the comintern's fatal policy of "social fascism" which brought the united front between the SPD and the KPD to final collapse; and so on.[109] This incidentally also applies to the Frankfurt School: for lack of a real analysis of the objective conditions for the defeat of the German workers' movement it finally sought to explain that defeat solely by means of an "analytical social psychology" (Fromm). (Compare also p. 277.)

The psychoanalytical interpretation of Reich and the German Freudo-Marxists provided an invaluable corrective to the *petit bourgeois* complex of feelings and super-ego ideologies which were also deeply embedded in the workers, to that mechanistic conception of class consciousness as voiced by Lukács and the Stalinist comintern. In order to destroy the historical transition of an irrational complex of feelings and ideologies one had—so Reich demanded—also to bind the *feelings* of those masses standing outside the party to the revolutionary movement, as the fascists knew how to do in such a masterly fashion. Therefore one had to tear the monopoly on psychology from the hands of bourgeois science and put it at the service of the workers' movement. This practical task of Marxist psychology lay, Reich felt, primarily in "speaking the language" of the masses. In *What Is Class Consciousness?* he confronted the abstract agitation and propaganda of the KPD, which derived from "high politics," with the demand that politics would again have to make a "connection with the little, banal, private everyday life and wishes of the broadest masses in all their variety. Only in this way can we succeed in creating a confluence of the objective sociological process and the subjective consciousness of human beings, of destroying the contradiction and the gulf between them . . ."[110] Not only the "economic laws of capital" and the great "interconnections in world politics" but also the everyday irrational complex of feelings and ideologies which separated the broad masses from communist organizations were to be put into the center of the agitational and propagandist process. Not only unemployment and the economic crisis but also "neurotic mass misery," not only the bourgeois state but also its psychological "structure factory," the bourgeois family, were to become objects of political campaigns.

The "Sex-Pol movement," which Reich initiated and which sought to make visible the connection between economic-political and sexual repression, contained the germs of a "cultural revolution" as the inalienable tactical element of the social and political revolution. Even though Sex-Pol practice, which primarily supported the "sexual struggle of the workers' youth," produced no spectacular success (not least of all because the KPD withdrew its support very shortly), it nonetheless possessed the correct basic insight that high capitalism had to be fought not only as an economically exploitative system but also one which in a historically new degree had deformed and neuroticized the instinctual and super-ego structures of the masses. The Sex-Pol program, the consistent "politicizing of the sexual question," even if in a "sexually and economically abbreviated manner," accounted for the historically new level of interiorization of bourgeois ideology and morality, that is, its anchoring through feeling in the psychosexual structure of the masses. It is to Reich's credit, with the help of psychoanalytic theory, to have grasped and practically employed Marx's statement that the "elimination of self-alienation follows the same course as self-alienation."

Late capitalism, however, to a large extent has blunted the tip of Reich's Sex-Pol program. In the wake of new profit and selling strategies of monopoly capitalism (compare also p. 213), the classic bourgeois sexual taboos, towards the overcoming of which Sex-Pol fought, are being increasingly dismantled. The degree to which modern capital utilizes sexuality itself to realize its programs would not have dawned on Reich. The "sexual revolution" which capitalism unloosened as a blind byproduct of its new revolution in turnover has largely undercut the demand for sexual freedom. That is why all new editions of the Sex-Pol movement today have become more or less obsolete.

Yet in other respects Reich's work is still pertinent, notably for today's Left. The abstract and objectivist propaganda and agitation of the KPD which he criticized for ignoring concrete psychology, that is, the concrete consciousness and need structure of the masses, seem to persist and dominate the language of the "New Left," especially its academic wing. Ernst Bloch's criticism of the propagandist practices of the communists in the twenties and thirties therefore is again relevant today: "A too abstract [. . .] Left [has] undernourished the masses [. . .] The Nazis speak deceptively but to human beings, the communists absolutely truthfully, but only of things."[111] It is not sufficient—this today's Left can learn from the mass-psychological practitioner Reich and not the theoretician of the orgasm—to analyze history and politics solely from the viewpoint of the objective rationality of capital movements; it is at least as important to take account of the frequently irrational reflexes of the rationality of capitalism in the consciousness of wage-earners. In countries where a large part of the wage-earning population is still blindly loyal to the parties of big capitalism and large landowners, the "split" between being and consciousness is no less great than during Reich's time. That is why Reich's warning to those on the Left who lightly dismiss psychology in the name of materialist rationality can still be endorsed today: "The more rational the behavior the narrower are the tasks for a psychology of the unconscious; the more irrational the further, the wider, the greater is sociology's need of psychology. This is particularly true for the behavior of the repressed classes during the class struggle."[112]

Reich's Naturalistic Misunderstanding of Marxism and Psychoanalysis

It is a well-known fact that Wilhelm Reich, the black sheep of the International Psychoanalytical Society as well as the German Communist Party, was excluded by both at the same time. The Reich case shows how unbridgeable the theoretical and practical gulf in fact is between Marxist and Freudian orthodoxy. Neither the IPS nor the KPD was in a position to criticize theories dialectically, to differentiate between the revolutionary questions he posed and the revisionist, that is, naturalistic deformation in his thinking. The fact that Reich's theoretical and practical attempt to mediate between Marxism and psychoanalysis was rejected *in toto* by both sides is probably the reason why in his late phase, during his emigration, he turned away from both. His late "rejection" of Marxism and psychoanalysis looks like an unconscious act of revenge on his spiritual "parents" whose dogmatic "heirs" rejected him, each for different reasons. His later theories, whether biological, sexual, mechanistic, or pertaining to the "orgone," which can be diagnosed only as scientifically camouflaged delusions, testify to the fact that his spirit was finally ground down between the Scylla of Stalinism and the Charybdis of Freudian orthodoxy. A critique of Reich which—as appears to be the case recently—emphatically unmasks these scientifically camouflaged phantasms for what they are, so as to demolish them once again, however makes things somewhat too easy for itself. A twin boycott on the part of Marxists and Freudians can no more explain Reich's theoretical confusion, or thereby excuse it (because in part his confusion can be traced to his early writings), than such a boycott is capable of discrediting his revolutionary beginnings and the progress of his thinking with respect to Stalinist as well as Freudian orthodoxy. The problematical nature, or even tragedy, of Wilhelm Reich consists in his attempt—so necessary and important in many ways—to find a third way between Stalinist economism and Freudian psychologism ending up as a naturalistic contraction of Marxist as well as psychoanalytical theory.

(1) Indeed it is to Reich's credit to have—in a certain sense—"Stood Freud upright." Thus he roundly denounced the metaphysical idealism in Freud's phylogenetic construction (especially in *Totem and Taboo*) and provided what was initially an enlightening materialistic model for the connection between sexual repression and economic exploitation. In *The Imposition of Sexual Morality*[113] Reich, in far-reaching agreement with the ethnological investigations and interpretations of Bachofen, Morgan, and Engels, described how, with the transition from matriarchal communal economy to patriarchal private property economic society, "cultural sexual morality" was internalized and institutionalized: a limitation of promiscuity, the enforcement of asceticism and monogamy, and the limitation of sexual satisfaction to the genital procreative function were interpreted as a "sexual-economic securing" of the privatization and monopolization of economic power. But these historical-materialistic explanations drifted into a sexual-economic naturalism in the end, which in a certain sense is the non-dialectic other side of Freud's metaphysical idealism. For Reich the "imposition of sexual morality" became the division between "healthy" nature and "diseased" culture. Reich understood history since the "origin of the family, of private property and the state" (Engels), only as "biopathy," as history of defection from nature, that is, from the "natural genital" life of the ur-communist society. His concept of history as an individual and collective history of denaturali-

zation—especially in his later writings—increasingly lost its historically materialist dimension. His therapeutic revolutionary program—on the individual level: creation of the "genital" character structure, that is, orgasmic potency, "self-regulation of sexual needs"; on the collective level: creation of a "democratic work" society, self-regulation of social production and distribution—probably had at its basis a naturalistic concept of history as well as of instinct. If it is the objective of individual therapy to "put the human animal in a position to accept nature in itself,"[114] then the goal of collective therapy is a "democratic work" society which "attempts [. . .] to remove the contradiction which a 'mis-development' of nature—6,000 years of exploitation, mysticism, and sexual repression—have caused in society."[115]

It is to Reich's credit to have refuted, and in a certain sense de-psychologized, the idealistic and cultural-pessimistic outgrowths of Freud's instinctual theory, such as Freud's reactionary Thanatos hypothesis which was based[116] on the presumption of a "primary masochism." But his own concept of instinct was far less complex than Freud's. Whereas Freud essentially understood the concept of instinct as an instrumental one "for the delimitation of the psychic from the physical," Reich on the other hand posited the naturalistic conception that the "physical and psychic basic functions, that we can grasp, are completely identical in the elements that represent life."[117] Whereas Freud's formulations of the concept of instinct were always careful and ambivalent, Reich simply made the hypothesis a dichotomy of "primary" natural biological and "secondary" drives that had become "asocial" through social repression. Whereas Freud developed his model of the psychic apparatus (id, ego, super-ego) first of all as a conflict model for the explanation of dreams, slips, and neuroses, Reich posited an anthopologically stratified model in which "biopathy," the history of the "pathological human animal," has become sedimented. Behind the strata of drives that have been deformed and perverted through "exploitation, mysticism, and sexual repression there live and work a natural sociability and sexuality, a spontaneous joy in work, a capacity to love. This last and third level which represents the biological heart of the human structure [. . .] is the only real hope which human beings have of eventually overcoming social misery."[118]

Reich's other accomplishment, the consistent development of Freud's only sketchily outlined "character typology" into a "character and resistance analysis," stands in the shadow of a naturalistic revision of the psychoanalytical concept of sexuality, that is, genitality. Reich's stylization of the "genital" character into a "healthy" character *ipso facto* not only reproduced Freud's mistake of having raised the psychology of the bourgeois entrepreneur ego to psychology as such. (See also p. 74.) It even lagged behind Freud's insight, which at least had culture-critical value, that the establishment of "genital primacy" over the anarchy of the partial instincts cost a high psychic price, namely, a preservation of the self and species (procreation); and of the polymorphous-perverse pleasure principle under a "castrating" reality principle. For according to Freud the whole body is basically originally a single "erogenous zone." While the partial instincts are anarchical at first, each of them wanting only pleasure, and only group around certain bodily zones (mouth, anus, genitals) with progressive maturation, the creation of "genital primacy" desexualizes the body, that is, polymorphous-perverse sexuality is pushed back in favor of genital procreation and performance. Reich overlooked the fact that the capitalist performance principle is what compels the "repressive genital principal at the cost of the partial drives, that is, what limits sexuality to the genital function of procreation and performance. Its ideal-utopian concept of an orgasmically potent 'genital' character therefore is derived from a 'conservative normality' ideal."[119] The same holds true for his concept of "mental health," which finally has the bourgeois ideology of performance at its basis. Thus he declared: "When we speak of mental health, we mean [. . .] a mental condition which is characterized by social performance and adjustment capacity."[120] Social "performance" and adjustment "capacity," however, mean in capitalist society the ability to work and compete.

Because Reich ignored the mental costs of a "genital primacy which guarantees a social performance and adjustment capacity," the dialectic disappeared from his concept of pathology, that is, neurosis, which is what distinguished Freud's conception. Whereas Reich reduced the problem of mental "health" and "normality" to one of "genital" or non-genital sexuality, Freud—and also Marcuse—emphasized the progressive, even subversive element of neurosis, that is, its negative element, perversion. "Perversion appears to offer a *promesse de bonheur*," writes Marcuse, "which is greater than 'normal sexuality.' Freud emphasizes the 'exclusive' character of deviations from the norm, their rejection of the sexual act as a purely procreative one. Perversions thus express a rebellion against the subjugation of sexuality under the command of the principle of procreation and against the institutions which guarantee this command [. . .] Perversions appear to reject the whole enslavement of the pleasure-ego by the reality-ego."[121]

For Reich on the other hand there was only a "healthy," "natural" genital character and a "pathological," neurotic pre-genital character. He was just as blind to the repressive element of bourgeois "genitality" as to the subversive element of the pre-genitality which he strove to thwart. Instead of pleading for a loosening of the "repressive genital principle," which would have been a presupposition for a free development and integration of the partial drives on a newer and higher stage (or for what Marcuse has called the "self-sublimation" of the instincts), he pleaded for a "therapeutic cleaning of the genital libido-object of pre-genital strivings."[122] With that he actually limited the subversive element of psychoanalysis, namely extending the concept of sexuality beyond what bourgeois genitality permitted, which was "rehabilitation of the partial drives" (Dahmer). By absolutizing the orgasm as the "high point of the sexual event" Reich simultaneously abstracted from specific pre-genital pleasure qualities the liberation of which—as in Marcuse—would mark the beginning of the utopia of a liberated Eros. Since he failed to differentiate between the natural-biological significance of the genital function (orgastic potency and procreative capacity) and its social and specifically cultural significance ("social performance and adjustment capability"), any other social interpretation of the genital function was impossible for him. However, it is more than likely that in a society whose forms of behavior are determined by cooperation and solidarity instead of by exploitation and competition, "genital primacy" will also acquire a qualitatively different mental significance. Dahmer thus observes: "If on the basis of a decrease in socially required work time and a consequent abundance of labor power, effective and unharmful contraceptives are developed, and the connection between genital primacy and procreation is severed, then the tyranny of the genital zone will be lessened. Reich separated sexuality (the pleasure process) from procreation, but simultaneously held onto genital primacy as a natural principle. Only through isolation of the genital function with respect to the meaning it has for human beings of a particular society and a particular class, of their wishes, fears, and illusions, does it become clinically and technically manipulable."[123]

Reich's reified concept of "genitality" also impressed its mark on his conception of female sexuality. His differentiation between "vaginal sexuality," meaning female submissiveness, and "clitoral sexuality" as something comparable to phallic, male activity, once more reproduced, this time on the level of female sexuality, a social role distribution of the sexes.

If Reich's progressive notion with respect to Freud originally consisted of his critique of "cultural sexual morality," which he combined with a Marxist critique of capitalist production relationships, the connection he made between political-social and sexual revolution fell apart in his later thinking. The Sex-Pol movement, which was still the practical expression of a "politicizing of the sexual question," from which Freud kept shying away, as well as Reich's orgasm and later orgone theory, again de-politicize the sexual question, that is, naturalize it. Reich's "sexual economy" finally degenerated into a "cure-all"; and the "sexual-eco-nomic self-steering of the organism," that is, the creation of orgastic potency, became the key to all problems endangering man. "The longed-for unity of and contradictoriness of culture and nature, work and love, morality and sexuality," he wrote, "remains a dream as long as human beings do not allow the biological demand for natural (orgastic) sexual gratification. And so will genuine democracy and responsible freedom remain an illusion."[124]

The naïve naturalism of Reich's "sexual economy" brought him—as Dahmer has shown—into the proximity of the "true socialists" of the nineteenth century: "Among the *petit-bourgeois* ideologies criticized by the Communist Manifesto there also belongs a group of 'true socialists' who were heavily influenced by Feuerbach's 'new religion,' the 'cult of abstract man.' What connects these 'true socialists' with Feuerbach (and with W. Reich) is their appeal to nature and what is natural as a norm. The critique of the idolatry of nature is [. . .] developed by Marx: 'The true socialist starts with the idea that the split between life and happiness has to stop. So as to find proof for this sentence he takes recourse to nature and imputes to it that it is devoid of this split, and from this he then derives the conclusion that since man has a natural body and possesses the general qualities of body, this split also should not exist in him.'"[125]

Reich's failure therefore was due not only to the economic obtuseness of Stalinist orthodoxy but primarily to his own naturalistic misunderstanding of psychoanalysis. He believed that he could simply eliminate its ideological dirt—for example, Freud's theory of the death instinct—and distill a "pure" science of the "instinctual nature of man as such"; but that way he was unable to grasp the ideological "trace elements" which were also part of Freud's "scientific" psychology, and which made Reich's "sexual economy" impure without his ever noticing. The progressive de-psychologization of Freud's instinctual theory now made it atrophy and biologically petrify. With a scaffolding of ontological categories Reich sought to grasp the "invariable" sexual-economic structure among "variable" changing social conditions. However, he only succeeded in reproducing the "scientistic self-misunderstanding of psychoanalysis" (Habermas). He did not understand that psychoanalysis is only the science of the pseudo-nature of bourgeois man, of the "individuated individual" (Marx) to whom his own character and diseases, his own capacities and incapabilities, what in reality is the socially mediated sedimentation of a "second nature," appears as nature as such. As Dahmer has observed: "Psychoanalysis has to do with data and connections of a pseudo-nature which comes into existence only through the self-abnegation of the subject under the pressure of social rules mediated by the family."[126] Psychoanalysis is neither in Freud nor Reich a natural science; rather it is a critique of pseudo-nature, a critique not only of natural processes—such as Reich thought—but also of "indigenous" psychological processes, which occur behind one's back, without the will or consciousness or control of human beings. This is its only and simultaneously its decisive relationship to a critique of political economy. (See also p. 150.) But this is precisely what Reich overlooked.

(2) Reich's naturalistic misunderstanding of psychoanalysis also largely determined his understanding of political economy. This can be demonstrated by his concept of fascism and Stalinism, but chiefly by his understanding of ideology.

Thus his revolutionary contribution *The Mass Psychology of Fascism,* a book with seven seals in the eyes of the Stalinist comintern, was simultaneously concerned with a step-by-step revision of Marxism's analysis of fascism. Although in 1933 Reich, with the appearance of *The Mass Psychology of Fascism,* still based himself on such a Marxist analysis of fascism with the Preface to the third edition the only remnant was the definition of fascism in "sexual-economic-biological" terms which have now almost entirely lost their social-historical dimension. In this Preface he outdid the previously Stalinist theory of "universal fascism," which he himself had fought so bitterly at one time and according to which almost all forms of political sovereignty from that of the bourgeoisie to that of the reformist workers' movement were designated as "fascist." Reich insisted that "Fascism [is] only a politically organized expression of the average human character structure [. . .] the mechanistic mystical character of human beings of our era creates the fascist parties and not vice versa [. . .] Fascism is not a political party but a certain way of viewing life, and an attitude to human beings, to love and to work."[127]

The political-economic basis of his concept of Stalinism likewise disappeared as it did from his concept of fascism. Reich knew that the "sexual revolution" was possible only on the basis of a "democratic work society" which he felt existed in revolutionary Soviet Union. But when he was forced to observe how the basis of "democratic work" in Soviet society was dismantled step by step in the wake of its Stalinization he was bitterly disappointed. He simply distinguished abstractly and naturalistically between two basic types of work: "the forcibly-unpleasurable and the naturally-pleasurable."[128] He did not comprehend the fact that in an economically and politically exhausted Soviet Union, "forcibly-unpleasurable" labor put decisive limits on the "naturally-pleasurable." Being an "anarchistic sexual theoretician" (Bernfeld), he could not imagine that certain historically determined forces do exist, and will continue to exist in a transitional socialist society, especially in one as underdeveloped as the Soviet Union. Rather he saw socialism as a repression-free paradise on earth, with no prohibitions on masturbation, voyeurism, anal-eroticism in children, with no pedagogical pressure to sublimate—in other words, a condition that makes possible the full unfolding of "complete genitality," one in which instinctual renunciation and sexual limitation have been *totally* eliminated.

Reich also seems to have been confused about the political-economic foundations of the process of ideology formation. It was to his credit to have augmented and differentiated the problem of ideology formation from a psychoanalytical viewpoint; yet his own concept of ideology remains psychologically obtuse. To have introduced the familial socialization process into the Marxist debate on "reflection" was an important contribution to the fight against Stalinist economism, since it could thus be concretely shown how economic processes are translated into mental ones. Yet the "analytical social psychology" which Fromm founded— after Reich—remained from a familial point of view limited. For example, Fromm has observed: "The family is the most essential medium through which the economic situation exercises its formative influence on the psyche of the individual."[129] Reich's "sexual economy" primarily took shape in a biological direction and Fromm's in an "analytical social-psychological" socialist direction. But both shared an almost exclusive concentration on the family as the "socialization factory" of the author-ity-bound character, and this closed their view to other dimensions of socialization. Both thereupon reproduced the narrow familial horizon of Freud's socialization theory which, strictly speaking, remained bound to the sphere of consumption. Thus all "socialization" and "modeling of instinctual character" (Haug) which immediately derived from capitalist production and the sphere of utility remained outside their purview. From this point of view W. Pieck's accusation against Reich, though it revealed a total ignorance of psychoanalytical matters, was not to be dismissed out of hand.

Although Reich's "sexual economy" pretends to explain the psychic effect of a relationship to production in the individual, that is the forma-tion of ideologies "in the human head," these relationships to production become effective for him exclusively through socializing agents: family, school, and church. Thus he wrote, for example: "A human being's way of feeling is altered by the limitation and repression of sexuality, this creates the religions that deny sexuality, and gradually the ruling class builds its own sexual-political organization, the church, with all its prede-cessors, which has as its sole objective the elimination of mankind's sexual desires and with it the least bit of happiness on earth."[130] Not only did Reich limit the economic and political function of the church in an inadmissible manner to the "sexual-political" sphere (after all, the me-dieval church was first of all an economic beneficiary of feudal land rents and the political and ideological guarantor of the feudal property relation-ship); he also had much too narrow a concept of the socially formative conditions of the anti-pleasure and anti-sensuality ideology which finally became the center of Christian, particularly of Protestant propaganda. It will be shown later (p. 127) that the "renunciation" and "repression" of sensuality results from the exchange principle itself, that it is already embedded in a (capitalist) commodity economy. The process of capital accumulation was a "renunciatory" process per se which had to be buttressed by a corresponding religious ideology, the Protestant ideology of renunciation, and a corresponding social character, "the anal retentive compulsive character."[131] The "sexual-political" organization of the church and the patriarchal monogamous family therefore were not the primary reason for the instinctual renunciation that is connected with the accumulation of capital, but only secured it secondarily.

Like "sexually renunciatory bourgeois morality," the "split between being and consciousness"—this Reich also overlooked from insufficient familiarity with political economy—is a necessary product of the economic development of a consumer society, too. According to Marx, the "fetish character" of the commodity (see also p. 137) itself produces that "inversion of consciousness" which Reich sought to explain solely by means of "sexual economy," that is, the psychoanalytical theory of socialization. The "inversion of consciousness" which necessarily results from the commodity character of social production is, so to speak, only reiterated by the "inversion of consciousness" that results from the socialization process of family, school, and church. If orthodox party communism therefore ignored this secondary ideology-forming process through bourgeois socialization agents, that is, underestimated their importance, Reich and the Freudo-Marxists (and the Frankfurt School, incidentally, as well: see p. 150) underestimated the importance of primary ideology formation, that is, the mystification process of the commodity economy itself. Reich, as it were, used a "double psychology," or in other words he confronted the critique of political economy with a psychoanalytical, that is, "sexual-economic" explanation of ideology, although in reality a critique of political economy is also a critique of psychology and ideology. When Reich wrote: "But in what manner does social ideology effect the individual? Marxist social theory had to leave this question open as outside its realm of competence [. . .],"[132] he foreshortened Marxist social theory of its psychological and ideological-critical potential. He seems to have been aware of the limits of a psychoanalytical critique of ideology when he declared that "the positive element and driving forces of class consciousness" lie outside their specific objective, though the "inhibitions of its development can only [!] be understood psychologically because they stem from irrational sources."[133] Yet this is precisely where he absolutized psychoanalytical competence, as he also did when he wrote: "It is clear that psychoanalysis and it alone can explain all irrational forms of behavior [. . .] such as mysticism of all kinds."[134] But precisely this is not clear. Inhibitions and deformations of class consciousness can be explained by psychoanalysis only to the extent that they are mediated through familial socialization processes, that is, disturbances: for example, the irrational "attachment to the leader" and loyalty to the group which results from the father and Oedipus complex, or the fascist camaraderie which results from repressed homosexuality, and so on. The inhibition of consciousness, however, which arises from a "mystification produced by the capitalist mode of production" (Marx; see also p. 152), from the mere appearance of equivalent exchange, the apparent "equality" of the "value of labor power" (= wages), lies outside the psychoanalytical purview.

A psychologistic and familialistic reduction of the psychoanalytical concept, however, has equally grave consequences for political strategy, as it does for its non-dialectical opposite, the economic reduction of the Stalinist concept of ideology. H. Wieser and J. Beyer have written: "Ideology as a 'reflection' mediated through social agencies which inverts real conditions (standing them on their head) bears from a psychoanalytical view the responsibility for the absence of class consciousness. For the anti-capitalist struggle this theoretical [. . .] evaluation has had the suggested strategic consequence. For if one makes obtuse institutions such as family, school, and media, which want to preserve capitalism, responsible for sabotaging class consciousness—and them alone—then the attempted creation and actualization of class consciousness will produce, and this is consistent with this theory, a struggle that is exclusively directed against these opponents."[135]

Not only Reich's Sex-Pol movement but also the anti-authoritarian phase of the student movement, which largely based itself on Reich, failed, among other reasons, because it reduced its struggle to the level of so-called "ideology factories." The non-dialectical negation of the anti-authoritarian phase through the "organized" phase,[136] however, had as its consequence that a psychological understanding of ideology in Reich's sense was negated by a traditional economic understanding of ideology in Pieck's sense. The struggle against the "ideology factories" slackened to the extent that it was taken up in the real factories.

In the meantime the political situation within the West German Left resembles that of the end of the twenties where every party fought in the other what it itself lacked. The old anti-authoritarian followers of Reich and the new "organized" followers of Pieck move—as in Dante's hell for the misers and spendthrifts[137]—in one and the same circle. Every time they encounter each other at the apogee and perigee of their dogmatic circle they scream furiously at each other: "Economist!" "Psychologist!"

Synopsis

Let us make a brief interim statement on the first part of the trial "In the Matter of Freud."

By playing off the conservative cultural philosopher and bourgeois anthropologist in Freud against the subversive sexual investigator and critic of ideology, orthodox-Marxist, that is, Stalinist, criticism missed— and as a consequence nearly all other Marxist critics have missed—the "combinative" character of Freud's work. J. M. Brohm thus observes: "Freud's work develops in fact out of the end of the era of bourgeois revolutions, at the same moment when the bourgeoisie has long since lost every revolutionary calling. His work consequently combines in a dialectical manner the rationalist materialism of the era of bourgeois revolutions (the progressive and critical materialism of a bourgeois revolutionary ideology which calls its objects by their names) with the ideology of the imperialist period, the period of ideological and theoretical disintegration."[138]

Thus the orthodox Marxist, or Stalinist, critique of Freud was always right yet always wrong. Rightly it objected that Freud's psychology did not stand on secure physiological footing; but at the same time it rejected, making an idealistic mistake—being itself mechanically obtuse in this respect—every relative psychological independent law as these manifested themselves in the phenomena Freud had discovered. With a certain justification orthodox Marxism grumbled about the eclectic metaphorical language of Freud's psychology. On the other hand, it showed no understanding whatever of his methodological problem, namely, the attempt to represent the unconscious, which withdraws from linguistic socialization, in the medium of language. Rightly orthodox Marxism denounced the crude idealism and biologism in the "foreign-political" relationships of

Freud's psychology, that is, in the interrelationship between instinctual and socio-economic structure. But in the process it missed the very dialectic of their "inner-political" relationships, that is, the dynamical conflict between id, ego, and super-ego. Orthodox Marxism correctly recognized in Freud's meta-psychological theory of instinct, in his theory of the death instinct, and in the nirvana principle, the inheritance of the decadent philosophy of Nietzsche and Schopenhauer. Yet it missed the materialistic-dialectical character of Freud's clinical psychology of conflict, his model of dreams, slips, and neuroses. It was right in criticizing the "pan-sexual" effusions of the libido theory; but simultaneously it overlooked its very materialistic principle of tracing back all "higher" moral and ethical values "in the human mind" to the "lower" psychosexual foundations. It was right in attacking the biologicalization and ontologization of the unconscious; on the other hand it failed to recognize the social dynamics of the unconscious, which "desires" rebellion against the "rule of colonizing reason"—or in other words the unconscious subversion of reified consciousness. Orthodox Marxism was right in rejecting Freud's cultural theory, which raised bourgeois neurosis to a historical principle, as the "product of bourgeois decadence"; yet it completely ignored Freud's revolutionary achievement of having confronted the biologistic and naturalistic concept of illness in bourgeois medicine with a genetic concept of illness which demonstrated the origin of psychic disturbances in early childhood traumas and psycho-social misdevelopments. Orthodox Marxism was right in attacking the sociological confusions of psychoanalysis, yet it overlooked the sociological substance of Freud's psychology in having found a (though in political and economic terms not completely clarified) concept for the psychology of the bourgeois individual, for the "individuated individual." Orthodox Marxism was right in denouncing the idealistic and psychological historical picture of psychoanalysis; yet in the process it failed to notice its substance which was critical of ideology and of culture, namely, the critique of "cultural sexual morality," of education and religion—which was felt as a profound threat by the bourgeois pedagogical, medical, and religious establishment.

The global Stalinist verdict against psychoanalysis derived on the one hand from immediate power considerations; for what political, cultural, and sexual restoration in the Stalinist era had to fear most of all was the culture-critical subversive side of psychoanalysis, its criticism of the Stalinist cult of personality and of the political prohibition on thought, the reintroduction of the bourgeois family structure, and the reconsolidation of "cultural sexual morality." On the other hand, Stalinist opposition to psychoanalysis also had some justification for its ideological reasons, for not only was Freud's fatalistic cultural philosophy irreconcilable with Marxist-Leninist theory, but the hedonistic pleasure principle of psychoanalysis was not reconcilable with the Stalinist reality principle of "primary socialist accumulation." Freud's radical individual psychology also stood in antagonistic contradiction to the proletarian ideology and the great collective performance in the Soviet Union. And finally, where Freud ventured to make political pronouncements, Stalinist criticism seemed to be proved correct: his bourgeois anti-Stalinism and his misunderstanding of Marxism as an economistic philosophy thus contributed to the fact that even the progressive side of his theories was condemned.

By rejecting psychoanalysis outright as a camouflaging product of the ruling imperialist ideology, the workers' movement that the Stalinist comintern led was deprived of any opportunity of mobilizing the enlightening and subversive side of psychoanalysis in its struggle against bourgeois ideology. The excommunication of a science whose "only goal and only contribution consists in making the unconscious conscious in psychic life" from the political theory and practice of the workers' movement proved costly, however; for the Stalinist concept of ideology, bereft of its psychological dimension, was blind to the irrational, indeed pathological reservoir from which the Nazi movement drew. Stalinist party communism had no conception of the nature of the psychic mechanism by means of which social and economic contradictions are translated into class consciousness or banished therefrom. Lacking a political psychology, it mistakenly fell into a Romantic psychologism that ignored the deep-reaching psychological and political ambivalance, the two blind spots, as it were, of the average *petit-bourgeois* and, partially, of also proletarian consciousness.

Reich's attempt to make psychoanalysis useful for the theory and practice of the workers' movement met with the bitter resistance of the comintern leadership. His psychoanalytical contribution to a differentiated derivation of an irrational-fascistic complex of feelings and ideologies in broad sectors of the *petit-bourgeoisie* and the workers from conditions relating to the familial socialization process was not recognized by the KPD. The reasons for this non-recognition, however, lay not only in the economistic understanding of ideology of the Stalinist KPD leadership but also in the psychological understanding of ideology of the socialist Freudians themselves. The "tragedy" of Wilhelm Reich consisted in the fact that every new, progressive tack in his thinking with respect to Marxist and Freudian orthodoxies went hand in hand with a revision, that is, naturalistic reduction of Marxist and psychoanalytical theory. Reich foundered primarily on his own naturalistic misunderstanding of psychoanalysis: as though it were in principle a science of the instinctual nature of man *as such* which was merely adulterated by Freud's bourgeois ideology. Reich failed to see that psychoanalysis was only the science of the pseudo-nature of the bourgeois individual, of the "individuated individual," to whom what in reality is the social sedimentation of his "second nature" appears as primal, as "instinctual nature."

However, one cannot criticize the traditional Marxist misunderstanding of psychoanalysis—as the case of Reich has taught us—without attacking its own false ideological understanding of itself. As long as psychoanalysis continues to misunderstand itself in Freud's sense as a "natural science," although in reality it is only the science of the pseudo-nature of the bourgeois individual, Marxist, e.g., Stalinist, resistance to it is justified. As long as psychoanalysis considers itself as more than it is in reality, Marxism in turn will consider psychoanalysis as less than it is. Traditional Marxist resistance to psychoanalysis can be dismantled, if at all, only when psychoanalysis itself questions its foundations. Psychoanalysis will not make itself appear trustworthy to Marxism merely by pretending to be a "natural science of the human psyche," as it has been trying to do all along, but only by putting its, as it were, hidden ideological cards on the table. But that means that instead of competing with historical materialism, psychoanalysis finally lets the latter look straight into its heart, so that its ideological and historical dimension, which it has concealed from itself, and which has entered nearly all its categories, can be laid bare. This we shall now attempt to do in the second part of the trial "In the Matter of Freud."

part two
With Marx Against the Bourgeois Ideology of Psychoanalysis

The truth is the totality.

HEGEL

3. Psychoanalytical Theory and Bourgeois Ideology

The "Projective" Historical Picture of Bourgeois Ideology

"It is apparent how the history of *industry*, industry as objectively existing, is the *open* book of man's essential powers, the observable present, human psychology [. . .] We have before us the objectified essential powers of man in the form of sensuous alien, useful objects— in the form of alienation—in ordinary industry [. . .] A psychology for which this book, that is, the most observably present and accessible part of history, remains closed, cannot become actual, substantial, and *real* science" (Marx[1]). As long as this "open book of man's essential progress" remains for psychoanalysis a volume with seven seals upon it, the latter cannot become "a genuine, significant, real science." It is, as it were, blind in one eye, and that is why it must absolutize what it sees with the other, consider it the whole, that is, the truth (in the Hegelian sense). Blind to "normal material industry," psychoanalysis considered its distorted and alienated reflection in the psyche of human beings as its "essence." Psychoanalysis suppresses the book of the "history of human industry" and instead opens its "appendix," the psychogram of the bourgeois soul: thus it considered what was only a distorted, alienated *impression* in the human psyche as the *original.*

Freud's historical construction is based as much on this "anthropological inversion" (R. Brückner[2]) as is his construction of instinctual theory. The outer reality, the "history of human industry," does not occur "objectively" in Freud, that is, independent and outside of the instinctual subject, but only in the form of the "reality principle," that is, intra-physically as represented through the ego, in other words super-ego. Outer reality, as it were, social relationships as determined by production, appears only on the surface of the psychic apparatus, on that topological layer where—according to Freud—the ego differentiates itself. Since Freud's theory admits social reality only inasmuch as it is represented intra-psychically, the theory finally was bound to mistake the intra-psychic representation of outer reality with reality itself. Thus the outer world with its social, political, and cultural institutions was finally interpreted as materialized projections of inner-psychic needs and their resistance which have been created in the childhood of the members of the society. Thus the patriarchal state and the patriarchal church appeared to the depth-psychological view as congealed, institutionalized projections of the "Oedipus complex." A deciphering of the intra-psychic reality, especially of its unconscious dimension, has therefore been accomplished by psychoanalysis at the cost of a progressive de-realization of outer-psychic reality. Dahmer writes: " 'Reality as principle' designated a blind spot in Freud's theory. Its attention focusses on the reification in the inside of the subjects; and because of this it loses sight of the objective reification of its social connection."[3]

After psychoanalysis had deciphered the symbolic representation of outer reality in the unconscious, it now sought with this symbolic language to interpret outer reality. Caught in this circle between the reality of the symbol and the symbolized reality psychoanalysis itself underwent a loss of reality, one that allowed it to "retrogress" further and further into the prehistory of the human species. E. Wulff comments: "In Freud there is a distinct tendency to put the true reality back into the furthest prehistory—of the human species, of the individual—but doing so extirpates the present. The actual present with its reality demand is only realized in a phantasizing, collective madness that has taken shape in the form of social institutions, laws, morality, religion; indeed, it has been created on the ground of a real history, but one that itself first has to be torn out from forgetfulness."[4]

Freud's picture of history, which still holds for orthodox psychoanalysis today, finally rests on a gigantic "projection" of the present into the past, of ontogenesis onto phylogenesis. The catch in Freud's historical construction is the Oedipus complex which takes place in the ontogenesis of every individual: the murder of the father which the Oedipal child commits symbolically in the bourgeois patriarchal family—according to Freud—is supposed to have *really* occurred in prehistory. This history of mankind—so Freud envisions it in *Totem and Taboo*—is a bloody, ever-recurring history of murder of fathers by sons. As brilliant as it is, his discovery that for the etiology of neuroses, say hysteria, it is relatively inconsequential whether the repressed "traumatic" sexual experience actually occurred or happened only in the imagination of the patient, may have led Freud to a gigantic short-circuiting of the psychological images and of historical reality. And it is precisely this short-circuiting which lends psychoanalysis its apocryphal traits.

That Freud lets the murder of the father be committed by a horde of brothers can only be considered—in view of the long-known ethnological investigations and discoveries of Bachofen, Morgan, and Engels regarding the primal communistic matriarchal societies—an expression of the ideological fulfillment of duty. Just as bourgeois national economy made an effort to interpret the pre-capitalist economic structure as a first step and "germinal cell" of capitalism itself, so it was the task of psychoanalysis to settle an anthropology of the bourgeoisie and the structure of the patriarchal family upon the prehistory of mankind. Just as national economists already detected private property where unlimited communal property was still the rule, so psychoanalysis sensed nineteenth-century bourgeois patriarchal anthropology where the matriarchy still dominated on the basis of communal property. Reiche observes: ". . . .Freud's historical construction [. . .] manifests its sense only if one deciphers the historical writing of bourgeois revolution as history written by a bourgeois historian working on his own, who would like to defend the accomplishments of the revolution and for this purpose has to project its ideals into a heroic period [. . .] Freud's primal father in truth bears the traits of a *pater familias* whose might in the feudal family bond has not yet been diminished by social and economic developments outside that union. The primal horde bears every imaginable resemblance to the outer (social) and inner (psychic) structure of the feudal family. The murder of the father occurs according to the classic sequence of all political revolutions which have brought the bourgeoisie to power. The brotherly horde bears the characteristics and the instinctual structure of the early bourgeoisie [. . .] The reality principle of this horde of brothers is a historical reality principle, namely, a performance principle as it is only possible and necessary in a commodity-producing society which is based on competition and capital."[5]

Freud's concept of instinct and libido also reflects—as Dieter Wyss remarks—in a certain sense the "spirit" of the capitalist era. The energetic models with which Freud sought to shore up the libido concept, such as with the concept of "psychic energy," have been borrowed from the concept of energy of natural science in the nineteenth century, which was only capable of quantitative distinctions and which expresses the abstract quantified rationality of the capitalist domination of nature itself. "The analogy between libido and capital is striking," according to D. Wyss.

"The former was regarded as the chief motor of the person, the latter as the chief motor of the economy [which, in contrast to the libido, it really was—author]. Both collect, can be diverted, or converted. The displacement of the "sum of excitation" along the gamut of the imagination corresponds to the possibilities for capital investment. It would be one-sided and materialistic to regard the stock exchange as godfather to the concept of energy in the nineteenth century—a concept which lies at the basis of the Freudian libido. But both the stock exchange and the concept of energy in the nineteenth century are children of the same 'spirit': the individual's technical domination of the earth, of nature."[6]

Especially Freud's understanding of nature, which is based on his psychology of the instincts, has its origins in a "commodity-producing society which is based on competition and capital" (R. Reiche). His conception of culture as a progressive neurosis in human history does not just coincide accidentally with Nietzsche's *Lebensphilosophie*, which is also disposed towards interpreting history only in terms of "case histories." Nietzsche and Freud both see in history the same dynamics as in neurosis: a growing sense of guilt whose cause in Nietzsche's view is the "genealogy of morals," in Freud "cultural sexual morality." Nietzsche's high point: "The world has been a madhouse for too long,"[7] corresponds with the gloomy conclusion that Freud reached in *Culture and Its Discontents:* "If civilization is a necessary course of development from the family to humanity as a whole, then—as a result of the inborn conflict arising from ambivalence—there is inextricably bound up with it an increase of the sense of guilt, which will perhaps reach heights that the individual finds hard to tolerate."[8] An interpretation of its own cultural and exploitative history as pathology is as characteristic of the philosophy of history as it is for the psychology of history.

The materialist foundation of Nietzsche's metaphor is the *workhouse,* which Marx already compared to the madhouse. Behind "cultural sexual morality" there hides in reality a rigid "work morality," that is, the specific need of the super-ego for punishment; there lurks the "conscience" of the Protestant citizen who has had to sacrifice a high degree of instinctual gratification in order to undergo the process of capital accumulation. (See also p. 83.) Freud's thesis that culture is paid for with an increasing renunciation of instinct is in a certain sense the psychoanalytical variation on the Protestant ideology of "innerworldly asceticism" (Max Weber). From the viewpoint of the accumulation of capital and the corresponding "abstinence theory," history can only be read as the history of a progressive instinctual renunciation. (See also p. 83.) The psychoanalytical bias that *every* culture is necessarily built on instinctual abstinence is, as it were, the pendant of the also widely disseminated economic prejudice that capital formation is only possible through savings.

Freud's theory of culture formulates the principle of bourgeois culture into a blind meta-psychological concept: progress as pathogenesis, the process of accumulation of capital as a "neuroticizing" life of suffering. For the progressive subsumption of the use value of human needs and gratifications under the rule of exchange value, of "abstract wealth," is identical with its progressive destruction, abstraction, and repression. (See also p. 147.)

Freud's theory of culture therefore should be limited to the culture of capitalist society. It is only barely applicable to culture in the sense of art, science, and higher education. The great cultures of the antique slave societies, for example, were not created by slaves but by members of the ruling class. The antique "representatives of culture," such as the Greek or Roman *patres,* were "completely free" as that word was understood at the time. According to Freud, these classes, which did not have to abstain from instinctual gratification, should have been culturally unproductive. Yet the opposite was the case. On the other hand, probably no system in recent history enforced a stricter abstinence on people than fascism. One seeks in vain for a cultural form of this society which might have corresponded to the level of its repression. Modern psychoanalytic ethnology meanwhile has also provided sufficient material to limit Freud's thesis—that culture *necessarily* is based on instinctual abstinence—specifically to the culture of capitalism and imperialism. Thus K. Michel cites the example of Agni culture which, "as it has been described to us, is not based on the repression of instinct but on every instinctual expression which finds its way into social life."[9]

Just as Freud's theory of "cultural neurosis" only reflects the abstinence ideology of the Protestant bourgeois who accumulates capital, so too his theory of aggression only reflects the dog-eat-dog law of capitalist competition. According to Kurnitzky the aggressive drive "is historically bound to a competitive and performance society [. . .] *Natural* selection, however, occurs in capitalists who are competing with each other and whose nature, no matter what, is a produced 'second nature,' one which in any event inflicts punishment and guilt feelings on human beings for their every memory of repressed instinctual wishes."[10]

Freud's theory of aggression, too, raises to the rank of a universal anthropological constant a clinical experience that is specific to one culture and society. Just as Freud projects the individual Oedipus drama in the bourgeois family onto the primal history of mankind, so he also derives a generally human aggression, e.g., the death instinct, from the clinically ascertainable destructive and self-destructive dynamics of certain neuroses which no society, not even a socialist one, could control: "With the elimination of private property one withdraws one of the instruments from human aggression, certainly one of the strongest but not *the* strongest. One will not have changed anything in the differences in power and influence which aggression misuses for its purposes."[11] Freud here mistakes such aggressive social forms of behavior as the murderous competition in the capital and labor markets, or the competition of the imperialist bourgeoisie among themselves, with the aggressive instinctual nature of man *as such*. Thus the aggressive and destructive dynamics of "imperialism as the highest stage of capitalism" (Lenin) appears to him as the expression of "human pleasure in aggression" independent of and beyond economic interest and class conflicts. Freud writes: "It [aggression] was not produced by property, ruled almost unchecked in primal times when property was still very sparse, manifests itself already in the crib when property has scarcely given up its primary anal form [. . .] If one eliminates the personal right to material goods, all that remains is the right growing out of sexual relationships which must become the source of the strongest dislike and of the most vehement animosity among individuals who are otherwise equal."[12]

The "anthropological inversion" of economic conflicts of interests and the psychological instinctual structure is evident: Freud regarded property solely as an instrument of human aggression instead of seeing the "source" of aggression in the antagonistic and class conflicts that result from it. In all of history human beings have slaughtered each other because of property, that is, because of property demands; however—until now, except in mythology—they have fought no wars over sexual privileges. And when Freud claimed that "aggression ruled almost exclusively in primal times when property was still sparse" he overlooked the fact that it was a very material scarcity that destroyed the unity of the primal communist society; that the struggle for the social surplus product split the primitive society into antagonistic classes; that the fight between the class which produced the social surplus product and the class which made it its "private" property was and is the actual and constant social driving force of "human aggression."

Freud's anthropologization of the aggressive instinct is in fact an unfortunate byproduct of the psychoanalytic theory. It is not for nothing that it is part of the ideological repertoire of every bourgeois psychoanalyst; for it is an excellent means of camouflaging real conflicts by seemingly indissoluble anthropological instinctual conflicts. The aggressive instinct, that is, "death instinct," which has been raised to the rank of an anthropological constant is—if regarded this way—"the bourgeois alternative to the proletarian theory of revolution, for it is the 'death instinct' of bourgeois society itself. [. . .] This society is destructive by basing itself on the dialectic of production and destruction, on the repression of the instinctual wishes in favor of the modern ability to perform."[13]

Mistaking the capitalistically "adulterated" instinctive structure for the "instinctual inheritance" of man as such—psychoanalysis's original sin—necessarily leads to "Social Darwinism" which is the conscious or unwitting philosophy of every bourgeois psychoanalyst. It provides munition for those for whom *homo homini lupus est* is the battle cry against socialism and which operates with the terror of "man's eternal wolf nature" in the interest of the genuine imperialist wolf. I. Deutscher observes: "To date psychoanalysis has been able to deal only with bourgeois man of the imperialist epoch. It represents him as man as such, treats his inner conflicts in a supra-historical manner as human conflicts in all epochs, in all social orders—as conflicts in human existence as such."[14]

The Bourgeois Barrier of Freud's Ego-Psychology

Freud acquired his first insight into the structure of neurosis while studying symptoms of an hysteria which owed its existence to the rigid sexual morality of the Victorian era. The realm of sexual life became one of the most important themes of the fantasy life of normal and neurotic human beings through its official taboos and discrimination. The creation of guilt feelings, which Freud could prove in all his patients, was furthered by the Victorian double standard: an official monogamous ideology on the one hand, a secret sexual libertinage and prostitution on the other. This specific social substratum, from which every specific sexual disturbance developed, was however not reflected by Freud when he formulated his theory. The time-bound nature of Victorian taboos and the symptoms resulting therefrom is becoming evident even now as hysteria is apparently on the wane. This can be traced back to a change in the form and function of sexuality in late capitalism, primarily to its "repressive desublimation" (Marcuse). The rigid taboos of the Victorian period have proved an obstacle to the utilization requirements of capital. Their "repressive loosening up," however, furthers the turnover of commodities. (See also p. 173.) A change in the form and function of neurosis which has become evident since Freud's time manifests itself in a relative increase in character neurosis and a relative decrease in symptom neurosis. The causes of this shift in the clinical structure of late-bourgeois society will be investigated elsewhere. (See p. 261.) In any event, the universal claim and the universal expansion of Freud's theory is contradicted by the historically limited specific social-clinical substratum from which it was developed. Haseloff thus comments: "However, it is clear that all these areas (education, penal law, art, religion, and finally culture) manifest their own structures, which cannot possibly be adequately designated by the axioms and expressions which came into existence in the therapeutic conflict with various (again time-bound) forms of hysteria."[15]

Freud not only ignored the specific social but—what was much more serious—the specific class character of his clinical material which formed the empirical foundation of his theoretical structure. His clients consisted entirely of the Viennese upper and middle classes which had been "hystericalized" by the decline of the Austro-Hungarian monarchy. The extrapolation of this class-specific symptom picture into a general theory of neurosis was further cemented by the selection of patients.[16] After several sensational cures more and more patients from the same substratum came to Freud and therefore the same or similar symptoms appeared. This "selection of clinical material from the Rayon of privileged alienation" (P. Brückner) was also impelled by the methodological requirements of psychoanalysis. Brückner states: "One should turn away patients—so Freud recommends in 1904—who do not have a certain level of education and a relatively dependable character." Since the man in bourgeois society who is a good man is the man who is able to pay, as Marx noted ironically, and on whom credit bestows the rights of a citizen, and since "'character' [. . .] and 'dependability' in the sense of punctual adherence to the appointment schedule is aided by the degree of disposable free time on his hand; and on the other hand since articulation (Freud's 'certain level of education') distributes itself specifically in one class (and was indispensable for the application as well as development of the psychoanalytic method), Freud lost sight of the consequences of wage labor for the make-up of consciousness, behavior, and instinctual structure, of everydayness—and with that necessarily of the corresponding consequences which ownership of the means of production, participation in revenues of the 'non-working owners,' have."[17]

In contrast to Freud, 74 per cent of whose patients came from the Viennese upper class, Adler primarily analyzed patients from the middle class (38 per cent) and lower class (36 per cent).[18] This entirely different class-specific stratum from which Adler's patients came also resulted, of course, in an entirely different clinical picture. What stood in the foreground for Freud's patients, who were freed from the need to participate in immediate production, was primarily the problematical nature of family dependencies, Oedipal conflicts, and the neurotic repression of instincts by bourgeois sexual morality. The symptomatic picture of the mostly *déclassé* and proletarian patients of Adler's, on the other hand, was the "inferiority complex" (Adler) that resulted from their social and economic underprivileged position. Their emotional problems therefore were primarily concentrated on overcoming their underprivileged status, on social mobility, that is, on "compensation" for their social "inferiority complex." That is why "sexual etiology" plays a comparatively less important role in Adler's theory and why he turned away from Freud's school. Although Adler was justly called a "revisionist" by Freudian orthodoxy because he denied the significance of the "sexual factor" in the formation of character and neuroses, he was socially more enlightened than they because he took greater account of the "social factor" in the formation of character and neuroses. However, Adler's as well as Freud's neurosis theories have one problem in common: both make their different class-specific "etiology"—the "inferiority complex" and the "Oedipus complex"—into a global motor of cultural neurosis.

According to Sohn-Rethel "a materialistic epistemology [. . .] should never speak about knowledge without considering its proper relationship to manual labor. Human thoughts have never won philosophic interest except as an activity separate from manual labor."[19] In fact one can also accuse Freud's theory of not having given "proper consideration" to its relationship to manual labor. Freud primarily analyzed the bourgeoisie, that is, the class of mental laborers. His clinical theory is therefore— speaking strictly—only a theory of the neurosis of mental labor. The capitalist division of labor and classes has surreptitiously entered his meta-psychological concepts without his having reflected on this matter. In that sense Freud's psychology is an unadmitted class psychology. At the same time—and this should be addressed once more to the vulgar Marxist critics of Freud—it is more than a class psychology. For the structural dynamics and economy of the unconscious in the intra-psychic mechanisms of dreams, slips, and neuroses, which Freud investigated, are also valid for the psychology of manual labor.

Not only did Freud fail to investigate the effect of wage labor on consciousness and instinctual structure; his concept of "work" also largely reflects the viewpoint of mental labor: work for him (incidentally, for Reich too) is "sublimated libido." To "sublimate" in work, however —in bourgeois society—is still the privilege of mental labor. According to Brückner: "After he felt extremely dependent in his position as an assistant at the clinic 'to have to be a machine for eleven hours so as to be a man for one hour,' Freud found later that he could not really imagine life as being pleasant without work: 'Fantasizing and work become one and the same thing for me. I don't amuse myself doing anything else,' this being 'free work' in Marx's sense. The fact that work only keeps most people alive by atrophying them [. . .], that their life activity loses all 'art character' (Freud's 'coinciding of work and fantasizing'), that its 'particular proficiency always becomes something abstract, indifferent' (Marx) [. . .] eludes his theoretic grasp because of his experience, re-mains extraneous to psychoanalysis."[20]

Freud's bourgeois-privileged concept of work, however, has quietly entered his psychology of the ego. The high intellectual and emotional "autonomy" of the psychoanalytical ego ideal, the "genital character," its superior capacity for sublimation, reflection, and abstraction, its highly developed capacity to control and integrate instinct, are luxurious attributes of mental labor. Anyway the fashioning of these brilliant "genital" qualities and potentialities not only presupposes a sunny child-hood but also a luxurious economic and social situation. Where—as in the upper ranks of bourgeois society—the "genital character," this idol of

Freud's psychology of the ego, is whittled the splinters are flying—way down below: for the "intellectual" ego-autonomy of the bourgeois minority presupposes the material wage dependency of the proletarian majority; "instinctual sublimation" on the one hand presupposes lifelong "instinctual abstinence" on the other; the capacity on the one side to "reflect and abstract" presupposes intellectual atrophy on the other. The wage laborer "together with his product surrenders his 'genital' qualities and potentialities to capital, which confronts him from now on with the omnipotence" of a half-automatic production process, with the "superiority" of highly developed machinery, with the "intelligence" of unattainable science. (See also p. 158f.) The "fate" of wage labor—"the separation of labor power from the personality of the worker, its transformation into a thing, into an object, which he sells on the market" (Lukács)[21]— is therefore irreconcilable with the "genital" personality ideal.

Conciliators between Marxism and psychoanalysis like Althusser[22] keep pointing out that the ego in Freud, as the locus of self-deception, and Marx's concept of the subject, as "character mask," actually negate the bourgeois ego, that is, concept of subject, by unmasking its autonomy as fictitious, in other words as the ideological product of the commodity society. And according to Althusser, Marx and Freud have recourse to one and the same subject which is only representative of the pretended structure—Marx's "character mask" on the one hand which is governed by economic forces of which it is not aware; and, on the other hand, the ego which is governed by unconscious (mostly sexual) instinctual forces (and "decentralized" in that sense). Yet with his concept of "genital character" Freud again lent support to the bourgeois illusion of autonomy which his concept of ego had just destroyed. The "genital character" ideal is based on the fiction of a free, autonomous ego which is in control of its instincts, which itself is an impossibility in capitalist society because that subject, no matter whether it thinks it is on the "genital" level or not, is in reality sub-ject (Latin: *subicere* = subjugate), that is, is determined by alien production and utilization conditions which are independent of it and its conscious control. This also holds true for the seemingly more autonomous "ego" of the capitalist.

For the social operation of the "economic character mask"—this is self-evident to the Marxist but cannot be said often enough to the Freudians—its individual instinctual or ego development is not at all relevant. Also the specific psychology of the id or ego of the capitalist cannot assert itself against the economic determination of the role it plays. The driving motive of its operation is neither its "Oedipus complex" nor its "inferiority complex," neither its "drive for power" nor its "acquisitive drive," neither its anal-sadistic nor its sado-masochistic character, neither its "need for recognition" nor its "need for security"; but it is the desire for money which drives him. "As the conscious representative of this movement," according to Marx, "the possessor of money becomes a capitalist. His person, or rather his pocket, is the point from which the money starts and to which it returns. The expansion of value which is the objective basis or mainspring of the circulation M-C-M* becomes his subjective aim, and it is only in so far as the appropriation of ever more and more wealth in the abstract becomes the sole motive of his operations, that he functions as a capitalist, that is, as capital personified and endowed with consciousness and a will."[23] And similarly, as Engels remarks, what matters "is not the good will of the individual capitalist whether he wants to engage himself [in the struggle concerning the length of the work day—author] or not, since the *competition* itself compels the most philanthropic among them to follow his colleagues."[24] Neither the subjective (libidinous or aggressive) "instinct" nor the subjective "will," neither individual "consciousness" nor the individual "unconscious" finally determines the behavior of the economic character mask; what does determine it are the compelling economic laws which transpire behind their back, mostly against their "will," and even against their "instincts"—even without their own awareness and in this sense "unconsciously."

Freudian psychology of the ego and its "genital" character idol should therefore be regarded as a scientific self-transfiguration and self-interpretation of the bourgeoisie in its liberal stage of ascendancy. The great bourgeois revolutions of the seventeenth and eighteenth centuries primarily had the objective of liberating small and medium-sized property owners from their feudal bonds. The accomplishment of the striving bourgeoisie—on the economic level: creation of the "free market," freedom of trade and freedom from custom duties; on the political level: constitution of parliamentary democracy and institutionalization of the bourgeois freedoms of assembly, association, thought, belief, and speech —also fashioned its psychological self-understanding of "freedom" and "autonomy." E. Wulff writes: "The bourgeois ego ideal of 'individual self-realization' thus is fashioned from the model of the businessman who acquires private property and defends his property and protects himself behind it; the demanded ego performance is correspondingly the excluding private acquisition of property. The ego determines itself under such circumstances as the most basic, actual, inalienable private property which no one can take away."[25]

The socially typical character of Freud's "individual ego" finds its clearest clinical expression in the phallic-narcissistic character syndrome. Psychoanalytic character investigation has precisely grasped the intrapsychic mechanism of the phallic-narcissistic character syndrome (also compare Reich's "Character Analysis"), yet its socially typical structure, in Wulff's sense, has eluded it to this day. Psychoanalysis explains the phallic-narcissistic syndrome purely in terms of individualistic psy-

*Money-Commodity-Money

chology: in the denial of heterosexual object love during the phallic phase, such as through the abrupt withdrawal of love on the part of the father or mother and consequently the introjection of the libido into its own ego. The phallic-narcissistic character accordingly is supposed to find gratification only through the lowering and humiliation of its love object, that is, by bringing itself into a compulsively competitive situation in which it keeps issuing forth as the stronger, smarter, more potent of the two.

Phallic competition—and the neuroses and character symptoms derived therefrom—seems to be more like a secondary sedimentation of the bourgeois competitive mechanism than a primary, invariable (biological) element of psychosexual instinctual development. The actual breeding ground of phallic competition is the social form of behavior of the small manufacturer (of the *petit bourgeois*) who has to fight tooth and nail to assert his product and simultaneously his "potency" on the "free market." There also exist competitive mechanisms among wage earners, primarily on the labor market where the sellers of the commodity "labor" confront each other as competitors, and in the factory where a differentiated wage scale and piece-work competition splits the entire class into competing groups; yet cooperation at the work place and proletarian solidarity represent a certain counterweight to the phallic bourgeois competitive principle.

Narcissistic self-esteem (which, in its clinical form, represents itself as an extreme egotism and authoritarianism, as extreme vanity, arrogance, and so on) like phallic competitiveness flourishes primarily in the class which, on the basis of its position in the production process, "considers itself something special." The literarily most articulated figure of the narcissistic egotist is the "Gyntian ego" (Ibsen[26]), which "is always sufficient unto itself," and whose material foundation is the "self-sufficiency" of private property, that is, of the social and cultural privileges deriving therefrom. Gynt's "narcissistic" character probably also has roots in his childhood and in his relationship to his mother. His permanent "narcissistic" attitude of "always only taking," however, is the primary expression of his class which "always only takes." So it is no accident that Gynt as a lover behaves just the same way as a capitalist, namely, as an exploiter. His "narcissistic character" is therefore identical with his exploitative character. Perhaps this is the reason why—according to Freud—narcissistic neuroses are scarcely or not at all "curable," for exploiters cannot be "cured" by putting them on a couch—they can only be opposed.

Narcissism is property interest directed to one's own person, as it were, the inverted, interiorized form of ownership interest. A narcissistic person loves primarily himself or what he is not, because he considers his thoughts, feelings, and judgments just as "unique" and inalienable as his material goods. A narcissistic fixation on one's own ego therefore cannot be explained alone from early childhood disappointments in love and in psychosexual misdevelopment. Rather it has its basis in the thoroughly profitable ("unconscious") conception of the bourgeois ego as an indivisible "private" monad, that is, in Stirner's terms, "the individual and his property."

"Narcissistic object selection" (Freud) projected this ideology of the "individual and his property" only onto the love object. This narcissistic projection finds its expression, among other ways, in an overestimation of the sexual object which—according to Freud—always occurs at the beginning of a love relationship. Yet an "overestimation of the love object" in reality only characterizes a bourgeois form of love: for just as property becomes the love object of the bourgeois, his love object also becomes his private property. The proletarian cannot afford to "overestimate" his love object because he is primarily interested in its use value. Thus the daughter of the estate-owner Puntila, in Brecht's play *Puntila and His Servant Matti,* is not "overestimated" by Matti, but is evaluated, that is, checked for her useful qualities. Eve does not pass the test because she is too "impractical."[27]

The general claims that Freud made for narcissism are valid in particular for the psychology of the bourgeoisie. His *Psychology of the Love Life* reflects the psychology of a class which was to mystify its love objects the more it made them into objects of exchange and exploitation. If it is to Freud's credit to have scientifically grasped the narcissistic "psychology of [bourgeois] love life," he became obtuse when he tried to raise his class-bound psychology to a psychology per se.

There is naturally a far lower incidence of narcissistic neuroses and character symptoms among the proletariat because the material foundation of narcissistic self-esteem, private property, and the social privileges deriving from it are lacking. The proletarian cannot appeal to his personal "uniqueness" because the labor market and the factory where he is nothing but the "personification of work time" (Marx) abstracts from him as a special person with special wishes, demands, and talents.

Therefore the Freudian psychology of the ego in general and the psychology of ego disturbances in particular, of which only the phallic-narcissistic syndrome has here been discussed, upon closer inspection turn out to be thoroughly determined by social and class circumstances, without these circumstances having been reflected upon by psychoanalysis. That is why Deutscher justly says that the "Freudian psychology of the ego is seen through the distorting prism of class psychology."[28]

Psychoanalytical Ethnocentrism

Freud's phylogenetic construction, through which the Oedipal drama runs like a thread from man's primal history to the industrial revolution, was dismantled, however, piece by piece by the post-Freudian schools.

The progress of the natural sciences and of ethnology in particular pulled the rug out from under its feet. Freud had sought to anchor his phylogenetic construction of the "return of the repressed" primal father with Haeckel's "biogenetic fundamental law" (the return of phylogenesis in ontogenesis). This attempt disintegrated completely when it turned out that Haeckel's law could no longer be maintained in its original form as Freud had understood it. Post-Freudian orthodoxy nevertheless sought to salvage the "universality of the Oedipus complex" by replacing the phylogenetic with an "ontogenetic universalism."[29] Accordingly every child, no matter what society or class he belongs to, was supposed to undergo the same psychosexual development whose high point is the same Oedipal constellation. Now phylogenesis became ontogenesis, that is, the absolutized psychosexual developmental scheme became the anchor of psychoanalytic historical construction. The ethnocentric parallelization of the various stages in psychosexual development, as derived from Freud, which allegedly corresponded to phases of human history (oral phase: herdsman culture, cannibalism; oral-sadistic phase: hunting culture; anal-retentive phase: building up of supplies, agriculture; and so on), allowed the most extraordinary phantasms to flourish among this generation of analysts. As examples we will cite only Roheim and Ferenczi's theories of capitalism.

According to Ferenczi, capitalism arose from the ontogenetic and phylogenetic transition from the oral to the anal phase. The clinically ascertainable relationship between money and anality he takes as the occasion for explaining the accumulation of use values and later of capital from anal eroticism. The "pleasure of owning more and more money" is —according to Ferenczi—a derivative of the "pleasure of collecting" by which every child is supposedly governed during the anal phase. The excrements retained are the "first savings of the individual [. . .] the pleasure in the intestinal content turns into pleasure in money which [. . .] is nothing but deliquefied non-smelling offal that glows." Whatever form money may take—paper, stocks, checks—the pleasure in owning it has "its deepest roots in coprophilia."[30]

Roheim, on the other hand, sees the creation of capitalism in a "regression of genitality into analism" whose source is the Oedipus complex, that is, castration fear: "For example, it is no accident that the god whom the Polynesians call Rongo, whose name means 'sacred' and 'money,' is the inventor of circumcision. Capitalism, which doubtless is a more highly developed type of social organization than previous ones, has its beginning in regression. But this regression implies an attenuation since it replaces the brutal, painful loss of the penis or its substitute, the foreskin, with the loss of excrements or their substitute, money [. . .]."[31]

The ludicrousness and contradictoriness of this "wild sociology" is quite self-evident: if the anal phase is a universal element in psychosexual development, how is it that capitalism has developed only in Western societies? If the anal phase is one of the earliest of childhood life, how is it that capitalism developed so late? The "wild sociology" of post-Freudian orthodoxy evoked, however, the strongest resistance among socialistically oriented Freudians. Reich administered massive criticism to the "wild interpretations" of Roheim. Fenichel energetically defended the primacy of the economy over psychology and Fromm totally refused to consider "libido" an independent instinct; rather he understood it as a "reaction to certain social situations."

What evolved out of the fight against the ethnocentric prejudices of the Freudians and post-Freudian orthodoxy finally was a "cultural psychoanalysis" which primarily invoked the investigations of the new American ethnology (Ruth Benedict, Margaret Mead, Fromm, Kardiner, Karen Horney, and others). This school of "cultural relativism" made an important contribution by insisting on the principle of "the relativity of cultures." It granted each culture something like a qualitative autonomy; that is, it sought to understand from the "inside" (Kardiner). The "culturalists" also did away with ontogenetic universalism: the psycho-affective development, as Freud described it, was for them only valid for children who live in our age and in our culture, but by no means did individual psychosexual phases of development constitute natural and universal elements of human instinctual development. Thus Mead confirms the thesis that Malinovsky maintained in his controversy with Jones that the Oedipus complex is not universal but dependent on concrete socio-economic conditions of each culture and family organization.[32] She was able to prove—just as Malinovsky had in matrilinear Trobriand society—that the Samoan and Arapesh cultures, for example, do not know an Oedipus complex in Freud's sense: in most matrilinear families of this culture the biological father does not acquire the function of sexual rival and the almighty authority because generally several male adults share the education and upkeep of the house community. Correspondingly, the child distributes his love or hatred among several persons simultaneously, for example on the father and the brother of the mother, since he has developed no strong Oedipal rivalry towards the father and no exclusive possessiveness towards the mother. He also experiences no trauma of separation and puberty crisis in the European sense. From this Mead concluded—as had Malinovsky before her—that the Oedipus structure in these societies was not a "basal structure." Similarly, Kardiner and Horney could demonstrate that in societies where the child was left completely unrestrained during defecation he developed no conflicts which can be related to the "anal phase" in Freud's theory.

"Cultural relativist psychoanalysis" also dismantled another ethnocentric myth of Freudian orthodoxy: that of the identity of neurotic and primitive man. Freud had given this formal identity between the psychology of the neurotic and that of the primitive as the reason for a functional similarity between symptom and rites. Freud, after all, understood social institutions, especially rites, rituals, as collective protection measures against the fear of "the power of the instinct." Whereas the primitive—so Freud presumed—protects himself by means of ritual against this fear and through so-called rites of puberty to overcome pubescent drives, the youth of our culture frequently manifest neurotic symptoms which represent for the psyche a kind of equivalent of ritual. But this equivalence in reality has a purely formal character: the social effects of the symptoms and rituals are in fact quite different, indeed opposite. "Even though taboo and phobia appear to have the same psycho-affective function," writes Nacht, "the phobiast is at a considerable disadvantage because his environment regards him as abnormal. The definition of neurosis implies that it occurs in a certain cultural setting."[33]

The qualitative social differences between the conceptual world of the neurotic and that of primitive man are described by Eisermann as follows: "The retreat from reality into an illusory world where only 'neurotic currency' counts is admittedly the specific quality of the neurotic. That is, "only what is thought most intensely, imagined with feeling, affects him, although his agreement with outer reality is nearly irrelevant" (Freud). The primitive, however, in Eisermann's view, "is 'organically' adjusted to his environment, in which he is highly capable of functioning and therefore 'healthy'; whereas what characterizes the neurotic is that he drops out of the social world. Neurosis, therefore, is not to be regarded as a retreat into the material world of imagination of the primitive but rather as a partial holding onto the formal imaginative function of the child."[34]

Besides, Freud's ethnocentrical construction which identified the world of the neurotic with that of primitive man had its eminently ideological and political significance of which he himself probably never quite became aware. This Freudian theorem was like a godsend to the ideologies of European and American imperialism—the age-old designation of the exploited peoples as "primitive cultures" thus acquired an additional psychoanalytic significance. What lay concealed behind this theory was the conception that extra-European cultures that had *de facto* become the prey of imperialism were in a certain sense "primitive," that is, "regressive" forms and gradations of European culture which permitted the latter to support their political and cultural claims to hegemony.

"Culturalist" psychoanalysis also revised Freud's conception of neurosis. In "The Neurotic Man in Our Time"[35] Karen Horney defined neurosis as "the disturbance of social relations between the ego and the other." Unlike Freud she did not see the root of neurotic fear in the "fear of one's own instinct" but in "social fear," in the fear of oppressive social conditions, for example in the economic principle of competition. Similarly, she questioned Freud's primacy of childhood over the personality structure of the adult by interpreting neurosis as "reactualization" of infantile conflict through recent social frustrations and conflicts. The "need for love" she did not explain any longer in id-psychological (that is, with reference to the libido) but in terms of the psychology of the ego, that is, as a means for the achievement of security and social recognition. Existential elements such as "female sexuality" and so-called "penis envy," which Freud had imputed, were also sociologically relativized. Horney and Deutsch traced penis envy back to the interiorized social inferiority complex of women in patriarchal cultures. This "culturalist" interpretation was far superior to Freud's biological conception according to which "penis envy" was a constituting element of "female sexuality."

As important as the contribution of the "cultural relativist" school was to the decentralization, demythologization, and debiologicalization of psychoanalysis, this new sociologically grounded ego-psychology and social psychology paved the way for a new social conformism whose value was the "adjustment" of human beings to "their" culture. The task of neurosis therapy now consisted—according to Horney—in integrating the person into this social environment and in motivating him to "activity" in the sense of the American performance principle. The "culturalist" school therefore took the road of "least resistance" in its process of de-archeologization, debiologicalization, and demystification of Freud's theory and while demolishing its subversive content it sociologized its depth-psychological dimension. The transposition of the id to ego psychology liquidates the subversiveness of the "id," of the unconscious. That is what constitutes the "revisionism" which Marcuse justly denounced in *Eros and Civilization.* [36]

But Marcuse, too, poured out the baby with the bath water in his critique of culturalist revisionism: for it is not sociologization and "culturalistic" relativization of Freud's theory of instincts that one should accuse the "culturalists" of. All one can charge them with here is that this necessary and initially progressive "revision" went hand in hand with the most banal conformist ideology. The actual "revisionist" scandal is not the necessary de-archeologization and the historicization of Freud's id-psychology but its opportunistic replacement by a psychology of the ego which in therapeutic practice led to social conformism. The demanded "primacy" of culture over biology, of the actual social environment over childhood experiences, is not what is reactionary, but that together with this "primacy" the pre-established harmony of the ego was based on the existing American un-culture and the existing milieu of capitalist exploitation.

Marcuse regained the subversive dimension of Freud's instinctual concept in *Eros and Civilization* but only at the price of remythologization and re-psychologization (although on a social-philo-sophically more enlightened level than Freud). He reactualized the social and culture-critical side of Freud's work, but at the same time he ap-pealed again to the apocryphal historical picture (such as in the simile of the murder of the primal father by the brother horde) and to Freud's fatalistic and universalistic cultural theory which the "revisionists," whom he had lambasted, had just relativized. So finally Marcuse is left in a position where he has no choice but to put the philosophical crown on Freud's mythology of the instinct, his mythological primal pictures of Orpheus and Narcissus, of Eros and Thanatos. Since Marcuse makes no attempt to differentiate between the historical materialist kernel of Freud's theory of instinct and neurosis and its culturally mythological and pessimistic extrapolation, that is, to historicize and to materialize the latter by means of a critique of political economy, his attempt to "save" Freud's theory gets stuck half-way. For it is to be "saved" only when and to the extent that it can be developed within the conditions of the capitalist process of production and accumulation. Marcuse's social-philosophical interpretation of Freud's work, on the other hand, is as far removed from any thought of political economy as Freud himself was. (Compare also R. Steigerwald's critique.)[37] In this respect Marcuse turns out to be still a faithful child of the Frankfurt School. (See also pp. 128f.)

The Secret Ideology of "Structural Psychoanalysis"

The only other among the post-Freudian schools which acquires a special importance, aside from the "culturalist" one, is that of "structural psychoanalysis," especially in the form it has developed in France (in Lacan and Foucault among others). Like the "culturalist" school, the structuralists have evolved during the struggle against the ideological and ethnocentric prejudices with which Freud's theory is laden. Their intent is to carve out the "abstraction of psychoanalysis in Freud's work" (Lacan). They seek to provide psychoanalysis with the "form of a science" by crystallizing its "invariable structural logic" which allegedly lies at the basis of all its concepts and objects.

Such structural formulation—and this is the achievement of the French school—has made an important contribution to the de-ideologization and demythologization of psychoanalysis. Thus, for example, Foucault con-vincingly dismantled certain long overdue Freudian myths with the help of a structuralist interpretation, for example the myth of the identity of the neurotic and the child, a myth in which the "culturalist" school was still caught. "It would undoubtedly be untenable to maintain," writes Foucault, "that the individual becomes a child again when he falls ill [. . .] but to maintain that the ill person's morbid personality manifests forms of behavior which are analogous to a younger age level is correct: normally integrated forms of behavior are liberated and privileged by the illness."[38]

Unlike Freud, Foucault does not conceive of pathological regression as a retreat into childhood, as a "recurrence" of earlier forms of behavior, but rather as a "subtractive process" which is characterized by an omission of certain functions of the normally highly integrated and highly complex total behavior. Foucault observes: "Thus what remains is not an early personality but an 'eliminated' personality [. . .] The pathological structure of the psyche is not *primary* but in the strictest sense of the word is *original.* "[39] Just as important is Foucault's attempt to formalize and systematize the disparate psychoanalytic and psychiatric world of concepts by grasping individual psychoanalytical and psychiatric symptom formations as concrete variations of an "invariable" pathological basic structure behind them. He thus develops a structuralist system of "pathologies" whose criterion is no longer some kind of nebulous pathological "essence" or "existence" but a "degree of pathological disintegration," that is, the watermark of regression: "Analysis according to the profundity of the illness is to be preferred to mere differentiation between illnesses: the sense of an illness can then be defined by the watermark which the process of regression has reached."[40] Foucault's "cycle of pathological disintegration"[41] begins with neurosis, then comes paranoia, then the psychoses, manic depression, schizophrenia, and finally dementia.

Although this systematization of pathological manifestations according to "degrees of disintegration" is far superior to a purely psychiatric phenomenology and the disparity of psychoanalysis's description of symptoms, it contains this weakness: the specific social triggers, which not only elicit "regression" and "pathological disintegration" but also determine the "watermark of regression" and the "degree of pathological disintegration," are not grasped at all. Structuralist psychoanalysis has indeed recognized the fact that "the content of an illness is the totality of flight and the defense mechanism by means of which an ill person replies to his (present) situation" (Foucault);[42] but it remains a completely open question as to which social "situation" is under consideration here and how it is constituted. (See also p. 193.) This procedure also automatically eliminated the subversive and socially critical element in Freud's concept of illness. The illnesses, the neuroses or psychoses, are no longer understood as the "expression of rebellion of the id against the outer world" (Freud), as "unconscious" opposition, as unwitting forms of resistance to certain social and cultural forces—for example, to cultural sexual morality or wage labor. (See also p. 208.) Rather they are now seen only under the aspect of their "variation" and their relationship to the "invariable" pathological basic structure. The specific social and class "variables" are taken into account during the course of the illness, but only abstractly, so to speak as a theoretical possibility, which is nowhere pinned down concretely in Foucault. But in this way certain "existential elements are smuggled in through the back door, under cover of "invariables" in the structuralist concept of illness. Thus Freud's concept of "neurotic anxiety" accidentally becomes in the hands of the structuralists an existentialist concept. According to Foucault: "In order that a contradiction is experienced in the anxiety-ridden mode of ambivalence, in order that a subject encloses itself in the circuit of pathological defense mechanisms during a conflict—for that to occur, anxiety which has transformed the ambiguity of a situation into the ambivalence of reactions must already be there. If anxiety describes the history of an individual, that is because it is the principle and the cause of this history."[43]

What was said of Foucault also applies to Lacan. The achievement of Lacan's school consists not only in having de-archeologized and demythologized Freud's theory of the unconscious with the help of structuralist logic but also in having fought the different philosophical-idealist and existentialist interpretations of the theory of the unconscious: of the unconscious as a "second form of consciousness"; of the unconscious as "bad faith" (Sartre); of the unconscious as a cancer-like remnant of a non-contemporaneous structure or as non-sense (Merleau-Ponty); of the unconscious as a biological-archetypical id (C. G. Jung). Lacan unmasked these idealist, existentialist, and phenomenological exploitations of the theory of the unconscious as "ideological misunderstandings" by insisting on the "actual primacy of language which is the only object and the only means of analytical practice" (Althusser[44]). Lacan pointed out that Freud's unconscious was already prestructured through the universal language code and its invariable logic. Althusser writes: "Lacan has shown that this transition from (in a border case) purely biological existence to human existence in the human child occurs under a law of order which [. . .] in its formal essence is alloyed with the order of language [. . .][45] All stages through which the human child goes are dominated by the law, by the code of human determination of communication or lack of communication, and his satisfactions inextinguishably and constitutively bear the sign of the law."[46] The invariable "order of language" (*ordre symbolique*), according to Lacan, also predetermines the general "invariable" psychosexual phases in which the social and class-specific determinants enter in each instance as special "variants." According to Althusser: "Where a superficial and biased reading of Freud only saw a happy and lawless childhood, a paradise of 'polymorphous perversity,' a kind of natural condition which is only arranged in biological phases [. . .] Lacan proves the effectiveness of order, of the law which awaits the newborn even before his birth and seizes him with his first scream so as to appoint his place and his role and the determinants imposed upon him."[47]

Such formulations also demonstrate the danger, that is, the ideological obtuseness of Lacan's school, which replaces the latent biological determinism of Freud with a new "structural" determinism, according to which the "place" and the "role" of the growing child is pre-embossed chiefly not by his "social role within the family organization" and his "position" (which means class situation) within the total social organism, but rather by a "code of human determinants," that is by the "symbolic order of language." Althusser thus observes: "Every tracing back of childhood traumata to biological frustration alone" turns out to be mistaken from a structuralist view "because the law that governs them disregards, as law, all content and only exists and is effective as law through this abstraction and because the child is governed by this rule and receives it with his first breath."[48] Although structural psychoanalysis largely has dismantled the biological myths and the secret bourgeois ideology of Freud, it too has had its secret myth and ideology, which is, however, so abstract that it is now scarcely tangible. The unproven anthropological premise of structural psychoanalysis is that there exists a psychosexual developmental structure which constitutes itself on the material of a previously formed language whose "invariability" cannot be eliminated either by social or class-specific "variables." For example, structural psychoanalysis understands the "Oedipus complex" as a general unrelinquishable element of this "invariable" psychosexual developmental structure which can only vary within each specific social and class formation. Althusser writes: "The 'Oedipal' is the dramatic structure [. . .] to which the law of culture subjects every accidental and inevitable candidate to humanity; it is a structure which not only contains the possibility but also the necessity of concrete variations in which it exists [. . .] The variations can be thought and recognized themselves in their nature as they derive from the structure of the invariable Oedipal constellation."[49]

The structural dualism of the "invariable" basic structure and the social and class-specific "variables" that imbue it, or—in Lacan's terminology—the dualism of "empty speech" and "filled speech," in a certain sense disregard, however, the laws of dialectical logic, and especially that law relating to a leap from quantity into quality. For example, it is imaginable that the effect of a certain quantity of (social and class-specific) variables on the "invariable" (psychosexual) developmental structure eliminates the "invariable" quality itself, so that one can no longer make out the difference between the real and the presumed (independent of social factors) "invariable" and the (however socially mediated) "variations." How should the "invariability of the Oedipus complex" be defined? What is it related to?

In a more recent investigation of the mental structure of a worker family in Naples, Anne Parsons reached the conclusion that the worker's children here do not live through an Oedipus phase in Freud's sense. She made the significant distinction that "two sides participate in the question of the Oedipus complex, the first being related to instinct and fantasy (of the child), the second to the identification and choice of object [. . .]"[50] In her opinion the "object side" of the Oedipus complex is directly influenced by the social structure and social norms, while only the "instinctual side" is independent of the social factor, that is, is "invariable." R. Reiche in his controversy with Anne Parsons puts the question even more consistently: "But this territorial gain for the 'social aspect' also gets stuck half-way, for it opposes the socially mediated 'object side' with the phase scheme of psychosexual development while pretending that this scheme and the underlying biological potential is a phylogenetic invariable structure [. . .] Is the sequence of the developmental phases really as variable as psychoanalysis describes it? Does the 'social factor' really influence only the 'object side'? [. . .] It is a necessary if also dangerous consequence of this thought that one drops the conception that there exists a biologically invariable catalogue of erogenous zones and therefore of instinctual sources and instinctual objectives which begin with the oral phase and find their fulfillment in the primacy of genitality [. . .] Not only the kind of instinctual satisfaction and instinctual repression, but also the quality of instinctual development follows biological as well as socially determined laws [. . .] Does the primacy of genitality, as psychoanalysis formulates it, or more precisely do the characterological and affective qualities, the object relationship and the relationship of ego and super-ego, which are attached to this concept, really constitute the highest step attainable? Or is this primacy not the product of a powerful ethnocentric bias, of an *a priori* option for a bourgeois picture of the world and for the capitalist mode of production?"[51]

Reiche's question also has to be put to structuralist psychoanalysis. Is what hides behind its claimed (or, at any event, quietly presumed) "invariability" of the psychosexual developmental structure, which reaches its apogee in the "Oedipus phase," perhaps only a most refined (because apparently devoid of ideology) "*a priori* option" for a bourgeois view of the world and the capitalist mode of production?

The Socially Typical Character of the Oedipus Complex

New investigations of comparative ethno-psychoanalysis appear to confirm the fact that not only the kind of instinctual gratification, and instinctual repression, but also the structure of instinctual development itself is influenced by "social factors." Among others, Parin and Morgenthaler could prove that psychosexual instinctual development in societies with a collective mode of production and a collective acquisition of property occurs in a way qualitatively different from that in the European realms of property and culture. The Dogon in West Africa, for example, do not have any phase in their childhood analogous to the "anal-sadistic complex" of Freud's theory. Parin writes: "The absence of any kind of active education to control the excremental function and to quiet the body in a sitting position obviates separation struggles from the mother and prevents stubbornness from developing into sadistically or masochistically inward-directed aggression."[52] The absence, that is, disregard, of the anal phase also has important consequences for the course of the Oedipal conflict. Dogon children do not go through an Oedipus-complex phase in Freud's sense, namely, with strong feelings of rivalry for the father and equally strong possessiveness towards the mother. The Oedipus complex in its typical manifestation seems rather to be tied to the patriarchal European and American culture whose economy is organized on the basis of private property. Parin writes: "The end result of the Oedipal phase acquires great importance in the social sphere of the Dogon, the Agni, and of occidental peoples generally. With us, however, the desire to possess the mother has a particular coloration and the conflict with the father as a disturbance of the dyade [the mother-child symbiosis—author] has an aggressive overtone. Even the sole 'possession' of the mother as an expression of sexual desire is a consequence of the education of the young child to performance and cleanliness. The first love feelings that are centered on a person manifest an anal-retentive overtone; they already bear the imprint of relationships arising out of production in a bourgeois world of possessions. Feelings of rivalry and anxieties also occur among the Dogon and Agni as soon as the dyade is disturbed. But the wish to kill the father is typical of European children whose rivalry in the struggle for separation from the mother and in that relating to toilet training has acquired a coloration of cruelty. The Dogon, who have no such anal training, know no such fantasies."[53]

Nor, according to Parin, is the fear of incest, which orthodox psychoanalysis had counted among the existentials of human beings, a genuine characteristic: "But incestual fear, too, which we interiorize in the form of rules about exogamy, each of which contains prohibitions against incest, and which we encounter in all societies that we know, we count—contrary to Freud's view—not among the causes (and not even with any certainty to the biology of mankind) but as a function and consequence of early socialization processes among which the Oedipal conflict has predominant significance."[54] The incest wish, which Freud proved existed in more or less developed form in the fantasies and dreams of many neurotics, becomes a pathogenetic factor in European culture only through the social eremiticism of the patriarchal nuclear family which only allows parents to serve as the sole objects of libido cathexis.

However, in patrilinear or matrilinear extended families of the Dogon and Agni the incest wish is defused through the possibility of collective object cathexis and horizontal identification with children of the same group of relatives; in other words, it is largely deprived of its pathological potential.

According to Parin, Oedipal rivalry and the exclusive claim to ownership of the mother—these being the constitutive elements of the occidental Oedipus complex—are the "consequence of educating the small child to perform and be clean." The anal-retentive character, which is what lends the Oedipus complex its *specific* stamp, thus is a socially typical one which bears the "stamp of conditions of production in the bourgeois world of possessions." If one looks for a corresponding political-economic reason for Reiche's question, then one must begin with the fact that in a highly developed commodity society the forms of instinctual development and object cathexis also *must* assume the "objectified form of commodities," that is, the form of possessions, alienation, and "competition."

Lukács writes: "The transformation of the commodity relation into a thing of 'ghostly objectivity' (Marx) cannot therefore content itself with the reduction of all objects for the gratification of human needs to commodities. It stamps its imprint upon the whole consciousness of man; his qualities and abilities are no longer an organic part of his personality, they are things which he can 'own' or 'dispose of' like the various objects of the external world. And there is no natural form in which human relations can be cast, no way in which man can bring his physical and psychic 'qualities' into play without their being subjected increasingly to this reifying process."[55]

It has already been shown how the "concrete form" of commodities largely structured the Freudian concept of ego. Almost all of the actions of the ego, especially in its clinical form, in the phallic-narcissistic character syndrome, let themselves be reduced to the "concrete form" of "owning," "selling," and "competing." It can be shown that the occidental Oedipus complex too, and its underlying "anal-retentive" character, are decisively fashioned by this "concrete form."

Psychoanalysis assigns a twin symbolism to defecation: it can have the meaning, as is demonstrable from dreams, symptoms, slips, and proverbial expressions, of "money" as well as of "gift." However, what enters into this dichotomous symbolism of excrement, without psychoanalysis being aware of it, is the ideology of private property. The "gift" concept itself is already marked by the "concrete form" of the commodity, inasmuch as "giving" is the opposite of "paying." One can only speak of a "gift" when one starts from the view of exchange. The gift is, so to speak, the exception to the rule of domination by the exchange principle. In non-commodity producing societies it would make no sense whatever to speak of the "gift" or "money" significance of excrement, for the category of "giving," that is, "paying," can only come into existence in an exchange society. Children, therefore, do not think of their bodily products as "gifts to the environment"—as psychoanalysis teaches—but if they do at all it is only because the opposite of "giving," "paying," "exchange," and "money" is already drilled into them at the earliest stage of their life as the ruling social form of behavior. Excrement has neither gift nor money significance for them in its natural state; and if it is now equipped with a twin symbolism in their dreams, in proverbial expressions, or in symptoms, that is because the double morality of commodity exchange has already become their flesh and blood.

Psychoanalysis therefore inverts the real problem: instead of investigating how and by which mechanisms the ideology of "private property" is anchored in the instinctual structure of the child it derives the "drive for possessions" from the "anal-retentive" complex, that is, from anal-reaction formations like the passion for collecting, greed, thriftiness, and so forth. The same holds true for so-called anal aggressiveness which—according to Freud—is bound to the "anal-sadistic" phase of instinctual development. In reality, the aggressiveness that corresponds to the anal phase derives from thinking about possession which is drilled into the child at the earliest age through the "castration fear" that what it "owns" will be "taken away." How does psychoanalysis manage to connect anal aggression, which it imputes as an anthropological constant, with the fact that children who have not been affected by the bourgeois drive for possession like to "give their (play) things away?" "Mine or yours? So it goes all day,/ Mine or yours? What a stupid question./ [. . .] Why do we have to fight?/ We could also split it/ so that everyone gets what everyone *needs*!"[56] In the nurseries of the Chinese people's communes, at any event, "anal-sadistic" aggression recedes in the same degree as the possessive pronouns "my" and "yours" lose their aggressive power together with their social basis.

Since classical psychoanalysis did not reflect on the connection between the bourgeois family structure and relationships dependent upon the capitalist ownership of property, it did not understand either how or in what form the bourgeois "possessive instinct," which is anchored in the "anal-retentive syndrome," co-determines the Western Oedipus complex. That is why it misunderstood the latter as a universal biological character. The sequence of psychosexual phases which reach their apogee in the Oedipus complex seemed to psychoanalysis in a certain sense an unvarying biological plan which itself is anchored in the instincts, although in reality it is a social and educational process which primarily has the following functions: to initiate the anal-retentive and aggressive modalities already in the small child, such being—according to Parin and Morgenthaler—part of the basic psychic equipment of a society determined by private property and ownership thinking (R. Reiche[57]); to anchor the mental disposition for wage labor early in the instinctual structure and to secure it through corresponding super-ego ideologies; and finally to train the ego early into the social role and power distribution of bourgeois society.

The two "socially typical" functions of psychosexual development which culminate in the Oedipus complex, as just now described, require brief elucidation. Reiche's question whether or not the "object relationships and the relationship of ego and super-ego, which are attached to this concept [. . .] are equivalent to an *a priori* option for the bourgeois picture of the world and for the capitalist manner of production" can be answered with an unequivocal yes if one follows the investigations of comparative ethnology. Parin comments: "One can say that it [the final outcome of the Oedipal conflict—author] perpetuates in our world the struggle that has become the Oedipal conflict, that it interiorizes the aggressive demand for submission and performance. If the authority of the father comprises the valid rules of our society and if these determine the family structure and if the initially wished-for identification with his authority succeeds, then a super-ego has been constituted which is separate from the ego and from the outer world which confronts the ego [. . .] In our society many preparations are made for the ego to make itself largely independent from the behavior of the outer world and therefore it enters a tense relationship with an interior authority (super-ego), which in an ideal case also acts independently from the behavior of the environment, but according to valid norms [. . .] The fashioning of a super-ego, however, is inevitable; but that it acts primarily by means of wages and punishment (guilt feelings) on the ego belongs to the particular qualities of our culture."[58]

In contrast to the Dogon and the Agni who form a "group ego" and a "clan conscience," which is the psychic organizational form that corresponds to their collective production and acquisition forms, the end result of the Oedipus conflict in Western culture is determined by the private economic organizational form: anal training (for performance and cleanliness) pre-molds the relationship with possession of material goods and the training of a super-ego morality which is oriented to private property. The enthronement of the parental super-ego as the "inheritance of the Oedipus complex" (Freud) simultaneously interiorizes those norms and forms of behavior—cleanliness, punctuality, zealousness, and endurance among others—which create the mental predisposition for wage labor. The Oedipal shackling of "infantile sexuality"—regarded in this way—is a first social training in the sense of capital which has a fundamental interest in the preservation of the patriarchal Oedipal family form as a breeding ground of cheap pliable labor.

The "latent conflict" between ego and super-ego, which is experienced as guilt feeling, is the adequate psychological reflection of the hierarchy of family power which reproduces the hierarchy of the social classes in microscopic form. As I. Caruso correctly remarked, Freud overlooked the fact that "a family relationship in a class society—already is a class relationship. In a class society, family relationships tend to eternalize the structures of class society while the latter, for the same purpose, creates a model for such relationships through the family—a model that is drilled into and introjected through the child."[59]

If the bourgeois family is a "neurosis factory," then that is so not primarily because of any "repressive sexual morality" holding sway in it, as Freud and Reich thought, but because it constitutes an "intimate" power relationship in which the social power relationship, that is, class relationship, is reproduced. Hörnle observes: "The bourgeois family order is a nicely terraced hierarchy, a small copy of the social order in the bourgeois state. At the head stands the father; he 'earns.' Under him is the mother, under both of them the children. This ranking is increased by the difference between the sexes. Mother and daughters have fewer rights than fathers and sons. In this way the family develops in the child early on the idea that such a stratification and division of society into the privileged and underprivileged, into those who give and those who serve, into those who are valuable and those who are less valuable, is quite natural and inescapable."[60]

The "latent conflict" between ego and super-ego thus is the result of a vertical identification of the child with the persons at the top of the hierarchy of family power. However, in contrast, among the Dogon and Agni a vertical identification with the matrilinear or patrilinear family head is largely neutralized by a horizontal identification with children from family groups who are on the same footing. The "group ego" and "clan conscience" that is created by horizontal identification thus lessens the repressive and extremely neurotic tensions between ego and super-ego in our culture, which reproduce in the individual himself the distribution of role and power, that is, the class tension of bourgeois society.

The relative independence of the ego from the social environment, its monadological character, can as previously mentioned be traced back to the exclusivity of the relationship to objects during the Oedipal phase. So the exclusive acquisition of the heterosexual love object already bears the marks of a social form of organization based on the exclusive, that is, "private," acquisition of the means of social production. Phallic Oedipal rivalry and aggression are the indigenous psychosexual sedimentation of a social form of behavior which is governed not by the principle of cooperation (as among the Agni and Dogon) but by the principle of competition. The competition, produced by the capital and labor market and permeating every sphere of bourgeois society, falls back onto the intra-family socialization process, onto the Oedipal parent-child relationship where it is interiorized as a psychosexual behavioral norm, that is, as "phallic" fixation.

Although Freud finally understood the Oedipus complex as a universal biological constant of human instinctual development, he appears to have doubted this conception. In a quite remarkable formulation he once described the Oedipus complex as a phenomenon produced by the social interaction of the parents: "The child takes both of its parents, and more particularly one of them, as the object of its erotic wishes. In so doing, it usually follows some indication from its parents, whose affection bears the closest characteristics of sexual activity, even though one that is inhibited in its aims. As a rule, the father prefers his daughter and a mother her son; the child reacts to this by wishing, if he is a son, to take his father's place, and, if she is a daughter, her father's."[61]

Here Freud at least allowed the possibility that the child does not select the parent of the opposite sex as the preferred (Oedipal) love object of its own volition but "follows some indication from its parents." Oedipal rivalry as a basis for an exclusive claim to the love object of the opposite sex therefore appears to be less a primary action on the part of the child than a secondary reaction to the (Oedipal) preferential treatment of a child of the opposite sex by its parents. Any heterosexual "object selection" on the part of the parents, however, is itself related to the gender-specific competitive mechanism. In other words, in bourgeois society erotic, intellectual, and other competition within the same gender is incomparably greater than the competition between the sexes. The bourgeois parents themselves have generally interiorized the competition between the different and same sexes to such a degree that they "automatically" bequeath their "special love" to the child of the opposite sex. Special and additional competition, of course, also obstructs homosexual eroticism. The social obstruction and taboo of homosexual eroticism necessarily has as a consequence the parents perceiving as "offensive" their erotic efforts towards the child of the same sex and therefore they subject it to a special form of censorship and repression. The social ostracism and repression of homosexuality is therefore one of the main reasons for the special turning of the parents towards the child of the opposite sex. In addition, there is the factor that both parents can in this way act out their sex-specific social roles: the father feels more drawn to the daughter than to the son because he can better act out his role as "superior man"; the mother prefers the son as an erotic object because she can act out her social "inferiority" role with respect to him, that is, she places the daughter into a secondary erotic rank equivalent to the latter's secondary social rank. And the child reacts to this unequal gender-specific treatment by his parents by himself turning more and more to the parent of the opposite sex.

Wilhelm Reich has emphasized the degree to which the kind and end result of the Oedius conflict depends on the specific social conditions affecting the child as he grows up: "The Oedipus situation not only con-

tains the instinctual attitudes but also the manner in which the child lives
through the Oedipus complex and overcomes it; for it is immediately
dependent on the general social ideology as well as on the position of the
parents in the process of production, which means that the destinies of the
Oedipus complex, like all others, are dependent on the economic structure of the society. Indeed, the fact that the Oedipus complex even came
to exist can be ascribed to the structure of the family as it is determined by
society."[62] It is obvious (not only to Freudians!) that the "position of the
parents in the production process" also largely determines their "feelings
towards" their children. For what holds true for the "relationship of
human beings to their work holds true for the relationship of human
beings to each other" (Marx[63]). All of these relationships—according to
Marx—are determined in bourgeois society, however, by "alienation,"
"foreignness," and animosity. So when Freud conceived of the "inimical" relationship of the child towards the parent of the same sex as an
"invariable" element of the Oedipal situation, he overlooked the fact that
this particular Oedipal animosity is only a reflection of that general
animosity and foreignness that determines people's relationship to their
work, to the product of this work, to themselves, and consequently to
other human beings. The foreignness and animosity of human beings in
their relationship to material inorganic products necessarily is reproduced
as well in their relationship to their physical living products, that is, their
children. This was manifest, for example, in proletarian families of the
nineteenth century: the parents treated their children as they themselves
were treated by capitalists, namely, as objects of economic utilization and
exploitation. As Marx observed, no one opposed laws that were designed
to limit child labor so much as those parents who thus utilized their
children. They were the "worst enemies of their children" and this social
animosity formed the decisive level of feeling in the Oedipal relationship
between father and son, mother and daughter. In other words, the emotional "Oedipal" attitude of the parents to their children precisely reflected their "position in the production process."

Since classical psychoanalysis and nearly all post-Freudian schools
remained stuck in their biological, ethnocentric, or structuralist prejudices and remained unclear as to the socio-economic determinants and
the socially typical character of the Oedipus complex, it was in the final
analysis also incapable of developing a social perspective on "overcoming the Oedipus complex." Only comparative ethno-psychoanalysts have
reached a somewhat closer understanding of the question what really
belongs to the biological foundation of the psychosexual instinctual development and what are only subsequent attempts to shore up ethnocentric prejudices biologically. The biological petrification of Freud's instinctual theory thus disintegrates bit by bit. In delineating the methodology of
comparative psychoanalysis, the relationship between forms of social

production and organization and the necessarily corresponding forms of instinctual development and object relationship in turn also permits the delineation of social conditions, that is, necessary changes, which can lead to new and "freer" forms of instinctual development, to qualitatively new object relationships, and to a new integration of instinct and consciousness. This methodology thus permits the formulation of those social conditions which are required for "overcoming the Oedipus complex" in its classic European form.

If the Oedipus complex in its classic manifestation is bound to the social matrix of the patriarchal nuclear family, then its prophylactic "overcoming" first of all presupposes the elimination of this family form. According to Marx and Engels, however, such an elimination of the bourgeois family is connected with the elimination of private property of the means of production. Only with the elimination of private property can wage labor and also that psychotic training institute, the bourgeois family, be eliminated. Only then—it follows—will a morality oriented towards egoistic owning and its psychosexual anchoring in an anal-retentive character syndrome lose its material basis. Finally, only the elimination of the family power hierarchy will create a presupposition for eliminating the bourgeois class hierarchy which persists in the family power hierarchy and its psychosexual anchoring by way of a vertical Oedipal identification with the father authority.

The "socialized" child who grows up in a communist extended family will be already integrated at an early stage into the social-production process, and he thus will develop qualitatively different collective object relationships from the child who grows up "privately" in a partiarchal nuclear family. Hörnle comments: "The child's entry into the sphere of social production also creates the mass-psychological prerequisite for a new communist education. The new social position of the child also changes the psychology of the adult masses towards children as well as the psychology of children towards adults."[64]

The foundation of communist education—the cooperative production and reproduction of social life—removes the ground from under a private, exclusive form of object relationship (as it is characteristic of the Oedipal relationship) and a vertical identification of the child (with authority above him in the family power hierarchy). It also furthers the socialization and collectivization of the object relationship, the emotional ties of the children to the educational collective, as well as their horizontal identification with the children of the same group of relatives, that is, the same production and house community. According to Hörnle: "The abode of the socialist future will be [. . .] the great airy extended house which is appointed with all the achievements of modern technology, where not only kitchen, heating, laundry, and housecleaning are centralized but where the great nurseries, playgrounds, baths, clubrooms, libraries, and ambulatory clinics offer entirely new educational possibilities for spirit and body. The 'dear old home' where the philistine feels comfortable and which as an educational foundation can only waken egocentric drives and individualistic attitudes is replaced by a collective extended house which is closely connected with the loci of production, school, and public life. Here is a breeding ground for a new collective care and education of the child, for a new collective father and mother instinct.''[65]

To the degree that social production and reproduction are organized on a cooperative basis, Oedipal rivalry, which reproduces the dog-eat-dog law of bourgeois competition, even in the child-parent relationship, will lose its social breeding ground. To the degree that private property and its psychology, an exclusive "drive for possessions," dies off, the Oedipal wish to possess the heterosexual love object will lose its neuroticizing exclusivity; and as the state "dies" the Oedipus complex will gradually die off too. Although the child will still experience an Oedipal conflict even here, it will occur only in the far less harmful form as described by Parin and Morgenthaler, namely, as a "transition," rich in conflict, "from the dyade (mother-child) to the tryade." In other words, the child will have to make its peace in the Oedipal phase with a horizontal integration into a tryade instead of a vertical submission to a fatherly rival. The super-ego in communist society therefore will no longer be "heir to the Oedipus complex," that is, product of a private and vertical identification with a father authority, but rather "heir" to the tryade, that is, to a "cooperative" polyade—in short, "heir" to social cooperation.

4. Psychoanalytic Therapy and Bourgeois Ideology

The Ambivalence of Freud's Theory—The Ambivalent Class Situation of the Analyst

Although in its beginnings psychoanalysis understood itself as a "governor of the unconscious in society," and although in a certain sense it appeared as the defender of neurosis, of subversive wishes and needs that asked to speak up, today it has degenerated into mere "adjustmental therapy." The example of analysis in the United States shows how the displacement of id by ego-psychology—as initiated by "culturalists"—neutralized the subversive element of Freud's theory. Modern "cultural" analysis (American vintage) pretends to take the side of the individual, yet by seeking to make the individual "healthy" and "able to work" it objectively sides with the capitalist social order where "ability to work" is one and the same with the exploitation of labor power. Although cultural analysis pretends to liberate sexuality from its "neurotic entanglements," its actual objective consists in taming "obstreperous" sexuality and diverting it into the standardized or prescribed form of the healthy American sex life. Thus Adorno says: "In the end not just the repressed, suppressed instinct but particularly the original instinct which seeks its own fulfillment appears as 'ill,' love as 'neurosis.' That practice of psychoanalysis which, according to its very own ideology, claims to heal neurosis and is already in agreement with what is the all-pervasive practice and tradition, disabuses human beings of love and happiness in favor of capacity for work and a *healthy sex life.* Happiness becomes infantilism [. . .] The demand for happiness [. . .] indeed begins to look 'archaic' as soon as it aims single-mindedly at the distorted figure who is split off from total fulfillment, at a somatically localizable satisfaction which turns into *some fun* that much more thoroughly the more assiduously the life of consciousness strives towards maturity."[66]

The question which Adorno leaves unanswered is whether psychoanalysis's "agreement with what is the all-pervasive practice," as is customary in the entire Western world, is to be traced back to a theory false and opportunistic in its broad outlines or to a false and opportunistic interpretation, that is, application of a basically correct theory. In reference to both we can say that the general ambivalence of Freud's theory towards culture and society as well as its onesided and opportunistic interpretation—application in therapeutic practice (especially at the hands of American revisionists) are the reasons why psychoanalysis was able to degenerate into adjustmental theory.

Psychoanalytic revisionism, no matter what form it takes—and here even Marcuse's attempt to save Freud's theory is of no avail—is part and parcel of this theory itself. The ambivalence of Freud's work manifests itself in the general reciprocity of subversive and reformist elements; an unequivocal text, such as the French Marxists recently thought they had found in Freud's work, does not exist. The actual contradiction of Freud consists in his having incessantly drawn the psychic balance of bourgeois society from the viewpoint of the neurotic individual but having capitulated in the end in face of social and political forces which produce "neurotic mass misery." His own class-indifferent viewpoint consequently made it possible for the subversive substance of his discoveries to be neutralized and incorporated by bourgeois society. Freud wrote: "[. . .] it is not the analyst's business to decide between parties."[67] His unremitting critique of the bourgeois educational system collapses into resigned reformism where it should also have taken sides politically: "Psychoanalytic education assumes an unasked-for responsibility when it attempts to make its charges into rebels [. . .] I even think revolutionary children are in no way desirable."[68] In his later writings Freud does not even ask for sexual liberation; rather he fears "a freedom of the instincts." For him culture is necessarily repressive. Although he recognizes the horrible forces chained by the super-ego, he does not consider their liberation worth striving for. His political and cultural scepticism finally also determined the principle behind his therapy, namely "liberation and shackling." In the antagonistic conflict between a denying reality (that is, its interiorized representative, the super-ego) and individual instinctual demands therapy has to take a middle course: "What attitude shall we adopt towards the sexual activity of early childhood? We know the responsibility we are incurring if we repress it, but we do not want to let it take its course without restriction. Among races of a low level of civilization and among lower strata of civilized races the sexuality of children seems to be given free reign. This probably proves a powerful protection against the subsequent development of neurosis in the individual. But does it not at the same time involve an extraordinary loss of potential for cultural achievement? There is a good deal to suggest that here we are faced by a new Scylla and Charybdis."[69]

Freud could not imagine a culture beyond instinctual suppression because his concept of culture finally remained caught up in the conceptions of bourgeois ideology. He was forced to stylize the contradiction between culture and sexuality, between denial and permissiveness, into an anthropological human destiny, into an inescapable Scylla and Charybdis, because he himself—politically, as a *petit bourgeois*—wavered between the Scylla and Charybdis of class contradiction. The general ambivalence of psychoanalytic theory as well as the reformism of psychoanalytic therapy therefore in the end are to be traced back to an "ambivalent" class situation and to the *petit-bourgeois* origins of Freud's school and of the psychoanalytic societies.

With time even the ambivalence of Freud's work has been erased and its reformist, *petit-bourgeois* side stylized into "official" psychoanalytic dogma. This opportunistic reduction can be traced to the particular ideological demands and class situation to which psychoanalytic societies were subjected by bourgeois society. So as to overcome its social ostracism psychoanalysis entered into a contract of "peaceful co-existence" with the bourgeois sciences—among others with reigning philosophy, sociology, and psychology. The political censorship of bourgeois institutions, of bourgeois pedagogy, of the church, and doctors among others finally also left its imprint in the minds of the analysts by allowing their "consciousness to censor itself." In the course of time these factors "repressed" that part of Freud's work not "fit for society" and therefore would have made difficult or prevented altogether its integration into bourgeois society.

So as to overcome their social isolation, psychoanalysts not only had to succumb to the ideological but also to the institutional pressure of the official academic sciences, which meant psychoanalysts had to organize themselves according to the academic model. K. Hartung and R. Wolff observe: "Since psychoanalysis did not enjoy the favor of the state it had only one choice: the institutionalization of its training. If, at the beginning, it was considered sufficient for the future analyst to 'experience the certain conviction of the existence of the unconscious' (Freud) in himself (something for which Freud even knew how to utilize his evening walks), the training was formalized more and more, cost more money, more years. The elitist mode of selection went practically undiscussed and was accepted without question: 'conditions for selection are a good intelligence, some [!] success in life, and successful social adjustment' [. . .]; just as uncritically accepted was the increasing dependency of the future analyst on his control analyst. Since the latter usually belonged to a particular school, Balint justly describes this process as 'super-ego intropression': the candidate subjects himself to an initiation rite; 'our training system has the objective that the candidate inevitably develops a weakness of the ego function and the formation and strengthening of a very special super-ego form' [. . .]."[70]

The formalized training of the analyst dangerously increased the systematization and formalization of the new teaching, an aspect which had its beginnings with Freud. Psychoanalysis developed more and more into a closed system whose striking characteristics, according to Fritz Riemann, are: "[. . .] perfectionist traits in the creation of technical rules and training conditions, emphasis on causal-genetic connections and deterministic recurrence compulsions in the psychic life, sought-for objective impersonality and authority of the analyst, intolerance of diversions from teaching. Understandably this construct with its firm tradition derived primarily from personalities with compulsive structural elements who found in it the security they sought."[71]

In the wake of the institutionalization of psychoanalytic training the critique of "sexual morality," which Freud himself still regarded as social criticism, lost more and more ground to the developing technocratic ideology of the modern psycho-specialist which dealt almost exclusively with problems of resistance, transference, and interpretative technique. To the degree that psychoanalytic societies were recognized as therapeutic and caretaker organizations like any other, they also made their peace with the economic conditions at whose mercy they, as "free" service institutions, were. J. M. Brohm has written: "Psychoanalysis as 'free enterprise' can do little else but cherish and eternalize those fundamental principles which are at the basis of 'free enterprise,' that is, primarily the law of supply and demand on the client and analyst market."[72] Like the professional organizations of the "free professions," whether of doctors, lawyers, or others, psychoanalytic societies are governed by the laws of the "free market place." As "free" service organizations they have an objective interest in securing the greatest possible turnover for themselves on the client market, that is, in maintaining the demand for mental illness which they want to heal, or even in increasing the demand. Since they depend on "solvent demand," they primarily treat patients from the upper and middle class. Neither they themselves nor their luxurious patients therefore can have any interest in a subversive, radical, enlightening psychoanalysis. J. M. Brohm declares: "The analyst from the *petit-bourgeois* strata exchanges his service, analysis on the couch, for a part of the income of his clients. Thus he absorbs the income of those who themselves absorb the labor power of the workers [. . .]. On the basis of this situation he does not become capable of imagining a situation that might differ from the one he himself is in: that of a parasite of surplus value [. . .] If one regards the analyst just like the psychiatrist, the doctor, the social worker, the psychologist, the psychological counsellor, the educator, and others who are responsible for re-socialization—in short, the total personnel who exist for the training, maintenance, care, and strengthening of the labor power of those who are actively productive, and moreover who exist for shackling them within the framework prescribed within the norms and laws—one sees that they all depend for their livelihood on the contradictions inherent in society and on actual neurotic social misery. World-wide 'neurotic misery' is their livelihood.''[73]

Their objective social position as "parasites of surplus value" is the real cause for the traditional liberalism and reformism of psychoanalysis. Its ideological barrier against Marxism is founded not so much in any theoretical "miscomprehensions" as in the expression of a fear that by siding with the socialist movement they would be cutting off the lucrative branch on which they are sitting.

The Class Character of the Analytical Cure

"Therapy cannot simply be understood as a technique, as an instrument in the hands of the psychiatrist (or psychoanalyst). Behind every form of treatment which a doctor prescribes stands a particular image vis-a-vis his patient. His behavior based on the image he maintains is tantamount to social, therefore political, behavior.''[74] Behind the so frequently implored "neutrality" of the analysts stands in reality a very definite system of social values and norms. Every analyst has a conscious or unconscious idea of "mental health" and "normalcy" which not only he himself must correspond to to a high degree ("So it makes good sense," wrote Freud, "if one demands from the analyst a higher degree of psychic normalcy [!] and correctness [. . .],")[75] but which influences the direction in which he therapizes his patient. That is why the cultural and moral conceptions he has interiorized enter into the principles of "analytical technique." Since most analysts have enjoyed a middle-class upbringing their principles are the cultural and moral conceptions of the middle class. Thus Freud was able to write as follows about the role of the analyst: "She [the patient] has to learn to overcome the pleasure principle [!] from him, the renunciation of proximate but socially not integrated gratification in favor of a remote, perhaps uncertain but psychologically as well as socially irreproachable one.''[76] Then the question arises: who decides what is "socially irreproachable" and what is not? At this point analysis becomes a political matter and every analyst, whether he admits it or not, becomes the advocate of a "reality principle" which can finally only be defined politically. The treated patient acquires this insight—if at all—usually only when the analysis is behind him or when it is broken off. Thomas L. thus declares: "Why is it that analysts know how I should behave and what is healthy for me? Where do they learn that? All they want is to cure faggots and people who hate the office. I believe they have quite a statistically normative view of people in our society, and that that fact sits inside them unconsciously just as it does inside us, and then they try to get you hopping so that you can better fulfill the expectations that you have made of yourself. But is that happiness?"[77]

The usually unconscious "inner social representative" of the analyst is finally also what determines the criteria of analyzability. Freud clearly formulated the principle of social selection: "One should not overlook a person's other qualities because of his illness, and should not turn away patients who have a certain degree of education and a relatively reliable character."[78] The criteria of analyzability thus are those relating to class and in fact not much has changed in this regard since Freud. Hartung and Wolff write: "According to Hollinshead/Redlich lower class patients constitute only 9.1% of the hospitalized cases under therapeutic psychoanalytic treatment in the state hospitals in the U. S. as opposed to 57% of patients from the middle and upper classes. One of the possible reasons for this seems to be the negative attitude of many psychotherapists toward these patients. They measure them against absolutized middle-class norms, feel repelled by their vulgar speech, their violent outbreaks, and sometimes also by their apathy and passivity."[79]

But what in fact happens among those who are about to be analyzed is not only a social but also a "character" selection. For the only candidates who have a chance to be analyzed, who do not give up despite a long period of waiting and the high price, are those who "believe" in analysis—despite all these obstacles. This has the consequence that many patients dramatize their symptoms immensely, even produce them, so as to become "believable" to the analyst. K. M. Michel remarks: "The symptoms the patients offer increase to the extent that the doctor or the medical institution appears disinterested. The motivation behind this is clear: the patient who, after all kinds of bothersome procedure, finds out nothing except that he is a 'case' but has little chance for a place on the couch, says to himself: 'They're treating me like everyone else, but I'm special. I'm in really bad shape, I need help desperately,' and then proceeds to produce the corresponding symptoms. More precisely, psychoanalytic practice itself ensures that those who want to let themselves be treated show the symptoms which first of all motivate them to undergo the analytic procedure."[80]

The patient's offer of heightened symptoms is matched by an increased price on the part of the analyst. Thus Freud, who seemed to have had a pretty good idea of capitalist laws insofar as they applied to his métier, declared: "As we know, we don't increase the patient's opinion of his treatment by giving it away for nothing,"[81] a statement that led many analysts to the opposite conclusion that the patient would evince that much greater interest in a cure the more difficult it became for him to pay for it. What is interesting in this connection is that, under altered economic conditions, "therapeutic necessities" also change overnight. Since the time when certain health insurances in some cases began to assume the cost of psychoanalytic treatment the "therapeutic" argument that the patient has to shortchange himself for the sake of his analysis, so as to "appreciate" it, falls automatically by the wayside.

On the other hand, the high price of analytic treatment already seems to be "therapy in itself." For the more expensive his "trouble" becomes for the middle or upper-class patient the more "valuable" does his soul appear as well. It is the high price of analysis which confirms the sickly bourgeois ego in its "uniqueness." According to Thomas L.: "Anyway, perhaps psychoanalysis only works because it is expensive. Because you think you're someone special, someone valuable. You're a problem and then you only let an expert take care of you. The more expensive your happiness becomes for you, the more there is probably to it. The high price per hour is so to speak a measuring stick of the value of your personality."[82]

Not only the criteria of analyzability—sufficient "free" time, "a certain level of education and a relatively reliable character" in the sense of punctual adherence to the payment and appointment schedules—but also the mode of the "analytic situation" itself has largely a class character. The strictly ritualized form of behavior between analyst and analysand seems to be formed more by elevated class norms than by scientific-therapeutic objectives. The rules of the psychoanalytic ceremony seem to be based more on Protestant ideology (which is particularly pervasive in the European and American middle classes) than tailored to the requirements of the patient. The abstinence rule is a case in point. Freud wrote thus: "As cruel as it may sound, we must make sure that the patient's suffering does not come to a premature end," since "every improvement in his suffering condition diminishes the driving force that works towards a cure."[83] Correspondingly, orthodox technique forbade the analyst to respond to strong emotional expressions by the patient. According to Freud: "In our technique we have so far maintained the rule that erotic satisfaction should not be afforded the patient."[84] And Freud led an embittered fight against Ferenczi who considered expressions of affection by the analyst reconcilable with analytic technique and consequently kissed patients and let himself be kissed by them. Although analysis promises to succeed only when the patient has succeeded in establishing a "positive transference" to the analyst, who then so to speak assumes the position of father or mother, this "transference" and the affections produced in this process, as a repetition of infantile conflict, nonetheless are—according to Freud—to occur "tactfully."

Patients who commit infractions against inner-analytic forms of behavior based on middle-class norms were considered "unanalyzable." But these patients—in the total balance—are the majority of all psychotherapeutic and psychiatric "cases," namely, "psychotics" who are primarily recruited from the proletarian lower classes. Hartung and Wolff state: "Psychoanalysis has developed along the lines of a genetic theory of mental illness which drew a line from neurosis as far as psychosis. Simultaneously it entered into a tacit division of labor with psychiatry and the brutality of the state institutions by condemning psychotics as 'unanalyzable.' "[85] In Freud's opinion and that of orthodox analysis, the psychotic is unable to establish a positive transference, "although the projection activity alone was sufficient proof of the constant transference activity of the psychotic, except that the analyst could not become the focus and object of this transference very easily."[86] Orthodox analysis did not ask itself the question whether—as I. Caruso says—"the first step to a further awakening of consciousness of these human beings should not rather be a social than an analytic step."[87] It did not occur to the analysts that this alleged "transference incapacity" of the proletarian psychotic was an expression of the "social distance" (F. C. Redlich) between doctor and patient, that is, an expression of an unconscious refusal to engage in "discrete," "tactful," and distanced inner-analytic forms of behavior. Hartung and Wolff continue: "The interpreting opposite simply has to assume a part of the ego function—analogous to the mother of early childhood—of the psychotic so as to be perceived as a potentially libidinous object in his world; the psychotic must, as Rosen says, really be 'mothered' before he accepts interpretation. It is easy to see that such an analytic situation is more demanding than normal bourgeois behavior on the basis of a contractual arrangement."[88]

Indeed, Freud was never able to provide a therapeutic reason for "tactful" and "discrete" inner-analytic behavior, no doubt because there finally only exists an ideological reason for it: that as a middle-class doctor and an "ascetic" scientist he himself made of his Protestant distress of "innerwordly asceticism" (Max Weber) his therapeutic virtue.

The "Analytical" Power "Situation"

According to Freud, the meaning of an analytical cure consists in a post-socialization in which the unsuccessful educational process of the individual is repeated under experimental conditions. The objective of therapy is to liberate the patient from his mostly unconscious emotional dependencies and fixations and to educate him into a conscious and autonomous subject. We have previously shown how the therapeutic goal of the "autonomous," "ego-strong" subject, acquired as it is from the model of the "free enterprise system" in its liberal stage of ascendancy, lacks every social basis from the standpoint of the wage-dependent patient. What is interesting here is the question by what means the emancipatory objective of analysis is itself effected in therapeutic practice. Is there a binding theory of "analytic technique" which would be adequate to this objective, or is it rather that this therapeutic practice itself contradicts the therapeutic objective?

The motor of the psychoanalytic process is the "regression" of the patient which is produced under experimental conditions (that of the "analytic situation"). This regression—as classic analysis understood it—is the prerequisite for the subsequent revision, that is, correction of an unsuccessful socializing process. In the words of René Spitz: "The patient comes to analysis as someone seeking help; he finds himself in a helpless situation. Out of this Freud created two nearly imperceptibly artful devices, which must be called brilliant in their simplicity, comprising as they do a surprising parallel to the situation of the infant. These two devices are: 1) The couch on which the patient lies entirely like an infant; he hears the analyst but does not see him; he directs his appeals and expressions like an infant into the empty room; exactly like an infant he is also vaguely aware of a shadowy creature to whom, depending on the changing analytic situation, he ascribes alternating roles, even identities. 2) The other device is the basic rule to say everything that comes to one's mind. In other words, one should concentrate one's perception upon the events in one's interior and report them without selection and censorship. This rule is more frequently broken than adhered to; but its result corresponds to the behavior of an infant who without selection and inhibitions transmits the events within his organism which he perceives through movements and sounds, through being quiet or excited. Like the infant the patient cannot become active, he is confined to his couch-children's bed. Only the analyst has the right to intervene or not."[89]

The artificially induced regressive status of the patient may have a stimulating effect on the repetition and making-conscious of childhood conflict, but the "analytic situation" on the "couch-children's bed" cements that regressive and passive attitude which is the "whole secret" of the neurosis, of which the neurotic wants to be healed. As analysand—and no therapeutic rationalization does anything to change this—he is regarded by the analyst as under age, the object of treatment. He is "ill," "neurotic," only because he still maintains a childish attitude; but how is the analytic cure to emancipate him from a childhood attitude which is reinforced, even institutionalized, by the "analytic situation"? The analysand is supposed to engage in a treatment whose rules he himself cannot determine, not even co-determine, rules whose sense is not explained to him. Rather he must produce "achievements," namely, constantly produce material which the analyst then interprets for him. Under the pain of having the analysis broken off (which usually turns out to be costly) he has to undergo an analytic ritual which appears to have only one recognizable meaning: to move the person of the analyst to a mystical distance.

This mystification is especially cemented by the prohibition of social contact between analyst and patient: the private life of the analyst should remain just as concealed from the analysand as his parents' life was to him as a child. This "analytic rule" may further the transference capacity of the patient but it simultaneously strengthens his childish belief in the almighty analyst father. When Freud said that "the doctor is supposed to remain obscure for the analyzed person and, like a reflector, show nothing but what is shown him,"[90] he stylized the doctor into a Delphic oracle whose "interpretation" eludes any control by the patient. The "analytic situation" transports him therefore into a state of artificial importance and dependency which once more doubles his family, job, and other dependencies, for whose sake he became ill. Wolf D. comments: "I had the feeling the man sits there somewhere and is picking his nose and does who knows what while the patient is reeling off his stuff, and you yourself simply have no way of controlling that any more. You don't know what he's doing, is he turning around, is he looking at you, or is he perhaps reading the paper? Sometimes you don't hear a single sound from him for hours."[91] The only thing that might have a therapeutically emancipatory effect on the patient, namely, conscious control and the ability to shape what happens within the "analytic situation," is precisely what he is prohibited from doing. Instead of being able to "control" his "interpreting" opposite, he is supposed to "trust" him blindly, create a "positive transference," as it is so nicely called. But what if the analyst, for example, is a political reactionary and—as did a well-known analyst in Berlin—prohibits his patient from participating in demonstrations or throwing stones at truncheon-swinging policemen? Is this form of self-defense of a political patient too much for an un- or pseudo-political analyst? Or is it rather a sign that the patient is no longer "analyzable" because he has already ceased to consider himself a patient in the sense of "suffering" and long-suffering (*pati* = suffer)?

K. M. Michel has pointed out that the "analytic situation" has been described as a "double-bind situation" by critics of psychoanalysis: "According to Jackson and Haley the only adequate reaction to the complex ritual of couch, free association, imposed spontaneity, fee, punctuality, and so on consists in rejecting this situation *in toto*. But this is precisely what the patient who is so urgently seeking help cannot do. And this, then, produces a very peculiar relationship between analyst and patient whose most important paradoxes are:

"(a) The patient regards the analyst as an expert who is, of course, supposed to explain to him what he should do. The analyst, however, transfers responsibility for the course of treatment to the patient and demands spontaneity from him while simultaneously establishing rules which completely circumscribe the patient's behavior. The patient thus practically is ordered to 'be spontaneous'!

"(b) Whatever the patient does in this situation occasions a paradoxical reaction on the part of the analyst. For example, if the patient claims that his condition has not improved the analyst ascribes this to his resistance but points out that it would be desirable if this situation provided the patient with better insight into his problem. If the patient says he feels better, the analyst interprets this as resistance and an attempt to elude treatment by a flight towards improvement before the real problem has been analyzed.

"(c) The patient is in a situation where he cannot behave as an adult but if he does behave like an adult the analyst interprets this as infantile and inappropriate [. . .]

"(d) [. . .] If the patient rejects any of the analyst's interpretations, the latter may reply that his interpretation refers to something of which the patient cannot be aware because it is unconscious to him. On the other hand, if the patient cites the unconscious as a reason for something, the analyst may also reject this assertion with the advice that the patient cannot speak about it because it is unconscious."[92]

The double-bind character of the "analytic situation" also becomes evident from the dichotomy of "assimilation" versus "acting out" which has been so much implored, especially in new psychoanalytic literature. The "acting out" of conflicts is despised by most psychoanalysts as "pathological." If the patient's unresolved conflicts withdraw from any conscious linguisitic assimilation/digestion, of course they cannot be resolved by being "acted out." But if "acting out" means breaking through a certain internalized social situation, of power and roles, then it may have—as Moreno's psychodrama shows—a "cathartic effect." If a shy and inhibited "patient," say a notorious stutterer, is suddenly pushed into the role of an aggressor through the artificial arrangement of a psychodrama and can act out his anxiety, that is, his interiorized hatred (onto the play-acted father authority, or boss, or whomever) by beginning to scream, which he would not do otherwise, then the cathartic effect in this instance is certainly greater than if he indulges himself in endless self-reflection about his "real" problem.

The prohibition of "acting out" within the analytic situation is what brings the patient into a "double-bind situation." He is supposed to learn to "assimilate" his infantile conflicts, which in reality are interiorized family and social-role conflicts, without being allowed to alter the framework of his new "analytic" role and power relationship. He is supposed to overcome his father without being allowed to question this new analyst father. If he does so anyway, his behavior is interpreted as "resistance" —something which, however, contradicts all psychoanalytic logic, the logic of transference. Just because the analysand "transfers" his unresolved father (mother, brother) relationship onto the analyst, the latter must also accept the rebellion against the father instead of remaining in mystic distance as the interpreting and untouchable "super-father" who has his back to the couch. The socially unemancipatory nature of Freud's neurosis theory holds, as we have said, that neurotic and other symptoms are traced back to an indigenously created infantile "trauma"; and it consequently does not understand them as indigenous symptomatic sedimentation of an intra-family role and power distribution which reproduces social role and class division in microcosm. The mechanistic concept of neurosis necessarily has as a consequence a mechanistic conception of therapy. For the irreversible separation of roles of analyst and analysand, of "healthy" and "ill," reproduces—even if in a different (namely, experimental) form and with other (namely, therapeutic) intentions—the irreversible separation of power and role in the family between "priviliged" and "underprivileged," "mature" and "immature," "superior" and "inferior," which made the patient ill in the first place. How is he to liberate himself from his neurosis, that is, from his internalized familial role and power situation if he cannot touch the new "analytic" role and power situation? If the "analytic situation" itself constitutes a "tactful" and "discrete" power relationship, then the final "cure" of the analysand can only consist in his becoming the subject instead of the object of analysis. But this presupposes that the analyst works along with his own negation—in fact, that from the very beginning he works towards the time when the analysand will redefine the analytic role relationship and constitute himself as a subject. This dialectical conception of analysis, this truly emancipatory elimination of the analytic situation, cannot be reconciled, however, with the traditional self-understanding of the orthodox analyst.

How sensitively patients react to a reversal of the analytic power and role relationship is shown in the tape recording that J.-P. Sartre published under the title *The Fool With the Tape Recorder or the Psychoanalyzed Psychoanalyst*. After many endless and futile sessions analysand A. suddenly started to precede the analyst's interpretations with his own and to confront the apparently "neutral" and "healthy" representative of the reality principle with his more personal "father" and "castration" complexes. Sartre made the following comment: "A. puts the question with admirable clarity: these 'endless psychoanalytic relationships, this dependency, this underlying relationship, this endless lying on the couch where the human being is totally exposed and falls back into childhood stammering, isn't that a use of violence, [. . .]' The inversion of the treatment through the patient shows that the analytic relationship is violent as such, independent of the doctor and the patient whom we happen to regard at the moment. If the situation is forcefully reversed, the analyst instantly becomes the analysand or, rather, someone who is in need of analysis: the force of the other and his own impotence transport him artificially into the situation of neurosis."[93]

The active rebellion of the analysand against the "analytic power relationship" (which is a surrogate for the other family and power-relationship situations which made him ill) the analyst vainly sought to interpret as "resistance" and as "pathological" defense; for the analysand now turned his back to the analyst as the latter had towards him. By doubting his self-understanding as "patient," as "forbearant" and "suffering" object (which was the actual reason for his illness), and conceiving of himself for the first time as a subject (which was the reason for his cure), he became healthy to the degree that the analyst became "ill." By reversing the social roles of authority and role distribution, of "healthy" and "ill," he consequently implored the political power which stands on the side of official "health": when he retained everything the analyst said and his interpretations on tape, thereby breaking the first commandment of the analytic contract, the commandment of discretion, the analyst called the police.

The Retreat into Psychoanalytical Inwardness

The idealistic tendency of Freud's theory to extirpate outer (social) reality in favor of intra-psychic reality has had grave consequences for psychoanalytic therapy. For the latter, too, "de-realizes" the actual social side of reality by devoting itself totally to the patient's past. In the analytic situation the patient's past is to be artificially reactivated in as sterile a state as possible, that is, uninfluenced by the actual experiences and problems he encounters in his daily existence. The analyst is like a chemist in that he wants to crystallize the "pure" pathological structure out of the diffuse "solution" of everyday life. Indeed, he desires nothing more than that the patient manifest his "abnormal reactions," if possible, only in the "analytic situation," that is, in "transference," and remain normal outside therapy. Freud has remarked: "We think it most undesirable if the patient acts outside the transference instead of remembering. The ideal conduct for our purposes would be that he should behave as normally as possible outside the treatment and express his abnormal reactions only in transference."[94]

This psycho-chemical "crystallization procedure," however, presupposes that the patient's "abnormal reactions" are not produced by the actual social situation (work, family, and so on) but exclusively by his past, his infantile instinctual destiny. But here the latent idealism of orthodox analysis manifests itself. For although analysis in the meantime admits that the patient only repeats his infantile history because he reacts to a *present* situation, that is, seeks to defend himself against an actual experience of displeasure, that is, anxiety, which results from his work, family, or marriage situation, it devotes itself almost exclusively to an investigation of his infantile history. Instead of lighting up the actual social situation which first triggered the patient's regression into the past, analysis engages in a "search for the lost time" of childhood. The classic technique thus reproduces the "idealism of the neurotic's understanding of the world" (Caruso) by entering fully into the loss of reality and retracing once more the entangled and devious paths of regression. For, according to Caruso, the neurotic acts "idealistically by pressing reality into the pattern of his supposed inwardness and psychoanalysis [. . .] repeats this movement of its object."[95]

But if the actual trigger of regression is screened out in the patient's social reality, the "unhappy past" indeed appears to determine the present in the sense of "predetermination"—something psychoanalysis is frequently accused of doing in any event, especially by those with an economicist prejudice. So the analysand Elke L. replies thus to the question whether she could also bring her present difficulties into analysis: "Sure, sure, but then he [the analyst] always said that doesn't interest me, he wanted to get to the root of it. What he would have liked best would have been if I had told him what I felt at my mother's breast. But I simply couldn't remember that."[96]

In the "pure," socially pristine depth-psychological view—pure, that is, of drawing social causal connections—a "terrible childhood" then becomes a "universal key" to the behavior and disturbances of the adult; and society consequently gets off scot-free. The deciding factor becomes not the social trauma of eight hours of alienated because outer determined labor but some individual "trauma" harking back to mother or father. Says Elke L.: "When I get excited about some asshole in the office because they treat you like dirt, then she [the analyst] only asks: Is that a man or a woman? and I say a man; and she says: 'Aha!'"[97] The analytical principle to reduce and de-actualize all immediate events and conflicts and find their infantile origin occasionally assumes manic traits. Elke L. continues: "For example, for Easter I was home in Berlin, and there my stepfather did something to my son, so that I haven't had anything to do with my family since. He behaved like a real pig, threw the kid twice across the room, something that actually isn't customary with us, but that was for her [the analyst] again a situation where I should have reacted differently; but I reacted the way I did, she felt, because I had re-experienced what I had once experienced in childhood."[98]

Neglect of a patient's actual social conflicts during analysis of his disturbances and symptoms necessarily leads to an overvaluation or—to use Freud's term—to an "over-determination" of his infantile prehistory. All the actual social triggers of mental illnesses, which still elude analytical interpretative technique, then have to be "projected" back into the patient's past. Although the determining role of infantile instinctual destiny for the formation of the adult personality structure is not in doubt, the mostly fatalistic role which the concepts of "formation" or "fixation" and of "recurrence compulsion" play in psychoanalysis derives in good part from the fact that—and in this respect one should also grant the validity of the Marxist charge of determinism—psychoanalysis never or only scarcely reflects on the "formative" influence of actual social factors, primarily the work situation, on the consciousness and behavior of adults. Analysis of infantile instinctual destiny runs the danger of degenerating into a "metaphysics of instincts." In this respect Freud already made a virtue of this calamity: "The theory of instincts is so to speak our mythology. The instincts are mythic creatures, grand in their indeterminateness. We cannot look away from them for a moment in our work and yet are never certain in the process that we see them distinctly."[99] The instincts are "grand in their indeterminateness" only as long as their determination by the class and work situation of the individual remains outside the purview of psychoanalysis.

According to more recent investigations, only 5 per cent of patients are cured in the sense that they appear halfway symptom-free and comparatively stable, that is, without recidivism. The high percentage of recidivism can be traced primarily to the fact that—measured against social reality—the therapeutic objectives themselves are "idealistic": for it is the very objective of therapy to help the ego-deficient patient to acquire that strength of ego and autonomy whose social basis has long since been liquidated. His reversion appears inevitable because whatever—if any— psychic autonomy he has won through analysis he has no way of taking advantage of in social practice, in his work, especially when he works for wages. Since it lacks any genuine room for social action his newly won ego-autonomy only hibernates in the ego-ideal. But this recreates the contradiction between real social (wage) dependency and the ideal of "personal" autonomy from which the patient grew ill in the first place. He moves in a circle.

There is no denying that psychoanalytic therapy can and must help in individual cases despite its immanent contradictions. The element of self-recognition which the psychoanalytic process stimulates may bring the privileged patient into the favorable position of being able to comprehend certain infantile compulsions that determine him (and possibly also to dismantle those compulsions). And if—again under the most favorable conditions—he is under analysis with a socially and politically enlightened analyst, he may even develop a critical consciousness about the social causes of his illness. But if the psychoanalytic cure above and beyond also envisions a new formation of character structure, then such a new formation will encounter obstacles wherever the disturbance or the compulsion that has to be removed arises primarily from social, that is, economic, determinants and not from a disturbance originating during infantile development. For example, the "anal retentive," truly clinical politeness and subaltern quality of the economic character-mask "salesman" (see also pp. 260f.) can neither be explained nor therapeutically revised through recourse to disturbances of his infantile instinctual development, such as an unconscious tendency to "anal submission," unless therapy frees the patient first of all from his subaltern economic compulsive role. As long as psychoanalytic theory does not know how to differentiate between qualities, that is, symptoms belonging to the inventory of the economic character mask and those which arise from an individual's infantile history, any practical therapy must come to nought. Even if in the wake of therapy certain cliches about behavior can be destroyed, these can harden again later on, if they belong to the social inventory, when the patient is released and reassumes his old social role, for example as a wage-dependent salesman.

Idealistic traits are not exclusively attached to therapeutic objectives but also adhere to therapeutic technique. Critics of psychoanalysis have often enough pointed out that psychoanalysis is still living in the conceptual world of animism with its trust in "verbal magic" and the "power of catharsis." Even Lévi-Strauss sees no principal difference between shamanist and psychoanalytical ritual.[100] Indeed, classic therapy fell prey at an early date to the illusion that one has grasped a repressed matter as soon as one has named it. Its "cathartic" and therapeutic effect, however, is produced by verbal expression only when it has practical material consequences in the life of the patient. What good is it to him if analysis brings a repressed hatred for his father back into his consciousness without his being able to express his actual hatred, say, of his boss or his "employer" because if he did he would be fired? What good is it to him if the old infantile hatred is brought forth from its suppressed state but the actual hatred which arises from his social or in other words wage dependency has to be repressed? What good is it to him if he cannot act out with his "verbal assimilation" his newly won social insights?

Indeed, orthodox analysis effects an immense retreat of the libido from the macrocosm of the outside world into the microcosm of the inner-world. According to Norman O. Brown:

"Orthodox psychoanalytical therapy fails to direct the libido back to the external world in the form of a project to change the world [. . .] Psychoanalytical consciousness, by returning to the microcosm of the inner world, puts at the disposal of the ego large quantities of libido that were previously in a state of repression. [. . .] And then what is the psychoanalytically conscious ego going to do with its newly discovered desires? Once the limitations of sublimation and the impossibility of 'rising above the crude life of the instincts' are recognized, orthodox psychoanalysis, as a result of its inability to transform itself into social criticism, has to send human desire back into repression again. Freud's earlier optimistic hopes of precluding repression through psychoanalytical consciousness are replaced by the theorem that psychoanalytical consciousness 'reconstructs the repressions from more solid material.' [. . .] And of course the institution of these new 'ego-systonic controls,' if we take Freud's theory of aggression seriously, means the internalization of the aggression released by all instinctual renunciation.''[101]

The new "ego-appropriate control" of those who have been churned through the mills of orthodox analysis for a few years expresses itself mostly in a clinical lack of aggression and in a frightening loss of spontaneity. Elke L. remarks: "I once told her [the analyst] if she integrated all aggressions the same way she would make a real Jesus freak out of me, I would do nothing bad to anyone anymore. But I don't want that. I still like to be angry at some people.''[102] This loss of spontaneity is the price of a "turning inward" of aggression, that is, of an auto-plastic ego transformation which is the objective of every analysis. This loss and ego transformation, and the means by which they are attained through verbal recall and assimilation, are finally expressions of class; for only those people are satisfied with a verbal "catharsis" who evidently have no need to change their real social situation. Only those people are interested in "auto-plastic ego transformation" who have no interest in "alloplastic" transformation, that is, in changes of social conditions. That is why Norman O. Brown rightly says: "Psychoanalysis, unless it is transformed into a critique of reality, resembles a psychosis in being autoplastic in its aim as well as in its faith in the magic word. [. . .] If psychoanalysis believes that with magic words and autoplastic ego-modifications it can escape the universal neurosis, it develops a private psychosis instead.''[103]

Freud once described the analytic situation as a civil war: "When the ego is weakened by internal conflict, we must come to its assistance. It is like a civil war which is to be decided with the help of a confederate from the outside. The analytical doctor and the weakened ego of the patient, leaning for support against the real outer world, are to form a party against the enemies, the instinctual demands of the id and the demands of conscience of the super-ego.''[104] The analytical situation is perhaps comparable to a civil war except that Freud's therapeutic strategy rather resembles a cease-fire which the reality principle (that is, its inner representative, the super-ego) makes at the cost of the id. But there is an alternative which Freud could not have recognized because of his ambivalent interpretation of the reality principle, namely, that the ego and the id must unite against reality. In other words, the lines must be redrawn in this "civil war"; in the conflict between ego, id, and reality, it is reality that must submit. This is the only possibility for psychoanalysis to be cured of its "private neurosis." Brown continues: "The only alternative [. . .] is to turn the aggression outward to the external world, as the energy working to change the world. Therapy is war."[105]

In this sense Thomas L.'s reason for breaking off his analysis is also a declaration of war: "Perhaps analysis as such failed, but somehow I found reality. On the other hand, if you want to get 'healthy' on the couch you somehow are a traitor to your class."[106] Instead of retreating to the ivory tower of psychoanalytic self-reflection, Thomas L. decided to "act out" his "private" conflicts socially: "I then extended my political activities into the work environment [. . .] and as that was naturally much more conflict-laden, because it did not take place in the treatment room with its thick carpets, there were tangible conflicts. I never really believed I was revolutionizing the world but after they didn't much like my politics I felt obligated to act completely in public and to agitate. This openness of course gave me tremendous psychic satisfaction. These conflicts, I think, are not really only mental, not only projections as analysis wants to make us believe; but they are good for you only if you don't just suffer but really get into the fray!"[107]

The Psychoanalytical Luxury Commodity: Understanding and Solidarity

Despite its repressive ritual, analysis does appear to have a "cathartic" effect on many patients. Otherwise the constantly rising demand for analysts, especially for group analysis, would remain inexplicable. But has this cathartic effect anything to do with the rules and rituals that are subsumed under the concept of "analytic technique"? That does not seem to be the case because—as K. M. Michel has demonstrated—there is no such thing as a generally valid and accepted "analytic technique."

Thus there are analysts who do without any ritual arrangement and only "interpret." Others do entirely without "interpretation" and let the patient stew in his own interpretations. And others again swear by the "therapeutic" power of silence, by a silent dipping into the "order of the symbolic" (Lacan), into the pre-verbal community of "unconscious discourse." It is the same with the rules of the cure, for example the abstinence rule. Conservative analysts forbid their patients erotic satisfaction within analysis and urge them not to enter into new libidinous ties during analysis. Progressive analysts, on the other hand, allow certain libidinous attachments by the patient within certain limits (kisses, small presents, and so on) and permit them to lead a "private" life outside analysis.

Analysts are completely at odds even on the question of what constitutes the actual pivotal point of the therapeutic process. Some consider it the making conscious of the Oedipal conflict, others the making conscious of conflicts which are pregenital and pre-Oedipal. K. M. Michel remarks: "The dilemma posits itself this way: Is the oral conflict the actual therapeutic concern or is it the Oedipal situation? [. . .] Put crudely: was 'it' the mother or the father?"[108] Elke L. observes: "[. . .] and he [the analyst] reduces the whole problem to my father [. . .] In the meantime I've entered a different therapy, and there it is suddenly completely certain that it has to do with my mother [. . .] The analysts don't know anything. But they know everything better. Their not knowing anything and their knowing everything better they take out on the patient."

The cathartic effect which analysis nonetheless has for many patients therefore consists not in an "analytic technique," no matter what form it takes, but rather in a very simple social fact: the "individualized individual," who has been "individualized" through bourgeois forms of behavior and principles of competition and exchange, experiences in the exclusive relationship with an analyst (or a "group") a temporary alleviation of his "individualization." The positive transference which is the condition for success of analysis maintains the patient in a state of dependency upon the analyst, but simultaneously it creates a trusting, understanding solidarity between the two. No analytic technique, no matter how complicated, but only this minimal solidarity in the analytic relationship between two people, is the whole "mystery" of analysis. Only in a society where, despite growing material affluence, more and more people live a "minimum mental existence" of mutual understanding, trust, communication, and solidarity can a specialized psychoanalytic society make its money from the psychic misery of masses of people. Many people experience in the hour of analysis the only situation in which someone actually listens to them, enters into them, takes them and their problems seriously. Thus Elke L. explains the question why analysis helped her at least to some extent: "Yes, you know, I can really gab with her when I have a problem with the child or something like that. And that helps me more than the other stuff."[109] And Ingrid B. replies to the same question: "I believe it was simply because everything was expressed and because the woman showed so much neutral understanding for everything."[110]

In a society governed by the exchange and profit principles (see also p. 142), people become so indifferent to one another that they themselves no longer produce a "neutral understanding" of others' problems necessary for a minimum psychic survival. Thus a special and therefore expensive service organization is required which approaches the "individualized individual" with, aside from monetary interest, also with "human interest"—now, however, for money. Psychoanalysis finds such an expensive market in our society because only within an exclusive and mystified communication with the analyst or the "group" is it possible to do what appears to become more and more impossible within "normal" social forms of behavior (in profession and family): to show one's true feelings, fears, and complexes, to go out of oneself, to let oneself go, to trust one or several persons without having to be afraid of being used or exploited in the process or of losing status. Thomas L. comments: "A therapy like that is a pretty artificial situation, and you don't get much out of it except one thing: that you should simply get outside yourself.[111] [. . .] It is like this, that you can't do that in society. You're afraid that if you let yourself go somehow, you are completely at their mercy."[112]

Since the economic character mask can afford psychology only outside the spheres of market and production, it perceives an exclusive, concealed relationship with the analyst or the "group" as temporary liberation. That is what lends a magical or mystical aura to the "analytic relationship" which so frequently seems like that of a secret society. Here the economic character mask can temporarily break through the neurotic character armor (Reich) which has been forged in the social competitive struggle; here it can finally be "human" if only in a regressive form. For human beings can afford to be human—like the estate-owner Puntila in Brecht's *Puntila and His Servant Matti*—only when they are drunk or when they are "ill." Only in an ill condition can and may they be what they otherwise, in a "normal" condition, on pain of economic ruin and social downfall may not be: weak, emotional, self-pitying, childish, melancholy, sad, depressed, dreamy, or—as psychoanalysis would say—regressive. Thomas L. remarks: "For we are, if we want to stay alive, somewhat regressive and immature in a society where the calculating capitalist, the soul of the small-time operator, is the ideal."[113]

The psychoanalytic cure—this constitutes its apparent but real catharsis—temporarily transforms the reified normal relationship of bourgeois individuals, who are "indifferent" towards each other and compete with each other, into an exclusive relationship of two or of a small group. If the "normal" emotional relationship between human beings has been "repressed" through abstract exchange or a money relationship (Wolf D.: "The money question played a big role in my development, namely, the question to what extent the child was given things, objects, and money instead of affection [. . .]"[114]), then the analyst offers the "ill person" in exchange for money a luxurious emotional relationship. Since the money character of human relationships robs them of their indigenous emotional character (see also p. 262), a special and therefore especially expensive effort is now required to create again a little feeling and understanding, a little human "interaction," at least at the edge of social reality. This is the business of psychoanalysis, no matter whether it is a question of classical individual psychoanalysis or modern group analysis. Thomas L. again observes: "I mean, psychoanalysis somehow profits from the condition that the individual is a fortress, an artificially limited area. That is completely clear to me: the individual in us is artificially isolated so that he can achieve more, then the pressure of suffering sets in, he has to get out in the form of work or aggression or domination of others, and then if you are poor you commit suicide or become dull or indifferent, or for a moment you are strong and defend yourself and you end up in jail or in an institution, depending; or you are educated and have money, then you go into analysis and let them give you for a lot of money what is rightfully yours: human understanding, undisturbed contact [. . .] Such contact, in case you get it, also influences you retroactively, and that is the 'cure.' That it takes some of us today five to ten years to learn to have an open, non-ironical, non-aggressive attitude to another person, and that this costs us 25 to 50 dollars an hour, throws light on our condition, on how out of the ordinary it is."[115]

Psychoanalysis throws light on the condition of our society inasmuch as what is normal and self-understood in non-reified societies is now sold as a luxury commodity, namely, an non-inimical, non-ironical, non-aggressive opening up to another person. Its business consists in trading in a luxury commodity which is becoming rarer and rarer in late capitalist society: "human understanding, undisturbed contact." To complain about the high price is indeed justified, but naïve. For the prospering psychoanalytic "soul factory" only follows the general capitalist price movements. The more reified, abstract, and inhuman the forms of social behavior become, the greater the demand for an exclusive psychoanalytic "soul massage" and the higher its price. As long as forms of social behavior depend on competition and exploitation, a "minimum psychic existence" of communication, contact, trust, and solidarity in the privileged upper and middle classes can only be produced by means of a business transaction and an exclusive "analytic" relationship of two or more in exchange. As long as the socialist movement has no new forms of communication and organization so as to counteract politically and therapeutically a growing mental misery, individual and group therapy—despite their mystification and repression—retain their partial justification.

Synopsis

Let us now draw up a brief balance sheet regarding the second part of the trial, "In the Matter of Freud."

The ideological obtuseness of psychoanalysis consists in its invariable mistaking of the bourgeois for man as such. Thus Freud's historical construction is nothing but a gigantic projection of the anthropology of the early bourgeoisie onto the pre- and primal history of mankind. His theory of culture encases a neuroticizing way of suffering and the Protestant spirit of capital accumulation, his theory of aggression the dog-eat-dog law of capitalist competition in a blind anthropological concept. His psychology of the ego too, his concept of an autonomous "genital character," turns out upon closer inspection to be an ideological self-transfiguration of the bourgeoisie during its liberal stage of ascendency. Similarly, the forms of ego disturbances that he registered should be regarded as psychological sedimentation of bourgeois forms of behavior which are fashioned by phallic competition, exclusionary possessive thinking, and monadological-narcissist individuation.

The scheme of psychosexual instinctual development which Freud claimed was universal (oral, anal, phallic), and which finds its apogee in the Oedipus complex, on closer inspection turns out to be an ethnocentric prejudice. And this prejudice is even now part of the concept of "invariable" which structural psychoanalysis has developed to impute a kind of "invariable" biological building plan to human instinctual development in which social and class-specific determinants enter only as "variables." The structure of the instinctual development itself as well as of its temporary end result, an exclusive claim of ownership of the mother and rivalry with the father in the "Oedipal" phase, already carries the imprint of bourgeois relationships within production; that is, they are fashioned by the "concrete form of the commodity," by "owning," by "alienation," and by "competition." The scheme of psychosexual development that Freud described should therefore not be regarded as a universal "invariable" but rather as a social-typical educational process which primarily has the following functions: to anchor, early in the instinctual structure of the child, "anal retentive" and aggressive modalities in relationship to possessions; to foster a psychosexual disposition towards wage labor; and to identify, with reference to the Oedipus complex, bourgeois power and class hierarchy with the authority of the father. Since psychoanalysis misunderstood the "Oedipus complex" as an anthropological-biological complex it could not develop a social perspective for "overcoming" it.

The bourgeois ideology and anthropology of Freud also entered and fashioned his model for therapy. The "analytical situation" and the rules and ritual of the cure are largely fashioned by the Protestant norms of the European and American middle class. "Social selection," which is effected by middle-class norms of behavior, is particularly harsh on proletarian patients, especially psychotics who are excluded by psychoanalytical societies as "unanalyzable." The emancipatory objective of analysis as such, namely, the creation of an autonomous ego structure, stands in crass contrast to the repressive means by which it is to be achieved: by a forced regression on the couch which keeps the patient in a state of immaturity and dependency and by the mystification of the analyst who possesses an absolute monopoly on interpretation and whose own ideal of "normalcy" and "health" is removed from any control or questioning by the patient. The screening out of the actual social situation of the patient from the "analytical process" throws the patient even further back into his past and robs him of any possibility of "assimilating" psychical conflicts and illnesses that result from his social (wage) dependency, not to speak of "acting them out." The frequent failure of therapy is primarily due to its idealistic conception, that is, in trust in word magic and in auto-plastic ego transformation which, of course, cannot eliminate the pathogenic social situation of the patient. Psychoanalytic prohibition on the "acting out" of conflicts finally produces a kind of "post-repression" and consequently a clinical lack of aggression which disposes the patient to even greater conformity to the existing social norms. Despite the repression and mystification attached to analysis it nevertheless appears to have a "cathartic" element for many patients. An "individuated individual" who has been individuated by the bourgeois principle of exchange and competition experiences in an exclusive relationship with the analyst or the group a certain trust and a certain solidarity which temporarily does away with his "individuation." The business of psychoanalysis therefore consists in trading "human contact," which is becoming increasingly rare in late capitalist society and is in fact a luxury commodity.

The general ambivalence of Freud's theory between materialist empiricism and bourgeois ideology as well as between reformism and opportunism in psychoanalytical therapy can finally be traced back to the ambivalent class situation, to the *petit-bourgeois* middle-class origins of Freud's school and of those psychoanalytic societies whose official recognition by bourgeois society was reimbursed by a progressive sacrifice of the subversive and culture-critical content of Freud's theory.

Does that mean that psychoanalysis has now become totally useless for historical materialism and the socialist movement? This would be a premature vulgar Marxist reduction. This is not the place to determine the task of an emancipatory psychoanalysis within the framework of today's socialist movement. Such would require a basic materialistic refounding chiefly of its concept of illness, which is something we shall attempt to do in Part Three.

The fact that bourgeois ideology and anthropology permeate almost all categories of psychoanalytical theory lets us first of all conclude that it cannot enter into a relationship with the theory of historical materialism. All attempts to "mediate" the Marxist and psychoanalytical systems of categories *must* founder on the fact that political-economic categories are historical-materialist categories, whereas psychoanalytical categories are largely blind, that is, they do not reflect their own historical and ideological content. Thus, to name only one example, it would be a theoretical impossibility to want to "mediate" the categories of Freud's psychology of the ego, which have gathered the *particular* psychology of one *class,* the liberal-enlightened bourgeoisie, into one blind concept, with the categories of political economy in *general.*

All attempts of psychoanalysis to accommodate itself to historical materialism in the form of a materialist dialectic, that is, as Marxist psychology in the Reichian manner, are—and this should be re-emphasized here—destined to failure. For they presuppose that one can extract ideological "alien components" from psychoanalysis and conserve the "pure" natural-scientific solution, the "pure" science of the instinctual nature of man *as such.* But this precisely is impossible. If one consistently mounted an attack upon the bourgeois ideology of psychoanalysis not much would eventually be left of it. Repeated recent attempts—by Lacan, Rappaport,[116] and others—to crystallize the "logical status" of psychoanalysis have encountered objective limits. For one cannot liquidate the ideological remnant of its significance, say in the category of the ego, without liquidating everything. If one seeks—like Rappaport—to develop the "logical status" of these categories one liquidates on the other hand their sociological substance. What remains is a totally formalized abstract system of categories which has lost the analytical strength of Freud's categories. The insolubly problematic nature, even the "tragedy," of psychoanalysis is that the power of what it says rests on the insoluble alloy of subversive science and bourgeois ideology, of materialist empiricism and bourgeois anthropology. Especially and only as a science of the pseudo-nature of bourgeois man, encasing the psychology of the "individuated individual" in a blind concept, is it irreplaceable for Marxism. The blindness of its categories towards its own historical and ideological content is, so to speak, the premise of its truth. Its monadological character reflects the fate of bourgeois individuation and socialization. In this sense—despite or precisely because of its ideological implications—psychoanalysis is a piece of indirect historical writing about bourgeois society, that is, it is written from the standpoint of the monadological bourgeois ego which is experiencing a new historical stage of socialization (see p. 159) as ego crisis, that is, as neurosis.

The problem of psychology, unsolved to this day from a Marxist viewpoint, cannot be remedied by separating psychology in the form of psychoanalysis from political economy as the Frankfurt School and the proponents of the theory of symbolic interaction wish, nor by trying to combine them at any price as the German Freudo-Marxist sought to do. What matters rather, on the one hand, is to pick up the beginnings, the seeds, of a materialist psychology and psychopathology that are strewn throughout Marx's *Capital* and to develop them further; and, on the other hand, to derive Freud's magnificent structural description of the "bourgeois soul," especially as a theory of illness and neurosis, from the laws of economic movement of bourgeois society itself. This—at least in the form of an outline—is now to be undertaken in Part Three.

part three
The Utilization of Capital and Psychic Impoverishment, or Society as Illness

Happiness is the subsequent fulfillment of a prehistoric wish. That is why wealth plays such a negligible role in happiness. Money was not a childhood wish.

FREUD

Prefatory Note

As we have said, the bourgeois barrier of Freud's theory of drives and libido lies in its biologistic and ethnocentric imputations of the instinctual nature of man *as such.* P. Brückner states: "Analysis of the modifications of human instinctual structures and of psychic apparatus in the course of the historical production and reproduction of society is *not* attached by Freud to the developed conditions of capitalism."[1] What is lacking, in other words, is an analysis of the historicity of the structure of social instincts and needs with regard to the historicity of the production of commodities. If, according to Marx, "the development of the five senses is a labor of the whole previous history of the world,"[2] then this also holds true for the development of the instinctual structure. The "psychic apparatus" (Freud), too, is the result of the "whole previous history of the world." The only methodological way, therefore, to make visible the historical and social-specific reality content of Freud's categories behind their biologistic and ethnocentric scaffolding is to develop a dialectic between the structure of social production and reproduction and the corresponding structure of social instincts and needs. This method simultaneously allows one step further in the emancipation of psychoanalysis from its mechanistic and idealistic "foreign policy" (as we said above). Its "inner-political" relationships, inasmuch as they pertain to the conflict psychology of the "individuated individual," can of course neither be verified nor falsified by means of a critique of political economy.

That analysis whose theme we have broached can here only be delineated in some of its essential aspects. In this process we are relying primarily on those remarks about the historical dialectic of money and the structure of need that can be found in Marx himself. Briefly, our main thesis is that the structure of social instincts and needs becomes, with the historical development of the structure of commodity and money, just as *abstract* as the latter. The "abstraction" of use values and of those useful needs and satisfactions which correspond to them and which lie at the root of the commodity and money form is in a certain sense to be regarded as the germinal political-economic cell of those processes of psychical "abstraction" which Freud described with his concept of "instinctual repression." Freud's theory of repression, regarded in this light, is the psychological complement of Marx's theory of commodities and money.

Freud—with some justification—was still able to investigate the social-ization process of the child from the standpoint of the *use* which the child makes of its instincts and instinctual objects. Interfamilial relationships, especially during the phase of primary socialization, are not yet imme-diately reified relations: this—as opposed to the reification that prevails in a (capitalist) exchange society—constitutes their progressive element. But this contradiction is also part of Freud's theory of instincts, espe-cially its concept of libido. This concept is on the one hand anachronistic because it does not and cannot reflect the effect of a general social reification onto the instinctual structure; for what specifically forecloses itself from its vision as a qualitative concept is the specific fate of sensuality in capitalism, its progressive disqualification and disrealization through the exchange principle. On the other hand, the blindness of Freud's libido concept is the prerequisite for his progressive, even uto-pian dimension, because this dimension clings to the "indestructible" *quality* of "childhood wishes" so as to defend them against all reified conceptions of pleasure, happiness, and love. This subversive, progres-sive dimension of the libido concept—as we have said—was totally ignored by orthodox Marxism.

If Freud's real greatness consists in having investigated the laws of psychosexual instinctual development and libido economy in the "preser-vation" of the bourgeois family, that is, where the use value of human relations still dominates, then his bourgeois weakness and obtuseness consists of his having also tried to apply his theory of use value, which is psychological at heart, where exchange value, and not use value any longer, dominates social relations; that is, where not a libido economy but a critique of political economy has the last word. A materialistic theory of illness therefore has to begin not as Freud with the exceptional case of use value within the family but vice versa, namely, from the normal exchange relations of the producer of social commodities. In contrast with Freud who derives "instinctual repression," or neurosis, only im-manently from the indigenous conditions of the bourgeois family, from the "Oedipal constellation," which appears to be a natural condition, a materialistic theory of illness has to derive interfamilial repressions and symptoms of illness primarily from an extrafamilial relationship of com-modity and exchange. It has to describe the process of reification which—

beginning with the commodity economy—seizes hold of the economy of the social libido at a certain developmental stage of the commodity society and finally also penetrates the "private sphere," the field of family socialization.

We are aware, of course, that the clinical phenomenon of "repression" is not simply identical with the political-economic phenomenon of "abstraction" of use values and of the usable needs and satisfactions related thereto. However, it can be shown that a necessary connection exists between the degree of abstraction which (capitalist) commodity society has reached in the course of its history and its degree of social instinctual repression. We are also aware that the concept of "repression" was applied by Freud only to specific instinctual needs, namely, sexual ones, whereas we are applying it in a much broader sense to all social needs which can be satisfied by the production of use value. This enlargement of the "repression" concept appears necessary, however, because its limitation to the sexual realm camouflages the extent of repression of social instincts and needs. For the historically developing money structure not only has deformed and perverted the sexual structure but also the entire structure of social needs. The enlargement of the "repression" concept is also supposed to guard against its pan-sexual misuse, a danger which Wilhelm Reich did not always avoid.

The beginning which we have here developed of a psychology founded in political economy does not compete with Freud's individual psychopathology, but seeks to place it within a historical-materialist founding context. It therefore does not negate the historical "etiology of neurosis" in the individual and family which Freud investigated, but rather seeks to plant it within the context of a historical-materialistic "etiology of neurosis." It seeks to derive the general condition under which modern psychology came into existence, that is, from the developmental laws of (capitalist) commodity society itself. This analysis finally seeks to make good on the demand that Baron made of the Marxists: "As Marxism is the inheritor and guardian of all that is valuable and progressive in bourgeois culture, it is the task of Marxism today to take up Freud's work where he left off [. . .] The Marxists, however, impressed by the achievements of Pavlov and his school, have turned their whole attention to the biological side of the matter and tend [. . .] to ignore Marx's revolutionary contribution to psychology, to the sociology of the psyche."[3] The theoretical foundation of the following chapters is "Marx's revolutionary contribution to psychology." In this sense it understands itself as a contribution to Marxist psychology. Simultaneously it attempts to take up "Freud's work where Freud left off," that is, to take literally the task which Freud designated but no longer completed, namely, a contribution to the "pathology of civilized communities" (Freud);[4] or more precisely, a contribution to the "pathology" of capitalist civilization.

Classic psychoanalysis thus far has done nothing but treat the ill person *within* society. Its theory consequently consisted in adjusting the alleged "patient" to an allegedly "healthy" society. It is the task of an emancipated psychoanalysis to treat society itself as an illness. It has to demonstrate that "therapy" is identical with the political struggle against an ill, because ill-making, society. We view what follows, therefore, as a contribution to the materialistic new-founding of an emancipatory psychoanalysis in the sense suggested by K. M. Michel: "Or is an emancipatory psychoanalytical practice thinkable which relates Freud's 'for we take a critical attitude to it [society]' not only to the ill-making elements of society, as its own system of symbols defines it, but to this system of symbols itself, to society as illness? Thus a (materialistically founded) psychoanalysis which declares total war on capitalist society?"[5]

5. On the Pathology of the Capitalist Commodity Society

The "Repression" of Use Value

According to Freud, "the basic driving force of human society is ultimately economic: since society does not have sufficient foodstuffs to maintain its members without their working it must limit the number of its members and divert its energies from sexual activity to work. This is the eternal and basic exigency of life which persists to this day."[6] This thoroughly materialistic perception by Freud has, however, an a-historical conception of work at its basis. For the capitalist development of the productive forces of work has mastered "ananke," the exigencies of life, up to a point, with the progressive overcoming of material shortages. Given the development of powers of production the economic motive for instinctual denial and instinctual repression would therefore also—according to Freud's logic—gradually have to disappear. Regarded in this fashion, it is actually quite incomprehensible that of all cultures the capitalist "culture," which has developed social wealth as none other before it, exacts such a high psychic toll, that is, imposes such a great instinctual denial on human beings.

Since Freud was not informed about the political economic foundations of capitalist "civilization," it also escaped him that the "economic" motive of human society itself is subject to historical transformation. If material scarcity of resources and means of production, the "exigencies of life," were the "economic motive" in pre-capitalist societies until the beginning of the capitalist age, then this motive historically recedes to the degree that material scarcity and poverty are also mastered with the development of the capitalist mode of production. The motive for instinctual denial and repression which predominates even now, however, is also an economic one. Yet it is no longer material destitution but the "repression" of use-value production by exchange-value production which itself is part and parcel of the dynamics of commodity production.

The political-economic primal cell for capitalist society's specific "form of repression" is therefore that of the commodity, that is, the commodity exchange. In exchange there occurs—according to Marx— that mystical transformation, that "transsubstantiation" in which the products of labor first turn into commodities, that is, are related to one another as "values." In exchange, particular, concrete, in and for itself unexchangeable and incomparable "private labor" is transcended by being related as "coagulation of undifferentiated abstract work," that is, as work time, to other particular, unexchangeable, and incomparable private labor. Marx states: "When they assume this money-shape, commodities strip off every trace of their natural use-value, and of the particular kind of labor to which they owe their creation, in order to transform themselves into the uniform, socially recognized incarnation of homogenous human labor."[7] This value form of the commodity, of the particular, concrete qualitative character of work, of its "natural use value," extends itself necessarily also onto the particular concrete qualitative needs and satisfactions which have been mediated through work.

Every act of exchange equates the incomparable qualities of two use values in a certain quantitative relationship to the relationship of the average social work-time that is objectified in them. This equation necessarily abstracts from the sensuous-concrete difference and diversity of the use values. If we abstract from the use value of manufactured products, "we make abstraction at the same time from the material elements and shapes that make the product a use-value; we see in it no longer a table, a house, yarn, or any other useful thing. Its existence as a material thing is put out of sight. Neither can it any longer be regarded as the product of the labor of the joiner, the mason, the spinner, or of any other definite kind of productive labor. Along with the useful qualities of the products themselves, we put out of sight both the useful character of the various kinds of labor embodied in them, and the concrete forms of that labor; there is nothing left but what is common to them all; all are reduced to one and the same sort of labor, human labor in the abstract."[8]

Exchange-value consciousness thus is indifferent, even blind to the sensuous-concrete quality and diversity of the use value; it "transcends" constantly the sensuous-qualitative world of useful things so as to discover on their invisible ground their "essence," that is, their "value." For an exchange-value consciousness each thing is only the physical husk of its "value substance," all its sensuous properties and particularities are, so to speak, only a "pantheistic" camouflage of the invariably same "monotheistic" principle of the "Holy Grail" which—according to Marx —"is the most glittering incarnation of its [capitalist society's] own life principle."[9]

The objective indifference of exchange value with regard to the sensuous particularity of use value necessarily reflects back on the need and instinctual structure of the individual that does the exchanging. As Haug observes: "A training in self-mastery to the point of indifference, as the preparation of sensuality adequate to the exchange principle, is the prerequisite for the execution of social relationships which reverberate from the exchange society into individual life."[10] The exchange principle therefore is inextricably bound to a certain animosity towards sensuality. "Abstract man," who is the personification of "abstract human labor," has just as abstract a relationship to his own sensuality as to the sensuality of use value. The abstraction of commodity and money and the disqualification and disrealization which it effects of the entire world of usable things are therefore the materialistic foundation of that psychic "process of abstraction" which Freud described with the concept of "repression." For the abstraction from the particularity, usefulness, and sensuousness of use value and the particular, useful, and concrete labor at its basis also has as a consequence the abstraction, that is, tendential "repression," of all particular, useful, sensuous needs and satisfactions which are bound to the use value. As Lukács remarks: "The relationship of men to each other and to the real objects of the genuine satisfaction of their needs— a relationship concealed in the immediate commodity relationship—fades into complete imperceptibility and unrecognizability."[11] Here he is sketching by means of political economy the historical process of the disqualification and disrealization of the social need and instinctual structure whose intrapsychic sedimentation Freud diagnosed with the concept of "repression."

The "repression of instinct" described by Freud, which one could also define as a psychological "process of abstraction," is a "real abstraction"[12] in A. Sohn-Rethel's sense. For "repression" does not occur on the level of consciousness but outside and without partaking of consciousness as a real process just as the value, that is, money, abstraction occurs outside and without the consciousness of the exchangers in the real process of exchange. Marx states: "They [the exchangers] do not know it, but they do it."[13] An exchange abstraction as "real abstraction" enters the exchangers' consciousness as little as its psychological complement, "repression," enters the consciousness of the repressing subject. An exchange-value consciousness and a "repressing" consciousness therefore suffer a "loss of reality" with regard to the sensuous-concrete objectivity of use value and the sensuous-concrete (instinctual) needs that are mediated by them.

The "real abstraction," that is, repression of the sensuous-concrete, natural-scientific use-form of things and the sensuous-concrete (instinctual) needs attached to them, which the exchange consciousness performs, makes itself potent in the autonomous form of exchange value. With a progressively increasing division of labor and the production of private commodities the exchange value acquires an existence separate from the product: as money. "In money," says Marx, "the value of the things is separated from their substance."[14] If exchange value, money, was at first—in the simple commodity production (CMC*)—only the mediator of a production that was chiefly aimed at use value, it finally becomes—in a fully developed capitalist commodity society (MCM)—the sole starting and end point: that is, the determining principle of production itself. Marx states: "The circuit CMC starts with one commodity, and finishes with another, which falls out of circulation and into consumption. Consumption, the satisfaction of wants, in one word, use value, is its end and aim. The circuit MCM, on the contrary, commences with money and ends with money. Its leading motive, and the goal that attracts it, is therefore mere exchange value."[15]

In capitalist commodity society (MCM) the economic motive of human society is thus inverted into its opposite: the actual purpose of production is no longer use value and the immediate satisfaction of needs and instincts but exchange value and with that the satisfaction of needs now only mediated through exchange value; that is, the renunciation of immediate satisfaction of needs and instinctual satisfaction. By becoming autonomous with respect to every particular commodity object and by becoming the "driving motive" of production, exchange value has unloosened itself from every concrete-sensuous immediate need.

Of course, particularly the slaves and the serfs of antique and medieval society also had to perform a high degree of "instinctual renunciation" in the form of slave and compulsory labor. But since the production here was still chiefly one of use values, production supplying bare essentials, the (instinctual) needs which were mediated through them could not yet "disappear into complete imperceptibility and unrecognizability" (Lukács). On the level of the antique, that is, feudal *natural* economy, social instinctual needs were also still immediately attached to use values and therefore had just as particular, concrete, and qualitative a character as natural-economic work itself. Marx writes: "Let us now transport ourselves [. . .] to the European middle ages shrouded in darkness. [. . .] Here the particular and natural form of labor, and not, as in a society based on production of commodities, its general abstract form is the

*Commodity-Money-Commodity

immediate social form of labor. Compulsory labor is just as properly measured by time, as commodity producing labor; but every serf knows that what he expends in the service of his lord, is a definite quantity of his own personal labor power. The tithe to be rendered to the priest is more matter of fact than his blessing. No matter, then, what we may think of the parts played by the different classes of people themselves in this society, the social relations between individuals in the performance of their labor, appear at all events as their own mutual personal relations, and are not disguised under the shape of social relations between the products of labor."[16]

In precapitalist societies, social relationships were still mythologically and religiously embellished master-servant relationships; but it was not yet—as in capitalist society—a case of objectified but of personal dependence relationships in which the social-instinctual and emotional structure was also embedded. The forms of economic exploitation were more brutal and more blatant in antique slave and feudal serf economy, but the slave and serf were not yet as "alienated" from their work and therefore from the real objects of their need and instinctual satisfaction as the "free wage-earner." To a degree, therefore, that a natural economy is replaced by a money economy and natural-economic work by commodity-producing work, by wage labor, the social need and instinctual structure also loosens itself from its immediate objects of concrete-sensuous satisfaction. To the degree that money as the "general commodity" "represses" the process of production and consumption as mediated by work, the social need and instinctual structure assumes the form of "abstract generality." As Marx declares: "As material representative of general wealth, as individualized exchange value, money must be the immediate object, purpose, and product of general work, the work of the individual. Work must immediately produce exchange value, that is, money. It must be wage labor. The craving for wealth, as everyone's drive, in that everyone wants to produce money, only produces general wealth [. . .] By virtue of the fact that wage labor, its immediate purpose, is money, general (abstract) wealth is posited as its purpose and object [. . .] By virtue of the fact that work is not a particular product which stands in a special relationship to the special needs of individuals, but is money, wealth in its general form, the individual's ability to work, has no limits; it is indifferent to its special quality and assumes any form which serves its purpose."[17] By raising itself to a general universal need, money becomes the global motor of "repression" of all the particular, concrete-sensuous needs and satisfactions which it originally (in the circuit CMC) still had to mediate. With the universal dissemination and development of the form of money, there develops therefore a structure of social needs which is as abstract and boundless as money itself. Although there also existed "boundless" needs within use-value production, such as greed which the middle ages counted among the deadly sins, yet this "boundless" need was still tied to immediate physical wealth, to real use values (such as clothes, jewelry, houses, livestock, and so on) and with that to a particular form of need satisfaction. The need for "abstract wealth," on the other hand, the lust for the accumulation of wealth as everyone's instinct, finds satisfaction only when it abstracts from all concrete particular use values; but at the same time it founders on its own contradiction because no particular use value provides it with satisfaction any longer. Greed for money, the "lust for accumulation of wealth," is therefore like an unending spiral. The more objects it acquires for itself through the possession of "abstract wealth" the more incapable it becomes of immediate concrete (instinctual) satisfaction. Since the "lust for the accumulation of wealth" has abstract wealth itself as objective and purpose it therefore no longer finds a qualitative barrier; it is rather the eternally dissatisfied, boundless, ill, lustful instinct as such.

The way the pursuit of abstract wealth "denatures" and "perverts" human instinctual nature has been described by Bertolt Brecht in *St. Joan of the Stockyards* with the example of Mauler, the monopolist on the Chicago meat market:

> "[. . .] There's no hindering this monster in his climb: nature to him is merchandise, even the air's for sale. What's in our stomach he resells to us. He gets rent out of caved-in houses, money from rotten meat; stone him, he is sure to change the stones to money; he's so wild for money so natural in this unnaturalness that even he cannot deny its power."[18]

The Character of Money and Lust

The character of lust attached to the character of the commodity, that is, of money, also puts its imprint on the structure of social needs and instincts. Marx portrayed this in the picture of Midas who in a certain sense is the mythological model, that is, bogey, of the man who suffers from the disease of lust. Midas, who like Dionysius wishes that everything he touches would turn to gold, becomes ill from insatiability. For the promise of absolute gratification turns into the impossibility of any kind of concrete satisfaction. He cannot eat or drink anything anymore, nor enjoy anything because everything he looks at turns into gold. As Ovid says: "Wealthy and miserable at one and the same time and benumbed by this strange misfortune/he wants to flee wealth and hates what he so recently desired./ Nothing stills his hunger now, his throat is parched with thirst./ Everywhere the loathsome gold he sought tortures him."[19] Midas, addict to gold and money, becomes ill because the more he "owns" the world the less he can acquire the actual world, the world of use values, of sensuous experience. The more power in the sense of "property" he acquires over the world of sensuous use values and satisfactions the more it slips from his senses, the less real, the more unsensuous, even "senseless" it becomes for him. The "boundlessness," the lust character of his needs, arises from the character of the commodity, that is, of money, which the whole actual world assumes under his hands. In the words of Kurnitzky: "Its [society's] fetish is the commodity which promises gratification but can never grant it, since it has only money value, but use value only for capital. It is waste product. Its image of salvation is the 'paradise of Midas,' death by gratification substitute."[20]

If, according to Freud, neurosis catches fire in the unbridgeable conflict between wish and reality, then Midas is the archetype of capital-psychosis. For the contradiction between the world as "abstract wealth" and the world as sensuous-concrete wealth that develops with the form of money reproduces itself—on the conscious level—as psychotic contradiction between fantasy and reality. According to Marx: "As general form of wealth money is confronted by the entire world of real valuables. Money is the pure abstraction of the same—pure fantasy. Where wealth appears to exist in complete material, palpable form as such, money only has its existence in my head, as a pure figment of my mind."[21]

The imaginary, hallucinatory power of "abstract wealth" finds very plastic expression in Charlie Chaplin's film *The Gold Rush.* Charlie and his companion have lost their way searching for gold in the snow-covered Alaskan mountains. By chance they come upon a broken-down log cabin where they spend the night. Charlie's gold-hungry companion, who has not eaten for weeks, is overcome by a hunger psychosis: he hallucinates Charlie as a fat, tasty chicken which he wants to shoot with his gun. Sensuous-actual wealth, in the form of a satisfying meal, exists for him, the gold addict, only as pure fantasy, as hallucination. Charlie, who is always more interested in erotic treasure than in gold, is better off in this case: he satisfies his hunger even with the most paltry use value: he cooks his shoes and eats them with pleasure after having first carefully removed the nails and licked them off.

The murderous effect of "abstract wealth," "death by gratification substitute," is an age-old theme of popular literature. In *A Thousand and One Nights* it is treated with ever new variations, for example in Sinbad the Seafarer and the Golden Ship of the Dead.[22] All those who murder, steal, cheat, and so forth for the sake of gold betray their humanity, are dehumanized, and come to a bad end. Only Sinbad, who finally is concerned with the treasure not of money but of love, remains alive. He, the adventurer, fighter, and lover who, so to speak, is the incarnation of living human wealth, of human sensuality, carries his dear "treasure" home alive while his rivals have to pay for their golden treasure with their lives.

The boundlessness, insatiability, and lustfulness of the structure of

social needs and instincts which began to predominate with the development of a money economy was also represented in many works of
literature in the middle ages, which saw its moral and religious nature
threatened (which, incidentally, is why money, banking, and usury were
left to the Jews, the "money" Jews) by advancing trade and by profiteer-
ing capitalism. So in Dante's *Divina Commedia* many punishments that are
meted out in hell have the sisyphean character of lust which is attached
to "abstract wealth." This is represented in the form of hellish "Tantalus
tortures." For example the counterfeiters in the thirtieth song of hell are
punished by "water addiction."[23]

The medieval counterfeiter who exploits social work by falsifying its
equivalent, money, that is, inflates its values, is in a certain sense the
atavistic-criminal prototype of the modern legal capitalist who exploits
social labor power by cheating workers of part of their value, namely,
surplus value. His hellish punishment, water addiction, which completely
denatures his body, has more than just symbolic character: the pursuit of
"abstract wealth," the money fetish, is payed for with the total loss of
sensuous wealth; lust for what is "most unnatural," money, with his own
denaturalization.

To the same degree that the particular concrete use value, the particular concrete instinctual object no longer affords any satisfaction, the fetish
for money itself assumes the function of the object of lust. In a certain
sense it fetishizes the entire instinctual structure of man by becoming the
dominating content of all his wishes and satisfactions. This too has
already been shown by Marx, in the image of the hoarder who in a certain
sense is the atavistic prototype of the accumulating capitalist: "In order
that gold may be held as money, and made to form a hoard, it must be
prevented from circulating, or from transforming itself into a means of
enjoyment. The hoarder, therefore, makes sacrifice of the lusts of the
flesh to his gold fetish. He acts in earnest up to the gospel of abstention.
On the other hand, he can withdraw from circulation no more than what
he has thrown into it in the shape of commodities. The more he produces,
the more he is able to sell. Hard work, saving, and avarice, are, therefore,
his three cardinal virtues, and to sell much and buy little the sum of his
political economy."[24]

The "cardinal virtues" of the hoarder are abstract, boundless "virtues" like the gold lust of Midas, which are characterized by their
incapacity for immediate instinctual satisfaction. His "zealousness" no
longer focuses on the acquisition of a particular concrete commodity but
its objective and purpose is "wealth in its general form." It therefore has
no limits. It is the same with "thrift" and "avarice": they are in a certain
sense the negation of the insatiable "pleasure lust" of Midas and are a
part of—according to Marx—gold lust. "The lust for pleasure in its
general form and avarice are two particular forms of the greed for

money."[25] That is why the pleasure addict and the miser in Dante's *Divina Commedia* are caught in the same circle of hell: both keep encountering each other at the Zenith and Nadir of their circle where they accuse each other bitterly every time. The one: "You miser!" The other: "You prodigal!"[26] The cyclical form of their tortuous way through hell, which brings them together time and again, expresses the futility and infinity, that is, the "recurrence compulsion" (Freud), of their instinctual drive which never achieves ultimate satisfaction.

The picture of the hoarder who "sacrifices his fleshly pleasures for the fetish of gold" contains—if you will—Freud's theory of neurosis *in nuce*. For this image provides the reason for the disciplining and submission of human sensuality under the exchange principle. The hoarder is the incarnation of endless "instinctual deferral" and "instinctual renunciation" in favor of an accumulation of abstract wealth—and from this viewpoint the archetype of capital-neurosis, the "neurotic human animal" whose "Faustian character" arises from the repression of his immediate sensual needs. Freud writes: "What appears in the minority of human individuals as an untiring impulsion toward further perfection can easily be understood as a result of instinctual repression upon which is based all that is most precious in human civilization. The repressed instinct never ceases to strive for complete satisfaction, which would consist in the repetition of primary experience of satisfaction. No substitutive or reactive formations and no sublimation will suffice to remove the repressed instinct's persisting tension; and it is the difference in amount between the pleasure of satisfaction which is demanded and that which is actually achieved that provides the driving factor which will permit no halting at any position attained, but, in the poet's words, 'presses ever forward unsubdued' (Mephistopheles, *Faust,* Part I, Sec. 4)."[27]

The restlessness, boundlessness, of this "Faustian" instinctual movement grows out of the restless, boundless character of an economic movement which abstracts from all concrete social needs and gratifications. The "untiring impulsion toward further perfection" is—in capitalist society—the urge for more and more "perfect" domination of nature *qua* exploitation and possession. But "this form of the destruction of nature, as it confronts us in the form of commodity, our second nature, as lifeless thing, suppresses and represses simultaneously the natural instinctual basis of human beings" (Kurnitzky[28]). To the same degree that economic gratification becomes a purpose in itself, that is, to the degree that its objective no longer consists in the satisfaction of an immediate concrete need, the accompanying instinctual movement becomes a purpose in itself as well, that is, it separates itself from its immediate concrete-sensuous (natural-economic) use objects.

The subjugation of human sensuality under the dictates of the exchange principle, of "abstract wealth"—as W. F. Haug has pointed out—has been very plastically described by Brecht in his *The Seven Deadly Sins of the Petit Bourgeoisie.* Step by step in her suffering life Anna relinquishes her sensual needs, especially her love needs, so as to assure herself of "abstract wealth" in the form of money. At the end of her life she is indeed "well off"—like the hoarder, but sensually just as broken as the latter, and "envious of everyone who could spend his days in idleness/with nothing to buy but pride/Enraged by each act of brutality/giving himself up to his instincts/A happy person, loving only the beloved and openly asking what he needs."[29] The "wealthier" and "more secure" Anna becomes, the poorer she becomes in sensual if uncertain pleasures. The more her sensual life becomes a utilitarian means, the more inimical to sensuality and the more "senseless" does it become. Regarded in this fashion, Anna's story is that of the neurotic life of suffering of the sensual human individual in capitalist exchange society.

The Accumulation of Capital and the "Anal-Compulsive Character"

Nearly all psychoanalytical theories of civilization describe capitalist culture above all as an anal one. This is absolutely proper except that the psychoanalytic theoreticians of capitalism usually never get beyond the most vulgar psychologism as, for example, when Ferenczi and Géza Roheim derive the economic function of money in a capitalist commodity economy from its psychological function within the libido economy instead of vice versa. The point of departure of all theories of psychoanalytical capitalism—according to R. Bastide—is the fact that money, that is, gold "in dreams and myths is always the symbol and substitute for excrement."[30] The association of money and anality also expresses itself in popular tales as that of the "donkey that shits gold" and in everyday expressions such as "stinking rich." In the psychoanalytical clinic excrement frequently acquires a fiduciary meaning; even a "fear of genital castration"—in the opinion of many psychoanalysts—can be transferred, via "anal displacement," to money.

In fact anal reaction formations play functionally a similar role in the libido economy to money in the capitalist commodity economy. According to Reich the "anal-compulsive character" distinguishes itself (also compare Reich's *Character Analysis*) by particularly rigid and abstract "virtues": by extreme orderliness, punctuality, a compulsion to cleanliness; by avarice, thriftiness, and a mania for hoarding; by a persistently calculating nature and consequently a profound general animosity to sensuality and an indifference of feeling, all of which generally build up genetically on the suppression of childhood anal eroticism and the rigid performance of excremental functions of cleaning and ordering ("regular" and "punctual" stool movement). As money as an autonomous

form of exchange value levels all use values, so do anal-reaction formations level all qualitative "emotional values." As money "as the radical
leveller extinguishes all differences" (Marx[31]), so the characterological
compulsions of the anal libido are "radical levellers" of all instinctual
objects and instinctual wishes whose "psychic energies" are bound in the
compulsive forms of their defense. Thus, for example, the repressed
(anal) erotic wish to "grovel in filth" or "to let oneself go" assumes the
form of a cleanliness compulsion or of compulsive retention and emotional blockage in the "anal-compulsive character syndrome." That
means that the repressed wish for a particular (anal) erotic "use activity"
transforms itself into the general and abstract form of a compulsive
activity. An anal-retentive character whose overt form of illness is the
compulsive neurotic thus compensates for the loss of qualitative relationship with instinctual objects by compulsively quantifying them and formal-
izing them. It formalizes the material of its repressed instinctual wishes
in its compulsion for order, cleanliness, and punctuality; and it quantifies
them in its obsession with avarice, thriftiness, and hoarding and in
calculating.

In *History and Class Consciousness* Lukács demonstrates that the
"principle of total calculability,"[32] the quantitative measurability of the
objective and subjective elements of the production process, of machinery and human labor power, was what made possible the victorious
advance of the capitalist mode of production. This principle of calculability and quantifiability extends not only to work performance, to the
determination of the value of labor, but also to its psychic economy.
However, what is most calculable and quantifiable within the libido
economy are the forms of characterological reaction of the anal libido.
The "retentive" (avarice, thriftiness, calculation, abstinence, "emotional
block") and "regulative" (order, cleanliness, and punctuality compulsions among others) behavioral compulsions of the anal-retentive character therefore represent the general characterological forms which   from
the viewpoint of utilization—are most easily calculated. That is why the
anal-compulsive character—as the "most calculable" and "most calculating" type of character—is only dominant in capitalist civilization.

Historically, the anal-retentive character becomes predominant only as
"social character" (Fromm) with the primary accumulation of capital;
and at first only within the class which was the bearer of this process,
within the bourgeoisie. The individual predecessor of the accumulating
bourgeoisie is—according to Marx—the aforementioned hoarder whose
cardinal virtues are immediate expressions of his economic function. As
"zealousness, thriftiness, greed, and acquisitive lust should—psychoanalytically—be understood as anal-reaction formations of the hoarder, so
these factors also predominate among capitalists as "abstract passions."
But "what with the former is only an individual mania is, within the

capitalist, an effect of the social mechanism in which he is only a cog."[33] The individual mania (of the hoarder) becomes a "social" mania, a manically accumulating "social character." For the capitalist, if possible, must limit his revenue and with that his need satisfaction so as to be able again to transform the surplus value he has drawn from work into capital instead of spending it lavishly. In the capitalist, therefore, "pleasure is subsumed under capital, the enjoying individual under the capitalizing one" (Marx[34]). The few means of enjoyment which the bourgeoisie allows itself during its ascendance "are especially appropriate to the bourgeois activity: tobacco, coffee, but primarily tea [. . .] The bourgeois needs a clear mind even during his intoxication" (Haug[35]). The "social character" of the early bourgeois, which is inimical to pleasure and sensuality, was primarily a psychological guarantee of his growing economic power. The bourgeois who had just emancipated himself from the feudal order could scarcely afford to give himself up to the feudal world of pleasure, to dissolution in the enjoyment of the moment. Only by providing the aristocracy with ever more and new means of pleasure and luxuries and always new products for feudal extravagance was he able "to acquire for himself the power the latter was losing" (Marx[36]).

The economic motive of accumulating wealth, which is no longer "use value and pleasure but only exchange value and its increase" (Marx[37]), finds its philosophical-moral guarantee in the "abstinence theory" of early Manchesterdom ("the more society progresses the more abstinence it requires"[38]) and its religious guarantee in the renunciatory ideology of Protestantism and its corresponding variations: Marx writes: "For a society based upon production of commodities, in which the producers in general enter into social relations with one another by treating their products as commodities and values, whereby they reduce their individual private labor to the standard of homogeneous human labor—for such a society, Christianity with its *cultus* of abstract man, more especially in its bourgeois developments, Protestantism, Deism, and so on, is the most fitting form of religion."[39]

Protestantism acquired importance for guaranteeing the capitalist modes of production especially because it changed almost all Catholic holidays into work days.[40] The actual mass-psychological function of Protestantism, however, consists in its having imposed—compared to Catholic feudal life and its emotional world—a new style of life and emotions appropriate for its own time which manifests itself by increasing inwardness, desexualization, suppression of the senses, and abstraction (also compare a Catholic and Protestant church, the Catholic and Protestant mass and liturgy, and so forth). If, according to Marx, Luther only fought the outward priest so as to install the inner priest in his place, then this expresses the social-psychological function of Protestantism: the transformation of social aggression against the new capitalist masters (also compare the German Peasant War which was not only anti-feudal but in part an anti-capitalist war directed against the German monopoly capitalists, Fugger and Welser) into moral and religious guilt feelings which constitute the social compulsive character capable of supporting the accumulation of capital. R. Reiche has remarked: "The forms of outward force would have been too uncertain for the process of capital formation: these forces always existed. If this process was to be effectively protected, particularly against the frequent initial setbacks due to economic crises, the outward forces had to be joined by inner compulsion [. . .] This compulsion can be described in its objective effect as reducing all human activity and qualities to their utilization in the process of production, that is, that all of them could be 'converted' into exchange relations. Subjectively, this compulsion had to have insight into the fact that nothing in the world is more self-evident next to work and the toil, effort, and distress associated with it—and the wages earned by it."[41] If Protestantism with its "cult of abstract man" is the adequate religious form, then a compulsive anal-retentive character—as the most abstract of all character types—is the most suitable characterological form in a society where "all human characteristics and qualities [. . .] are converted to their exchange relations." If Protestantism is, so to speak, a collective "compulsive neurosis" (as Freud said of religion as such), then the "Protestant ethic" (Max Weber[42]) is the religious reflection of that conscientiousness (that is, the fear of a punishing super-ego in contrast to "fear of the loss of love") which—according to Freud—constitutes the anal-compulsive character. The flight into the "collective compulsive neurosis" of Protestantism, that is, into the individual straightjacket of the "anal-retentive" character (as "social character"), is therefore the adequate religious, that is, characterological expression of the social-instinctual renunciation tied up with the accumulation of capital on the one hand and the development of wage labor on the other. To the degree that "the enjoying individual is subsumed under the capitalizing one" there arises a structure of social ego and instinct where the anal-reaction formations and defense mechanism, the psychosexual capacities for instinctual control, instinctual deferral, and renunciation become the dominating "character qualities" whereas oral character qualities, that is, the psychosexual capacity for surrendering oneself, for pleasure, for intoxication, begin to degenerate.

This also becomes clear from those attributes which psychoanalytical literature associates even today with the concept of the ego. All of its positive associations are—according to R. Reiche—"grouped around control, domination, decision, limitation, comprehensiveness, overview, subordination, watchfulness; all negative associations go in the direction of dissolution, inability to draw a limit, letting oneself go [. . .] The category of the ego only unlocks its secret meaning when regarded in the context of a social formation that is based on competition; it is bound to the commodity-selling, market-oriented bourgeois who must defeat his opponent but by emotionally neutral means, that is, without directly killing him."[43] The psychosexual, that is, characterological pendant to the "emotionally neutral means" with which the bourgeois defeats his competitor is the "emotional neutrality" and emotional blockage of the "anal-retentive" character mask which is distinguished by a strict superego that in extreme cases takes the form of a "compulsive neurosis." The neurosis punishes with guilt feelings every "temptation," every recidivism into a feudal and natural-economic enjoyment of pleasure and sensuality.

Once production has climbed beyond the primary rung, the capitalist too can afford a certain measure of extravagance and pleasure. At a certain level of development and accumulation he can translate a part of his surplus value into pleasurable means without endangering the process of capital formation.

According to Marx: "When a certain stage of development has been reached, a conventional degree of prodigality, which is also an exhibition of wealth, and consequently a source of credit, becomes a business necessity to the 'unfortunate' capitalist. Luxury enters into capital's expenses of representation."[44] For the "instinctual destiny" of the capitalizing individual this produces a conflict with grave consequences. Marx continues: "One portion of the surplus value is consumed by the capitalist as revenue, the other is employed as capital, is accumulated. Given the mass of surplus value, then, the larger the one of these parts, the smaller is the other. *Caeteris paribus,* the ratio of these parts determines the magnitude of the accumulation. [. . .] But along with this growth, there is at the same time developed in his breast, a Faustian conflict between the passion for accumulation, and the desire for enjoyment."[45]

The psychology of the capitalizing individual is from then on determined by the unceasing conflict betweeen his (calculating) reason, his "ego" function, which is intent on accumulation, that is, on instinctual renunciation and deferral; and his (passionate) feelings, his "id" function, which is intent on enjoyment and extravagance, that is, on immediate instinctual gratification. The "Faustian" conflict between accumulation and the "urge for pleasure" expresses itself—on the level of the psychic apparatus—as a neuroticizing conflict between "anal-retentive" control and the oral need for surrender and pleasure. But the capitalist's mania for pleasure no longer has the character of an unlimited surrender to the world of feudal pleasures; it is now under the domination of the hard calculus of the market. Extravagance is no longer enjoyed for its own sake—as it still was in feudal society—but as part of business. Marx comments: "Although, therefore, the prodigality of the capitalist never possesses the bona-fide character of the open-handed feudal lord's prodigality, but, on the contrary, has always lurking behind it the most sordid avarice and the most anxious calculation, yet his expenditure grows with his accumulation, without the one necessarily restricting the other."[46] The "prodigality" of the capitalist is only the other side of his avarice; both qualities are based on "calculation." Calculated "retention" as well as calculated "spending" and "prodigality" have nothing in common with the immediate satisfaction of needs. The "conventional degree of prodigality" therefore does not eliminate "anal-retentive" compulsive avarice, thriftiness, calculation, and so on, but only reproduces the anal level in another form. "Prodigality," "luxury," is only a means of representation, that is, a means of power. "Enjoyment" therefore stands in the service of capital power, is therefore—as psychoanalysis understands it—soldered to the "anal-acquisitive instinct." "Enjoyment" as representation, that is, a means of power. "Enjoyment" therefore stands shackles of the anal-retentive character structure, but merely supplements and complements it.

To the degree that the psychology of the capitalizing individual is subsumed under the dictate of the hard, exacting, and precisely calculating market, his "calculating being" also extends itself to all human relationships. "Calculation is not only related to the amount of money which is spent on pleasure and puts a limit on enjoyment; it also governs human relations [. . .] an equivalence exchange degrades human relations to a losing business: what you invest would not prove a loss but you invest so as to earn."[47]

The working class, on the other hand, did not at first have to interiorize the consumption and instinctual abstinence of the accumulating bourgeois since, lacking all means of production, it could not itself accumulate, and thus had nothing to abstain from. It lived from hand to mouth. For centuries on end the bourgeoisie also sought vainly to impose its Protestant ideology and its psychology of "anal-retentive" achievement on wage laborers who in the sixteenth, seventeenth, and eighteenth centuries frequently only worked a three-day week, that is, just long enough to earn as much as they needed to subsist on. Thus the ideologists of English capital complained time and again about the lack of a work morality in the developing wage-labor class. As Marx quotes from another source: "That mankind in general is naturally inclined to ease and indolence, we fatally experience to be true, from the conduct of our manufacturing populace who do not labor, upon an average, above four days in a week, unless provisions happen to be very dear [. . .] ."[48] Only when the bourgeoisie acquired the power of the state and enacted the six-day week and twelve-hour day, Sunday and night shifts, child and woman labor, were the capitalist work morality and its corresponding "social character" also imposed on wage laborers.

As distinct from the bourgeois "compulsive character," which ultimately is based on the priority of the "accumulative instinct," the proletarian "compulsive character" constitutes itself only in the process of capitalist labor; that is, it is the social-psychological sedimentation of the work-and-shop organization which is determined by the capitalist division of labor. As Marx states: "It is clear that this direct dependence of the operations, and therefore of the laborers, on each other, compels each one of them to spend on his work no more than the necessary time; and thus a continuity, uniformity, regularity, order, and even intensity of labor, of quite a different kind, is begotten than is to be found in an independent handicraft or even in simple cooperation."[49]

The new compulsive "virtues of labor" which are imposed as social norms through the development of the capitalist organization and division of labor, that is, social "character virtues," have a grave effect on those practices relating to education and socialization, especially of the worker families. By suppressing and disciplining the "polymorphous perverse" sexuality of childhood, the family prepares the child early on for his life role as "wage laborer" and for the "barracks discipline" which goes hand in hand with the development of the factory system. Marx says: "The technical subordination of the workman to the uniform motion of the instruments of labor, and the peculiar composition of the body of the working people, consisting as it does of individuals of both sexes and of all ages, give rise to a barracks discipline, which is elaborated into a complete system in the factory, and which fully develops the aforementioned labor of overseeing, thereby dividing the working people into operatives and overseers, into private soldiers and sergeants of an industrial army."[50]

The "barracks discipline" within the developing capitalist factory system must be pre-molded and guaranteed technically through the socialization and education of the worker child according to rigid conceptions of order, cleanliness, and authority. (See also p. 190.) The suppression of the polymorphous perverse sexuality of childhood by "cultural sexual morality" is a social-technical means of repression that is part and parcel of the logic of capital and anchors the psychic disposition to wage labor at an early age in the instinctual structure of the growing wage laborer. The "cultural sexual morality" which Freud made responsible for the massive creation of neurosis is therefore the historical twin of a developing capitalist Protestant "work morality."

The new compulsion for work and achievement, which the militarily organized capital factory system imposed on wage laborers, also puts its stamp on the structure of social instincts in general and on sexuality in particular. R. Reiche has noted: "Sexuality is lastingly fashioned under the domination of the anal character and the economic principle which is its basis. In reality sexuality seems to be something that is separate from work and yet can only be attained by means of work; it acquires a reward character like good food on holidays, getting up late on Sunday, like money as such. This demeans sexuality to a work process. Thus it becomes like work: low, dirty, mechanical, and measured according to categories of achievement which are foreign to the nature of pleasure."[51]

This "anal character" of capitalist culture, which demeans pleasure and libido itself to a work process, finds its most brilliant literary expression in Mauler's monologue in Brecht's *St. Joan of the Stockyards:*

> *"And as for the thing made of sweat and money*
> *which we have erected in these cities:*
> *now it looks as if a man*
> *had made a building, the biggest in the world and*
> *the costliest and most practical, but*
> *by mistake and because it was cheap he used dog shit*
> *for material, so that it would be pretty hard*
> *to stay there and at last his only claim*
> *to fame was that he had made the biggest stink in the world.*
> *Anyone who gets out of a building like that*
> *should be a cheerful man."*[52]

Capitalist Rationality and the Pathic Gap Between "Ego" and "Id," "Reason" and "Feeling"

The abstraction of money is in a certain sense a secularized form of the Christian abstraction of the human being which finds its purest expression in Protestantism. The Christian-Protestant abstraction and the resulting dichotomous division into a "pure" (good) world of abstract virtue and an "impure" (sinful) world of passions and instinct is an adequate religious reflection of the abstraction of value, that is, money and the resulting dichotomy into a world of "abstract wealth" and the "repressed world of sensuous-concrete wealth." This dichotomous picture of the world, created by a commodity society, also reflects itself in Freud's dichotomous psychology of the ego and the id. This is the blind theoretical reflex of that dichotomy of the "bourgeois soul" which arises from the production of commodities, from the exchange principle, namely, the dichotomous split between calculating and abstracting reason and the incalculable, unquantifiable sensuousness which is repressed. Freud declares: "The ego represents what one could call reason and prudence, in contrast to the id which contains the passions [. . .] The id cannot say what is wants [. . .] We are lived by unknown, ungovernable powers."[53]

Of course Freud explains—and this constitutes his psychologism—the dichotomous division of the bourgeois soul within the soul's own terms; he conceives of "reason," "thinking," *"ratio,"* only intra-psychologically as special functions of the ego which have as one function the "checking of reality." Specifically Western rationality—especially in its abstract, reified form—is not, however, primarily an intra-psychological, that is, as Freud thought, an achievement of the ego but rather a reflex of the abstract relation of exchange and money in the mind of economic subjects. That is why Adorno is correct in saying that "specific social determinants have emancipated themselves from psychology through the injection of abstract determinants between persons such as, especially, the equivalence exchange and by the domination of an organ built according to the model of such determinants which have freed themselves from control by human beings, by reason."[54] Sohn-Rethel's more recent investigations into the connection between the "commodity form" and the "form of thought" also confirm[55] that specifically Western rationalist abstraction and capacity for thinking cannot be explained by means of the soul but must be derived primarily from "(abstract) determinants that have freed themselves from the control of human beings."

Psychological relationships between human beings necessarily assume the form of their economic relations in capitalist commodity society, that is, the form of "abstract" exchange relationships. The commodity exchange brings individuals into a relationship of "formal equality" with each other, and therefore of "indifference." According to Marx: "The mutual and all-sided dependence of individuals who are indifferent toward each other constitutes their social connection."[56] This has grave consequences for the psychology of the private producers who produce in isolation and independently of each other. Lukács remarks: "The act of exchange in its formal generality [. . .] also negates the use value as use value, also creates that relationship of 'abstract equality' between concretely unequal, even incomparable material [. . .] Thus the subject of the exchange is just as abstract, formal, and reified as its object."[57] The formal abstration of the exchange act condemns human "interaction"— at least in the sphere of production and circulation—to a brutal indifference" (Engels[58]). The psychological make-up of the subject for exchange intercourse therefore tendentially enforces the splitting of the totality of his psychic function; one part of his psychic activity, the ego, must subject itself to the "formal equality" of commodity traffic and the logic of the exchange (of accumulation, of profit), that is, to make calculating reason its own so as to be socially "adjusted." The other half of psychic activity, the "passions," "sensuousness," and the "instinctual nature" of man is shunted off into the incalculable (and therefore rebellious) psychological remnant of the private sphere, that is, into the underground of the "personality," into the "id." For individual egos which have been isolated and atomized by the exchange relationship can only have social intercourse with each other when they eliminate their "personal" feelings in the process, according to the motto: "No sentiment in money matters!" That is how the seller of the commodity known as labor power speaks to his buyer, the capitalist: "I demand a work day of normal length, and I demand it without any appeal to your heart, for in money matters sentiment is out of place. You may be a model citizen, perhaps a member of the Society for the Prevention to Cruelty to Animals, and in the odor of sanctity to boot; but the thing that you represent face to face with me has no heart in its breast" (Marx).[59]

The "sentiments," the "heart," or in Freud's terminology the "functions of the id" have to be eliminated as incalculable emotional ballast from this exchange. The id—regarded this way—is the petrified psychological sedimentation of the reified subject into which all wishes, drives, and feelings have sunk; and these have been cut off from the traffic of social commodity and exchange. Adorno writes: "What deposits itself in the subconscious is whatever falls behind in the subject, what has to pay the bill for progress and enlightenment [of capitalist reason—author]. The anachronism becomes timeless."[60]

The dichotomous split in the "bourgeois soul" between the rationally calculating function of the ego and the incalculably passionate function of the id reproduces itself—with the development of a commodity society —on an ever and ever higher level. To the degree that labor power is subsumed as commodity and the process of social labor under the process of utilizing capital, the human passions, the "id" functions—from the viewpoint of the rational calculating ego—only look like "disturbance factors," as "sources of errors" in the process of production. Lukács notes: "With the modern 'psychological' analysis of the work process (in Taylorism) this rational mechanization extends right into the worker's 'soul'; even his psychological attributes are separated from his total personality and placed in opposition to it so as to facilitate their integration into specialized rational systems and their reduction into statistically viable concepts. [. . .] In consequence of the rationalization of the work process the human qualities and idiosyncrasies of the worker appear increasingly as *mere sources of error* when contrasted with these abstract special laws functioning according to rational predictions."[61] For the psychology of the reified subject this means that the emotional, affective function of the "id" as an incalculable part of the commodity of labor power has to be 'split off,' indeed castrated from it. If according to Lukács the "tearing apart of the object of production necessarily entails a simultaneous tearing apart of its subject,"[62] then this "fissure" in the subject expresses itself in the "pathic gap" between its "rational" ego functions and its "irrational" id functions which the ego represents to itself as "unknown, ungovernable powers" (Freud). In Adorno's words: "The subject dissects itself into the machinery of social production, which has its continuation in his inner being; and into an undissolved remnant which degenerates into a curiosity as an impotent special sphere with regard to the proliferating 'rational' component [. . .] Its psychology appears usually as nothing but a 'disturbance' and is fended off repeatedly by the drastic tutelage of 'reason,' in which situations of objective social interest embody themselves. The objectives of the ego are no longer identical with primary instinctual objectives, can no longer be translated back into those, and frequently contradict them."[63]

The pathic gap, the dysfunction between "ego" and "id," which is the basis of neurosis, therefore comes into existence only in the course of the development of a capitalist mode of production which compels a progressive subsumption of any kind of spontaneity, emotion, or instinct under the rationalism of capital. Baran writes: "If man became subjugated in early history through exploitation and domination, the principle of the capitalist order demanded that he learn to count with care and calculation [. . .] What has remained of his elementary emotionalism and originality, after his master's whip had chastized him for centuries, now came under the far more systematic, more unrelieved pressure of the hard, precisely calculable capitalist market."[64]

Taking human feelings, suffering, and passions into consideration is pure "sentimentality" from the viewpoint of capital, and so they do not appear in its balance sheets. On the occasion of the introduction of bookkeeping in the sixteenth century, the monopoly capitalist Fugger therefore declared quite consistently: "Bookkeeping is the soul of capital, the greatest invention of humanity; one is no longer distracted by minutiae, sentimentality, and consideration for all sorts of persons and things. One only sees the money, and money must multiply itself."[65] The "elementary emotionalism and originality of human beings" (Baran) was for capital only a bothersome obstacle on the way to the total calculability of the objective and subjective elements of the production and utilization process. It therefore had to be broken, and what remained of it became the psychic "remnant," a "curiosity" repressed into the underground of the personality that had become a commodity, that is, into the "id."

According to Lukács, "it was capitalism that first of all produced with its uniform economic structure for the entire society a structure of consciousness at once formal and uniform for the whole [. . .]."[66] But it has also—one could amplify Lukács's insight—produced a psychological structure both formal and uniform, namely, the tendential dissociation of "ego" and "id," of reason and passion, of a *"ratio"* molded by a calculating and quantifying exchange principle, and a remnant of feeling that is still attached to use value (from the standpoint of capital). According to SPK Heidelberg: "So as to uphold the misrelationship between the degree of development of the productive forces and that of the production relationship in favor of capital accumulation the total functionalization and subjugation of human needs by the 'natural laws' of capital production and destruction is necessary. In the individual this contradiction reflects itself in the separation and opposition of reason and feeling [. . .]

The constant functional disturbance of these incompatible mechanisms of feeling and reason expresses itself in illness. The mind of capital expresses itself in the rationalization of the factories, while the enlargement of the productive forces is expressed through the intensification of exploitation and through the violent upholding of production relationships. The individual therefore experiences the violence of rationality of capital through the mediating agent of illness."[67]

The psychology of the reified individual who is tendentially governed by the abstract law of exchange appears only as "psychological disturbance," as dysfunction between "ego" and "id," reason and feeling, that is, as "illness." That is why Freud's dichotomous theory of psychology and neurosis forges the (although political-economically blind) concept not only for the individual but also for the collective state of affairs. At its root this clinical individual psychology is also—and let this be addressed once more to orthodox anti-Freudian Marxists—and *especially* a social and mass psychology.

In his essay "Is the Oedipus Complex Universal?" R. Reiche expounds the interesting thesis that Freud's clinical concepts, such as "repression," contain a historical dimension which cannot be meta-psychologically dissolved: "In practice Freud perhaps felt this when he writes that one cannot place repression on the same level with other defense mechanisms: 'In any event, it is something special which is more distinctly separated from the other defense mechanisms than they are from each other' (*G. W.* XVI, p. 81). Anna Freud approaches the conclusion that there is a natural repertoire of defense mechanisms which the psychic apparatus has at its disposal and which are then deployed by the healthy or ill personality in this or that mixture [. . .] I believe that the exceptional position of repression with regard to the other defense mechanisms is a historical product; it corresponds to the particular reality principle of industrial-capitalist societies."[68]

Thus, according to Reiche, "repression" is by no means an actual biological, that is, universal defense mechanism in Anna Freud's sense, but rather a social-typical defense mechanism. However, Reiche did not further elaborate *why* in a bourgeois psychology of the ego, "defense mechanisms" particularly and among them especially the technique of "repression" play such a predominant role.

The fact that bourgeois ego psychology is primarily a psychology of "defense mechanisms," among which represssion appears to dominate, is most intimately related to the reification structure of the subject in capitalist society. It is characteristic for the psychology of the reified subject that its immediate sensuous (instinctual) needs have to be rejected in extreme ways by the "ego," the psychic representative of calculating and abstracting reason. What is "rejected" is what is irreconcilable with the laws and forms of behavior in a (capitalist) commodity society.

Translated into Freudian terminology that means: "Among these wishful impulses derived from infancy, which can neither be destroyed nor inhibited, there are some whose fulfillment would be a contradiction of the purposive ideas of secondary thinking. The fulfillment of these wishes would no longer generate an effect of pleasure but of unpleasure; and it is precisely this transformation of affect which constitutes the essense of what we term repression."[69] Since "the reification structure sinks deeper and more fatefully and constitutively into human consciousness in the course of the development of capitalism" (Lukács[70]), the "wishful impulses derived from infancy, which can neither be destroyed nor inhibited," enter into an increasingly greater opposition to the "purposive ideas of secondary thinking," that is, to the principle of calculating and abstract reason. The ego, that is, super-ego—as the intra-psychic agency of "secondary thinking"—is, so to speak, the psychological police force which has to keep these "primary" wishes and instincts away from consciousness. The super-ego therefore tendentially persecutes and punishes all the immediate sensuous-concrete instinctual wishes which withdraw from the abstract process of capitalist reason, that is, those desires that desire use value as use value. But these are primarily those infantile wishes which take form during the "preservation" of the family, those "childhood wishes" whose repression—according to Freud—form the individual historical foundation of every neurotic illness. For childhood wishes still are immediately attached to sensuous-concrete wealth, that is, to the natural-economic use form of things and human individuals. Happiness for a child is primarily redemption of an erotic and not of a money wish. Freud states: "Happiness is the subsequent fulfillment of a prehistorical [that is, infantile—author] wish. That is why wealth plays such a negligible role in happiness. Money was not a childhood wish."[71] The program with which the monopoly capitalist Fugger introduced the capitalist era at the beginning of the sixteenth century is therefore the "unhappiest" in the world from the viewpoint of the "childhood wishes." Fugger writes: "Now only money is noted. Not wagon or shiploads any more, cannons, cloth, flour, wool, copper. Nothing but money. Commodities, animals, people, everything turns into capital that must multiply."[72]

The central content of bourgeois socialization from now on consists in putting the sensuous-concrete natural-economic use form of childhood wishes through the wringer of "abstract reason." The "primary" structure of sensuous need and instinct in the child must be long worked over by "secondary thinking" until it unloosens itself from its immediate sensuous-concrete instinctual objects and is at the disposal of "abstract work," of wage labor, and of its only instinctual objective, "abstract wealth," in the form of money. According to R. Reiche: "That is the permanent function of terror in the family: to work people over in such a way as to dispose them to wage labor = to alienated labor = to being capable only of a crippled articulation of their needs; and then maintain this dispostion each day by continually crippling all needs which aim above and beyond themselves."[73]

The historical process of subjugating human sensuality and instincts to the dictates of the exchange principle, of "abstract wealth," has to be perpetrated anew in terms of technical socialization on each individual child. In this sense one can say that ontogenesis "repeats" phylogenesis. But this law should not be understood biologically, as Freud did under the influence of Haeckel's "fundamental biogenetic law," but rather as a question of an historical "recurrence compulsion" which is rooted in capitalism itself. The abstract structure of needs and instincts structure which became predominant with the accumulation of capital has to be newly re-anchored in every new-born being, in every future capitalist and wage laborer. That is the reason for the historical continuity, the conservative violence of the bourgeois patriarchal family which so far has outlasted all revolutionary transformations in history. Thus, as long as the predominant form of social labor continues to be wage labor in transitional socialist societies, especially revisionist ones (although not wage labor for private capital but for state capital), in the sense of "alienated," that is, abstract labor, the patriarchal nuclear family—as a psychological training institute for wage labor—cannot be eliminated.

But let us return to R. Reiche's thesis that the "defense mechanisms" of the ego, especially that of repression, "contain a historical dimension which cannot be meta-psychologically dissolved." The historical unfolding of the contradiction between use and exchange value, between the world of sensuous-concrete wealth and that of "abstract wealth," necessarily reflects itself—at a certain stage of development—in the psychology of the capitalist commodity owner and producer: namely as a pathogenic contradiction between the immediate sensuousness and instinctuality of the "id" and the abstract and calculating reason of the "ego," that is, super-ego, between the particular concrete natural-economic use form of the "libido," or "childhood wishes," and their abstract exchange, that is, forms of defense, or "symptoms." Repression is the pathogenetic force which first produces this contradiction in the subject and simultaneously "solves" it by banning one aspect of it, the particular concrete instinctual wish, from a consciousness that has become abstract.

Every symptom—according to Freud—is a compromise between an instinctual wish of the "id" and the moral interjection of the ego, that is, super-ego. The "return of the repressed" in the symptom therefore has the same meaning as the "return" of the repressed sensuous-concrete natural-economic "use form" of the libido, or "childhood wishes." This constitutes the progressive, even subversive side of the symptom, the subversive element of neurosis (that is, psychosis). Seen in this way, in the neurotic (or delusionary) symptom, the repressed natural-economic use form of the libido rebels against the economic and libido-economic forces against which they "defend." Defense against repression seems to be—in its social-typical manifestation and meaning for a bourgeois psychology of the ego, for the psychology of the reified subject—an intra-psychic continuation of the economic processes of defense, that is, repression, which constantly occur in the sphere of production and circulation in a (capitalist) commodity society: thus the "repression" of sensuous-concrete wealth by "abstract wealth," of "sensuous-concrete" (instinctual) needs and satisfactions by a structure of needs and satisfactions which is becoming more and more abstract.

"Emotional Illness" as an Unconscious Protest Against Capital's "Unemotional Payment in Cash"

To the degree that the universe of social relations is reified and, therefore, de-eroticized by the invasion of capitalist reason, human eroticism can, tendentiously, only hibernate in the "imagination," in the fantasy of human beings. "Fantasy," which Freud called a "preservation in the realm of the soul," becomes a kind of psychic sub-culture where "childhood wishes" which have been suppressed by capitalist reality and the utilization principle eke out henceforth their illegal existence.

The neurotic (that is, psychotic) and the artist differ, according to Freud, only in that the latter transforms and objectifies the "childhood wishes" that have been retained in his fantasy into socially acceptable and honored forms; whereas the former can express them only in socially unacceptable forms, honor them only in the form of neurotic (or delusionary) symptoms, that is, in discriminated form. Cooper writes: "All metaphors of paranoia are a poetic protest against this invasion. This poetic protest, whose quality of course varies, is not however acknowledged by society, and if it is uttered too vehemently, psychiatry assumes the treatment."[74]

Every neurotic (or delusionary) symptom is, according to Freud, the expression of a libidinous retreat from outer reality into the psychic inner world. If the nature of the libido consists in "creating larger and larger units," that is, more and more comprehensive human connections, contacts, or communications, then the character of commodity and money in social forms of intercourse enforces the libido's retreat into the illegality of the symptom, into the sub-culture of mental illness. Freud seems to have had something similar in mind when he wrote that "neurosis like psychosis is thus an expression of the rebellion of the id against the outer world, its displeasure or, if you will, its inability to adjust itself to real exigency."[75] But since Freud lacked a materialistic concept of the "outside world," of the reality principle, he could not tell with precision what actually constituted the "real exigency" against which neurosis and psychosis rebel.

Since "the structure of reification sinks more deeply and fatefully and constitutively into the consciousness of human beings in the course of the development of capitalism" (Lukács), the libido, that is, the natural-economic use world of feeling which is still immediately attached to use value, enters into an ever-increasing conflict with the "reality principle" of abstract calculating reason. "Love," "poetry," and madness become only symptoms of the "displeasure at, or, so to speak, inability" of human beings to subject themselves to the dictates of calculating reason. Shakespeare knew this long before Freud. Thus Theseus says in *A Midsummer Night's Dream:* "Lovers and madmen have such seething brains,/Such shaping fantasies, that apprehend/More than cool reason ever comprehends. The lunatic, the lover and the poet/Are of imagination all compact."[76] The "cooler reason" with which love, poetry, and madness enter into diseased conflict is the reason of the primal accumulation of capital which found its first great literary expression in Shakespeare's work. This conflict, which was just arising during Shakespeare's time, comes into full flower only in high capitalism; and the dramas and novels of the nineteenth and the beginning of the twentieth century are correspondingly full of examples of how the libido, the natural-economic use form of desire, comes into sharper and sharper conflict with the "cooler reason" of an advancing capitalist reality principle. With the replacement of a natural economy by a money economy the former natural-economic "owners," the owners of land and estates, also suffer a loss of identity. This has been brilliantly portrayed in Chekhov's *The Cherry Orchard.*

In *The Cherry Orchard* the imposition of a ground rent on the "sound world" of natural-economic use-value production becomes the trigger of a family, that is, identity crisis which may be regarded as a "case history" of the pathology of capitalist commodity society. H. Lange writes: "Andreevna Ranevskaja, who owns an estate near Moscow, spends several years in France, primarily in Paris. But one day in spring when the cherry trees blossom on her estate she returns to it. Tired of unnamed distractions, here on her estate she recalls her childhood, here she enjoys as ever her flowering cherry orchard, here she finds peace and identity, here the walls and the countryside still bear the physiognomy of their owner. This natural-economic self-certainty and restfulness, however, already contain the capitalist worm in the person of the businessman Lopachin who is the son of one of Ranevskaja's serfs and who has become rich through speculation. Still acutely remembering the times of serfdom, Lopachin tries to save Ranevskaja as an estate owner; that is, he suggests to her to convert part of her property into ground rent: the cherry orchard should be cut down and rented out in parcels to summer vacationers from the city [. . .] Ranevskaja refuses. Whoever cuts down the cherry orchard, she says, also cuts down her identity, the estate is she herself, she might just as well have stayed in Paris and have lived like a prostitute by selling her body, her identity, her physiognomy. In short: the estate is auctioned off because it is heavily indebted; and the new owner who immediately has the cherry orchard cut down and parcelled out is, of course, Lopachin. The whole play demonstrates with classic clarity how capitalist ground rent intervenes between the countryside and the owner of the countryside; how man and nature, landowners as well as their social dependents, lose their identity together with their immediate environment and, thereby, also themselves. From Ranevskaja's viewpoint the cherry orchard, as the surplus of a natural-economic way of life, can be enjoyed, remembered. The cherry orchard as ground rent, cut down and parcelled out as capital investment, drives Lopachin and Ranevskaja as well as her dependents into the anonymity of capitalist commodity society[. . .]."[77]

The melancholy which overcomes Ranevskaja at the sight of her beloved cherry orchard is the expression—from Lopachin's, that is, the capitalist's viewpoint—of a morbid holding on to a piece of natural-economic reality which, through the imposition of ground rent, has long since been capitalized and de-realized. Since the cherry orchard has value only inasmuch as it provides ground rent, that is, exchange value, the emotional value attached to it is now anachronistic, can only survive in the fantasy of the former owner whose imagination has been shaped by a natural economy. Ranevskaja becomes "sentimental" and "melancholy," that is, "emotionally ill," because her emotional world has been expropriated together with her natural-economic world of possessions. Lopachin on the other hand, the representative of the capitalist reality principle, is "healthy" in the sense that he is protected against every "regression" into the old natural-economic emotional ambience; that is, he has made the abstract calculating reason of accumulation entirely his own. H. Lange comments: "Where Ranevskaja goes slowly but surely blind, psychically and emotionally, at the sight of her countryside, Lopachin has long since been blind, blindness has already become second nature for him. He does not have to see the cherry orchard, he enjoys the cherry orchard in its alienated form, as ground rent, as bank balance, as net profit in Charkov. Lopachin, the new owner, who reckons the net-profit poppy at the sight of a blooming poppy field [. . .], has no time, neither for beauty of landscape nor for the melancholy of the dying petty aristocracy, nor for his bride, for time is money. He is compelled by but one law: the accumulation of capital."[78]

To the degree that "abstract wealth" becomes his only requirement, his only pleasure, Lopachin loses all sensuous-concrete (natural-economic) pleasure, pain, and passion. To the degree that he become the new master, that is, owner of the "cherry orchard," it disappears from his senses; it exists for him only in a de-sensualized, castrated, abstract form: as ground rent, as bank balance. From Ranevskaja's viewpoint, that is, from the natural-economic viewpoint, his "health" is therefore total "illness," his capitalist "happiness" total unhappiness, total neurosis.

The economic background of he creation of a psychosis is mirrored in similar fashion in Ibsen's *The Wild Duck.* H. Lange writes: "Werle, big businessman, mine owner, and so on, imputes an economic crime, the cutting down of state-owned forests, to his friend Lieutenant Ekdal. Ekdal has to go to prison, his bourgeois existence is destroyed. After serving his time, Ekdal lives, supported by Werle's charity, with his son Hjalmar on whom Werle has foisted a housekeeper, an illegitimate daughter, and training as a photographer. The repressive metaphor which Ibsen imposes on the Ekdals like a gravestone is without equal in late bourgeois literature: far from his beloved woods, without his lieutenant's commission, old Ekdal, next to the studio, erects a forest of painted cardboard and puts a few rabbits next to it which, while reeking of schnaps, his lieutenant's jacket over his shoulders, he shoots. A wild duck with a broken wing that swims in a tub full of water is supposed to dissimulate free nature for the Ekdals, where the father once was happy as hunter and free man until he accidentally cut down the state forest. Young Werle, who would like to disabuse the Ekdals of this lie which his father has foisted on them, and which his father caused to happen, only ends up disabusing them of the remnant of their natural-economic bliss [. . .]."[79]

In his fantasy Ekdal tries to maintain the natural-economic reality which he has long since lost. Holding on to his "childhood wishes" is here identical with the old holding on to a "natural-economic state of bliss" which, long since devoid of a real social basis, becomes autonomous as a hallucinatory, that is, psychotic, world of mere appearance.

The neuroticizing contradiction between capitalist rationality and natural-economic sentimentality is also the theme of Brecht's *Puntila and His Servant Matti.* Estate-owner Puntila is constantly torn between calculating (capitalist) reason and "private" humanitarianism, that is, melancholy sentimentality. Puntila can be human, full of feeling, poetic, in love, only when he is "drunk," that is, temporarily slips out of his economic character mask. Only in this condition does he have a sense for nature, art, friendship, and love. As soon as he is sober again, that is, is again the sober personification of his capital function, he regrets horribly all the sentiments, feelings, and good deeds to which he succumbed. He feels "healthy" only in that condition which society calls "ill," namely, when intoxicated; while he is truly ill only in a condition of complete "accountability" as calculating capitalist, for whom other people's strengths and weaknesses are only material strong or weak for exploitation. That is why he fears those "attacks of senseless sobriety" during which he sinks to the level of an animal: "But it gets even worse, because during these attacks of total, senseless sobriety I sink down to the level of an animal. I have no inhibitions left at all. Brother, what I do in such a state you can't make me responsible for anymore at all. It's not as if I had a heart in my breast and keep telling myself that I am ill. In a state like that I am directly responsible. Do you know what that means, brother, to be responsible? A responsible human being is a human being of whom you can expect anything. For example, he's capable of forgetting the well being of his children; he's lost all sense for friendship; he's ready to walk across his own corpse. That is because he's responsible, as the lawyers call it."[80] Puntila's "accountable" condition, that is, his condition of "calculating exploitation," is however the chronically ill normal condition of capitalist society.

Similarly Mauler, the aforementioned monopolist of the Chicago meat-market (in Brecht's *St. Joan of the Stockyards),* demonstrates the schizophrenic split of the "bourgeois soul." As personification of the function of capital he must suppress his "human feelings" (for St. Joan and her social-relief program) so as not to be ruined by the competition. Mauler, whose heart is rent with pity when one of his cattle is slaughtered but not when one of his workers is fired ("I have pity for cattle but not for men"), does not so much demonstrate the "eternally human" Faustian conflict between libidinous and aggressive drives, between Eros and Thanatos (Freud); rather a social conflict of interest is the reason for his private neurosis. "A twofold power cuts and tears within my breast, like a jagged, deep-thrust knife; I'm drawn to what is truly great, free from self and the profit rate, and yet impelled to business life all unawares!"[81]

The capitalist soul can afford humanity and love only upon punishment of economic ruin. From·a capitalist viewpoint "love" and "passion" always look like a "business risk" and in this sense like weakness, dumbness, stupidity, misfortune, illness, even neurosis. Regarded in this fashion, neurosis, that is, psychosis, would be only a definition, a label, from the standpoint of capitalist reality, namely, the rentability principle. Regarded from the viewpoint of the id, however, the non-calculable and therefore irrational passions, neurosis, that is, psychosis, or "emotional illness" would be an unconscious rebellion against the "unemotional payment in cash" (Marx[82]) to which capital has reduced all social relationships.

Capital Mystification and Psychological Mystification

As we stated above, Freudo-Marxist theoreticians of mediation as well as (neo-) Adornitic* theoreticians of "cooperation," that is, "interaction,"

*See Translator's Note.

supported the authority of psychoanalysis with the argument—among others—that psychoanalysis alone can grasp and investigate irrational, mystical, and pathological consciousness and behavior. As has been said, both schools eliminated the psychological dimension from political economy. For, to be precise, psychoanalysis, that is, the theory of psychoanalytic interaction, can only grasp those irrational and mystical elements of consciousness which have been mediated through the process of family socialization, not those that arise from the commodity character of social production. However, now in late capitalism and its particular blindness, consciousness mystified by the "fetish character" of the commodity (of money, of capital) is acquiring increasing significance. Simultaneously—and this is important for the foundation of a materialist theory of illness—it can be shown that that consciousness mystified by the economic relationship of wage, commodity, money, and capital is related, albeit in a very mediated way, with the mystification of psycho-pathological consciousness as discovered by Freud.

The individual products of the producers enter into social intercourse, under the conditions of commodity production, that is, only by discarding their sensuous-concrete use character and assuming the character of equality, of "formal generality." Commodities realize their social life only in exchange because "commodity owners are not a part of the community of production and can relate to each other only by means of their products."[83] The relationship between persons that is contained in the exchange value is therefore a "relationship concealed under a physical husk." This objectification of persons and personification of objects, this real inversion of object and subject, arises immediately out of the character of social work which establishes the exchange value. Marx states: "The social relation of production appears as something existing apart from individual human beings, and the distinctive relations into which they enter in the course of production in society appears as the specific properties of a thing—it is this perverted appearance, this prosaically real, and by no means imaginary, mystification that is characteristic of all social forms of labor-positing exchange value. This perverted appearance manifests itself merely in a more striking manner in money than it does in commodities."[84]

The reification and inversion contained in the simple value form (CC) is still visible with relative ease by the producers: for it seizes only the exchange relationship between two definite particular commodities. But to the degree that the simple value form progresses to a general equivalence, or money, form, the reification and inversion immanent in the equivalence value establishing work assumes palpable form. One can no longer detect in money the fact that it expresses a relationship grounded in social production. One can no longer detect in the form in which money appears the fact that it represents social work, for it assumes "the form of a natural thing with definite qualities" (Marx[85]). The social relationship is therefore swallowed up by the "general commodity." In Marx's words: "What appears to happen is, not that gold becomes money, in consequence of all other commodities expressing their value therein; but, on the contrary, that all other commodities universally express their values in gold, because it is money. The intermediate steps of the process vanish in the result and leave no trace behind."[86] This false appearance confirms once and for all the fact that the place of value formation seems to be in the sphere of circulation and not where it actually occurs: in the sphere of production. Any consciousness which has remained attached to equivalence exchange has been "stood on its head."

The inversion of consciousness reproduces itself in capitalist commodity society (MCM) on a new level; for "under the capitalist mode of production and in the case of capital, which forms its dominant category, its determining production relationship, this enchanted and perverted world develops still more" (Marx).[87] In the production of simple commodities (CMC) the equivalence is genuinely given as an equality of quantitative value between two commodities insofar as these are exchanged in their objectified work time. The equivalence is mere appearance on this level only insofar as it occurs between two qualitatively unequal and incomparable products.

The production of capitalist commodities (MCM), however, produces, besides this simple, also an additional appearance: the appearance of equivalence not only of qualitatively but also of quantitatively unequal and incomparable commodities. As in a simple commodity society, so in a capitalist commodity society it also appears as though commodity owners with equal rights confront each other on the market to sell their commodities according to the principle of equivalence exchange. On the one hand are the money owner and buyer of labor power, on the other the owner and seller of the commodity of labor power. The latter *appears* to receive the "value of his work" in the form of a wage from the capitalist. But in fact, the wage which the capitalist pays the worker for the use of his labor power is less than the value which his labor power produces. This particular use value, labor power, creates *more* value than what corresponds to the value of labor power, that is, than what corresponds to its cost of reproduction. Marx observes: "The wage-form thus extinguishes every trace of the division of the working-day into necessary labor and surplus labor, into paid and unpaid labor. In *corvée,* the labor of the worker for himself and his compulsory labor for his lord differ in space and time in the clearest possible way. In slave labor, even that part of the working day in which the slave is only replacing the value of his own means of existence, in which, therefore, in fact, he works for himself alone, appears as labor for his master. All the slave's labor appears as unpaid labor. In wage-labor, on the contrary, even surplus-labor, or unpaid labor, appears as paid. [. . .] This phenomenal form which makes the actual relation invisible, and indeed, shows the direct opposite of that relation, forms the basis of all the juridical notions of both laborer and capitalist, of all the mystifications of the capitalist mode of production, of all its illusions as to liberty, of all the apologetic shifts of the vulgar economist."[88] This twin appearance of equivalence between qualitatively and quantitatively unequal and incomparable values makes the mystification of the capitalist mode of production incomparably more effective than that of the production of simple commodities which only knew the simple appearance of equivalence between qualitatively incomparable use values.

With the separation of the capacity to work from its realization, the subsumption of the process of social work under the process of utilizing capital, and the application of a social-productive power of work at higher and higher levels in the form of machinery and large industry, there finally arises for consciousness, which has remained attached to equivalence exchange, the appearance of the autonomous productive power of capital. Marx states: "The power of labor, which maintains value, appears as the self-sustaining power of capital itself, the value-creating power of labor as the self-utilizing power of capital, and, all in all, according to its definition, objectified work appears as the applicator of living work."[89]

Mystification reaches its apogee in interest-bearing capital; for money here appears itself to be hatching money, according to the motto which every bank recommends to its customers: "Let your money work for you!" In interest-bearing capital which—according to Marx—is the most "conceptless form of capital" the value-creating power of labor appears totally extinguished. Marx states: "Capital appears as a mysterious and self-creating source of interest—the source of its own increase. [. . .] In interest-bearing capital, therefore, this automatic fetish, self-expanding value, money-generating money, are brought out in their pure state and in this form it no longer bears the birthmark of its origins."[90]

The inversion of social relationships immanent in work—work that transforms exchange value in a relationship between things—reproduces itself on a higher and higher level with the historical development of the commodity category. It reproduces itself, therefore, also on a higher and higher level of consciousness. The "enchanted, inverted, topsy-turvy world where Monsieur le Capital and Madame la Terre do their mischief as social characters and as nothing but things" (Marx[91]) also stands social consciousness on its head. The more the real nature of capital retreats behind its fetish-like appearance, the greater becomes the "deficiency in consciousness" in the capital agent and wage laborer. Social consciousness suffers an increasing loss of reality as the reality of capital, its real production process, conceals itself. This process is "repressed" in the sense that it is no longer "conceivable," in the sense that it can no longer be grasped by means of a concept—as Marx says of interest-bearing capital, the most fetishized and reified form of capital. "All reification is a form of forgetfulness" (Adorno-Horkheimer[92]). In this sense one can say that the fetish of capital produces an "amnesia" of huge dimensions, a general social loss of memory and "disturbance of consciousness" or—to speak with Lorenzer—a general "destruction of language." Indeed this "inverted and enchanted" consciousness succumbs, so to speak to a gigantic "projection," for it regards as standing outside and independent of itself and as a threatening alien power what in fact is the product of its own activity.

As the reified subject regards its own productive power as the alien power of capital existing outside itself, so it conversely mistakes capital's independent impulse to utilize for its own psychological impulse. The inversion of subject and object which arises from the mystification of capital reproduces itself in the inner being of the subject as psychological mystification: it regards as its own "personal" will, its own original "impulse," what in reality is only an objective application of the will immanent in the "compulsive" laws of economics, what is only a reflection of the "impulse to love" of capital. Marx writes: "As a capitalist, he is only capital personified. His soul is the soul of capital. But capital has one single life impulse, the tendency to create value and surplus value; to make its constant factor, the means of production, absorb the greatest possible amount of surplus labor."[93] What in reality is only the socially mediated sediment of his "second nature" therefore appears to the reified subject as its "inmost" nature, as "instinctual nature." It holds on the more firmly to its own unexchangeable "character" the more it petrifies into an "economic character mask."

The psychological mystification arising from capital mystification is characteristic of psychopathology (of the reified subject). Just as the products of the subject's material activity assume the form of a natural and thing-like power existing outside itself, and governing it instead of it governing them, so likewise with the products of its mental activity. Marx asks: "Why is it that their [human beings'] conditions become autonomous over against them, that the power of of their own life overpowers them?"[94] But this question refers not only to their material products—this would be a materialistic reduction!—but also to the products of their ideas and desires in the widest possible sense. P. Brückner appears to have something similar in mind when he writes, under the influence of Marx, that " 'our own product has raised itself on its hind feet against us'—the active human being is overwhelmed by the results of his production [. . .] The consolidation of these products acquires material power over us which outgrows our control [. . .] and 'the complete subjugation of individuality under social determinants which assume the form of material forces' (so Marx in the *Grundrisse*) enters determinately into the structure, laws, and regulations of the psychic processes—and this consolidation must also reproduce itself, via many mediations and within the framework of the naturally given constitution, in the psychic apparatus.''[95]

How the inversion that Brückner cites—''our own product has raised itself on its hind feet against us'' (Marx)—enters determinately into the structure, laws, and regulation of the psychic process Marx himself already sketched in his theory of religion. From a Marxist viewpoint, religion is the idealistic, that is illusionary reflection of those autonomous alien powers which really govern the life of human beings. In his analysis of commodity fetishism Marx makes an explicit comparison between the becoming autonomous of the materialist and the becoming autonomous of the idealistic (religious) products of human beings: ''In order, therefore, to find an analogy, we must have recourse to the mist-enveloped regions of the religious world. In that world the productions of the human brain appear as independent beings endowed with life, and entering into relation both with one another and the human race. So it is in the world of commodities with the products of men's hands.''[96]

But, as in the mist-enveloped regions of the religious world, the wishful products of the human brain also ''appear as independent beings endowed with life, and entering into relation both with one another and the human race,'' so in the ''mist-enveloped regions'' of the psychological, that is, psycho-pathological world. In the process of repression, regression, and symptom formation, the wishful ''products of the human brain'' assume the ''phantasmagoric form'' of an alien power which rules men instead of their governing them. In paranoia, for example, according to Freud, autonomous love desires assume the form of a persecution complex. The paranoiac constantly sees himself threatened and persecuted by alien forces which in reality are products of his own fantasy. By means of certain rituals and characterological reaction formations the compulsive neurotic defends himself furiously against his repressed sexual desires which lead a phantom-like existence in his unconscious. As psychic activity becomes autonomous, or more precisely, in the splitting off (''castration'') of these products of psychic fission from their producer, is the nature of all psychopathology under which Freud also subsumed, and by no means in last place, religion.

If religion is the ''fantastic reflection, in the mind, of those outer forces which govern everyday life'' (Lenin[97]), then neurosis, that is, psychosis, is the ''fantastic reflection'' of these outer forces in the inner being. If ''earthly powers'' assume the ''form of supernatural ones'' (Lenin), thus ''earthly powers'' here assume the form of subterranean, unconscious ones. Neurosis, that is, psychosis, regarded in this way is an internalized form of religion (which is what Freud appeared to have in mind when he called neurosis a ''private religion'') and religion an externalized and collective form of neurosis, that is, psychosis (which Freud, too, seemed to suggest when he called religion a "collective compulsive neurosis").

The process in which the products of idealistic (religious) and psychic fission (neurosis and psychosis) become autonomous with regard to their producer would thus be—if given one common denominator—only different reflexes of the same social movement: the becoming autonomous of material products, commodities, with regard to their producers. Marx's statement to the effect that "our own product has stood itself on its hind feet against us" therefore means *in toto:* not only the physical but also the psychic, the wish-product, has "stood itself on its hind feet against us" in the form of religion, that is, neurosis. Just as in the commodity "their [human beings'] social action takes the form of the action of objects which rule the producers instead of being ruled by them" (Marx[98]), so the religious, that is, psychopathological fission action is also removed from their conscious control.

However, there exists not only a functional but also a historical connection between the religious and the psychopathological autonomy of "products of the human brain." With regard to "religious reflex" the psychopathological reflex stands like a modern over against an anachronistic form of "reflection" of those "alien forces that govern the everyday life of man" (Lenin). According to Lenin, the "foundation of the religious reflex" exists as long as "in today's bourgeois society human beings are determined by the means of production, which they produce themselves, as by an alien power."[99] Yet there is historical change in that form in which the means of production which they produced themselves is reflected as "alien power." Religious fear loses its basis in the same degree as the imagined omnipotence of the God-Father *imago* is refuted by the genuine omnipotence of scientific reason which takes effect in the process of capitalist production and transforms itself into a generalized "abstract" fear, the "neurotic" fear which is, so to speak, a secularized and de-personalized form of religious fear, in the wake of the objectification, de-personalization, and anonymity of social domination. If—according to Freud—"neurosis in our time has replaced the monastery,"[100] then this statement expresses the fact that the religious form of escape from the world has been tendentiously replaced by another, by neurotic escape from the world. Since the irrationality of capitalist society in its entirety can be projected less and less into the "mist-enveloped regions of the religious world," it is increasingly *introjected* into the modern "mist-enveloped region" of the unconscious world. It is, so to speak, a question of a "landslide" in the superstructure; a process in which the uppermost is turned into what is lowest. In other words, the "high" form of religious reflex (of the "alien social powers") is transformed into the "lower" form of psychopathological reflex; the modern psychoneurotic (that is, psychotic) no longer believes in hell, but he has a "hellish" fear of his own repressed, that is, autonomous, instinctual wishes. He is not frightened by the "holy spirit" but by the "unholy" (because now "alien" to him) "spirits" of the unconscious. He hopes for "redemption" not from his own sins, it is true, but from his "symptoms." Not the priest now but the psychoanalyst affords him absolution.

Regarded in this fashion, neurosis and psychosis, would be the adequate psychological reflection of a society where, on the one hand, the autonomous means of production grow into a more and more threatening "alien force," and on the other the anachronistic "religious" reflex of this alien power is necessarily secularized, made anonymous, and replaced by the modern profane form of the psychological reflex.

The Crisis of Capitalism and the "Prevalence of Neuroses"

Since Freud—and with him the enlightened European bourgeoisie—in the final analysis "repressed" the "economic motif" from the phenomena of illness that he diagnosed, he could base his "etiology of neurosis" only in the circumscribed private realm of the family. Since he did not reflect upon the dialectical relationship between certain social forms of production and the family forms corresponding to them, he had to treat his clinical findings, in supra-historical fashion, as expressions of universal human instinctual conflicts. A historical-materialist "etiology of neurosis," on the other hand, must develop Freud's clinical findings out of the crisis of a particular historical familial form which itself is the expression of a much more comprehensive economic and social crisis: the crisis of capitalism in its imperialist phase.

In feudal society and early capitalism the patriarchal-monogamous nuclear family still had a rational basis because it was primarily a community of production and commodity. In the small shop of the artisan or farmer the father was the owner of the means of production which—*qua* the right of inheritance—were bequeathed to the son. The forced monogamy of the wife—as only proof of fatherhood—stood in the service of the inheritance of private property. The father's right of educating and training the women and children also derived from his disposal over the means of agricultural production. The patriarchal-monogamous family, the small shop of the artisan or farmer, were not liquidated until the accumulation and concentration of capital and the socialization of work had reached a higher and higher level; and it was at that point that the community of family production transformed itself into a "pure," "terrorist" community of education. With the separation of family reproduction from the productive expenditure of labor power (in the factory), with the separation of living and work place, and with the tendency to become indifferent towards the specific content of (wage) labor, there was also effected a complete revolution in familial relationships. Hörnle writes:

"Marriage becomes a 'pure money relationship.' And the more or less passable previous harmony, which was based on the recognized leadership of the man and the subordination of the women and children, is replaced by the daily quarrel which, often enough, degenerates into an embittered fight of all against all. The marital peace which had been guaranteed by the daily habit of working together and the legal status of the man as the owner of the means of production is replaced by indifference, mistrust, dislike, even in many cases by open hatred. Marital fidelity, now devoid of an economic rationale, is replaced by habitual adultery and prostitution."[101]

The exchange relationships which govern every sphere of bourgeois society also permeate familial relationships. Thus in the *haute bourgeois* family the securing of property and the representation of wealth stand in the foreground of such familial relationships. For the middle classes who no longer possess any property capable of accumulating capital, this contradiction between a sheltered family life and the exchange principle in society expresses itself in a strong insecurity in all familial relationships. (See also p. 188.) For the proletariat the family at any event existed only as an empty model, as a "bourgeois phrase," as Marx and Engels said in *The Communist Manifesto:* "The bourgeois platitudes about family and education, about the fond relationship between parents and children, become that much more nauseating the more all family ties of the proletarians are sundered, as a consequence of the effects of large industry, into simple objects of trade and instruments of work."[102]

Although the interests of the family members are no longer determined by the mutual production of necessary consumer goods, the ideals of obedience, piety, and marital fidelity of the early bourgeois family remains in existence. The sharpening contradiction between the anachronistic ideology and psychology of the patriarchal nuclear family and its increasing lack of a social and economic foundation mirrors itself in the innumerable family crises and family tragedies which have been sufficiently treated in the literature of the late nineteenth and early twentieth centuries. The classic objective of the socialization of the bourgeois family, the creation of autonomous individuals who are capable of a reflective use of paternal norms, was robbed of its social foundation by the increasing dependency and indebtedness of small and middling property owners. The increasing socialization of work and capital (in the form of trusts, corporations, and huge concerns) and the de-personalization and anonymity of social domination which it entailed, also disempowered the old patriarchal family authority. The ideal of autonomy it represented persisted only in the ego-ideal of the middle classes which had lost their economic and social autonomy. The sharpening of the contradiction between real degradation, that is, proletarization, and the "personal" ideal of autonomy here left its mark as "ego-crisis" and "ego-

weakness." The forms of ego disturbance which psychoanalysis registered therefore reflected the crisis of the bourgeois class itself: the
reproductive conditions of the bourgeois individual- and competitive-ego
can no longer be assured in the wake of the degradation and proletarization of formerly bourgeois and *petit bourgeois* strata. E. Wulff states:
"One can expect 'classic' ego disturbances of the kind described, that is,
disturbances of 'ego-consciousness,' only in societies whose authorities
over and practices of socialization mold such an individual ego as a
socially typical structure."[103] The classic bourgeois individual reacted to
the new historical level of his socialization with "disturbances" which
Freud called "neurosis": this is the sociological and historical kernel of
his neurosis theory, a kernel which he himself suppressed.

By destroying its social and economic foundation, developing monopoly capitalism not only transformed the classic bourgeois family into a
breeding ground of psychic crises and disturbances; but through its
elements of immanent social and political crisis it created a social "atmosphere" which favored the massive creation of neurosis. According to
Sapir: "What counts for us is to emphasize the undisputed fact that an
atmosphere which socially favors the massive creation of psychoneurosis
is, on the one hand, an atmosphere of compulsion and disenfranchisement, and, on the other, one of satiated idleness which excludes all healthy
initiative and purposefulness. At the lower level of the pyramid of modern
bourgeois society the phenomena that belong to the first category are
sufficiently assured by mass unemployment, fascism, and the other marvels of the capitalist regime; at the upper level of the same pyramid the
various phenomena of the second category follow inevitably from the
growth of monopolist undertakings and the displacement of numerous
bourgeois into the category of pensioners—all of them elements which
repress the entrepreneurial spirit which was so highly developed in the
pre-imperialist phase of capitalism [. . .]."[104]

Competitive capitalism with its "entrepreneurial spirit" still intact
assured a relative protection against "mental illness" in the sense of
"capacity for work," that is, with the active participation of the owners
of capital in the instigation and management of such enterprises. However, the parasitical "idleness" of large and small stockholders who now
existed as pensioners, as dividend collectors (isolated from their possessions), produced a social "atmosphere" which favors neurotic flight from
reality, isolation, and apathy. In the lower social strata, however, the
growing rate of mental illness was the result of a sharpening social and
political crisis, of mass unemployment on the one hand, of growing
political repression and fascistization on the other. The social anxieties
and the insecurity here left their mark in the higher incidence of mental
illness. (Interesting is Sapir's explanation of the common denominator of
both "categories" of illness: parasitical idleness, that is, privileged "un-

employment" in the upper classes, and enforced idleness, that is forced unemployment, in the lower classes. In both cases, elimination from the immediate process of production, absence from concrete work, conjures up the danger of a neuroticizing isolation and flight from reality.)

Since Freud lacked a category to comprehend the elements of social and economic crisis in a monopoly capitalist system, his theory of illness, that is, neurosis, remained stuck in a set of explanations derived from familial psychology. Still, he provided *one* model of neurosis which contains the germ of the social and political set of explanations which he surpressed. Thus Reuben Osborn reminds us that Freud—in his early definition of repressive forces—once compared the dynamic structure of the psychic apparatus with the caste structure, that is, class society: "The mind was pictured as a kind of three-storey dwelling. On the top floor were the respectable members of the conscious family. Below them were the pre-conscious people, quiet decent folk, who were permitted to visit the neighbors above. True, a policeman stood on the stairs between but was a genial soul, rarely forbidding passage. But the characters on the ground floor were a tumultuous uncultured crowd, noisily clamoring to pass the overworked policeman between them and the pre-conscious level. Occasionally one slipped by, generally in a disguise that represented him as a harmless person and when night had brought a relaxation of the policeman's vigilance. These policemen were a picturesque representation of the repressive forces."[105]

The class structure of capitalist society appears in the psychic structure of the individual as refracted by a prism: "policemen" represent the "censor," that is, the "forces of repression"; the "inhabitants of the ground floor" what has to be repressed, that is, what *is* repressed. The latter seek to penetrate to the top floor where the members of the conscious family live, so as to become conscious themselves. Freud's dynamic model of neurosis—regarded in this way—is a disguised political model, the model of an impeded revolution.

According to this model, the qualitative and quantitative extent of the neurosis is directly proportional to the strength of the "censor," that is, the social and political "repressive forces." However, in a class society the power of these "repressive forces" is finally an expression of a relationship based on social power, that is, it depends on the development of the class struggle. Mental illness of all kinds therefore begins to become prevalent primarily in such historical epochs where social contradictions are frozen, that is, particularly epochs of political reaction. If social contradictions cannot be resolved "progressively," by taking on the form of a class struggle , then they must be solved "regressively" by being repressed from consciousness, that is, by assuming the rigid form of neurosis. Since the sharpening of class contradictions could no longer be solved (except in Russia) by the method of socialist revolution, they had to be massively "repressed" and interiorized in neurosis.

The "ego weakness" of the bourgeoisie in its imperialist phase was primarily due to the fact that it was no longer master in its own house. For the workers' movement, which grew rapidly in the late nineteenth and early twentieth centuries, threatened the bourgeoisie with social "castration" to an unimaginable extent. The "castrator" who haunts the anxiety-ridden dreams of Freud's *haute-bourgeois* patients indeed wielded hammer and sickle and indeed seemed to attack the "sex," that is, the property of the exploiting classes. The "spectre" making the rounds of Europe pursued the bourgeois into his sleep. Since the imperialist bourgeoisie had become reactionary to the degree that it had fulfilled its "historical mission," the accumulation of capital, and since the bourgeois relationships based on property and production had begun to shackle the further development of productive forces, the bourgeoisie yearned for the past where its "historical mission" and also its self-confidence as a class was still undisputed. Neurosis here was primarily the individual sediment of a social regression of a class which clung to its past, to its historical childhood, because the future no longer belonged to it. The decadent and insecure bourgeoisie wanted, so to speak, to crawl back into the womb because the proletariat blocked its forward passage.

But the incidence of mental illness also increased among the proletariat, which was incapable of giving effective political expression to its emancipatory needs after the unsuccessful revolution of 1918. According to the estimates of the German Sexpol,[106] at the beginning of the thirties some 60 per cent of working men and up to 90 per cent of working women suffered mental illness and sexual disturbances. Wilhelm Reich sought to explain the increasing rate of mental illness and neurosis by suggesting the "adoption of a bourgeois sexual morality" by the proletariat, which was amplified by fascism with its *"völkisch"* familial and sexual politics. The "prevalence of neuroses" (Reich) in the fascist and imperialist era, however, is very insufficiently explained by the theory of "sexual repression." Since Reich, as we have noted, lacked a dialectical concept of mental illness and neurosis, his explanation, too, remains stuck in a world of naturalistic sexual economy.

The "prevalence of neurosis" and psychic disturbances in the fascist era was the product of suppression and repression not only of sexual but of all emancipatory social, political, and cultural needs by the totalitarian state. The German people, so to speak, had swallowed the stick with which it was being beaten; that was what made them ill. Regarded psychologically, the fascist state was the historical apogee of a dictatorship of the "super-ego" in German history, the historical high point of the fortification of a national compulsive neurosis.

Fascist ideology and propaganda were, in other words, a social-compulsive ritual staged by means of the totalitarian state which had to "defend against" the "return of the repressed" revolution of 1918. This social-compulsive syndrome contained the suppressed, emancipatory passions of the dependent classes just as much as a compulsive totalitarian form of their defense. Simultaneously, an increasing rate of mental illness and neurosis in the era of fascism was a kind of passive resistance to a system whose *"völkisch* health" was identical with the anti-Semitic extermination campaigns within and the imperialist wars of conquest without. Since the German workers, too, were no longer in a position, after the destruction of their party and fighting organization, to undertake offensive anti-fascist resistance and underground movements, many of them withdrew into the passive resistance of "neurosis," into the "legal" underground of mental illness.

6. On the Pathology of the Capitalist Organization of Work

According to our presentation, the "neurosis of civilized man," which Freud deciphered only in psychological terms, comes into existence in a historical process in which the capitalist owners of commodity "shape the world according to their image." The "evil spirits," the "Pandora's box," of the commodity form were set free historically only after they had articulated all regions of social production and reproduction according to to their laws, that is, according to the laws of exchange and profit. To the degree that commodity becomes a "universal category" (Lukács), the pathogenetic character attached to it becomes universal as well.

Up to this point we have developed the "pathogenetic dynamic" inherent in capitalism from the reification structure which is part and parcel of the commodity form; that is, we have described the dialectic between a historically developing structure of commodity and money and the structure of social needs and instincts only in its *general* form. Now we want to try to demonstrate the *particular* pathogenetic effects of the commodity structure on industrial wage-laborers in the capitalist work process. For, as we have said, a materialistic theory of illness has to begin, not with Freud's concept of libido, but with the category of "work."

I. *"INDUSTRIAL PATHOLOGY"*

The Blind Spot of All Bourgeois Theories of Illness

All bourgeois theories of illness, whether it is a question of psychoanalysis, of psychosomatic medicine, factory psychology, labor medicine, or the newer medical sociology, contain the same basic flaw: they assiduously overlook or euphemistically circumscribe the primary social breeding ground of illness, namely, capitalist relationships grounded in work. They discover the cause of mental diseases in all sorts of derivative or epiphenomena: in the "Oedipus complex" (Freud), in a "bad work atmosphere" (Bornemann), in an "environment of technical-industrial civilization" (Mitscherlich), in "social role tensions" (Parsons), and so on; but not in the capitalist organization of work. A euphemistic camouflaging of the pathology of the capitalist organization of work is as old as capitalism itself.

Engels has cited, as the chief witness of such euphemisms, the author of a work entitled *The Philosophy of Manufacturing* who describes child labor in various English manufacturing centers in 1835 in the rhapsodic terms of a romantic poet: "I have visited many factories, both in Manchester and in the surrounding districts, during a period of several months, entering the spinning rooms, unexpectedly, and often alone, at different times of day, and I never saw a single instance of corporeal chastisement, inflicted on a child, nor indeed did I even see children in ill-humor. They seemed to be always cheerful and alert, taking pleasure in the light play of their muscles—enjoying the mobility natural to their age. The scene of industry, so far from exciting sad emotion in my mind, was always exhilarating."[107]

Although devoid of such romantic flair in its transfiguration of capitalist work, modern factory psychology nevertheless finds itself on the same level as the fascist cynicism that "work makes free." Thus, for example, in the words of Bornemann: "Factory work, which is well articulated and performed according to the principle of the division of labor, need not make the human being into a slave of his work, since with good automatization work moves almost to the periphery of consciousness and the human being actually is freed again for intellectual labor. (Hans Sachs rhymed his verses to the rhythm of his shoemaker's hammer; Spinoza thought up a philosophical system while grinding his lenses)."[108]

Modern factory psychology traces mental illness primarily to disturbances and unpleasantness in the "factory climate." According to Bornemann, the functions of a "good factory climate" look like this: "A good leadership style, uniform cooperation and communication, and so forth increase the individual's satisfaction with his work and thus his pleasure in working: but it also raises production. [!] Pleasure in one's own work is a prerequisite and expression of individual satisfaction and of productive work."[109] A "therapeutic" concept of bourgeois factory psychology consists in creating a "less abrasive" course of production by binding the individual worker that much more strongly to his alienated labor, by improving his relationship with his superior and by "climatic" modifications in the factory or office. What is supposed to become "healthy" is not the worker but the factory, and that in the sense of a "healthy" increase of production and profit. In short, the "primacy of the individual," the primacy of his physical and mental health, is subordinated to "productivity."

The concept of health and illness in positivistic medical sociology is as opportunistic as that of bourgeois factory psychology, and the extent to which it is shaped by the capitalist principle of achievement becomes clear from Parson's definition of health as the "condition of optimal achievement capacity in an individual," that is, of illness as "a generalized disturbance of life." Parson's abstract medical-sociological role theory tacitly accepts a concrete distribution of roles within capitalist class society: "Psychic conditions of health and illness are personal conditions, defined in terms of the relevance to humanity's ability to fulfill institutionalized roles."[110] According to Parsons, every kind of non-adjustment to an "institutionalized role," for example to that of wage earner, would be identical with "illness." Thus it becomes self-evident that Parson's positivist theory of roles amounts to a most bald-faced apology for existing power relationships.

As opposed to classical medicine's concept of illness, and that of bourgeois factory psychology and of positivist medical sociology, the psychosomatic concept of illness is, at least socially, considerably more enlightened. The starting point of A. Mitscherlich's theory of psychosomatic illness is that in "modern industrial society" the incidence of medical illness has not decreased despite the success of the medical sciences. More and more patients come to doctors with disturbances which can no longer be diagnosed with the methods of classical medicine, not to speak of being cured. This leads Mitscherlich to the conclusion that "the life forms of society have created new conditions for illness out of themselves which are related to the environment of technical industrial civilization."[111] If only in a very abstract manner, Mitscherlich at least accepts factors of psycho-sociological illness which have been totally neglected by traditional medicine: "From the viewpoint of sociology, illness, no matter how it manifests itself, is an opportunity for the individual to express his non-correspondence with social demands; illness for the individual in a helpless situation is an opportunity to react."[112]

According to this definition, illness is a symptom of the conflict between the individual and society, a conflict that can express itself psychically, somatically, and psychosomatically. But this psychosomatic concept of illness—which is a progressive one in contrast with those of classical medicine—nonetheless remains blind to the real social causes of illness which are given only abstract and vague designations. "Technology" as such, "technical industrial civilization," can scarcely be made reponsible for the increasing incidence of illness; for these were what made possible the successes of modern medicine in the first place. Not the "environment of technological industrial civilization" but the capitalist organization of technology and of industrial labor is the main reason for the increasing incidence of illness which Mitscherlich records.

From a social point of view, Mitscherlich's poorly defined concept of illness results in a therapy which is nothing more than moderate reformism. The therapeutic objective—an increase of the autonomous freedom of the individual in expressing his instinctual wishes—is supposed to be achieved by means of widening the autonomy of the ego, by a deepening of insight into the motives for his actions, and by making conscious his previously unconscious repressed feelings. The "autonomous freedom of the individual" thus is supposed to be created by psychoanalytical navelgazing instead of by a struggle for the social prerequisities of such autonomy. Mitscherlich's therapy therefore only reproduces the reformism and idealism of classic psychoanalytic therapy: protest against the social compulsion which expresses itself in psychosomatic illness is again throttled and internalized in therapy: not society, but the patient, is altered.

In recent years, however, the rate of illness among workers has increased to such an extent that capitalism, too, has developed great interest in elucidating "pathogenetic social factors." Production decreases due to mounting illness worry even the highest capitalist health authorities. Thus did R. T. Collins (Chairman of the Joint Committee on Mental Health in Industry, American Medical Association) arrived at the following conclusion at a congress of the National Health Council in the United States: "Mental disease is a more frequent reason for absence from the job than any physical illness, except for the simple cold. Some 80 to 90 per cent of the employees who are let go today are dismissed for social inabilities [. . .] that is, inability to get along with other people. One of four workers [. . .] has mental problems which manifest themselves in absence from work, in accidents, in alcoholism, illness, dissatisfaction with the job and disputes with colleagues and superiors."[113] The tactic of official capitalist "health apostles" to make the patients themselves responsible for their mental illness as their "private problem" (for example, as their inability to get along with other people) is just as clear as is their serious concern about the rapidly spreading phenomenon of shirking work by falling ill. On the one hand, capital has an increasing interest in investigating "pathogenetic social factors" so as to control the ever intensifying decrease in production through illness by means of corresponding prophylactic measures; on the other hand, it must camouflage the true causes of mental mass misery so as to prevent a politicization process at the root.

All recent investigations of the etiology of mental illness at the site of work, mostly commissioned by industry itself, contain this contradiction. However, we can differentiate between two directions that the investigations of new theories of medical sociology and epidemical sociology are taking.

The first, purely apologetic, direction explains the increase of mental disturbance among the work force as a consequence of "misdirected self-love" in the sense of psychoanalytical ego psychology (American vintage), or of an "unsatisfactory factory climate" in the sense of bourgeois factory psychology, or of "failed adjustment" in the sense of positivist medical sociology. The conditions to which adjustment cannot be made are exculpated, the "non-adjusted" person is the culprit. Such an explanation, for example, reads like this: "Many people in the shop have not learned [. . .] to accept and respect genuine authority. They believe in the idea that how they think something should be done is the only correct way [. . .] They turn an inadequacy into a complaint and a complaint into a problem [. . .] The employee who makes problems will often abruptly manifest psychosomatic symptoms."[114] The psychosomatic problem thus remains the "private concern of the private person." Psychoanalytically oriented authors interpret the increased frequency of psychosomatic disturbances among employess in the accustomed manner via the father and Oedipus complex. According to Levinson & Co. the mentally disturbed worker transfers his "negative relationship with his father" onto the factory. The employee then feels "that the organization owes him something. He consistently exploits his environment [. . .] Such a person has developed forms of rationalizing his behavior which calm his conscience and free him from his obligations."[115]

The second, more progressive, direction of medical-epidemicological investigation at least has come somewhat closer to the pathology of the capitalist work organization in seeking to investigate which factors at the work site correlate most of all with mental illnesses.

Thus a study by Alphen de Veer (1955) produced the result that particular workers with monotonous activities, little room for independent decisions, and strong concentration on the movement of the machine show the highest degree of mental disturbance.[116] Gadourek in his 1965 study found that dissatisfaction with the required work, the lower social status of the work performed, plus the fact that the workers are watched during their work correlates with the highest incidence of psychosomatic disturbances.[117] Kornhauser (1965) in a study performed on Detroit factory workers reached the conclusion that unskilled workers with repetitious jobs, after skilled and unskilled workers with non-repetitious jobs, have the lowest incidence of mental health. The factor that correlates most strongly with mental illness is "the impossibility of employing one's talent in one's work."[118] Correspondingly, psychosomatic disturbances increase among workers of lower qualification. According to Planz, stomach ulcer is to be found particularly among "employees from the lower social strata who are weighed down with a job where they have only superiors but no subordinates."[119] Stomach ulcer has become the measuring rod of psychosomatic illness among the working population and "the population which suffers from cancer comes more frequently from the lowest social strata, the unskilled. Female workers from the lower strata, unskilled women, are the ones who most frequently suffer, physically and mentally, from obesity."[120]

But such progressive bourgeois medical epidemology, too, suffers from positivist simplification by replacing the structural connection between the capitalist organization of work and mental wretchedness with a point-by-point connection between individual pathogenetic factors at the work site and mental disturbance. The totality of these etiological factors provides at best a compound picture but not a structural and genetic picture of industrial pathology.

The Capitalist Division of Labor and the "Division of the Individual"

The young Marx, with his "theory of alienation," had already developed the *Grundriss* of a materialist theory of illness. As he shows in his economic-political writings, the modern worker is "alienated" from his product, from the act of production, from other people, and therefore also from himself. According to Marx, compulsive labor is identical with the human individual's "loss of self." The "alien character [of labor] is obvious from the fact that as soon as no physical or other pressure exists, labor is avoided like the plague. External labor, labor in which man is externalized, is labor of self-sacrifice, of penance."[121] With the loss of the object of his work the worker suffers—in Freud's terminology—a corresponding loss of identity. Marx writes: "The workers neither have command over the organization of their work nor over its products. They are a body that is ruled by an alien will [. . .][122] Their process of realization is simultaneously a process of disrealization[123] [. . .] the complete extraction of the human inner being as complete emptying out, universal objectification as total alienation."[124]

It is remarkable—and this fact appears to have escaped the Freudians to this day—that the "young" Marx described wage labor quite explicitly in terms of pathology. "To be sure, labor produces marvels for the wealthy, but it produces deprivation for the workers [. . .] It produces intelligence, but for the worker it produces imbecility and cretinism."[125] Since his relationship to the object of his work is not an "active" one, not one of "acquisition," he becomes a "spiritually as well as physically dehumanized being." Since his relationship to nature and to human beings is not one of "free, conscious activity, " he loses himself, and his instincts become animalistic. "The worker, therefore, feels at ease only outside work, and during work he is outside himself. He is at home when he is not working and when he is working he is not at home. His work, therefore, is not voluntary, but coerced forced labor. It is not the satisfaction of a need but only a *means* to satisfy other needs. [. . .] The result, therefore, is that man (the worker) feels that he is acting freely only in his animal functions—eating, drinking,and procreating, or at most in his shelter and finery—while in his human functions he feels only like an animal. The animalistic becomes the human and the human the animalistic."[126] The social basis of the "neurotic human animal" which Freud himself repressed is therefore the "work animal" which is alienated from itself. Marx observes: "Life for the worker becomes only a means to work. In his work the worker is never worker but only work animal."[127]

In *Capital* Marx finally represented the historical process of "man's alienation from himself" which is identical with his case history. The pathogenetic dimension of "work" appears historically in the same degree as the full development of commodity production, when the capacity to work is *separated* from its conditions for realization and the social labor process is subsumed under the process of utilizing capital. According to Marx: "The means of production are at once changed into means for the absorption of the labor of others. It is now no longer the laborer that employs the means of production, but the means of production that employ the laborer. Instead of being consumed by him as material elements of his productive activity, they consume him as the ferment necessary to their own life process, and the life process of capital consists only in its movement as value constantly expanding, constantly multiplying itself."[128] With the separation of the capacity to work from its conditions for realization the producers, too, are "separated" from their objectified qualitative capacities and potentialities as contained in the work product. The "separation of labor power from the personality of the worker, its transformation into an object which he sells on the market place"[129] (Lukács), is therefore the actual materialist basis of what Freud in individual psychopathology diagnosed as the "castration complex." The "castration complex," which—according to Freud—lies at the basis of all psychopathological phenomena, arises, if you take Marx at his word, from the "castrating" quality of wage labor: the worker's own activity "as alien and not belonging to him, activity as passivity, power as weakness, procreation as emasculation, the worker's *own* physical and spiritual energy, his personal life—for what else is life but activity— as an activity turned against him, independent of him, and not belonging to him" (Marx[130]). Fear of castration is certainly not a primal, so to speak "biological" fear, but rather the reflex of that social "castration" which permeates the "preservation" of the family, which consists in the fact that the wage laborer with his product is simultaneously "separated" from his genital qualities and potency which now confront him as an alien power. "Intelligence in production expands in one direction because it vanishes in many others. What is lost by detail laborers is concentrated in the capital that employs them. It is a result of the division of labor in manufactures, that the laborer is brought face to face with the intellectual potencies of the material process of production, as the property of another, and as a ruling power."[131]

Marx described the pathogenetic effect of the developing division of labor in the following fashion, using the example of the transition from handicraft to manufacture production: "Some crippling of body and mind is inseparable even from the division of labor in society as a whole. Since, however, manufacture carries this social separation of branches of labor much further, and also, by its peculiar division, attacks the individual at the very roots of his life, it is the first to afford the materials for, and to give a start to, industrial pathology."[132] And Marx suggests in this connection that the subsuming of the worker under the manufacturing division of labor has as a consequence the splintering of all his productive capacities and talents, that is, the "abnormal" partialization of his total need and instinctual structure. For manufacture "converts the laborer into a crippled monstrosity, by forcing his detail dexterity at the expense of a world of productive capabilities and instincts; as in the States of La Plata they butcher a whole beast for the sake of his hide or his tallow. Not only is detail work distributed to different individuals, but the individual himself is made the automatic motor of a fractional operation, and the absurd fable of Menenius Agrippa, which makes man a mere fragment of his own body, becomes realized."[133]

The capitalist form of the division of labor finally drives the fragmentation and partialization of the objective and subjective elements of the production process even further. According to Lukács: "It has already been pointed out that the division of labor disrupts every organically unified process of work and life and breaks it down into its components. This enables the artificially isolated partial functions to be performed in the most rational manner by 'specialists' who are especially adapted mentally and physically for the purpose. This has the effect of making these partial functions autonomous and so they tend to develop through their own momentum and in accordance with their own special laws independently of the other partial functions of society (or that part of the society to which they belong)."[134] In the same degree as the "organic unity" of the process of life and work is destroyed, so is the "organic unity" of the working individual destroyed: he himself is "divided." As little as individual acts of detail work—in the consciousness of the detail worker—still come together into the "organic unity" of the product, that little do his "fragmented and partialized" capacities and qualities still fit together into an "organic unity" of the person. Thus it is no longer possible to create an integration of partial psychic functions, of "partial drives," into an "organic unity" of the "structure of genital instincts and character." There reproduces itself in the psychic apparatus a "similar rational-inhuman division of labor as was found in the factory" (Lukács[135]), namely, the dissection of the psychosexual totality (that is, genitality) into individual partial psychic functions, into their "partialized" instinctual aspects. The "rationalization and isolation of (industrial and bureaucratic) partial functions, which become autonomous with regard to the entire process of production and administration, necessarily goes hand in hand with the fact that the accompanying emotional and cognitive functions also become autonomous. The "repetition compulsion" of industrial and bureaucratic detail work continues in the inner being—as in an extreme "clinical" repetition compulsion—in the form of thoughts and feelings of the Sisyphean detail worker. The "psychic impoverishment" of the weakened and ill ego, its impoverishment of free, mobile instinctual energy that might be capable of object cathexis (as psychoanalysis says), is therefore the adequate psychological reflex of the "impoverishment of the workers of their individual productive energies," which is determined by the "enrichment of the total worker, that is, of capital with social productive power" (Marx [136]). Regarded this way, industrial pathology is the materialist foundation of the "psychopathology of (capitalist) everyday life" (Freud).

Capitalist "Regression Machinery"

According to Foucault a structural mark of every illness is that the complex coordinated reactions in consciousness and behavior are replaced by simple stereotypical and automatic forms of behavior which increase as the former are eliminated. "Illness eliminates the complex, less stable functions that are dependent on the will by increasing simple, stable, and automatic functions."[137] This structural description, of course, abstracts—that is the blind spot of structural psychoanalysis—from concrete social triggers and causes of "pathological disintegration." If illness, "regression"—according to Foucault—is determined by "the emergence of certain automatic modes of reaction" and by the disappearance of complex and coordinated modes of consciousness and behavior, then he designates, without either knowing or wanting to, the nature of "industrial pathology": for the capitalist form of division of labor, on the one hand, has as one effect the work process as a whole becoming more and more complex, coordinated, and qualified; but the work of a large part of the work force becomes simpler, more automatic, involuntary. A picture of the behavior and reactions of the disqualified worker is abstract and regressive in the sense that his complex "higher" technical, intellectual, and psychological functions are replaced by simpler, "lower" functions. The increasing disqualification of large realms of industrial and bureaucratic work is, therefore, a main cause of industrial pathology.

Work on the half-automatic machine produces a mental state that could be described with Freud's concept of the "day dream." Sartre observes: "Investigations from the initial period of the use of half-automated machines have shown that specialized women workers surrender to sexual fantasies while working. They thought of the room, the bed, the night, everything that is relevant to being alone with their partner. But it was the machine inside them, which dreams this tenderness. For the kind of attention demanded of them by their work neither permitted them distraction (to think of something else) nor complete concentration (thinking decelerates the movement in this case). The machinery conversely demands and produces in human beings a semi-automatism which complements them [. . .] The mind is put under stress without being fully employed, it is limited to a lateral control, the body functions 'mechanically' and yet remains watched [. . .] Every single act of attention, every thought system must be repressed, so as not to hinder the lateral control function, and not to slow down the movements. So all one can do is surrender to passivity."[138]

So it is a case of a half-waking state during which the conscious censor, as a consequence of the "function of lateral control," is neither entirely eliminated nor entirely functions. So neither the functions of the ego (reflection, development of thought) nor the functions of the id (sexual fantasies among others) develop fully; the mechanical "recurrence compulsion" of the machine reproduces itself on all levels of the psychological apparatus; mental activity stagnates. The fact that primarily women —as the most unqualified and therefore cheapest labor power—suffer most from the consequences of mechanization and automation (under capitalist conditions) the capitalist "apostles of health" justify by citing alleged sex-specific differences. Thus, according to the opinion of many doctors, women are particularly predestined to piece work: "Women are less suited for hard manual labor but more for work that requires quickness, fine coordination, agile movements, and a constantly hovering attentiveness. These natural [!] talents of women the economy has used to develop a particular kind of women's work: automated work preparation."[139] Indeed, according to the medicine men of capitalism, the automated production process with its rhythmic work preparation is virtually destined for the "emotional" and "sensitive" weaker sex. "Rhythmic work movements are already initially directed to their continuation and success. This constitutes the inner connection of perception and movement [!], of voluntary activity and the enlivening, stimulating beat of the work rhythm. This experience is a joyful feeling for the women, and encourages them to the uninhibited—but not unresisting—continuation of their activity. They possess a high sensitivity towards disturbance rhythmic procedures [which of course includes cigarette breaks, small talk, and other pauses—author]. The other women experience a feeling of monotony and displeasure." That of course is then her private concern: "Whether some experiences are monotonous has nothing to do with the organization of work but with the inner structure of the worker [!]."[140]

The German government medical director Dr. Buckup has accomplished the ideological feat of ascribing women's suitability for automated work to their particular talent for fantasizing: "A woman is generally better suited than a man for activities connected with many rationalization measures in assembly-line work which occur without great demands on one's work capacity and precision. However, the prerequisite is that the work that has to be performed automates itself while it is being performed, that is, must be abstracted from attentiveness and thought processes. A woman, after all—who is more gifted in fantasy than man [!]—is capable of performing the most monotonous work by personally disinvolving herself from her work and she compensates for its monotony with wish-fulfillment dreams and other like thoughts."[141]

In reality, abstraction from the processes of attention and thought and the fact that related psychic activity becomes autonomous becomes a more and more decisive element of industrial pathology. According to Sartre: "The woman worker thinks of sexual surrender because the machine demands that she live her conscious life in passivity, and so as to maintain attentiveness which is capable of adjusting itself without ever mobilizing itself in active thought. Of course, this circling of fantasy can assume different aspects, attach itself to different objects [. . .] The essential thing is that the object of these fantasies is simultaneously the subject itself, that both constantly go over into each other. If the woman [. . .] stops dozing and thinks of her man or lover, work stops or slows down. That is why women practically are prevented from thinking of their children—objects of their care and concern [. . .]."[142]

Work on a half-automated machine does not absorb all one's attentive (or cathexic) energy (Freud), yet just enough so that female workers cannot produce quite enough energy for complete "object cathexis" (thinking of their husband or their children)—except at the price of a slowdown or stoppage of work. The permanent withdrawal of mental "attention" and cathexic energy by half-automated work processes drives the "libido" back to regressive levels. Day-dreaming or dozing during work is an expression of enforced "regression."

Wage-dependent patients, therefore, do not fall ill because of an "unassimilated past"—as bourgeois psychoanalysis would say—but from the ever-present and "recurring" power of alienating labor. They regress not because they are fixated on some kind of pre-genital state of instinctual development (as psychoanalysis would say); rather their existence as the "wage slaves of capital," as the "automatic cogs of detail labor" (Marx), is identical *per se* with a regressive existence. Marx writes: "Machinery is put to wrong use, with the object of transforming the workman, from his very childhood, into part of a detail machine. In this way, not only are the expenses of his reproduction considerably lessened, but at the same time his helpless dependence upon the factory as a whole, and therefore upon the capitalist, is rendered complete."[143] Not an "unassimilated Oedipus complex" but capitalist machinery, whose blind appendix they are, drives the workers' thinking and feeling farther and farther back into the past. P. Schneider observes: "Among young women you can see that their resistance hasn't been broken yet by the machines. You recognize by the energy and the fury of their movements the eight-hour fight which they conduct for their bodily and psychic autonomy. Their body, as it were, still retains its own rhythm which they match against the machine. Things are different with older women who have been sitting at the machine for ten or twenty years. The machine has subjugated their body, wrinkled their face, made their hands defenseless [. . .] Most of the time the noise from the machine roars into their defenseless head, drives them back to habits and wishes of long ago. American experiments have shown that piece work is performed with the greatest alacrity if consciousness is eliminated by music. So it is a question of a kind of work which precisely does not require the cooperation but the cessation, that is, the becoming autonomous, of mental activity. One can imagine what kind of force is lent the old, inculcated compulsions to cleanliness and family rituals from the fact that the machines constantly throw the mental movements of the women back to their starting point. Piece-work machines are regression instruments pure and simple."[144]

Splitting off, becoming autonomous, and "repressing" mental activity to the minimal remnant necessary for exercising the detail function is what constitutes the nature of industrial pathology. Indeed, the capitalist machines of regression sometimes determine mental activity even when its access to motility is blocked, during sleep, while the workers are dreaming. Wallraff comments: "Some are pursued by their work into their sleep. One fellow told me [. . .] that the assembly line wouldn't let go of him even at night. He often sits up in his sleep and mechanically performs the movements and manipulations which he must perform stereotypically during the day."[145] Moreover it is remarkable that the psychoanalysis of dream life (especially of working patients) is invariably sounded out for sexual symbols and wishes, but never for the "unassimilated remnants of the day" in the sense of psychically unassimilated recent experiences at the work site.

The regressive and pathogenetic effect of work at a half-automated machine thus refutes all psychoanalytic, that is, psycho-therapeutic, illusions about "ego reinforcement" and "ego strengthening" and "ego autonomy" for wage-dependent "patients." The classic objective of psychoanalytic therapy—"Where there was id should become ego" (Freud)—remains illusory as long as work on capitalist regression machines maintains mental activity in a "twilight state" between consciousness and unconsciousness and drives it constantly back into the ever-present "past" of "endless work agony" (Engels).

The Intensification of Work and the Increase of "Functional Illness"

In *Illness as Conflict* A. Mitscherlich remarks that alone "in 1954, some 100,000 persons in the Federal Republic left the work process prematurely owing to heart and circulatory damage [. . .] Functional illnesses constitute 30 to 50 per cent of all cases of illness that require treatment from a general practitioner or specialist [. . .] Of course, no statistic can answer the question how many of the 100,000 persons who had to quit work in 1954 due to heart and circulatory disturbances became unfit because of so-called organ neuroses[. . .]."[146]

In the meantime West German public-health officials can no longer suppress the fact of an increasing rate of "functional" illness among the wage-dependent population. The medical "interim report" of 1970 mentions alarming figures: for 63.9 percent of the men and 71.1 percent of the women from a total of 50,000 employees (of which, however, only 63 percent allowed themselves to be checked), therapeutic measures were considered necessary. "Heart and circulatory illnesses occupy first place. Next are pathological findings of the skeleton and muscles, stomach and intestinal tract, kidneys and genitals and the respiratory organs. The percentage of formerly unknown illnesses first discovered by the check-up represented 14.2 per cent among the men and 13.3 per cent among the women. The newly discovered pathological findings are not related to age."[147] The increase in the death rate due to "functional" illnesses corresponds to these findings: in 1967 in the Federal Republic some 144,647 men died of cardiovascular and circulatory diseases.[148]

The "interim report," of course, has nothing to say about the true economic and social causes of these "functional" and "pathological" mass symptoms. The rapid current increase of psychosomatic disturbances and pathological defects in the working population is to be traced primarily to structural changes in the late-capitalist production process and to new techniques of surplus-value exploitation.

Technical know-how, physical strength, and individual agility were necessary during the early and high-capitalist era; but in the third industrial revolution, when work became increasingly marked by repetitious detail, monotonousness and extreme nervous strain began to predominate. With growing technicalization and automation the significance of manual labor is disappearing to the same degree as the share of technically controlling "mental work" in industrial production is increasing. This produces an increasing shift of the main emphasis from physical to the "functional," that is, mental realm. The new qualifications that begin to predominate today are an ability for concentrated attention and the highest possible degree of responsibility in the control and correction of complicated half- or fully automated machines. However, the new qualifications of industrial mental labor are associated with an increasing experience of monotony. The highly mechanized and automated work process has banished the last rudiments of creativity from the wage-labor environment. The easing of work in the sense of its (partial) liberation from heavy physical labor and strain simultaneously has imposed a complete vacuity on such work. This is something that Marx has already described: "At the same time that factory work exhausts the nervous system to the uttermost, it does away with the many-sided play of the muscles, and confiscates every atom of freedom, both in bodily and intellectual activity. Even the lightening of labor becomes a sort of torture, since the machine does not free the laborer from work, but deprives the work of all interest."[149] American auto workers who are are increasingly becoming partly automated appendages of fully automated machines express this quite bluntly: "[. . .] here in the new factory the machines control us."[150] Fiat workers from Mirafiori near Turino who were interviewed by a group of the Movimento Studentesco in 1969 had this to say about their work: "Not for people, for robots only; it's piece work and demands more than physical effort, that is, nervous strain, in other words: it has a negative effect on the human nervous system."[151] And another: "I believe if we go on like this, that is, until it becomes an unbearable rhythm, that sooner or later we will end up in a sanatorium. In other words: one is working at the limit of one's energies."[152]

The servicing of a machine at a highly mechanized and rationalized work site requires less physical energy but the service requirements are accelerated by the increased scope of the realm of work, that is, by the acceleration of the assembly line. Since the automated machines watch autonomously over the most important variables in the production process and react to critical situations with meaningful corrective actions, the fact that workers are bound to *one* machine also becomes increasingly unprofitable from the viewpoint of capital. The workers' activity there-fore is extended to the control and correction of several simultaneously operating automatic production processes. But that is why the strain on the nerves of the worker is increased, for he must now have his eyes everywhere and do several things at once. This is what workers at an automated textile mill had to say about their extended sphere of activity: "Now with 26 looms I am unhappy. We have too many looms. That is a great strain on my nerves, they are going to pieces in the process. When you've worked for two to three hours you are simply done in[. . .] You are also responsible for the product, for the stuff that's got faults. You have 20 looms and sometimes the material is of pretty poor quality, and then something starts to go wrong and you run back and forth and start to boil over and your whole body trembles."[153]

The increasing replacement of industrial manual labor by mental labor and the acceleration of service requirements in connection with the extension of the field of activity—these structural changes in a highly developed production process are to be made chiefly responsible for the shift from organic to "functional" illnesses: "the 'relief' of the muscle-power machine is confronted by the 'strain' of the nervous automaton. What is to be feared is chronic hyper-irritation of the vegetative nervous system which first leads to functional disturbances and subsequently to organic damages of all kinds [. . .]."[154] The modern highly mechanized and automated work process has therefore pushed back the classic occupational diseases (such as tuberculosis, consumption, silicosis) to the same degree as it has increased the functional illnesses of the "nervous automaton." Thus in the sphere of work there simply is no such thing as the "repressive assimilation of 'modern nervousness'" (R. Reiche).[155] On the contrary, "modern nervousness" (Freud) has reached a histori-cally new highpoint (although for reasons other than Freud's).

The compulsion towards maximum profit makes it necessary to keep the machines running the entire week if possible, night and day. For it is in the interest of capital to extract the maximum mass of surplus value out of its labor power and to amortize its plant in the shortest possible time, and in a legally regulated workday this can only be achieved by means of shift work. Symanowski/Vilmar provide the following report about shift work on "family life" and on the physical and mental health of these workers: "Right at the beginning the head foreman told me that the shift was responsible for the ruin of many marriages, and several workers confirmed this to us later on. It becomes impossible to go on living together. What is particularly crucial is the missing Sunday where you can go meet people and the inhuman rhythm of the shift work. When father comes home the children are asleep, and when they come home from school he is leaving. The children's chief experience is of their father tearing open the bedroom door and screaming 'shut up!' If both husband and wife are doing shift labor, they scarcely see each other at all under present-day arrangements of the eight-to nine-hour shift."[156]

The incommensurability of work time with the natural rhythm of day and night also creates havoc with the entire vegetative nervous system: "[. . .] A large percentage of the shift workers have something wrong with their stomachs because the organism cannot adjust itself to constant change."[157] The shift worker loses all feeling for the natural change from day to night because he always has to sleep and wake up at different times, and the artificially lighted factory halls completely disconcert him about the time of day. "In the long run this way of life produces injuries to mental and physical health, such as heart, circulatory, and stomach troubles, sleeplessness, and nervous irritability."[158] The psychic, that is, functional disturbances of the shift worker are primarily, then, consequence of insufficient social communication within the family as well as within the larger groups which presuppose a normal sense of rhythm to daily life. If, according to Foucault, "disturbances of the form of time in this morbid world" are characterized "by time no longer running forward nor running at all,"[159] then he characterizes precisely the sense of time of the shift worker which Wallraff has described in the following manner: "The horrible thing is that time-off is basically nothing but a second factory. Whoever has to last out eight hours of work with no concrete objective can no longer divide his life into two realms [. . .] The off-days are nothing but waiting for the next shift."[160] The worker's sense of time becomes "pathological" in Foucault's sense, for the "accumulation of the past [past work in this instance—author] can no longer dissolve for him; and, therefore, past and present can no longer run towards the future."[161]

A further important contributing factor for the increase of "functional" disturbances and of "modern nervousness" is the historical shift in emphasis in various techniques of surplus-value exploitation. Since the organized workers movement fought for and won the eight-hour day, capital is no longer in a position to increase its profit by extending the work day, as it was still able to do in the nineteenth century—that is, by heightening the increase in *absolute* surplus value. Since then it seeks to increase the *relative* surplus value by means of an uninterrupted rationalization of production, through increasing the rate of piece work, and through more and more rational methods of work-site evaluation (Refa, MTM, and so on). In the wake of the third industrial revolution the exploitation of relative surplus value has increased grandiosely through the constant rationalization and intensification of work. The new forms of such work-intensive exploitation, however, also have as a consequence an intensified mental exploitation and impoverishment.

Among the most intensive and pathogenic means of rationalization are new systems for evaluating work performance, for example the MTM system. This system, which has been introduced into many large industrial enterprises, "is based on the presupposition that there exists a measurable minimum of necessary movement for each step in the work process. For each of these steps a time norm is constructed which is supposed to be achieved by every human being on earth no matter whether he or she be a giant or a dwarf, a pregnant woman or a Turkish carpetmaker."[162] The decisive advantage of these "measuring methods" for the entrepreneur is that they give the appearance of objective control of performance which the worker can no longer find fault with. The data, once it has been gathered, for every basic step, fixed in the tables and kept as standardized measures in a safe of the MTM Company in Pennsylvania, in a certain sense assumes the rank of primal clock. However, for the worker the MTM system means that he has no time left for any kind of subjective expression of tiredness, sadness, being in love, and so forth. All his real needs and feelings are, so to speak, standardized away. In this instance he experiences concretely and sensuously that he is nothing but the "personification of mere work time" (Marx).

With its higher work norms the MTM system simultaneously introduces higher quotas of illness. Peter Schneider writes: "Chronic injuries to women who work on the assembly line are: injuries to the spinal discs, tendonitis, and stomach and gall bladder illnesses, which are of course aggravated by the increase of the piece-work rate. At times the women help themselves by massaging each other's necks and back muscles, or they let their upper body and arms hang down slack for a while. But they know it doesn't help much. One woman said to me: 'All of us here develop some kind of tic sooner or later. And most of the time it doesn't stop there, we get it in the head too!' Another girl expressed her feelings about the advantages of the new system in the following way: 'Sometimes I just feel like jumping up from my place and screaming until I keel over . . .' "[163]

New work-site evaluation systems produce a time-neurosis of massive proportions: on the one hand the workers are afraid of not achieving the "advance time"; on the other hand, they are afraid that if they do, the piece-work rate will be increased; and this combination of factors produces constant nervousness and irritation which find expression in a significant increase in the number of accidents at work. Every year in the Federal Republic there are some 2.5 million accidents on the job which result in an incapacity for work for an average of at least three days. From 1950 until 1969, nearly 145,000 workers lost their lives in accidents, and the accident rate is still climbing. In some professions (for example, in mining) there is a yearly increase of 12 percent.[164] What is revealing in this regard is the connection between work days lost through strikes and those lost through illness and accidents. In England, for example, 311 million work days were lost through illness and accidents in 1967 as opposed to 3 million through strikes.[165] A comparison of the number of work-related accidents per 1,000 workers in the Federal Republic and the German Democratic Republic indicates both the cost to capitalism and the intensification of labor that is exacted: in the Federal Republic the rate is 97.3; in the German Democratic Republic, 41.2 accidents per worker.[166] Besides insufficient protective measures which, from the viewpoint of capital, belong to the *faux frais de production* (cold cost), motivation presumably also plays a role in this connection: work accidents appear in many instances as a kind of unconscious surrogate action in lieu of consciously unexpressed protest against the inhuman capitalist organization of work and its constant intensification. The refusal to participate any longer in a certain sense assumes the form of unconsciously produced self-mutilation.

One measure of the physical wear and tear on the workers as a consequence of the intensification of work is also the high rate at which they are becoming invalids. According to Gerns, "roughly two-thirds of workers and employees become invalids before they reach legal retirement age [. . .] How devastating the consequences of the enormous intensity of work are is also expressed by the fact that in the Federal Republic the average life expectancy of men after their third decade declines despite all the achievements of medical science. Especially striking is the great increase of heart and circulatory illnesses as the cause of death. This indicates a change in the strain of work which more and more becomes a hyper-strain on the psyche."[167]

Noise disturbances also play a role in the increase of functional illnesses. Medical investigation of these disturbances shows that vegetative reflexes begin to occur at a noise level of 65 decibels, with the consequence that the entire vegetative nervous system of the organism is redirected. This also means a displacement of the endocrine system, the glandular functions, and so on [. . .] as well as a decrease in gastric juices and changes in the adrenal gland."[168] Lehman quotes an investigation by Jansen which compares two groups of workers one of which was exposed to a high level of noise whereas the other was not. The group of steelworkers exposed to the high-decibel level manifested a distinctly higher rate of disturbances affecting the circulation, heart, digestive tract, and general equilibrium. According to Kieselbach and others, "prolonged exposure to intensive noise levels leads to lasting changes in the vegetative nervous system which can assume the character of clinical symptoms."[169]

A further cause of functional illness is the constant fear of unemployment among wage-dependent workers. Thus Halliday (according to Pflanz)[170] was able to show that the insecurity produced by unemployment manifests itself in an increase in psychosomatic disturbances.

Middle-aged employees are especially hard hit by fears of this kind since they have a much more difficult time finding re-employment. Unemployed patients who were tested by Pflanz had a higher incidence of headache, disturbed sleep, and ulcers. Gadourek[171] and Kornhouser[172] both found a correlation between psychosomatic disturbances and fear of losing one's job. This social fear, which can assume functional symptoms, intensifies during the periodic recessions of the capitalist economic cycle which the entrepreneurs—as we know—use to increase discipline and intimidate the workers.

As long as the working class does not rebel against these new and intensified forms of exploitation, heart, stomach, and circulatory diseases of individual workers will rebel for them. Even though the worker may still "go along'," his circulation, in any event, will not. Even if he says, "Actually I feel all right," his stomach ulcer will prove the contrary. Peter Schneider comments: "[. . .] Women put a distance between their illness and themselves, that is, they invent reasons for it which have nothing to do with the job and which lie far in the past. Often this illness serves as an expression of unconscious or conscious protest against the drudgery of their job."[173] As long as the industrial or bureaucratic detail worker permits a situation in which he "is realized as only a fragment of his body" (Marx), that bodily fragment (heart, stomach, kidney) goes on strike instead of the whole man, that is, he falls ill. The repressed class conflict is "somatized," that is, assumes the unconscious and self-destructive form of "organ neurosis."

The Utilization of the "Diseased Commodity"

As we have said, it is scarcely possible any longer for capitalist "public health services" to conceal the increasing symptoms of pathology among the working population today. However, it very much suppresses the true social causes of these new "industrial" diseases. It is not interested in a really massive prophylaxis if only because it operates on a capitalist basis, that is, the profit motive. The development of a capitalist "health industry" obeys the general laws of capital accumulation. The kind and extent of its "health services" are not determined by the requirements of a defective work force but by the need for profit by the industries wielding such prophylaxis. Only inasmuch as they become a deficit for production do massive illnesses, therefore, come under consideration for the public-health administrators. Thus the previously mentioned Chairman of the Joint Committee on Mental Health bemoaned the high rate of schizophrenia among the American working population especially because "of the average loss of 94.3 days of work, which makes evident that this disturbance is of notable significance for industry."[174]

A capitalist "public-health service" has the sole task of repairing defective labor power so as to make it useful again for capital. Since the cost for medical services in the sense of capital are *faux frais de production,* the lowest possible estimate is put upon them. The acute shortage of doctors and nursing personnel in all capitalist countries is proof of this. Therefore it is part of the logic of capital to shift the costs of repair of the "commodity labor" onto the working class itself.

Indeed, health insurance is only in appearance paid half by the worker and half by the capitalist. According to T. Ripke: "In reality the capitalist writes off 'his' share as well as that of the worker as part of the wages or supplementary social contributions. Both parts are part of the wage."[175] The health insurance which the worker buys is an unconcealed "part wage" and that which the capitalist pays for is a camouflaged "part wage." The services of various medical organizations (such as factory doctors) therefore are not a "gift" of capital to the defective work force; rather they constitute—inasmuch as they are paid for by the working class through health insurance—an equivalent for the money deducted from their wages.

Just as a "healthy" work force becomes "ill" by becoming the object of ruthless capital utilization, so an "ill" labor force can be repaired only if it subjects itself to the conditions for utilization incumbent on the "diseased commodity." Capitalist "public-health services" do not comprise an autonomous organization interested in public health for purely humanitarian reasons. Rather, nationalized or not, they are the distribution center, embellished with humanitarian ideology, of various branches of industry which live off the utilization of the "diseased commodity," the chemical and pharmaceutical industries in particular. According to SPK: "The patient as the consumer of products of the pharmaceutical industry becomes an object of secondary exploitation. This interlocking of the sectors of production and 'service' is characteristic of capitalist society. In every instance, the person, whether he is a 'healthy' worker in a factory or a patient in a clinic or under a doctor's care, is only a means of economic compulsions and purposes. These economic mechanisms give the lie to all medical liberalism."[176]

The pharmaceutical industry and its suppliers, the chemical industry, therefore are interested in a constantly rising demand for medical services, that is, in an expanding market of patients. This branch of capital therefore definitely has no very great interest in developing a truly perfect state of national health since its business is, of course, disease. Indeed, it can be proved that the profit rate of the pharmaceutical industry rose at the same rate in recent years as the rate of "functional" illness on the part of the work force. The largest medical supplier in the world, Hoffmann-La Roche, increased its turnover per year (in Swiss Francs) from 1.4 billion in 1962 to 5.0 in 1970. The stock-exchange price of the

La Roche shares rose from 73,000 Swiss Francs in 1960 to 194,000 Swiss Francs in 1971. Dividends increased from 280 in 1960 to 1,000 in 1970. The cause of this fabulous turnover and profit increase is the extraordinarily high rate of use of "psychotropic substances" with which the workers have recently been seeking to anesthetize the psychic misery in a highly rationalized work process.[177]

The increasing number of "functional" and "habit-forming" illnesses (see also p. 209) thus serve the special function of injecting capital on the behalf of the relevant capitalist firms, in that the constantly increasing demand for psychotropic substances, for medicine and medical instruments, provides a shot in the arm for totally new pharmaceutical and medical industries. If one wanted to exaggerate, one could say that today almost as much profit is made from "diseased" as from "healthy" labor power. According to SPK Heidelberg: "His [the patient's] illness is taken away from him, is bureaucratically administered and radiologically analyzed, and surgically treated, and translated into capital, into the capital of the construction industry (hospitals, doctor's villas), of the chemical and pharmaceutical industry (test tubes, medicines), of the electrical industry (x-ray and electrocardiac machines, and encephalographs, electroshock apparatuses), of the glass industry (laboratory instruments)."[178]

The profit rate of the "health industry" in the meantime is so high that even other branches of industry are entering into the "business of illness." Thus, for example, the Siemens Company (electrical appliances), of whom it certainly cannot be said that the "nation's health" is its specialty, proclaimed that "Our house thus profits not only from the general growth of our industrial society but just as much from the physical and psychic consequences which this society, if it wishes to continue to grow and exist, happens to demand [. . .] Also, the fact that many of our citizens fear they are becoming incapable of withstanding increasing stress reflects itself in our busy order department. That is why some time ago we entered the business of diagnosis—with a 26 per cent participation we became the main stockholder of the Deutschen Klinik für Diagnostik AG. This first German Mayo Clinic investigates the health and performance primarily of leaders of the economy, of high officials, of solvent and private persons" (Siemens Festschrift).[179]

However, not only industry profits from the utilization of the "diseased commodity" but to an increasing degree the doctors themselves. In *Der Arzt und sein Geld* ("The Doctor and his Money"), Doctor E. Wulff writes about the average income of the settled general practictioner in the Federal Republic: "In 1968 his turnover averaged 123,000 DM of which 30 per cent had to be deducted for business expenses. In 1970, after new arrangements had been reached with the insurance plans which raised the doctors' income by an average of 15 percent, the gross rose to an average of 142,000 DM. If one deducts 30 percent from this sum, one arrives at an average income of 100,000 DM."[180] The increasing interdependence between doctors and entrepreneurs is determined in part by the key position of the pharmaceutical industry, which pays high fees to doctors for prescribing their pharmaceutical products; but the doctors themselves, who look for suitable investment of their astronomical incomes, have in recent times become direct participants in corporations, industrial undertakings, and the like. Their patients become, so to speak, co-entrepreneurs; or at any rate doctors let their customers work twice for them.

The increasing identity of interest between entrepreneurial organizations and professional medical associations also becomes evident from the increase of entrepreneurial and doctors' income on the one hand and the "increase of the degree of illness of the West German worker" on the other: they have been nearly proportional in the last few years. Since 1960 the income of the entrepreneurs rose twice and three times as much as wages, while the income of doctors rose roughly three times as fast as the national income. E. Wulff states: "From 1963 to 1967 the income of doctors rose by roughly 66 per cent. The national income per citizen rose by only 21 per cent."[181] With the increase in profits, there also rose, as can be proved, the number of patients. A further indication of this is provided by the Statistical Yearbook, according to which "the life and, therewith, also the social-security expectancy of men between 60 and 65 has been clearly decreasing since 1950."[182]

The increasing rate of illness of the working population, which is primarily a consequence of the constant intensification of work, guarantees the pharmaceutical and chemical industries, as well as doctors, not only a constantly increasing demand for pharmaceutical preparations and medical services; it also functions at the same time as an increasingly significant shock absorber for the crises of the capitalist economy in general. For a constantly increasing defection from work through illness makes the creation of a potentially revolutionary army of unemployed— in a period of depression—very difficult, if not impossible. The number of work hours lost each year through illness could be easily translated into an unemployment quota which would by far exceed a critical limit. Moreover, in economically critical periods, social-security deductions, which constitute roughly 35 per cent of net wages in the Federal Republic, are made available by the state household as investment assistance to the economy. The social-security deductions therefore serve the state as an "unlimited shock absorber for the prophylaxis of crises."[183]

On the other hand, "shirking work through illness" appears recently to have become a half-official, at any event subversive, form of struggle, or more precisely: the "wildcat strike" of the European and American working class against which not only the "medicine men" of capital but also the capitalists themselves are powerless. Thus a young Italian Fiat worker reports: "And then there was this kind of struggling which wasn't really organized, but—what do I know?—is really spontaneous, yet somewhere deep in the consciousness of the workers: staying away, calling in sick *en masse,* and not going to work. That's pretty rough on Fiat, because Fiat never experienced such a high percentage of illness, not when there wasn't an epidemic which forced workers to stay in bed. In other words: massive shirking of work. Something like that never happened before. Even Agnelli [the boss of Fiat] was forced to admit that 18,000 workers were ill at the same time, and that means: 18,000 workers might be the entire work force of the Alfa Romeo plant which calls in sick. As a consequence the doctors sounded an alarm, and as a reply the figure of 18,000 workers who shirked work quickly rose to 27,000."[184]

II. *PSYCHOSIS—FLIGHT FROM WAGE LABOR*

On the Class Character of Mental Illness

Interpretations and theories of psychoanalysis *not* specific to class or strata "are true only insofar as they reflect the overlapping truth of the commodity-producing society" (R. Reiche[185]). Freud's non-class-oriented psychology of the id and ego is also "true" only in this general sense. It turns false where it is concerned with individuals whose instinctual and character development is mainly determined by their class situation, that is, by their relationship to the means of production. Wilhelm Reich's *Character Analysis,* which quite consistently developed Freud's theory, deriving character symptoms and resistance from fixation on certain psychosexual phases (such as the "anal-compulsive character" or the "phallic-narcissistic character") is also devoid of any class- and strata-specific differentiation.

The same holds true for the psychoanalytic theory of illness. But it is self-evident that the "mental illness" of the *owner* of the means of production has other causes and forms than the mental illness of those who work on these means. In other words, in a class society mental illness, too, has a class character. This is precisely what Ziffel means in Brecht's *Refugee Conversations* when he says, sardonically, to his friend Kalle: "It is of undeniable credit to psychoanalysis to have discovered a soul in the owning class."[186] And when Kalle described to him the "case" of a major industrialist who always felt guilty because "as a child he had had something with his nanny, something very complicated," but had always felt very relieved after psychoanalysis, Ziffel replies suspiciously: "Just between you and me, I don't believe it when a capitalist has a bad conscience in certain plays. In my opinion this can only happen if they've missed ripping someone off somewhere along the line."[187]

More recent research into socialization is providing the materialist fibre for Freud's class- and strata-unspecific theory of character, that is, developing class and strata-specific determinants in the formation of clinical and characterological symptoms. A strata- and class-specific psychology and psychopathology primarily have to represent the dialectic between the social content of (instinctual) desire and the class- and strata-specific forms of its defense. Accordingly, one would have to investigate in each case whether the "main emphasis of the contradiction" within the symptom lies on the side of the "id" or of the "super-ego," on the side of instinctual desire or its defense. This method can also be applied to the Freudian differentiation between neurosis and psychosis.

According to Freud, in neurosis the "id" is in conflict with the "ego," that is, super-ego, which represses the instinctual wish in the name of the frustrating reality. It is characteristic of neurosis that "all our analyses go to show that transference neurosis originates from our ego's refusing to accept a powerful instinctual impulse in the id or to help it find a motor outlet, or from the ego forbidding that impulse the object at which it is aiming. In such a case the ego defends itself against the instinctual impulse by the mechanism of repression. The repressed material struggles against this fate. It creates for itself, along paths over which the ego has no power, a substitutive representation (which forces itself upon the ego by way of a compromise)—the symptom. The ego finds its unity threatened and impaired by this intruder, and it continues to struggle against the symptom, just as it fended off the original instinctual impulse. All this produces the picture of neurosis."[188]

Conversely, in psychosis the ego stands in the service of the id, the instinctual wish; that is, it renounces the frustrating reality so as to replace it with its own delusionary reality. Freud comments: "The ego creates, autocratically, a new external and internal world and there can be no doubt of the fact that this new world is constructed in accordance with the id's wishful impulses, and that the motive of this dissociation from the external world is some very serious frustration by the reality of a wish—a frustration which seems intolerable. The close affinity of this psychosis to normal dreams is unmistakable." The outcome of the psychic conflict depends, according to Freud, "on whether in a conflictual tension of this kind, the ego remains true to its dependence on the external world and attempts to silence the id, or whether it lets itself be overcome by the id and thus torn away from reality (psychosis)."[189]

Thus in the case of neurosis the "main emphasis in the contradiction" between the id and (super-) ego lies on the side of the (super-) ego at whose behest the instinctual wishes are repressed; in psychosis, on the other hand, it lies on the side of the id which renounces the moral demands and norms of the (super-) ego, that is, of reality, so as to create its own delusionary reality. But which side wins the upper hand in the struggle between id and (super-) ego and then determines the symptom picture largely depends on the power relationship of the psychic authorities which, finally, and this Freud no longer reflected upon, express a social and power and class relationship.

In fact Langner and Michael[190] were able to prove that psychotic disturbances and pathological personality characteristics are significantly more frequent among the lower class, but neurotic disturbances on the other hand are significantly more frequent among the middle and upper classes (of American society). Hollingshead's and Redlich's so-called "New Haven Study"[191] also shows that in the bourgeois upper and middle classes neuroses predominate, whereas among the proletarian lower classes psychosis is clearly over-represented. Miller and Swanson trace this phenomenon to the different strata-specific "defense mechanisms of the ego" (Anna Freud). "Rigid educational techniques appear to further a defensive identification and the construction of an externalized super-ego. Subjected to such an education, the child tends to learn defense mechanisms of a renunciatory type. Thus in situations of extreme stress it will seek refuge in psychotic conflict solutions. Conversely, permissive educational practice furthers an anaclitic identification with the caretaker and thus the formation of a relatively well-internalized super-ego. In this case the child tends to learn defense mechanisms of a repressive type. In case of conflict it will tend toward neurosis. If it is true that rigid educational techniques are preferred in the lower classes and permissive techniques among the upper classes, this would provide us with an explanation for the strata-specific kinds of illness to which Hollingshead and Redlich (1958), Myers and Roberts (1959), as well as Sanua (1961) have referred."[192]

Super-ego formation (externalized or internalized), which is decisive for the outcome of the psychic conflict (neurosis or psychosis), thus is largely determined by class- and strata-specific socialization. In the middle class the formation of a "relatively well-internalized super-ego" is supported by strong feelings of social insecurity. M. N. Schönwetter writes: "The insecurity, which has its reason in the father's profession, can make his educational behavior take the form that he perceives his son's sexual strivings in the Oedipal phase as threatening and competitive, and therefore represses them strongly. At the same time he demands of his child that he identify with him, so as to achieve the self-esteem which his professional situation does not provide. This attitude, rejecting as it does sexual demands and simultaneously demanding identification, leads to the development of feelings of animosity on the child's part towards the father, and the child represses these feelings through the erection of a strong super-ego. It appears to make sense that this provides the basis for neurotic tendencies as they can be found more frequently in the middle class than in the working class."[193]

Since social position in the middle-class family is generally based on professional status (especially among officials of some sort, high-level employees, and those with "professions") and not on capital-earning property, this status can be maintained only through similar qualifications among the children. M. N. Schönwetter comments: "At a relatively early age the child is confronted with achievement-related expectations [. . .] The development of self-control as the main problem of education is not [as in the working class—author] defined as following externally determined rules but as the autonomous control of spontaneous emotional reactions and as the autonomous following of internalized expectations relating to behavior. The control of one's own needs in favor of future gratification (instinctual deferral) is forced upon the child on the basis of parental expectations."[194]

Since the middle and lower-middle classes have long since been robbed of their economic self-sufficiency, they seek to maintain their self-confidence by compulsively clinging to the straws of bourgeois ideology concerning achievement and upward mobility. Their anal-retentive behavior compulsion (compulsive control and emotional blockage, and so on) results primarily from the extreme contradiction between their ego and their ego ideal: the more inescapable their *déclassé* position and proletarization, the greater their longing to rise to the status of the property owning bourgeoisie. The psychological ambivalence of the bourgeois middle stratum, which disposes its members to (compulsively) neurotic super-ego formations, therefore results in the final analysis from their ambivalence as a class which neither has control of the means of production nor works with them directly.

But the typically middle-class way of working is also important for the "etiology" of middle-class neurosis. The tendency to social "aphasia" is incomparably greater among the middle-class professions than among proletarians because of the former's mostly individualistic and isolated mode of work. The proletarian participates in "combinative" and "cooperative" work which destroys him physically and mentally, yet offers a certain counterweight to neurotic isolation. There would be no explaining otherwise why significantly higher rates of neurosis can be found especially among middle-class intellectuals (primarily students): the individual ideology of socially upward mobility and the compulsive need to achieve, its generally isolated form of work, and its extremely long dependency on parents and family here produce a comparatively greater disposition for neurosis.

In contrast to the middle-class child, who internalizes the individualistic and achievement-oriented norms and expectations of his parents at an early age, the worker's child is socialized more in the direction of obeying rules and norms that come from the outside, and which prepare it for later work in the factory. M. N. Schönwetter states: "The material and mental stress to which the parents are subjected in their professional and family lives explains why limitations of behavior and disciplinary actions are overemphasized in the educational process. The expectation that outwardly imposed rules are kept is expressed in the high value placed on such qualities as cleanliness, orderliness, and good manners, as well as in an emphasis on obedience which corresponds to the virtues demanded at the place of work, thereby preparing the child at an early age for his future job role."[195]

The proletarian parents impose the same rigid, externally set norms onto their children to which they themselves must submit in the production process. But, in contrast to middle-class families, where "love-oriented" educational practices (that is, punishment by withdrawal of love) predominate, "power-oriented" educational practices predominate in the working-class family (that is, direct physical punishment and chastisement), which reproduces the everyday experience of the parents in the production process. "Permissive" middle-class educational practices indeed appear to be psychologically impossible for the proletarian family, as Hörnle has already pointed out: "But how are the masses of proletarian parents [. . .] going to do without chastising and ordering their children about as long as they are forced to contend with their small apartment, the constant threat of the landlord, nagging neighbors, worrying to death by financial fears, exhausted by their job? [. . .] Even the best-intentioned pedagogical measures founder on the inevitable consequences of the material and spiritual poverty of the proletariat, on its dependency and servitude. A command automatically takes the place of winsome friendliness, nervous quarreling the place of patient leading."[196]

The predominantly "power-oriented" educational practices in the working-class family, and the permanent use of aggression up to and including the use of physical violence, prevent compulsive instinctual control—which is so characteristic of the middle class—that is, the internalization of aggressions. M. N. Schönwetter observes: "The educational practices that predominate among the working class increase the aggressiveness of their children but largely prevent the internalization of parental norms."[197] The absence of guilt feelings, by means of which external punishment is internalized, and the diminished tendency to repress aggression and turn them against oneself, have as a consequence a more externalized form of super-ego formation. This seems to be one of the reasons why (compulsive) neurotic illnesses are relatively less frequent among the working class than in the middle class.

The fact that the super-ego is relatively well internalized in the middle class, however, not only has to do with the specific, that is, "permissive" educational practice but also with the specific ideology of these classes: for they must constantly rationalize their true social status as exploiters, that is, as a parasitical class, and compensate for it morally. The exploiting class always has greater need of "morality" than the exploited class. That is why its "super-ego morality" is better internalized. The super-ego formation in the dominated and exploited classes, on the other hand, resembles an ideological and psychological colonization where the morality of the rulers is assimilated as the ruling morality. But because the proletarian super-ego—as a product of ideological colonization—is largely determined by alien sources, it remains more "external" than the (petit-) bourgeois super-ego.

Finally, the significantly higher rate of neurosis in the middle and upper classes—as paradoxical as this may sound at first—is an expression of a class privilege. For a preoccupation with "interior illness" can be afforded only by a class which lives off the concrete material "externalization" of another class. The working classes, on whose talent, concentration, self-control, persistence, and activity the production and reproduction of social life depends, can much less afford attacks of hysteria, melancholy, breakdowns, and phobias of all kinds. Working and "falling ill" are mutually self-excluding, for to be absent-minded, hysterical, melancholy, paranoid, phobic, and the like means not to be able to guarantee the reproduction of one's own labor power. In concrete terms this means that one loses one's job, that one is out on the street, slips down to the level of the lumpen proletariat. Although, as has been shown, mental illness and disturbances are also increasing significantly among the working population of the capitalist world, yet the workers as long as they are part of the work process can far less afford to manifest psychoneurosis because the social consequences are much graver for them than for the middle and upper classes. As a consequence, sensitivity to illness lessens significantly among the lower classes, as Koos was able to prove in his "Investigations of Differentiated Sensitivity to Somatic Illness."[198]

Koos confronted his test people with a selected list of easily recognizable symptoms such as headaches, backaches, chronic tiredness, coughing, lack of appetite, and so forth, asking them whether any of the listed symptoms were considered significant and should be called to the doctor's attention. "The test persons were divided into three groups. Group I: upper class; group II: middle class; group III: lower class. The result: members of the first group uniformly affirmed the significance of the symptoms; members of the second group in general showed a lower sensitivity; but in contrast, group III demonstrated a marked indifference to most symptoms."[199]

A community nurse, who had very precise knowledge of the town where the investigation was conducted, gave the following explanation for the low sensitivity of group III: "That is pretty much what I would have expected. The poor people in our area don't know much about illness [. . .] Why should they worry about backaches, tiredness, and stiffness? My God, poor people always have them, they are poorly fed, poorly cared for after birth, with too much work. I would have been surprised if they had said anything different."[200] One person explained the low sensitivity of the lower classes this way: "How do I know how much something is going to cost if something is wrong with me? When I start treatment I'll probably lose my job and my family won't have anything to live on."[201]

The significant decrease in sensitivity to somatic illnesses which Koos found in the lower classes can be easily transposed to mental, psychoneurotic, and psychosomatic illnesses. This becomes evident from the comments of the test persons that the lower classes do not consider mental and somatic illnesses as "psychic ailments," but at most as feeling done in, as defective labor power which can no longer achieve its own reproduction. K. Hartung and R. Wolff write: "The one who is done in cannot count on increased interest in his person, but rather must fear that his reproduction possibilities are threatened [. . .] For the lower classes there exist no psychic illnesses up to a certain degree, but only demoralization, alcoholism, or feeling upset, rotten, or over-irritated, simply because there is no money to transform it into a purely mental illness and to reproduce oneself at one and the same time. A 'turning' into 'psychosis' seems to be less a mental illness than an escape into the hospital."[202]

There are also frequent psychic breakdowns in the lower classes when the contradiction between true socialization and living conditions and the actual standard, which is middle-class oriented, has become too great. Thus H. Berndt in her essay "On the Sociogenesis of Psychiatric Illness" reaches the conclusion that the "members of the [American] lower classes in their striving must assume the values of the middle class, so as to be socially and economically successful. But the norms and the educational system of the lower class, on the basis of which the adjustment has to be made, is inferior to the corresponding middle-class system. Psychotic breakdowns follow with much greater frequency in the pursuit of this [middle class] objective because the members of the lower class have not yet been sufficiently educated (socialized) for middle-class norms and, therefore, have to adjust compulsively to norms which do not do justice to their living conditions."[203]

The predominance of a psychotic type of conflict solution in the lower classes cannot therefore be solely explained—as do Swanson, Miller, Gottschalch, M. N. Schönwetter, *et al.*—with customary rigid educational techniques and the resultant externalized form of super-ego formation. New, more progressive research into socialization runs the danger of regarding flight into psychosis solely as a problem specifically related to the socialization of one class. The decisive question is why the psychotic regresses so far that a social way out of his regression seems scarcely possible any more. For in contrast to the neurotic who usually regresses to the phallic, anal, or more rarely to the oral stage of his instinctual development, the psychotic regresses to the very earliest phase of his childhood development, which psychoanalysis designates as oral, narcissistic, and autistic. If one starts out from Foucault's "cycle of pathological disintegration," then psychosis and schizophrenia are almost at the end of this cycle, that is, the water mark of psychic regression is there at its lowest. Of course, structural psychoanalysis does not provide us with any information about what specific social causes and conditions provoke this deepest level of regression. If, according to Foucault, regression "is an individual's answer to a present situation," then one can assume that the "degree of psychological disintegration," that is, the deepest level of regression, is also a measure of the social situation of the ill individual. The proletarian psychotic regresses farther than the middle-class neurotic because social reality is much more oppressive for him, that is, the degree of instinctual renunciation is much greater and, therefore, the "loss of reality" is also much greater for him than for the middle-class neurotic. Whereas the latter can go on living relatively undisturbed and continue to work with his stomach ulcer and paranoia, the former is usually totally incapable of acting and working; that is, he immediately lands in the "booby hatch." A member of the lower class has *really* to break down before the state will care for him; he cannot afford the "luxury" of a neurosis because otherwise no one takes care of him and his family. He has to "flip out" completely if he wants the health insurance to do something for him.

The extremely low water mark of regression in the (proletarian) psychotic therefore cannot be solely explained with his specific social condition but only within the totality of his proletarian living conditions. The proletarian psychotic regresses to such an extreme degree because "the way forward" is completely blocked off for him. The degree of his regression is the degree of his impotence and simultaneously a measure of his (unconscious) psychic resistance to his real living conditions. He mistakes his ego with the outer world and the outer world with his ego (like an infant who cannot yet distinguish between his mother's breast and himself) so as to fend off his fear of it. And for this, in fact, he has every reason: for the "external world" produced by him and his kind really confronts him not only in his imagination but also in reality as an "alien power," as "alien working conditions," as capital that dominates him, as a state that controls him. (See also p. 206.) He has to develop extreme defense mechanisms so as to protect himself from this now autonomous social power that is totally removed from his control and influence. His extreme defense mechanisms, like paranoia, contain such an excessive "rationality" that society has to call it "mad." He becomes paranoiac because he sees the spectres that *really* sit at the back of his neck and the neck of his kind magnified a hundredfold. His "negativism"—as psychoanalysis says—which expresses itself in a total "rejection" of positive expressions of feeling and transference (which is why psychoanalysis has condemned him as "unanalyzable"), can be understood as the patient's adequate reply to the objective disinterest and the animosity of society towards him. Basically, psychoanalysis has known this a long time. Nearly every general representation of schizophrenia contains hints along this line: "One should not forget that one must assume that the possible reason for the autistic withdrawal of many schizophrenics from the world are well-founded fears and disappointments in their early life. With this as the background, the fear of animosity and of being left alone by other people, together with a fear of the individual's own immensely dammed-up agressions, often produces the effect of incredible hypersensitivity, or clairvoyance for the inimical feelings in the environment (Stierling)." (Hartung and Wolff[204]).

The proletarian psychotic really switches on the invisible electric wire with which society, that is, the upper classes, have always fenced themselves off from him and his kind: this is the whole "secret" of his "negativism," which has been so much implored. Since he is the only one who lacks the possibility "of singing the melody of these petrified conditions" (Marx),[205] he himself becomes petrified: he flees into "catatonia," into total rigidity, so as not to become a "psychopathic criminal" or psychopathic revolutionary. Because he cannot really break through the surrounding social barriers, he seeks to break through them in his imagination. Of this Freud appears to have had a presentiment when he wrote: "It can hardly be doubted that the world of phantasy plays the same part in psychosis and that there, too, it is the storehouse from which the materials or the pattern for building the new reality are derived."[206]

Looked at in this way, it is not at all surprising and requires no major "scientific" explanation why the rate of psychosis is significantly higher among the lower classes than among the middle or upper classes: since the proletariat more than anyone else has to suffer under capitalist reality, it has *objectively* (even if not always subjectively) the greatest interest in its renewal. But as long—as a consequence of its political and organizational weaknesses—it cannot really change social reality, the isolated proletarian instead will change his concept of reality, that is, create a delusionary picture of the world.

Schizophrenia as Viewed by Classical and Modern Psychoanalysis

The connection between the proletarian class structure and the solution to psychotic conflict is to be more clearly demonstrated with the example of schizophrenia and of drug psychosis which to an increasing degree today determine the clinical picture of late capitalism.

The development of research into schizophrenia, however, has assumed such proportions in recent years that it cannot be completely covered within the framework of this book. As far as we know, the best representation and critique of classical and modern research of this type is to be found in *Kursbuch 28* ("Das Elend mit der Psyche" I, Psychiatrie) by Klaus Hartung and Renate Wolff, on whom we draw in the following.

Classical repressive psychiatry has undergone radical criticism in recent years by progressive psychoanalysts such as Laing and Cooper in England, Basaglia in Italy, Lacan and Polack in France (to name only the best known). Classical psychoanalysis considers the psychotic incurable from the onset; correspondingly, it only allowed itself a single task, which was to put the label "crazy," "psychopathic," "mentally ill," or the like on the psychotic's unconscious rebellion against unbearable living conditions, so as to keep him—within the condition of total disenfranchisement —in "total institutions" (Basaglia) called mental institutions, Hartung and Wolff write: "Who is mentally ill has always been determined by others [. . .] The mentally ill were an example by which society demonstrated the governability of the rebellious unconscious."[207] The history of psychoanalysis is "one of the methods by which society made psychic resistance to dominant living conditions disappear by making psychotics disappear."[208]

According to Laing, there is no such condition as schizophrenia; rather, this is merely a label for a defense mechanism that psychoanalysis as the governor of official health creates. Hartung and Wolff comment: "What others have perpetrated on the schizophrenic is subsumed under the nature of schizophrenia [. . .] The only interesting aspect of every designation of schizophrenia is the other's behavior towards the schizophrenic, which is supposed to be fixed by this definition.[209] [. . .] We have no language for what the schizophrenic wants. Nor is it allowed to be articulated."[210]

The psychotic was always considered a danger by society because, in contrast to the neurotic whose drives are shackled by a strongly internalized and rigid super-ego, the psychotic tends to impulsive outbreaks and actions in which his rebellious unconscious manifests itself. Unlike the usually shy and inhibited neurotic, the psychotic is unable to count on society's help because his "delusion," his "being possessed," is perceived as a profound threat by society. Moser writes: "For the psychopath is [. . .] the exemplary criminal inasmuch as it is a question of theft, robbery, aggression, instinctuality, ruthlessness, uninhibitedness, and so forth. He embodies the negative picture of the conforming, well-adjusted human individual [. . .] Many actions performed by psychopaths constitute something like the essence of criminality in the usual sense, of unfettered, insurgent, provocative audacity and insurrection."[211]

In the person of the psychopath society always persecuted the distorted, unconscious, and anarchic picture of the revolutionary, just as— vice versa—it identifies the revolutionary with "psychopaths" and "madmen." That is why the psychopath must first of all be "bound," put in chains, shackled, beaten, tortured, and put into a "total institution."

To this day society treats the psychopath as though it had to exorcise the devil. It defends against the radicalness of his psychic resistance, of his "symptom," with correspondingly radical means. Hartung and Wolff comment: "Society reacted that much more radically to madmen since it probably always perceived that madness contained something radical [. . .] The question that Laing poses is one that could probably have been raised at all times: who is more dangerous to humanity, the psychotic who believes the bomb is inside him or the bomber pilot?"[212]

The "circle of illness" then came to a close in the "total institution." By becoming the complete object of an institutional hierarchy the "patient" in the institution reproduces a hundredfold what happened to make him "ill" and "mad" in the first place. His most virulent symptoms are usually disguised and unconscious attempts to rebel against a social condition (within as well as outside the "total institution") in which he is totally determined by alien forces. Progressive psychiatry has formulated the concept of "institutional artifact" for this syndrome, which means that certain always recurring typical symptoms and chronic manifestations of an illness—for example, catatonic "rigidity" which the old custodial psychiatry regarded as "inherited," as quasi-natural events— in reality are products of the institutional situation. Hartung and Wolff write: "One discovers that the 'clinical cases' are cases of the particular clinic."[213] Newer, progressive (especially Anglo-Saxon) research into schizophrenia in the meantime has refuted the classical conception of "inherited mental illness" through a genetic-psychoanalytic interpretation. It has been able to show that schizophrenic symptoms are the result of certain family constellations to which the child is exposed during primary socialization. Particularly are so-called "double-bind" situations regarded as specific for the schizophrenogene family, which means contradictions between the content of the signals of different levels of communication, such as between words and wordless behavior. A "double-bind" situation exists, for example, when a verbal demand the mother makes of her child is confronted by a simultaneous prohibition on the (gestic or mimic) level of expression to fulfill that demand. The child, which does not know whether it should or should not approach the mother, enters a "schizophrenic" situation which it cannot assimilate. Such "double-bind" situations usually result from deep-reaching disturbances of the parental relationship, primarily when the mother herself has ambivalent (half-tender, half-inimical) feelings towards her child or when the positive affect of the mother is negated by rejection or inimical behavior by the father. The constant up and down of the emotional climate of the parents creates in the child's memory contradictory conceptions. Since the parental authorities are themselves contradictory, saying simultaneously yes and no, as it were, the child cannot identify itself with them; the parents, rather, are "introjected," that is, both sides are absorbed into the ego without being assimilated, which produces a complete loss of orientation in the child. By later "transferring" such ambivalent parental introjection onto persons, authorities, and institutions, the child constantly reproduces the "schizophrenogene" family constellation outside the family. Since it was unable to create a positive object relationship, that is, identification, in any phase of its psychosexual development, it falls back into the earliest phases of its development: it becomes "autistic."

Typical for the "schizophrenogene" family is its character as "pseudo-community," that is, as "torture society." In such a family no one speaks as he really thinks and no one acts as he really wants to. All conflicts are disguised, that is, carried out at the cost of the "weakest" family member. He or she becomes the black sheep of the family onto whom the other family members, that is, the parents, project their own unacknowledged aggressions, that is, unresolved problems. The usually concealed conflict between parents is carried out in the psyche of the child: this psyche is "split." The inability to become unhappy with one another creates the need to make a defenseless victim "go crazy." According to Hartung and Wolff: "In this sense the schizophrenic child is the symptom of, that is to say, the reason for an irrational situation. Schizophrenia tells the truth about the family, from which the family still manages to escape because schizophrenia is an illness.[214] [. . .] The difference between the schizophrenic and the normal person consists in the schizophrenic no longer being able to bear the family. During an attempt to retrace a schizophrenic process, the authors described the destructive quality of normal socialization."[215]

The child which has been made "crazy" in this way attempts to break out of its schizophrenic situation by randomly applying violence to the parents, to all authorities, the caretakers, the doctors, and its whole environment onto which it projects its inimical relationship to its primary referent persons. This anarchic, violent attempt at liberation keeps recurring as "schizophrenic thrust." Cooper writes: "In such a case the only possible condition remains the arbitrary, sudden, irrational, aggressive self-activation by the child. This child, which may be 20, 30, 40, or 50 years old, becomes aggressive towards its mother, because this remains its sole means of tearing itself away from her."[216] The "schizophrenic thrust" is usually followed by a long phase of "catatonic rigidity." This expresses the collapse of the attempted rebellion and the simultaneous turning inward of the aggression. Catatonia is nothing but total resignation in the face of repeated failure in the attempt to rebel against the interiorized family power relationship. Catatonic rigidity and schizophrenic thrust are both radical "self-protective mechanisms" against the unbearable living conditions within and outside the family. Laing states: "In our opinion, experience and behavior, if they are regarded as schizophrenic, without exception represent a special strategy which someone invents to make an unbearable situation bearable."[217]

This genetic-psychoanalytic interpretation of schizophrenia as the product of disturbances in primary socialization, which again are expression of disturbances in interfamilial relationships, represents a great step forward with regard to the traditional psychoanalytic conception of schizophrenia as an "inherited" mental illness. Yet the psychoanalytical contribution to the elucidation of schizophrenia necessarily remains as limited as the psychoanalytical method itself. Even the progressive, psychoanalytically oriented psychology of Laing, Cooper, and others conceals the superimposed social causes of schizophrenia, by viewing the family—as Freud did—as an isolated social system, as an extra-territorial realm whose entanglement with the socio-economic system is neglected. It has not yet, in other words, analyzed familial structures with regard to relationships which result from the processes of production and the social structures of power.

According to G. Vinnai, "double-bind" situations which are characteristic for the "schizophrenogene" family can be traced to the contradictions of capitalist society itself. Here are his most important theses: "First of all, what psychopathology classifies as schizophrenia [identity diffusion, serious contact disturbances, ambivalence in emotional attitudes, blockage of thought processes, stereotyped behavior patterns, destruction of space-time experience, and the like—author] represent an extreme variation of injured identity which can be found in all members of capitalist society. Secondly, serious identity disturbances in our society can be found particularly among members of the working class. According to our investigations, the rate of schizophrenia is highest among the lowest factions of the working class [. . .] Thirdly, 'double-bind' situations should be interpreted together with the contradiction between productive powers and production relationships. Institutionalized social compulsions, which are a given with the condition of capitalism, make it by and large impossible for the workers to follow maxims of collective solidarity which would be appropriate to their objective interests; at the same time the situation with regard to how their interests are realized makes it impossible for them to orient themselves according to bourgeois-individualistic maxims which contain a constant prohibition against solidarity [. . .] Fourthly, the pathogenetic dimensions of primary socialization have their analogies in the realm of educational socialization [. . .] The workingclass child experiences the discrepancy between the norms of the working class and bourgeois norms, which are institutionalized in school, as 'double-bind' situations which it cannot interpret and which it cannot escape [. . .] Fifthly, 'double-bind' constellations in the socialization process are followed by the identity-destroying contradiction between the demands of collective work achievements, which correspond to the rationality of the productive powers, and the simultaneous demands of factory organization which conforms to the interests of capital and destroys solidarity; a contradiction which the isolated worker, who is not organized to fight, cannot overcome rationally. The pseudo-community of the family is the preliminary stage of the 'factory family' with its social-partnership ideology which camouflages the antagonism between the interests of the owners of the means of production and the workers [. . .]."[218]

Regarded in this way, the schizophrenic "double-bind" situation is an extreme individual expression of corresponding social "double-bind" constellations, that is, a disguised class contradiction to which proletarian children and parents are particularly exposed at school, training, and work. "Schizophrenogene" consciousness is nothing else but destroyed, or impeded, class consciousness.

According to J. Roth's estimate, roughly 600,000 people suffer from "schizophrenia" in the Federal Republic at present, the overwhelming majority of them coming from the proletarian lower classes. Disregarding the fact that a schizophrenic from the lower class has far fewer opportunities to be properly treated than a schizophrenic from the middle class, it is nevertheless true that the rate of recidivism among proletarian schizophrenia is much higher as well. Between 1951 and 1961 the recidivism rate in Rhenish state hospitals increased by 315 per cent. "Although two-thirds of them no longer showed any productive symptoms upon release, the results of subsequent checkups after one year were not encouraging: 41 per cent had to be readmitted because of a social crisis in connection with delusionary symptoms."[219]

To grasp the connection between "delusionary symptoms" and "social crisis," that is, social situation, is the concern of a further sociologically oriented direction within new, progressive research on schizophrenia. This direction, in contrast with psychoanalytically oriented research, focusses its main attention on those "pathogenetic social factors" which correlate significantly with an increase of schizophrenia. Thus Faris and Dunham[220] discovered through their investigations in major American cities a higher percentage of schizophrenia in sections of cities which manifested a high degree of "social disorganization." As criteria for the construct of "social disorganization" Faris and Dunham used the prevalence of one-family houses, whether owned or rented, a larger percentage of foreign-born Americans, a higher child-mortality rate, and so forth, which led them to the conclusion that the outbreak of schizophrenia is facilitated in areas where the inhabitants are exposed to a high degree of "social isolation." Leighton and others[221] showed that a lower level of educational and professional training is connected with a higher incidence of psychotic disturbances. Professor Häfner[222] was able to show in similar studies in the Federal Republic that a significant increase of psychic illness, primarily of psychosis, appears in parts of cities where the living standards are the lowest.

Even though most of these investigations agree that a significantly higher rate of psychosis among the lower classes is an immediate expression of their underprivileged status, they nonetheless "use as the basis for their evaluation a middle-class standard [. . .] If it is noted that a high degree of psychotic illness depends on the 'stability of an area,' and if stability is defined as a decreasing child-mortality rate, a higher degree of education, the ownership of a house, this means first of all that the lower class lives somewhere else or has been successfully evicted from the area. Such a concept serves credit investigators, policemen, and personnel departments" (Hartung and Wolff[223]).

Like psychoanalytically oriented "double-bind" research, sociological efforts to isolate the "pathogenetic social factors'" of schizophrenia represent definite progress with regard to the classic psychoanalytical description of it as "incurable mental illness." Yet socially enlightened research on schizophrenia too, by and large, accommodates the interests of an enlightened capitalism which is increasingly concerned with the reintegration of labor power from the lower class which is threatened by mental disintegration in the production process. Recent greater public interest in schizophrenia, in the form of public investment and reformistic re-socialization programs, derives less from strictly humanitarian impulses than from capital's concern that it is losing large segments of the working class, especially among its cheapest labor power, through an escape into psychosis. Public investments in the prophylactic fight against "pathogenetic social factors"—as in increased public-health services, the elimination of "social isolation" through better working opportunities within each district, the construction of "community centers," youth and sport clubs, and the like—as well as reform programs (particularly in Holland and Great Britain) for the re-socialization of schizophrenics: work therapy, group therapy, family therapy, the concept of the "therapeutic community," which envisions a democratization and liberalization of the institutional hierarchy—all of this has merely the function of attenuating the effect of "pathogenetic social factors." However, all these attempts are unable to eliminate the "pathogenic" class situation (especially "pathogenetic" capitalist working conditions) of those who seek to escape it through a flight into psychosis.

The "Clinical" Industry and the "Industrial" Clinic

It becomes evident from recent, sociologically oriented research into schizophrenia that the unskilled worker is statistically most likely to become a schizophrenic case; the worker who usually lives in a slum in a city or in a miserable apartment complex. Such research, however, generally looks for the "pathogenetic factors" only in the sphere of reproduction, in the living or family situation; the production sphere, that is, capitalist working conditions, is left unconsidered with noticeably unanimous consistency by the researchers.

One look at the psychoanalytical diagnosis of schizophrenia, however, suffices to make one realize the determining influence of capitalist working conditions on, as it is so nicely called, the "schizophrenic syndrome." For example, one of the standard psychoanalytical determinations of schizophrenia reads like this: "Schizophrenia simplex one usually calls cases which verge on being defective but lack an impressive spectrum of psychopathological manifestations, a bland gradual depletion of verve, initiative, and adjustment to life and its tasks. Frequently the patients are morose, lacking in affect, depressively moody, not infrequently hypochondriacs or temporarily marked by co-anesthetic complaints, sometimes they show fleeting signs of paranoiac relationships with various individuals, mistrust, and hypersensitivity without productively closed delusion."[224] According to Hartung and Wolff, this psychiatric description of schizophrenia is nothing but "an exact duplicate of the life situation of a worker after twenty years at the assembly line."[225] The "bland, gradual depletion of verve, initiative," was what Marx described in connection with the capitalist organization of work: "[. . .] Constant labor of one uniform kind disturbs the intensity and flow of a man's animal spirits, which find recreation and delight in mere change of activity."[226] As long as workers in such a situation are still in a position to describe their mental state themselves they have no need of a psychiatrist; for they know better than he why they go "crazy." For example, regarding the auto workers in Detroit: "They say: 'this here is prison. You can't imagine it.' They say: 'It's worse here than in prison. In prison at least there are moments when you can rest [. . .]' They say: 'I have to fit seven bolts, eight hours a day always the same bolts. I am twenty-six. When I die I will be mad" (quoted from A. Gorz[227]).

In any event, "communicatory disturbances" diagnosed and labelled as "schizophrenic," which —as in catatonic schizophrenia—can go so far as a complete disruption of contact, cannot be exclusively explained by "social isolation" within the sphere of reproduction, the living and family situation, as most American and British investigators tend to do. These disturbances are chiefly the consequence of increasing "social isolation" within the sphere of production itself which is what first produces the "social isolation" within the living and family situation. The increasing lack of communication in a para-militarily organized and psychologically sealed-off work process, where every human contact during work tendentiously leads to a decrease of output and is made notoriously difficult by watchdog supervisors, is to be made co-responsible for the rapid increase of schizophrenic communicatory disturbances within the last few years. According to Rabehl and Heilmann: "The utilization process under monopoly-capitalist conditions enforced a renewed atomization of the working class especially within and by means of the character of the labor process. The struggle of the workers increasingly forces capital to halt the decrease of the profit rate by shortening the work day, increasing relative surplus value, or in other words by intensifying work. For the working class this means the danger of renewed atomization, a division of the workers from each other during the work process by means of cleverly designed control systems evaluating work site, wage groups, piece work, and so on, with all sorts of fateful effects on the solidarity and class consciousness of the proletariat."[228]

If "renewed atomization," this social isolation through and during the work process (such as, for example, individual piece work where it is particularly strong), is doubled by a corresponding psychological isolation at home; and if work stress in the factory is made twice as great by work stress in the family, then a schizophrenic breakdown cannot be far off. In such a case the diagnosis "lack of incentive, inhibited modulation, lacking in affect"—these being labels for schizophrenia—actually only signify the normal case, the normal proletarian state of affairs: "A twenty-six-year-old mother became schizophrenic when she was pregnant with her fifth child and when her husband, on whom she was extremely dependent, remained away from home day and night, staying at the shop, and paying no further attention to her. The patient said: 'I was ill the first time when I noticed that I was in my fourth month and with my fifth child. I was very worried, because at that time the work also became too much for me. Look, besides the four children and the housework I also have to renovate the house, inside and out. I was very ambitious. But I had to do everything myself. So that when I noticed that I was pregnant I thought I couldn't bear the responsibility anymore. That happened six months after my husband opened his own shop. He became extremely busy. He had to leave the house at four in the morning and didn't finish work until 9 or 10 in the evening. We hardly speak to each other anymore. That was too much for me. I had to leave the house or go somewhere I didn't have so much responsibility anymore. But my husband wouldn't have agreed to that.' "[229]

This "case," representative of a hundred thousand just like it, demonstrates that "schizophrenic reaction"—as repressive psychoanalysis labels it—means nothing but the refusal to go on, to continue to vegetate under inhuman living and working conditions. And in fact the dominant psychoanalysis has no other criteria for mental "health" than the capacity to work. Leavy and Freedman state: "Psychoanalysis understands work as an indicator of health."[230] And "a human being who is not working is either regarded as ill or as morally reprehensible."[231] Dominant repressive psychoanalysis labels as "ill," "psychopathic," or "mad" everyone who tries to withdraw consciously or unconsciously from the "madness" of the machinery of capitalist utilization. It understands the "inability to sell labor power as illness. But what does 'incapacity to work' mean? [. . .] Evidently labor power which is becoming rebellious [. . .] We maintain that every psychoanalytical diagnosis tracks down and punishes a refusal [. . .] to go along, to keep selling labor power. Taking the side of the health of the patient is taking the side of the interest of capital" (Hartung and Wolff[232]).

Wage earners generally have internalized this capitalist ideology of "health" = capacity-to-work to such a degree that they themselves consider themselves "ill" when they are not working, although it is the capitalist organization of work which makes them ill. According to Leavy and Freedman: "Our patients' complaint that their self-confidence is depressed is far more frequent when their symptoms prevent them from going to work. In a society where everyone works, not working suffices to produce feelings of guilt and depression."[233] What stands behind the feeling of "guilt and depression" is the quite justifiable fear of being fired for being "ill" after a long absence from one's job. For it is pretty usual entrepreneurial practice during crises or recessions to let those workers go first who have most frequently called in "ill." For wage earners being "ill" is the only opportunity he or she has temporarily to withdraw from wage labor, that is, from the exploitation of his or her labor power. Conversely anyone who does not go along, that is, who does not let himself or herself be exploited, is regarded as "ill" in the sense of "crazy." If psychosis, "schizophrenia"—from the wage earner's viewpoint—is nothing but the unconscious refusal to go on, to keep selling himself as labor power, then conversely—from the viewpoint of capital, of utilization—it is a "scientific" synonym, a "label" for defective, unprofitable labor power which is becoming rebellious.

The modern "social-psychiatric" concept of "health" has the capitalist concept of work capacity = exploitability just as much as its basis as did classic repressive psychoanalysis. Although modern social psychoanalysis—in contrast to the old custodial psychoanalysis which lacked any conception of psychotherapy—also seeks to introduce the relationship of patient to environment in psychiatric diagnosis and therapy; and although it has subjected classical psychiatry to a sharp critique in this respect— for the latter's principle of releasing the patient unprepared led to so-called "revolving-door" psychiatry; those who had been discharged had to be re-admitted after several months or years—nevertheless its own concept of "social" rehabilitation is basically only a therapeutically prettified partaking of the interests of capital.

The most essential implement of such "rehabilitation" is so-called "work therapy," which means nothing but enabling the "ill" worker to sell his labor power again. The clinics therefore draw up contracts with individual firms which in this way acquire extremely cheap labor power. In Frankfurt, for example, patients are folding prospectuses for Delacroix and Nestlé; their monthly wage averages between 15 and 20 DM. In Königslutter patients are tying hairnets for Solida. Their monthly wage is 35 DM. In Warstein curtain rings are produced for the Mescheder firm of Nölle: the monthly wage averages between 50 and 60 DM. [234] These examples could easily be multiplied.

Re-socialization through work thus is a useful method for bringing cheap labor power onto the market and helping industry achieve maximum profits. As long as mental illness is suffered and feared primarily as the inability to work in a society which measures health exclusively in terms of the individual's capacity to work = exploitability, work therapy might make some sense; that is, it might prevent the total exclusion of the patient through his inability to work. As long as the self-esteem and identity of the wage earner are alone assured by the price of his labor power and the quality of his work, they might protect him against a total loss of identity. Yet the work therapy which has recently been practiced under the cover of reform protects the ill person neither from inhuman and nor from alienated working conditions, nor does it assure that they can qualify their labor power. J. Roth writes: "Work therapy as the most essential therapeutic instrument of established modernistically adorned repressive psychiatry pursues the sole objective of repairing the person who became ill because of production conditions and its conflicts, so that (a) the patient can be used smoothly and efficiently in the production process, and (b) the patient can give himself up as an involuntary object to order and regulations. Those who leave the institutions are work objects fixated on authority, are willing and adjusted, and have learned skills which serve the sole purpose of the state apparatus and of industry." [235]

Group dynamics are playing an increasingly greater role in the "rehabilitation" of defective labor power. Psychiatric institutes in Sweden in the fifties worked out new group-dynamic methods for the integration of institutionalized patients which had the effect of "refocussing the protest against hospitals and society, with the help of conservative individual psychology, into a protest against the patient's own illness." [236] In fall 1969 a large insurance firm began to implement these findings for factory purposes with a "mental-health campaign." Financed by the Swedish employer's association, this campaign in the meantime has 300 psychologists, sociologists, and psychotherapists working for it, who describe their objective in this way: "The goal of rehabilitation is, if possible, to get the patient to return to this place of work. But one can succeed in this effort only if it is supported by a prognosis. Otherwise one runs the danger of disappointing or antagonizing the worker with frequent failures."[237] It is clear who sets the tone of this "mental-health campaign." "As a result of this effort, factory management expects as fast and vigorous an increase in production as possible from psychotherapists."[238]

Industry has always enjoyed an excellent relationship with psychiatry, especially since the latter provided it with labor power at cut-rate prices which capital, moreover, could chalk up as a "therapeutic charitable act." The history of industry provides sufficient examples of the fact that institutionalized patients have for a long time been regarded as a secret "industrial reserve army." Karl Marx has described how the personnel of British insane asylums, no matter how "mad," were employed during the expansionist phase of British industry, except that at that time there was no talk of work therapy. It was a question of blatant maximum exploitation of the cheapest labor power. The recruiting of "madmen" for industrial production thus is by no means an invention of Nazi ideology. It results necessarily from the utilization laws and utilization problems of capital, that is, it is immanent to the capitalist economy itself.

When and how someone is "ill" or "mad," that is, incapable of assuring the reproduction of his labor power, has never been a question of ideology but always one of economics. When capitalist economy demanded it, ideology was given a 180-degree turn. Of this Nazi psychiatry provides the best proof. "During the Nazi era ill persons [. . .] in the university clinic, right here in Heidelberg, were psychiatrically and surgically checked (owing to the 'freedom of science') as to whether they should continue to be treated in the gas chambers that had been specially constructed for them, or whether they should 'only' be sterilized—all of this, as we know, to maintain the purity of the race. The owners of the large concerns were satisfied by this argument as becomes evident from the fact that the means necessary for the gas chambers and the 'freedom of science' were forthcoming. Regardless of this, gas chambers are of course much more economical: short-term boarding costs from the point of arrival until the time of murder. You can tear down the insane asylums, all you need for Germany are a few gas chambers. However, towards the end of the war there was a complete turnabout. Production in the armaments plants suffered from numerous insufficiencies. Despite the lynch justice of factory enforcers, the ambition of the prisoners of war began to wane, and their readiness to perform 'violent' acts in the form of sabotage, pilfering of food, and the like was increasing. At that point Heidelberg Professor Carl Schneider [. . .] sent the following urgent message to the *Führer's* headquarters: a large percentage of patients in the institutions were eager to work, capable of working, not at all violent, and politically reliable. Therefore, it was of inestimable importance for the accelerated drive for final victory to use these patients instead of p.o.w.'s in armament production."[239] In the final phase of fascist rule an unreliable, rebellious labor force, the p.o.w.'s, were to be replaced by reliable labor power, the "madmen" and the "ill." Industry, especially the armaments industry, had entered a crisis and had an acute shortage of exploitable human material.

That is how the circle connecting "modern" psychiatry and "modern" industry closes: the former provides the latter with psychiatric "cases" by ruining the mental health and therewith the labor power of the workers; the former rebuilds the defective labor power, under the label "work therapy," so that it can be sold back to industry at a cut-rate price. While the "clinical" spirit has always been at home in the capitalist factory (as Marx showed when he compared the "workhouse" with the "madhouse"), conversely the spirit of industry is now invading the clinics. Thus a doctor of the state hospital in Königslutter makes the following summary: "We have to make our patients fit for the assembly line." And the Süchteln therapeutician Bruno Blombeck, who drills recuperating patients in four- to six-week courses on the work bench, says quite openly: "We instill work discipline and time discipline."[240]

Indeed, the house rules, say, of the Rhenish day-clinic Rheydt do not differ essentially from the house rules of the Siemens firm. Both function according to the same wage-punishment system. The day-clinic punishes: "Intentional slowdowns, subversion of work morality, negligence of bodily care, bad table manners, smoking at other than designated times [. . .]."[241] In the apprentice workshops of the Siemens firm the following rules obtain: "Cleanliness, no talking, sitting, or leaning while working, proper requests for permissions to go to the toilet, no reading of newspapers even during pauses, smoking prohibited also for those over sixteen, and in part also within a two-kilometer radius of the factory; no inappropriate modish dress or abnormal length of hair; and so on."[242]

So the "healthy" and the "ill" worker share the condition of (wage) dependency and disenfranchisement, which differ only in degree—the "healthy" worker, say, still has a union that supports him, the "ill" worker who has been admitted into an institution does not. Both share the social conditions under which they "work," that is, become ill and become healthy, that is, must become capable of working again, as determined by alien forces. Such determination by alien forces, however, is the cause and nature of all mental illness in capitalism, be it the temporary alcoholism of the "normal" worker, be it the chronic alcoholism of his colleague at the withdrawal station, be it the latent schizophrenia of the "healthy" piece worker or the manifest schizophrenia of his fellow worker in the institution.

The "industrial" clinic and "clinical" industry are historical twins of the capitalist mode of production. That is why one cannot be fought without the other. The most striking and successful example of such a fight is described in Franco Basaglia's book *The Total Institution.*[243] In 1961 a doctors' collective began a seven-year process of transforming an

institution in Gorizia (Italy) which until then had been led along traditional lines. Basaglia and his collective started with the position that "the
'mentally ill' person was primarily 'ill' because he was excluded, had
been left in the lurch by everyone, a human being without rights with
whom one could do as one pleased."[244] The *therapy* was that the doctors,
the caretaker personnel, and the patients *together* organized the fight
against the "total institution": they eliminated the clinical hierarchy,
doctors and caretakers no longer considered themselves jailers of the
patients; the patients themselves decided about the kind and duration of
their treatment; they received appropriate work and education inside the
clinic and could participate in all cultural events (film, theater, music,
dance) that interested them. The "therapeutic" success was very impressive: patients who had long since been given up as "hopeless cases" by
classical psychiatry began to revive in the same degree as they felt treated
as human beings.

Here is an excerpt from an interview with a "chronically ill patient."
"QUESTION: All the doors are open today. Can you move about as you
please? MARGHERITA: Yes, today. But it wasn't always like that, there
was a time when we weren't allowed to. QUESTION: Were you tied down?
MARGHERITA: With the straightjacket. Later on they also tied our feet
together. QUESTION: Why? MARGHERITA: Because I leapt about, flailed
about, I behaved like the devil. I simply liked doing that and they thought
I was ill, so that they would have to tie me down . . . QUESTION:
Something inside you revolted, but you weren't allowed to express it?
MARGHERITA: Yes, we were afraid we'd be constrained again . . . QUES-
TION: And then when the bars were removed . . . MARGHERITA: We
thought, isn't that a funny feeling after all these years . . . we felt relieved.
QUESTION: And what are you doing in the clinic community now?
MARGHERITA: Afternoons I go to school, and as far as work is concerned
I work in the EEG laboratory. QUESTION: So that is your work, and when
you don't work you play music? MARGHERITA: Yes, I belong to the
chorus. We practice twice a week and on Saturdays there's a film,
Sundays a dance and sometimes we go on outings . . ."[245]

The "self-organization" of the "patients" thus becomes a political
model for the self-organization of the supposedly "healthy"; the social
transformation within the total institution becomes a historical sign for a
social transformation outside the "total institution."

Drug Psychosis

In the last years the mass media have reported an "alarming" increase
in the consumption of narcotics and of narcotic-related crimes in the
Federal Republic. Between 1969 and 1970 alone narcotic-related crimes

in the Hamburg area increased from 4,761 to 16,104. In Hamburg between 14,000 to 15,000 students from ages 14 to 21 (of a total student population of 110,000) regularly take narcotics. At Hamburg vocational training schools one out of five students is presently taking narcotics. These figures for the Hamburg region[246] signify a trend which is representative for the rest of the Federal Republic. In April 1972 the Federal Republic already had a total of 250,000 youthful narcotics consumers.[247]

Official drug statistics and drug reporting, however, only seeks to attach the increasing drug wave to the youthful masses, to the young apprentices, to high-school and university students, while concealing the fact that the consumption of light drugs, more precisely, of "psychotropic substances," that is, pain-relieving tablets and chemicals with euphoric effect, is also increasing steadily among the adult population. A representative survey of 2,000 adults in 1961, conducted by the Allensbacher Institut, showed that within a 14-day period 60 per cent of those surveyed regularly consumed medicine with psychotropic effects.[248] Some 32 per cent of the men and 15 per cent of the women surveyed at a Swiss watch factory, it was found, regularly took pain-relieving medication. It was estimated that the demands upon concentration, agility, and work rhythm were from medium high to high among three-quarters of the workers. Among women surveyed a greater frequency of total demand was noted than among men.[249]

"Like every symptom produced by society, addiction contains two elements: a positive one, in that a solution of a certain problem has at least been attempted, which a normal person will simply ignore; and a negative one, which expresses itself in the compulsiveness of the attempt to solve the problem."[250] The testimony of nearly all opiate addicts and fixers reveals that they become completely dependent on the drug only *after* they have "flipped out," that is, run away from home, left school, or given up their apprenticeship or job; or vice versa, that they took drugs so long and in such amounts until they left school, ran away from home, or were forced to give up their job or apprenticeship. Whatever the direction in which the casual chain between "flipping out" and drug addiction runs, it appears in any event to be a compulsive, that is, unsuccessful individual attempt to break out of certain social (family, wage) dependencies which were felt to be unbearable. In a certain sense the narcotics addict exchanges his socially dependent relationship (especially that of wage labor) for a psycho-chemical dependency whose euphoria (at least at the beginning of the addiction) allows him to experience feelings of happiness.

That is also why there is a greater frequency of drug addiction in social strata and institutions where social compulsions and dependencies are the greatest. Prisons, reformatories, so-called "welfare homes," and psychiatric institutions among others have a higher percentage of drug addicts than any other institutions. Thus two-thirds of all inhabitants of "welfare homes" are narcotics consumers.[251] The drug wave, which until recently had been regarded as a middle-class phenomenon in the Federal Republic, as "chic" addiction of psychedelic students, is visibly spreading to the proletariat. According to figures published in the *Frankfurter Rundschau* (of December 9, 1970), "the number of drug-addicted students is receding while the number of vocational students, that is, of youth who are part of the working population, is on a definite increase. Moreover, one can observe that the social standing of the younger age levels is decreasing."

The increasing use of psycho-pharmaceuticals among the working population can be chiefly traced back to the physical and mental exhaustion resulting from half-automated work processes, to increasing "functional" illnesses and "organ neuroses" which can be endured, that is, anesthetized, only by chemical stimulants, by so-called "happy pills." "Frau Heinrich is 33 years old, has done piece work for AEG for 12 years [. . .] During this period she has worked her way up to an hourly wage of 5 DM. Beside her, in a shelf of her machine, she has a regular drug store, pain-killers of all kinds, for different degrees of pain, to suppress the pain, in order that she might fulfill her quota."[252]

So the immense increase in the consumption of psycho-pharmaceuticals is not to be traced back to the "chic" addiction of psychedelic youth, but to heightened conditions of work and exploitation in capitalist production. With the entry of psycho-pharmaceuticals into capitalist production, factory managers have killed several birds with one stone. For one, the effect of "happy pills" increases work capacity, that is, it guarantees the maximum exploitation of labor power. For the great majority of workers the "happy pill," therefore, is not a "way out" from an achievement-oriented society, but rather the most certain means of their subjugation under its conditions. According to J. Neye: "In contrast to comparable substances, the specific effect of psycho-pharmaceuticals consists in their ability to increase the absolute surplus value during a relatively constant mode of work and an unchanging production relationship with regard to the main 'variable,' the human individual. The specific utilization problems of capital in its present stage of the third industrial revolution thus explain the immanence of psycho-pharmaceuticals to the system."[253] On the other hand, the euphoric effect of speed pills camouflages the worst consequences of rationalized and automated production on the mental health of the workers. Psycho-pharmaceuticals serve as "sunglasses for the soul," liberate hidden energies, that is, they have the effect of letting one perform repulsive and alienated labor with pleasure. When the worker, as Marx says, "only feels together outside work and during work beside himself," then "speed" transmits to him the sensation, that is, illusion, that he also feels "together" while he is working.

The increasing demand for psychotropic substances also cranks up the whole new chemical and pharmaceutical industries whose profit rate is increasing at the same rate of psychosomatic and addictive illnesses among workers.

Proof of this is the increasing turnover of the medical concern Hoffmann-La Roche (already extensively documented on pp. 202f) which is primarily based on the high rate of profit produced by psychotropic substances, which constitute 50 per cent of total pharmaceutical production of this, the largest of all pharmaceutical concerns.[254] Capitalism thus is interested in the "drug wave" as long as its speed-pill market cranks up the capacity of the wage earner to produce. Proof of this is also provided by the advertising outlay of the pharmaceutical industry. According to expert estimates the advertising budget of the pharmaceutical industry in the Federal Republic was a half-billion DM in 1969.[255] Capitalist interest in the creation of the "drug wave" is also demonstrated in the recent campaign for the tranquilizer Adumbran. On the accompanying order form one can read: "Adumbran—for your nervous patients who want to and must remain capable of working."

Thus on the one hand the large concerns (and not only the pharmaceutical concerns) are stoking the drug wave with every means at their command, and on the other "illegal" drug consumers and "illegal" drug traffickers are criminalized. However, "illegal" drug-dealers are criminalized only because they compete with legal dealers, that is, the pharmaceutical concerns, on the black market of drugs; and "illegal" drug consumers are criminalized because they generally become "dropouts" from the capitalist work process. The legislators thus do not really punish the drug consumer, who is indispensable for the maximum exploitation of labor power today, but only those who "take off" on the drug wave, that is, withdraw from legal exploitation. That constitutes the hypocrisy of capitalist drug "morality."

As we have said, today's trend is for younger and younger age groups, especially of children of working-class mothers, to escape into drug psychosis. The primary reason for this is that working mothers are so unnerved by their work in the office or factory that they are frequently unable to devote sufficient attention and love to their children—especially during the first five years of their life which are so important for the development of the personality. For many youths drugs thus become a "surrogate mother."

Thus the case histories of *all* drug addicts show a high degree of oral disturbances which can be traced back to early experiences of loneliness and isolation. U. Ehebald says: "And here, in fact, we come upon the causes for personality disturbances which lead to drug addiction, which at first are only related to the early child-parent relationship, yet are indirectly dependent on today's production relationship which has exploitation, especially of the woman, as a consequence. The so-called equality of women forces the repeated realization on us that these women who will be mothers one day or who are already mothers are subjected to the same merciless and inhuman forces of the economic system as the men. The women are robbed of the opportunity to be with their children until they are ready to enter collective education."[256]

Added to these injuries during primary socialization, which are increasing among the lower social strata most exposed to capitalist work stress, is the high incidence of broken homes. Most drug addicts are "welfare" children, that is, suffer from all kinds of neglect. A new form of neglect which is characteristic of the case history of many drug addicts is so-called "affluent neglect." "This refers to those parents who are more intent on making money than caring for their children. They do not love their children, who are a bother. They calm their guilty conscience by buying off the children with money, saying: Leave me alone."[257]

The typical work and family situation of many (especially proletarian) drug addicts that has been sketched here results in definite psychic motivation, symptoms, and behavior patterns which also characterize the "drug scene." The manic-depressive psychology of many opiate addicts becomes clear only on the basis of a (previously described) social situation. Most opiate addicts come from the proletarian strata where the psychotic type of conflict solution (as we showed) appears to dominate. The manic "high" of the proletarian addict, which is frequently accompanied by elements of "megalomania," should therefore be regarded as an individually successful attempt to overcome the class barriers in his imagination which he cannot overcome in reality. For his wishes and fantasies are not "megalomaniacal" in an absolute, but only in a relative, sense, because of his confined class situation and his lack of opportunity. The sense of inferiority which is peculiar to this type of addict is the reverse side of this megalomania, and thus should be regarded as an exaggerated form of the "social inferiority complex" which bourgeois society inflicts on the lower classes. Regarded from this perspective, the drug addiction of the proletarian youth, whose actual motivation is "status seeking," is a compulsive attempt to negate his own "low" class status in his imagination. As long as this status is not eliminated through an organized struggle for a new classless society, the individual, impotent proletarian's attempt to break out of his class situation will continue to end in psychosis.

7. On the Pathology of the Capitalist "Consumer Society"

The pathogenetic picture of late capitalism is determined not only by the sphere of production but also increasingly by the sphere of reproduction, that is, of consumption. If "industrial pathology" is the basis of the "psycho-pathology of (late capitalist) everyday life" (Freud), then there arises on this basis a corresponding "superstructure" from which entirely new pathogenetic effects are emanating today. For the solution of its problems relating to realization, such as sales, monopoly capitalism unlooscns—as never before—an inflationary world of "beautiful appearances," of infinite "promises of happiness and use value" (W. F. Haug), which has serious consequences for the consciousness and psychology of the consumer, especially the young. As Haug has demonstrated in his book *Zur Kritik der Warenästhetik* ("On the Critique of Commodity Esthetics"),[258] the instinctual structure of whole generations of buyers, as a blind side-effect of the interests of capitalist utilization, is subjected to an increasingly compulsive molding process based on commodity esthetics which, as we will show, also lastingly determines the picture of social pathology.

The picture of massive clinical behavior and symptoms produced by the capitalist "reality principle," by a lifelong compulsion to perform wage labor, is so to speak camouflaged by the capitalistically perverted "pleasure principle" of a totally unfettered mania for buying. Whereas the "industrial pathology" produced by the production process primarily contains a pathology of disturbances which has always included an element of refusal, of unconscious rebellion against the (capitalist) reality principle, the pathology of the "sphere of consumption" appears as a pathology of perfect, highly integrated pictures of models and behavior from which every element of refusal and resistance appear to have vanished. Thus, whereas we were previously dealing with a pathology of mental dysfunction which is still experienced by the victims as real suffering, unhappiness, pain, and the like, we are dealing here with a pathology of total mental functionalism (in the sense demanded by the process of capitalist utilization) which everywhere is experienced as a feeling of happiness, as a psychedelic "euphoria of consumption." If the pathology resulting from capital's immediate productive function can still be described as a palpable and, in the classical sense, "clinical" picture of (neurotic, psychotic, psychosomatic, and other) behavior disturbances, the pathology resulting from the sales function of capital can no longer be grasped by means of classical clinical concepts. Confronted with this difficulty, it became necessary for the author to formulate new concepts such as "commodity psychosis" or "the compulsive character of commodity esthetics" which seek to elucidate the pathogenetic dimension of late capitalist commodity economy. In this regard we took particular recourse to W. F. Haug's analysis of the commodity esthetic in terms of the "molding of sensuousness" whose extensive political-economic basis was, however, not recapitulated here, especially since Haug himself has already provided it.

The Estheticization of the Commodity and the "Phantasmal Buyer"

According to W. F. Haug, the origin of the commodity esthetic is initiated in a contradiction in the exchange relationship, though it was monopoly capitalism which inflated the "phantasmal" world of commodity appearances so that it determines social perceptions and the instinctual structure more and more lastingly. The tendency towards the esthetic packaging of the commodity results necessarily from the immanent contradiction between use value and exchange value. Whereas the commodity has real use value for the buyer, whose acquisition of it is the actual point of the purchase, for the seller it is nothing but a means for the purpose of realizing its exchange value in the form of money. From the viewpoint of exchange value, use value therefore is nothing but bait. Haug writes: "A tendency begins with the contradiction between use value and exchange value, distributed among various persons, which drives its use form, the shape of the commodity, into newer and newer transformations. From this point on two things are produced when commodities are made: first of all, use value; secondly, and as an extra, the appearance of use value [. . .] From the viewpoint of exchange value, everything depends until the end, that is, upon the completion of the sales contract, on the promise of use value in the commodity [. . .] The esthetic component of the commodity in the broadest sense—sensuous appearance and sense of use value—here becomes detached. Appearance becomes ever more important for the transaction—and factually more important than what is fact. What only *is* fact but does not look like fact is not bought. But what *appears* to be fact is bought. In the system of selling and buying, esthetic appearance, the promise of use value in the commodity, looms as the actual sales function of the commodity."[259]

With the development of monopoly capitalism, where private capital seeks to subjugate a use value entirely, the "appearance of the commodity" also assumes gigantic proportions in the form of supra-regional advertising. Haug writes: "With innumerable and nameless everyday products it was always the generally valid use value which was suppressed as a bothersome obstacle standing in the way of utilizing interests. When private capital subjugates a particular use value, [. . .] the commodity esthetic becomes detached from the commodity itself which by packaging is increased and disseminated everywhere through advertising."[260] To the same degree that the commodity esthetic is detached from the commodity itself there comes into existence an autonomous "abstract" sensuousness with regard to the material use value from which it has been divorced, an inflationary world of "beautiful appearances," an endless "promise of use value" (Haug) and happiness which transport the consumer masses into a psychotropic, quasi-religious make-believe world.

In this sense a monopolistic commodity society, whose religious aura has become an anachronism, is much more aura-like, much more mystical than the old medieval society which reeked of religion. Since in medieval society the social relationship of producers to their products was still clear and transparent and, therefore, could not yet "assume a phantastic form different from their reality" (Marx[261]), it required a sphere of religious production separate from material production, which itself had to produce a "phantasmal" appearance since the sphere of material production did not yet produce one all by itself. Conversely, in monopolistic commodity society the sphere of religion, which is external and separate from material production, becomes superfluous because commodity production now creates out of itself a "phantasmal world of appearances" on a much higher level than religion was ever capable of doing. For in late capitalism "the production of mere appearance is no longer confined to certain places that represent the sacred or power, but form a totality of sensuousness of which soon not a single element will not have been subjected to the capitalist process of utilization" (Haug).[262]

When Roland Barthes in *Myths of the Everyday*[263] compared "the creation of the great French Deesse-Citroenne with the creation of the great Gothic cathedrals," then he has failed to explain why the one was a purely subsidized venture while the other a pure profit undertaking. Yet this comparison expresses the insight that religious mystification, which once was protected from the profane sphere of material production, has so to speak dissolved in this sphere, has profanized itself and generalized itself as commodity mystification. O. Münzeberg writes: "Detroit, the city of the perverse American automobile. The new monarchs: General Motors, Ford, and Chrysler. There instead of saying 'by God' the people say 'by Ford,' expressing their quasi-religious respect of the new gods. The administrative headquarters of Ford in Dearborn is entered like a cathedral. The holy of holies, the car of the year, a two-seater sports car, stands on a sacred ramp and is called Boss 302. The priests of capital seal off the production site—as Catholic priests conceal the cross during the Good Friday liturgy—for two months from public view. The resurrection celebration, the psychological fact, is celebrated on September 1, when the *top car,* the holiest of all, the idol for the coming year, is revealed."[264]

The historically new extent of the mystification and estheticization of the commodity world in the service of realizing commodity capitalism has as a necessary consequence a "displacement" (Freud) of the libidinous energies of the world of objectified persons onto the world of personified objects, or commodity fetishes. Since the universe of social relationships as naked exchange and money relationship is less and less subject to cathexis, the universe of personified objects, of commodities, itself becomes the "substitute" object of libidinous energies. The libido evaporates, as it were, from the human commodity skin. The commodity bodies and their multiple appearances which have been peeled off the human become ever so many "focuses of suggestion" for the social libido household.

Monopoly capital has transformed its metropolises into huge stage sets on which the "monarchs," the heroes and stars of the world of commodity, in a certain sense present an uninterrupted Aristotelian "theatre of empathy" (Brecht). The corridors and displays of the supermarkets become the cult, that is, art shrines of the commodity world, which are entirely calculated to arouse the consumer's empathy. This "empathy" absorbs itself in the staged appearance of the commodity so as to be "removed" from the mundane everyday existence of alienated production. Marketing has created its own concept for a commodity-esthetic use of bourgeois "empathy esthetics," namely, that of the "buying experience." Haug comments: "The advertising of shop-construction capital speaks with a threatening undertone: whoever wants to sell must transmit experience [. . .] He (the buyer) 'should not stand at a distance.' 'He should be a participant' goes one of the fundamental laws of business. The commodity on display, its being seen, the buying process, and all the elements constituting and surrounding it are fashioned into a conception of a total theatrical work of art whose effects are calculated with the public's readiness to buy in mind. Thus the sales location as stage is determined by its function to transmit experiences to the public which stimulate a heightened buying behavior."[265]

The "sales location as stage of experience" has an immediate effect on the buyer's ability to experience. The "dissolution of the commodity into a process of experience" has the effect that the consumer tends only to "experience" what is transmitted to him previously in the commodity category, that is, what can be expressed in commodity categories. That becomes manifest even when he does not have to deal with the nature of the commodity but only with nature itself. Even where his experience is still "original" in the sense of "primal" and the object of his experience is still "natural" in the sense of "pristine," the "commodity soul" speaks out of him, of which Marx spoke half-jokingly, half-seriously. Thus the tourist, the buyer of a "vacation" commodity, usually is only able to perceive that segment from nature which has been transmitted to him beforehand in its technically reproducible and buyable form. H. M. Enzensberger writes: "Tourism is an industry whose product is identical with its advertising: its consumers are simultaneously its employees. The colorful shots which the tourist takes differ only in their modalities from those which he acquires as postcards and sends off. They are the trip itself which he has undertaken. The world of which he catches sight is *a priori* reproduction. All he receives is an imitation. He confirms the fact of the poster, which was what tempted him in the first place."[266]

The sensuous waste and impoverishment of late capitalist consumers of the commodity increases to the degree that the commodity world itself unfetters its total sensuousness. The field of perception and experience of human beings tends to shrivel to that realm which is populated with pictures of the commodity esthetic, which intervenes like a filter between the human senses and nature—and nature itself appears only as the "golden background of the commodity." The consumer's senses visibly transform themselves into "receptors" of mere buying signals. The sensuousness of the consumer thus becomes more and more a medium," a passive "membrane" of the commodity; its monopolized foreign language becomes a second "mother tongue."

The buyer's psychological interior tends to transform itself into a "field of associations," into a psychological "colony" of the external commodity world. According to Haug, the tendency goes so far that the commodity's use-value character is increasingly pushed back by its un-, that is, half-conscious, associated "significance" character (one could say: by its artistic character). Haug declares: "The phenomena described here will increase according to their quantity and insistent significance; according to their quality they will have as their effect that the structure of the use value of commodities is displaced even further in the direction of an overemphasis on relations to needs of a fantastic kind. More and more goods will increasingly change in a direction at whose extremity stands the 'thing which merely signifies.' The expression 'thing which merely signifies' is supposed to indicate that the degree of reality and the nature of the commodity itself as use value are displaced at a distance from an 'external object which satisfies definite human needs through its physical attributes' (Marx) by simply appearing as what it is, and in the direction of an increasing accentuation of what signifies and relates in the commodity. The weight will shift further away from the immediate material, from purposeful use value, to thoughts, feelings, associations which one identifies with the commodity or which one assumes others will identify with it. As packaging and advertising surround the commodity with an aura of associations, the auras of commodity association and need satisfaction will be molded in accordance with their supposed use value."[267]

To the degree that the real use value of commodities decreases through their planned deterioration, their imaginary, their ideal value in a certain sense increases. It is a kind of "irony of the fate" of capitalist commodity economy that the more matter and human material it sells, the more "idealistic," even "phantastic" it becomes. The real material use value often enough only has the function of expressing an idea, an association which inspires the buyer to buy. Since he has to decide between competing commodities of the same kind, which no longer can be distinguished by their use value, he selects that commodity which gives off the most promising "aura"; that is, within the same genre of commodities—and this holds true for detergents as much as for "political messages"—he only has a choice between competing names, forms, pictures, in short between "phantasma" appearances. The "competitive appearances" (Haug) of the commodities offering themselves to the buyer thus educates him more and more to be an "idealist," or "phantast," who chases after ideas, associations, figments of the imagination, and hallucinations, which circle around the visibly decreasing core of material use value in the commodity.

The "phantasmal" world of commodity associations resembles the psychotic world of associations in that it seeks ever more perfect ways of circumventing the buyer's critical censorship, that is, the function of "testing reality." The relationship of the buyer to the commodity world thus becomes more and more unreal. W. Alf writes: "The commodities offer, and in this are comparable to the style of Louis XV, an increasingly more glittering and thinner skin, which promises more and more but keeps fewer and fewer promises [. . .] The commodities themselves accomplish less and less of what they actually should perform: if the ideology of happiness were not constantly provided together with the commodity it would scarcely produce feelings of happiness anymore."[268] The buyer tends to become the "commodity psychotic" who denies the visibly real and essential decreasing use value of the commodity to the same degree that he is deceived about its use-value appearance, its promise of happiness. Regarded in this manner, the buyer suffers an increasing "loss of reality" with respect to the world of commodities. His buying behavior acquires more and more "phantastic," indeed almost "delusionary" attributes.

Commodity Euphoria and Drug Euphoria

Since external markets are being increasingly blocked off by the expansion of socialist camps and anti-imperialist liberation movements in the Third World countries, monopoly capitalism today is increasingly dependent on the intensive exploitation and opening up of its interior markets. The new sales strategies resulting from the realization and sales problems of monopoly capital have grave consequences for the psychology of the consumer, in particular the young consumer. The rigid Protestant renunciatory type who held the Bible in one hand and the savings book in the other put up too much "character resistance" to the excessive sales strategies of capital. Therefore, this type had to be correspondingly "remolded," that is, loosened up and unthawed so as to enable capital "to entice the golden birds out of its pockets" (Marx[269]) that much more easily. The religious conscience in its Protestant ascetic form had to be dismantled because it turned into an obstacle to the realization interests of capital: today it tends to be replaced by the "bad conscience" not to follow the "categorical imperatives" of the newest commodity offering. Capital can no longer use the "anal-retentive" middle-class renunciatory morality which still functioned in the classic phase of capitalism (at least not in the sphere of circulation and consumption). Instead it entices the rigid Protestant compulsive character away from the ascetic church bench into the lascivious armchair of industrial trade fairs, puts the "Beatles" up against the religious "song of renunciation," modern "pop" against the old stucco, the sex star against the Virgin Mary, in short: a profitable "paradise" of consumption on earth against the unprofitable "paradise in the beyond."

This process of re-education and remolding of the classical anal-retentive compulsive character into a "highly variable commodity fetishist" (who can be addressed and seduced at any given moment) has been described by R. Reiche as a "process of replacement of rigid functionalism by repressive desublimation." Reiche states: "Individuals must learn to consume; to consume whenever the system wants it, and to consume what the system wants. The classic anal-compulsive character must be loosened up."[270] According to Reiche, this new "repressively loosened up" social character is a purely "genital façade. The instinctual structure of these individuals has been insufficiently prepared for 'genital primacy.' But it does not appear that they become addicted because of instinctual restrictions [such as the classic pervert—author] but because of insufficient training of the instincts and ego."[271]

As problematical as the concept of "genital façade" may be (see pp. 236f), because it still depends on Freud's fiction of the "genital character" and was developed only out of the conditions of the sphere of realization, that is, consumption, Reiche's description is correct in that consumer behavior, especially that of the younger middle class, is today assuming a regressive form, that is, the form of addiction. The commodity character appended to the addictive character also puts its stamp on the instinctual structure of the consumer. As we showed elsewhere, the dominant characterological qualities of the classical social character, which asserted itself with the accumulation of capital, were the anal-defense mechanisms and reaction formations; whereas the qualities of "oral" character, such as the psychosexual capacity for enjoyment, sensuality, self-surrender, and intoxication were correspondingly repressed. Today, however, these "oral" character modalities are again hauled out of their repressed state by the unending sensuous appeal of a psychotropical commodity landscape. Of course, the late-capitalist "oral"-addictive character, which has to perform a maximum of consumption, no longer has anything in common with the feudal pleasure character. Where the latter was still able sensuously to acquire the feudal pleasures of the natural-economic world, the former falls into increasing dependency on a totally abstract, commodity-esthetic sensuousness determined by alien forces; and this keeps the oral-addictive character tied to a moronic circle between pseudo-and non-gratification, so as to spur its wearer on to ever newer "achievements" in consumption.

According to Freud, religion, art, and narcotics are some of the "great substitute gratifications" of human beings.[272] The ideological function of religion and (bourgeois) art as external realms of superstructure, the production of a "phantasmagorical world of appearances" and its mass-psychological function, the ritualistic exhibition of collective substitute gratifications (for the frustrations of real life)—all these, however, tend to be replaced by the immanent religiosity, esthetic and narcotic, of the world of commodities. That also alters the traditional relationship of basis and superstructure: to the same degree that the cupola of St. Peter becomes an advertisement for the commodity of heaven and the stories of religious martyrs are replaced by the faces of happy dolls of the world of commodities, so art and religion too become (from the standpoint of capital) increasingly superfluous outside this world. Capital has liberated the "great substitute gratifications" of man from their religious and artistic ghetto, profaned and enmassed them by everywhere staging the "song" of the commodity and the Aristotelian "empathic theater of the commodity." By combining a religious, artistic, and narcotic "state of euphoria" with "commodity euphoria" it provides a synthesis of all the "great substitute gratifications" of man.

Walter Benjamin has already described the estheticizing, mystifying, and narcoticizing atmosphere which the metropolises of the capitalist commodity society disseminate everywhere in his work *Charles Baudelaire: A Lyric Poet in the Era of High Capitalism:* "Baudelaire was a connoisseur of narcotics, yet one of their most important social effects probably escaped him. It consists in the charm displayed by addicts under the influence of drugs. Commodities derive the same effect from the crowd that surges around and intoxicates them. The concentration of costumes which makes the market, which in turn makes the commodity into a commodity, enhances its attractiveness to the average buyer. When Baudelaire speaks of the 'big cities' state of religious intoxication,' the commodity is probably the unnamed subject of this state."[273] And Benjamin describes how the *flaneur* of the "second empire" who was formerly still interested in the usefulness of things and human beings ("in stones, gas lanterns, and fiacres") and protested as a total "personality" against the "division of labor" in the production of industrial commodities, is finally corrupted by the "narcotics commodity." "The *flaneur* [in his decline—author] is at the mercy of the crowds. With that he shares the situation of the commodity [. . .] It pervades him blissfully like an opiate which can indemnify him for many humiliations. The euphoria to which the *flaneur* surrenders is that of the commodity with the buzz of the crowd around it."[274]

This "state of religious intoxication in the big cities" meantime appears to be reaching its absolute apogee within the late capitalist commodity landscape: wherever the Dionysian "gods of happiness" engaged by capital start up the "song of their commodity" they awaken the voluptuousness of those from whom they want to profit. Wherever they manifest the "sacredness of the commodity" they enchant with their "sex appeal" so as to transport the buyer into a quasi-religious erective state of euphoria.

In fact, American research has shown that housewives make 50 per cent of their supermarket purchases on impulse, that is, purchases are no longer motivated by rational need. The buyers are so blinded by the "sensuous-supra-sensuous" appearance of the commodity world that their critical capacities fail them. Indeed, corresponding commodity-esthetic arrangements systematically switch them off. Thus—to name only one example—the Color Research Institute of Chicago specializes in the design of packages with depth effect and lets no package come on the market which has not been subjected to special "eye-catching tests." Although buyers feel particularly "free" in supermarkets, because they apparently "serve themselves," that is, can choose "freely," in reality advertising strategies have long since acquired control over their buying reflexes. According to Vance Packard, the El Dorado of the supermarket transports the buyer, especially women, into a "trance-like" state which resembles the initial stage of hypnosis.[275]

Regarded psychoanalytically, the state of hypnosis, that is, euphoria, is a slightly psychotic condition where the ego denies a part of reality so as to surrender itself to the hallucinatory wish, that is, the substitute world of the "id." In contrast to the genuine psychotic, who produces his hallucinatory world of appearances of his own accord, that is, from the wishful conceptions of the id, the "commodity psychosis" delegates its hallucinatory power in a certain sense to the "phantasmagorical as-if world" of commodities which usurps the psychotic's own power to imagine and to wish. As the former is overwhelmed by the unfettered images of his inner world, so the latter is overwhelmed by the unfettered commodity-esthetic models of an anonymous external world. As the former loses his way in the labyrinth of his own unsatisfied (childhood) wishes, so the latter loses his way in the labyrinth of fungible consumer wishes constantly being stimulated in him, and which leave him dissatisfied because they are no longer his own. Yet whereas the true psychotic withdraws more or less completely from external reality so as to surrender himself entirely to his own psychic inner and wish-fulfillment world, the "commodity psychotic" has switched off all his own wish lights, so as to immerse himself completely in the psychedlic light of the commodity scene. His mental inner world, so to speak, becomes the "inner world of the outer world" of commodities, that is, an internal dark room which is only illuminated by the glare of the external commodity world. The "psychic apparatus" is in a certain sense reconstructed into a "screen" for the commodity movie that is running outside.

The commodity, however, retains its psychedelic, that is, psychic, power only within the ritual of buying. Since the commodity's real use value shrinks to the same degree that its use value sparkles in ever new colors of "esthetic innovation" (Haug) on its surface, euphoria is necessarily followed by hangover. Brecht has already described this effect: "When we pass by a haberdashery the clothes in the window usually look so beautiful that you know at once: esthetics has been at play here, esthetically trained people designed this, and their chief purpose was to design something tasteful. Moreover, the clothes on display here are showing us their best side. They have been made chiefly for the display window and manifest how vile they really are only when they are bought and worn. Then it becomes very quickly apparent that they were not made for coarse reality. The material is poor, that is, it won't last long, and will quickly change its appearance. The old suit is the new one's brother, and he takes care of his brother."[276]

Outside the buying relationship the commodity loses its psychedelic, that is, "psychotic" power. Once the commodity movie has ended the sober buyer stands in front of his use-value dummy as before the left-over shambles of his self-delusion. R. Heuer writes: "Aside from profit, capital —before the end of its history—is interested in only one side-effect of its products: in their beautiful frustration. It produces only [at least in the area of the consumer goods—author] beautifully tasting emetics. Things which satisfy just long enough so that the next act of buying can be performed as quickly as possible, namely, before the uselessness of what has just been bought is fully realized. That is the classic picture of addiction: it is the experience which always promises more and keeps less; but in the end the only thing it promises is promising itself."[277]

Drug addiction is one extreme on the wide scale of addiction which late capitalist commodity society produces. Hash, LSD, drug euphoria, which especially seizes the younger consumers today, produce a "hypnoid state" (Vance Packard) in which the consumer is driven to his ultimate limit in the commodity world. Regarded this way, illegal hash, LSD, and the drug scene are only an extension of the legal commodity scene where everyone more or less becomes "addicted": whether to nicotine, alcohol, Coca-Cola, television, or whatever. Not only the "outcast" society of drug addicts but also the entire "inside" society of late capitalist commodity consumers finds itself on a somnambulistic trip which, of course, ends each time at the prosaic cash registers of the large department stores.

Particularly are young consumers exposed to the crossfire of various advertising campaigns. The more psychedelic the ads the better the sales. The advertising ideologies designed for youth, however, increasingly assume the character of drug-consumer ideologies. If Marx called religion "the opium of the people," then late capitalist consumer society has reversed this sentence again: the narcotic consumer and the psychotropic commodity consumer need no religious ideology any more. Both are so intoxicated by the commodity-, that is, drug-world's promise of happiness that they experience the "beyond" already in the "here and now." The genuine and the commodity opium have become "the religion of the people" today.

That is why the official fight against drug addiction is so extremely hypocritical. For the only thing that is fought is the illegal and therefore unprofitable ultimate limit of addiction, but not its daily, legal, profitable form.

The actual fascination of drug psychosis as an extreme case of "commodity psychosis" consists in the highly dynamic effect which occurs

because of the "displacement" and "condensation" (Freud) of unconscious thoughts and conceptions in a dream-, that is, euphoric state.
Osborn writes: "In a peculiar way, dream life [and also euphoria—au-
thor] is more closely connected to the dynamic nature of reality than
waking life. For consciousness tends to represent the processes of the
environment as rigid and distinct [. . .] On the other side, dream life
represents its content in the form of highly dramatized actions [. . .]."[278]
The susceptibility, especially of young consumers, to hallucinogens can
be traced, among other reasons, to the fact that their social relationships,
which have petrified to pure exchange and money relationships, are
artificially dynamized and dramatized in the hallucinogenic states of
dream and euphoria.

Looked at in this way, the artificial dynamics and dramatics of the state
of intoxication are a regressive attempt to break out from the real waste-
land and petrification of late capitalist exchange society.

The dynamicization of reality in the state of euphoria is simultaneously
connected to a highly sensuous concretization: whereas in the waking
state concrete reality is predominantly assimilated in abstract concepts,
in the dream, that is, in euphoria, abstract thoughts, the "dream
thoughts" (Freud), are brought into a highly concrete and sensuous form
through the "displacement" and "condensation" of the "dream work."
If one regards the hash-, LSD-, opium-, or otherwise artificially induced
dreams, that is, euphoria, of the young workers from this aspect, then it
looks like a helplessly regressive attempt to compensate, through sensuous concretization, for their work which is more and more abstract and
determined by alien forces.

The psychedelic commodity landscape has a similar, though in its
dosage, much lesser effect. Its images too appear to be created according
to the laws of Freud's "dream analysis"; they too are marked by an
extremely high degree of condensation. The more "over-determined" the
visual display of the commodities, that is, the more that conscious and
unconscious wishes and longings are "condensed" in their pictorial
elements, the greater is their "adhesion," that is, their advertising value.
The word as advertising message now only has a secondary function; it
is no longer a match for the "over-determined" pictorial language of the
commodity esthetic. Just as drugs produce an artificial internal dream
state through a regressive revivification of visual memories, so the psychotropic commodity world produces, through fixating its pictorial-visual
appearance on the consumer, an artificial and external condition for the
dream. The dream pictures of the commodity esthetic are in a certain
sense the consumer's standardized and enmassed dream pictures projected onto the surface of the commodity after having been previously
cheated away from him by marketing and advertising psychology, and the
like. Fixation and regression to the "sensuous level of recognition" (Mao

Tse-tung[279])—this the real and the commodity dream have in common—leads to a blocking of a "rational recognition" of those social relationships which have assumed "the form of a relationship of things" in the commodity. The price paid for making the drug and commodity consumer visually sensitive is the immobilization of language: faced with the suggestive power of the images which the commodity world falsely promises him, the psychedelic buyer is as speechless as the dreamer and drug addict.

The bourgeoisie reacts finally with such horror to the drug addict because it recognizes in him the "Janus face" of its own economic movement: the "euphoria," the "pleasure" on the one hand, and (economic and mental) ruin on the other side. The drug addict, who usually also has to deal, that is, make as many consumers as possible dependent on drugs so as to be able to finance his habit, therefore develops the ultimate interpretation of a "free market," of a "free" exchange of commodities: "Every man speculates on creating a new need for the other, to put him in a new state of dependency, so as to lead him to a new way of pleasure and, therefore, of economic ruin" (Marx[280]).

Drug addiction is the psychological mirror image of "economic" addiction, the addiction to profit which arises from the compulsive laws of commodity production. As indifferent as the drug addict is towards all individual needs which do not serve the satisfaction of his addiction, that indifferent is the capitalist towards all social needs (for example, the shortening of the work week) which do not serve the satisfaction of his profit addiction. The only need here for a higher "high" and "flash" corresponds there to the only need for a higher and higher rate of profit. Total addiction, and total indifference towards everything that does not serve the satisfaction of that addiction: these are the two pathological poles of the drug and "commodity soul."

The "Commodity Doll" and the "Sex Doll"

As already discussed, the exchange principle is connected with a certain animosity towards sensuousness, a notorious indifference to the sensuous diversity of the use value and the sensuous needs and satisfactions transmitted by it. The abstraction of sensuousness reproduces itself with the development of (capital) commodity society on a higher and higher level. Sexual sensuousness, too, is subjected to this abstraction process to the degree that it is seized as a sales function by capital. The compulsion to make uniform and to standardize production, which is a given with production on an enlarged scale, also extends itself to the industrial production of sex, that is, to the production of sexualized commodities. Haug writes: "Sexual sensuousness can be utilized by industrial capital only in abstract form, in its massive reproducibility."[281] Sexualized commodities can realize their particular erotic use value (under capitalist conditions) only when they assume the "form of abstract generality," that is, offer themselves to sexual needs in a generalized, abstract, standardized form. Haug adds: "The sexual need and the offer to satisfy it are despecified. In a certain sense, the sexual forms of the commodity begin to resemble money, with which Freud, in this connection, compared anxiety: they become freely convertible into all things. Exchange value takes sexuality into its service and transforms it into exchange value. The façades of sexual happiness become the most frequently worn dress of the commodity, or else the golden background on which the commodity appears."[282]

The sexualized commodity doll holds the mirror of its surface up to the consumer for as long a time as necessary until the consumer finally recognizes himself in it. In the process of this imperceptible mimicry he sloughs off everything that still reminds of his individual, unchangeable facial and character traits, so as to step forth purified into the purgatory of standardized mass production as refined sexual-exchange value. The sexualized commodity doll and the "sex doll" that have been sloughed off from it therefore play the same role in the esthetic of capital commodity society as money in the economy of commodity society: if money is the general economic equivalent in which all dead commodities represent their exchange value, then the sex doll is the general esthetic equivalent in which the living commodities represent their interchangeability. That is why money and credit advertisements today increasingly assume the form of sexual advertisements: "Sex is simply normal and just as modern as owning securities. The person who lets his money collect dust in a savings account is just as unmodern as the sexually inhibited person" (Twen).

The despecification of sexual forms and the simultaneous dollification of human facial and character traits manifests itself in the pornographic portrayal of the commodity world just as in the promiscuous sexual practice of the (middle-class) sex and porno consumer. The "sexual grand sale" in the form of "porno, pop, and group sex," celebrated by the sales apparatus as "sexual revolution," does not prove the sexual libertinage of a progressive culture; it only proves that department store capital achieves a greater turnover with nudity today than with bourgeois modesty. The pornographication of the entire sphere of consumption, like the promiscuous convertability of sexual objects, means, however, the total abstraction of use value from sexuality. This becomes especially clear from the Leigh Report which Reiche quotes: "It is characteristic of all the cases that Leigh describes that each individual solves the discontent he feels in his life by means of a kind of permanent sporting event. Even when he becomes addicted, which is usually the case, he does not understand this addiction as an unfulfillment of his life practice but as increased sporting enthusiasm. The dominant form of sexual behavior, clinging to one partner, or better, the compulsive sense of duty to use one partner, is only seemingly eliminated by a compulsive anarchy and indifference in choice towards all partners [. . .] As a result sexuality is brought radically into the capitalist commodity form, whose adequate expression is its advertising value and the unending increase in consumption. Translated into the category of sexuality, this increase in consumption means: individual commodities do not satisfy me, they leave me dissatisfied because I can only consume them but cannot really use them. So at least I want 'really' to consume them, affix them with the highest possible exchange value and advertise them, photograph them, make them into a series, treat them sadistically, and so on . . ."[283]

The capitalist form of promiscuity strikingly demonstrates how the commodity and money structure of social needs and gratifications increasingly also determines the sexual structure. Money craving and promiscuous sexual greed have the same movement: what is longed for is not the particular erotic use value of the sexual object but the general undifferentiated abstract form which appears in its promiscuous convertability. This kind of sexual lust, despecified and dequalified, is then preferably measured in concepts of money and achievement, that is, in quantified concepts (also compare Reiche on American "dating"[284]), just as, conversely, the potency of money becomes the measure of sexual potency. H. M. Plato observes: "As far as I am concerned, there is a connection between potency and money. The gold doll increases the potency of the one who has her as a treasure. Increase of money and increase of potency go hand in hand [. . .] You can make the doll dance with money. The dance around the golden doll is the dance around strength, around total power."[285]

The promiscuous exchange of partners is in a certain sense the last consequence of equivalence exchange. The sexual indifference of the late capitalist sex and porno consumer is the extreme psychological expression of the equivalence of their economic value and of indifference to abstract exchange relations. The high rate of frigidity and psychic impotence (primarily among middle-class sex and porno consumers) proves that the "hoarfrost of the commodity economy" (Walter Benjamin[286]) penetrates even the most intimate sexual expressions and can go so far as the "unfeeling isolation of the individual in his private interests" (F. Engels[287]).

A consumer society therefore can behave more freely towards sexuality because its subversive content is being increasingly liquidated by capitalist coordination and by making all sexual appearance and content uniform. The less able sex and porno consumers are to break through a "naked" exchange and money relationship to which all social relationships are reduced, the more voyeuristically they behave towards the nakedness of the human body. The "sexual education" which capital today injects into its sex and porno consumers is, therefore, the exact counterpiece to Brecht's "Love Education": "But girls, I recommend/ some enticement in your screams/carnal I love my soul/soulless my flesh."[288] Where interested business capital sets free taboo bourgeois sexuality, where it bares piece by piece the flesh as a tempting packaging of the commodity, this dialectic of "carnal" and "soulful" love goes awry: neither the "capital soul" nor the flesh bared by capital "breathes a soul" into those who depend on love.

The "sexual revolution" which is being propelled under the sign of the "sales revolution" contributes even further to the fragmentation and partialization of the instinctual structure. With every acquisition the buyer is, so to speak, promised a "beloved" or at least part of her: breasts, legs, thighs. Thus business capital today brings the erotic shards, which "cultural sexual morality" used to keep in the dark, into broad daylight, that is, neon light, since even the exhibition of fetishized fragments of the commodity doll is still profitable. The tendency to a fragmentation of the instinctual structure in the wake of the progressive specialization and fragmentation of industrial labor is made even sharper by the "partial tease" of the commodity esthetic within the sphere of circulation. The commodity-esthetic molding of sensuality, therefore, contributes decisively to the regressive autonomy of the "partial drives."

In order to illustrate the mechanism of instinctual regression, Freud once compared the instinctual structure to a system of communication tubes whose "genital" main channel is blocked to the degree that excess pressure is created in its "pregenital" subsidiary channels. Thus the appearance of sexual use value in the world of commodities also produces an immense excess pressure in the "subsidiary channels" of the instinctual structure: libidinous energy is pushed off into the subsidiary channels of the libido, that is, it is driven into an exhibitionist and voyeurist fixation. Haug writes: "The use value of pure sexual appearance, for example, resides in the gratification of curiosity. With seeming gratification through mere sexual appearance it is characteristic that the demand for appearance is reproduced simultaneously with gratification and the compulsive fixation [. . .] Here the only form of use value suitable for massive utilization has a retroactive effect on the need structure of human beings, that is, in voyeuristic fixation."[289]

On the other hand, the more fractionalized and fragmented the instinctual structure of the industrial detail worker and detail eroticist becomes, their demand increases for erotic models which embody the sensual "totality" so far denied them. The whole "artistry" of the late capitalist sales apparatus consists in putting the "sales objects" of the commodity, that is, sex doll together in such a way that its seams and fragments become invisible. The body of a car, that is, of a sex doll, becomes more expensive, iridescent, and "total" just as the sensual "motor" of its consumers becomes ever more ready for the junkheap. The "technocracy of sensuality" (Haug), which allows the late capitalist commodity world to sparkle and resound in all colors and sounds, simultaneously signifies the increased dismantling of sensuality on the consumer's part. The more colorful, tricky, and differentiated the face of the commodity, the paler, more uniform, more monotonous, and poorer does the buyer become.

Three thousand years ago human beings danced around the "golden calf," that is, around the incarnation of "abstract" wealth. Today it is abstract wealth itself, the commodity and gold doll, which dances before its consumer's eyes in the display window, on the television screen, and elsewhere. In the course of the history of commodity society, the "golden calf" in a certain sense revealed itself to be a "Trojan horse" that came to life to the same degree as it sapped its devotees' life and liveliness.

The Discipline of Anal Achievement and Oral Addiction

"Private property has made us so stupid and one-sided that an object is ours only if we have it, if it exists for us as capital or is immediately possessed by us [. . .] Hence *all* the physical and spiritual senses have been replaced by the simple alienation of them all, the sense of *having*."[290] Late capitalist "consumer society" has completely fulfilled Marx's statement: the entire objective world of use values, which man can no longer "acquire," has been replaced by the world of commodity fetishes which he now can only "have," that is, buy. The sense of "owning," of buying, has become the "sense par excellence," the "sense of all senses," the "sense" of late capitalist society as such. The identity of buying and loving is the perverse identity of the "commodity soul" which today speaks even out of the "child's soul."

The atrophy and impoverishment of human sensuality has historically increased to the degree that the process of reification, that is, of the abstraction of the particular, concrete (natural-economic) use form of work and the particular concrete needs and satisfactions mediated by it, has increased. What appears to contradict this is that fully developed commodity production, especially if late capitalist, has aroused and also gratified entirely new kinds of needs which, for example in the middle ages, due to economic and technical underdevelopment, did not even exist. The pathology of capitalist commodity society does not consist in the fact that its level of social-need satisfaction has sunk quantitatively and absolutely. On the contrary: it has risen quantitatively and absolutely with the development of the forces of production. What is pathological is that the production of constantly new needs and satisfactions goes hand in hand with the destruction of the psychosexual capacity for *qualitative* need, that is, *ultimate* satisfaction.

The consumer's act of buying, choosing from one display window over another, from one fashion, one catalogue, one movie over the next, increasingly assumes the character of substitute-, that is, fore-pleasure. In the act of buying the consumer seeks to acquire a surrogate fraction of what the producers have taken away from him. The commodity fetish thus in a certain sense becomes the fig leaf over his expropriation, over his "being stripped" as a producer. The more he is able to buy, that is, the more frequently he can change his fetishist attributes, the less expropriated, or "castrated," he seems, the greater seems his individual potency. Marx writes: "Everything that the national economist takes of your life and humanity he replaces in the form of money and wealth, and everything that you can do your money can do: it can eat, drink, go to the ball, to the theater; it knows how to subjugate art, scholarship, historical rarities, political power; it can travel; it can acquire everything for you; it can buy all of that, it is the true potency."[291] The commodity, e.g., money fetish, becomes the surrogate as such of phallic satisfaction, the totalitarian substitute object for the totality of human potencies and capacities which its owners as well as its producers have lost. For them the cleavage between the world of abstract riches and the world of sensuous-concrete wealth, between the accumulation of abstract exchange values and the sensuous acquisition of concrete use values, becomes deeper and deeper. Thus late capitalist consumer society increasingly resembles the paradise of Midas: objectively speaking, the more opportunities for satisfaction man has, the less satisfied he becomes.

Capitalism today has reached a stage where (as once before during the transition from feudalism to early capitalism) it touches on the foundations of social character. Through the increasing fragmentation of industrial labor and the capacities and qualities linked with it, through an increasingly more obtrusive commodity-esthetic "partial"-tease within the "sphere of consumption," and through a growing loss of authority in classic socialization agencies (primarily the family), the instinctual structure of today's youth is increasingly "loosened up," that is, disintegrated. The progressive partialization and fragmentation of the instinctual structure has the consequence of making it less and less possible to achieve mature and firm object relationships with the sexual partner. The content of the sexual object relationship becomes as "indifferent" and fungible as the content of work. This "indifference" in relation to work, to consumer objects, to the sexual partner, reflecting as it does the totalitarian character of the commodity relationship, is the actual reason for the massive regressive behavior and symptoms that one can find among today's youth. As we have already noted, R. Reiche classified this new "regressive" social character as "genital façade": "The instinctual structure of these individuals has been insufficiently prepared for 'genital primacy' [. . .] These individuals are to be 'intentionally' equipped with weak egos and then made pliable in adolescence with intentional sexual loosening-up exercises. These 'loosenings'—which is what they are from a historical perspective—are individually tied to a deficient training of the instincts, that is, to an inability to hold the partial drives together."[292] However, a "deficient instinctual education," that is, an "inability to hold the partial drives together," is not primarily the consequence of the failure of classic socialization authorities (among others, the family). The regressive "loosening up" of the instinctual structure expresses the invasion of the commodity relation to its deepest levels. The total leveling, emptying out, and abstraction of social relationships tied up with the commodity character also increasingly hollows out the instinctual structure, that is, the psychosexual capacity for the libidinous cathexis of objects. For the abstraction of the particular, concrete (natural-economic) use form of libidinous relations and objects (see also pp. 149f) is identical with the loss of their sensuous totality, which comes into existence only through the ensemble of different partial drives, different sensuous partial functions such as seeing, tasting, smelling, touching. Since the totality of sensuous partial functions has been repressed through the totalitarian "sense" of the commodity, and since all "spiritual and physical senses" have been repressed by the "sense of having" (Marx), the instinctual structure too remains rudimentary and underdeveloped.

As correct as R. Reiche's finding is that the instinctual fate of young (especially middle-class) consumers occurs only on a quasi-regressive pregenital level, as wrong, however, is the rigid and mechanistic alternative of the "anal-compulsive character" which is supposedly historically superseded, and of the "seemingly genital" addictive character which is developing into the dominant social character. The absolutization of the concept of addiction necessarily results from the fact that Reiche investigated only specific instinctual molding within the sphere of consumption. Although the classic "anal-compulsive character" with its rigid behavioral stereotypes is also increasingly loosened up through structural changes within the production process—by means of an ever higher disposition towards changing work demands—yet the late capitalist production process with its rigid work and achievement compulsions still keeps creating anal-retentive behavior and character compulsions (instinctual deferral as well as instinctual abstinence, orderliness, punctuality, and cleanliness compulsions). In the sphere of production capital still swings the piece-work whip while it offers the carrot, so to speak, only in the sphere of consumption: on the one hand, it still requires a rigid renunciatory character, that of maximum work achievement; and on the other, a repressively "loosened up" addictive character which has to produce a maximum of consumption. On the one hand, the instinctual wishes are more and more repressed through the intensification and abstraction of work; and on the other, they are increasingly provoked by more and more obtrusive and "psychedelic" appeals to buy. P. Schneider writes: "In the first place, late capitalism must strengthen its censorship over mobilized desires, convince the workers as producers that they have no right to these desires roused and shaped by selling machinery, that they must work and toil. But it must break the dam it has just erected before these desires flood consciousness with ever new images of capitalist wish fulfillment, so as to retain the worker as consumer of his alienated product; late capitalism needs both: it must mobilize guilt feelings against capitalist desires as well as capitalist desires against guilt feelings."[293]

What is characteristic for the instinctual fate of youthful "social character" that R. Reiche has in mind is that one instinctual extreme, the "anal-retentive" achievement compulsion, is alternately negated and retained by the other, namely, "oral" (consumption) addiction. The extreme tension of the producer in the work process necessarily creates its pathogenetic counter-movement: extreme relaxation and slackening off in "psychedelic euphoria." The zigzag-like instinctual movement, which falls from one extreme into the other in capital's rhythm of production and circulation, tends to destroy every secure psychosexual foundation, every dialectic of instinctual sequence, and thus also the capacity for the creation of mature and firm relationships to objects. U. Ehebald writes: "In this world [. . .] where adults, as it were, are forced into *anal* positions, where achievement, possession, and power are the only objectives worth striving for, the capacity to love is lost more and more. Thus the relationship between adults and children is more and more determined by the demands of achievement and not by love. At best youths and adults can still love in an orally addictive way in such a world of consumption and ownership [. . .] Thus sexuality, too, is consumed addictively. But that is the sheer opposite of a mature object relationship."[294]

Torn between compulsive instinctual repression in the sphere of production and compulsive instinctual unshackling in consumption, the working consumers enter into a kind of unending "double-bind" situation. This "schizophrenic" contradiction between the discipline of "anal" achievement and "oral" addiction is characteristic for the behavior of the "seemingly genitally" organized youthful "social character."

The Compulsive Character of "Commodity Esthetics"

The inversion of social qualities into "natural characteristics" resulting from the "fetish character" of the commodity today extends itself increasingly into the psychology of the "economic character mask." This is particularly true for the wage-dependent agents of capital, the sales personnel. Of these employees and sales persons "an effort is required that they make a show of this commodity (their labor power); and their appearance, the look of the employees of capital, plays in their situation the same role as the commodity esthetic does for commodity owners [. . .] What is a function of the realization of its commodity capital for the department-store capitalist, the look of his sales agents, becomes for them a sales function of their commodity labor power" (Haug[295]).

At the end of the twenties, Krakauer in his book *The Employees* described the compulsion to commodity esthetic display by sales agents. The increasing social insecurity of the middle class in the twenties forced many employees and secretaries to further the salability of their commodity labor power, which was in little demand, by displaying themselves as esthetic commodities. "Afraid to be withdrawn as used commodity goods, the ladies and gentlemen color their hair, and people in their forties take up sports so as to remain slim," wrote Krakauer (quoted in Haug[296]). Yet not only the personal appearance of the sales person but also his behavior, indeed his whole psychology, is finally subsumed under the sales function. This must become second nature to him just because he is unself-sufficient and sells in someone else's name. His notorious politeness and friendliness, his apparent concern, his flattery and ever-pleasing subservience—all these calculating elements of his sales function assume the form of characterological qualities out of fear of not "being accepted" by the customer. Standing under the sway of his sales function, he must constantly mimic a "pleasant," "friendly," "youthful" mien and repress all "natural" qualities, needs, and feelings which contradict this function. For, from the perspective of realization, all his "personal" feelings, all temporary moodiness, fears, and aggressions are only "nuisance factors" of his sales function. The economic character mask of the sales person therefore contains a clinical symptom, a clinical "character resistance" of the kind Wilhelm Reich once described in a patient who tried to fend off his repressed hatred for his father with a compulsive undying smile.[297] Here the clinical "keep-smiling" mask was the expression of an individual characterological misdevelopment; with sales personnel it is the expression and consequence of an economically determined function which the sales person, as psychologically "healthy" as he may otherwise be, cannot escape. As the personification of the sales function he must constantly put on a "good face" to a "rotten game," that is, conceal his real primary feelings, forms of expression, and behavior behind his "second face" as molded by commodity esthetics.

The increasing division within the sphere of circulation, which has as its consequence a corresponding division of labor within the sales function, leaves its trace in the face of the salesman mask, too. Haug writes: "Display and staging of the commodity, arrangement of sales site, its architecture, the lighting conditions, the colors, the sound façade, the aromas, the sales personnel, their outward appearance, the sales event—every element of the transformation of the commodity and the circumstances under which this occurs is calculated and functional.''[298] Like the capacities and functions of the industrial detail worker, those of the industrial detail sales person, too, become more and more specialized, fragmented, monotonous. Every salesman represents a more and more moronic element of the totality of the sales function: one person sits at the cash register, the other is solely occupied arranging the goods, another creating favorable lighting conditions, and so forth. The "compulsive character" of the esthetically molded sales and behavior function thus reproduces itself on a narrower and narrower field. With this the "face" of the sales mask also becomes smaller and more monotonous.

The buyer's appearance, like the sales person's, also succumbs increasingly to this compulsive molding process based on commodity esthetics. For on the work and "love market" the competing bidders must advertise themselves as best they can to maintain their market value or to increase it. Haug comments: "To personified capital its customers appear as buyers of packaging in which they will sell themselves. His own function is that of a jobber of packaging for the self-sale of his woman buyers."[299] This is also demonstrated by the strategies it offers the buyer for "success in love." An entire industrial branch, the so-called "beauty industry," which in the Federal Republic has the highest rate of growth and profit, is busy preparing the female—but to an increasing extent also the male—customer for "success" on the commodity stage. The cosmetics industry promises "to make every girl into a goddess"[300] and the textile industry advises women to offer themselves beautifully packaged in ever new variations.

The appearance of the buyer is constantly remolded in the economic rhythm of the textile, cosmetics and other industries. The face, thus, becomes less and less the personal expression of the human being, but rather the buyer's means of advertising himself, a means that is externally determined; for the buyer would like to appear as "pleasant" as possible, so as to make an effect that will be an incentive to "buying" him. Oddities in his appearance or in the expression of his facial mask, the traits of his "own" character, are more and more extinguished. Haug writes: "Packaging as 'goddess' functions simultaneously as a glittering 'straight-jacket,' as glittering compensation for the condition of subjugation and degradation to a being of second rank [. . .] In the process of acquiring such a face another face was lost [. . .]"[301] Thus there comes into existence a new social "compulsive character"—not in the psychoanalytical sense, in the sense of a fixation on certain (pregenital) libido positions (as in the classic anal-compulsive character), but in the sense of a highly variable, commodity-esthetic character mask *everything* of which it expresses is constantly subjected to the circulatory rhythm of capital, to a permanent revolution. R. Reiche observes: "He must constantly change his fetishist attributes and, under certain circumstances, just as rapidly the sexual object to which he affixes the fetishes [. . .] The manipulative fashion, which cannot even be put on a par with fashion in the old sense, provides the model for this type while it shackles it to fore-pleasure. Advertising not only prescribes the kind of clothes he has to wear and the foci of partial erotization (maxi- or mini-skirt) with which he and his partner must decorate themselves to be worthy of love; it also prescribes his complexion, the color and shape of his hair, the gestures he or his partner have to perform for specific activities such as the smoking of cigars or cigarettes, dancing, holding of whisky glasses, love making, walking on the street, so that his actual identity value remains high on the price index. All these accessories, to which individual qualities have sunk and become simultaneously fetishized, for which reason an object was worth loving, can, in case of doubt, change their appearance from one day to the next, and switch over to their exact opposite. The type under discussion is thus not actually perverse [. . .] He is merely a highly variable fetishist. The alacrity with which he changes his fetishes is finally a function of the circulatory speed of capital."[302]

The dominant and simultaneously uniform model according to which this highly variable commodity-esthetic character mask is molded is that of youth. According to Haug: "Youth becomes the pattern of the picture, not only of those who have success in business but also of the sexually attractive person who therefore appears successful and happy. Once more a circular compulsive function sets in. First there is anxiety over being dropped by capital for reasons of age. This fear was 'capitalistically' removed by offering commodities which promised to provide a youthful appearance. Soon no one could 'underbid' this standard of youthful appearance in adults without making a repulsive impression and therefore being rejected. [. . .] The consequence is — on the pain of sexual senility and isolation—a universally spreading compulsion to the 'cosmetic' of human beings and the appointment of their interior."[303]

Since youthfulness has been seized and enmassed by capital as a sales function, everyone who does not want to be defeated in the competitive struggle must undergo a kind of "compulsive" rejuvenation. The face as the mirror of the real experiences, sufferings, fears, and hopes of the human being, as the mirror of what his life and his aging has really been like, thus visibly retreats behind the facial mask, that is, has been trimmed to look youthful. This facial mask petrifies into a living commodity larvae amidst the rejuvenating commodity landscape. The same thing happens that happened to the old people in a Ray Bradbury science-fiction novel[304] who are put on a carrousel and become one year younger per revolution. Those who have been compulsively rejuvenated, however, become schizophrenic, because they look and are treated like children yet think and feel like old people. Thus the process of capital utilization condemns whole generations of sellers and buyers to "compulsive rejuvenation," that is, to a regression in appearance, behavior, and instinctual structure whose extent not even Freud could have imagined. For here it is not a case of individual, that is, individual-historical regression, which might be explicable with unresolved infantile conflicts, but of a massive regression resulting from the sales function of commodities, especially of the commodity of labor power. The compulsive rejuvenation of the new commodity-esthetic compulsive character, which is most marked in wage-dependent sales personnel, thus becomes the dominant trend of "infantile society."

The Depth-Psychological Invasion of Commodity Esthetics

It is characteristic of the pathology of the "consumer society" that what becomes decisive—by way of the massive formation of instinctual and character structures—is less and less the specific fate of individual socialization, the "fate" of primary instinctual development, but increasingly of the secondary socialization, that is, commodity-esthetic training in the sense of maximum functionalism for the capitalist realization process. This secondary socialization increasingly penetrates the instinctual structure of human beings to his most secret fears and longings, tearing down age-old taboos, asserting entirely new standards of what is "beautiful," "youthful," "clean," and the like, and revolutionizing the appearance and self-representation of entire generations of buyers and sellers.

A particularly drastic example of this is the incursion into the deepest level of the "personality" by the expanding cosmetics industry's reconditioning of the sense of smell. Classic psychoanalysis derived the kinds and characteristics of the sense of smell and the conceptions of what is considered "clean," that is, "repulsive," from the more or less strong repression of anal eroticism (which itself was dependent on a specifically rigid or permissive educational style during the anal phase). The cosmetics industry in a certain sense has performed a secondary socialization of the sense of smell which by far outranks the effects of the primary one. Haug writes: "A drastic example of this is the introduction of 'intimate sprays' and other means against the smell of one's own body. A true campaign has succeeded in disseminating a social antipathy against smells, primarily all sexually stimulating body smells, and to radicalize this antipathy. In this regard one should note the specific effect of these means on human senses, for when these means are used the stimulation threshold is lowered, that is, the banned odors are perceived much more strongly. Where they still crop up now and then, their irrefutable perception has now been antipathetically fixed. Now the body smells nauseatingly. Fear-drenched nausea, which is caused by a nauseating smell, leads to panic-stricken rejection and avoidance, that is, the antipathy which has been developed in this way tends to spread aggressively. Thus there comes into existence a new social norm anchored immediately and overpoweringly in the individual's senses, a norm of what is normal, clean, and of what is repulsive, low."[305]

What determines anal-reaction formations regarding what is "clean," that is, nauseating, therefore is less and less the quality of primary anal training, but rather the blind realization interests of those industrial branches which exploit anal fears. What holds true for the norms of that which is regarded with antipathy holds true for sympathizable norms and their models. If, according to Freud, the adult's "choice of the beloved" is decisively formed by his infantile object relationships and identification, then the significance of these primary infantile formations is largely relativized today by the secondary commodity-esthetic shaping of the instinctual structure, if not revised. Which sexual object is perceived as "beautiful" and "desirable," or as "repulsive" or "hateful," is decided less and less by the quality of the primary Oedipal and pre-Oedipal choice of object and increasingly by the dictates of commodity-esthetically produced models which increasingly affect the deepest reaches of the "personality."

The fact that the erotic models of entire generations of buyers have been molded by the blind realization laws of capital is shown by the model of "youthfulness" which we have already described. This model did not merely enforce an entirely new standard of what is "beautiful" and "youthful," but it also produced a new "social fear," the fear of growing old. The fear of aging has its rational base in that "young dynamic" labor power has a considerably higher market value than when it has deteriorated with age. The life of workers who have been expelled from the capitalist production process—with social security and pensions on which they can barely survive—is a bogey, however, for every young worker. The yearning for youthfulness therefore arises from a system where the old have nothing to laugh about and where aging means the same thing as declining economic and social status, becoming *déclassé*, and social isolation. The constant repression of old, used-up people by "young dynamic" labor power lends the fear of aging a truly traumatic dimension. Indeed, one could phrase it more pointedly and say that the classic childhood fears which Freud described are losing in importance compared to the trauma of old age. In any event, the psychology of the adult worker today is stamped more by this secondarily produced "social fear" than by the infantile fears stimulated during his primary socialization which psychoanalysis alone considers relevant.

The picture of what is "masculine," like the picture of what is "beautiful'' and "youthful," is also less and less determined by the classic Oedipal "imagines" which the family socialization process produces; rather, the character of what is "masculine" today succumbs to an anonymous shaping by commodity esthetics which increasingly withdraws from the influence of the agents of personal socialization (parents, teachers, and others). What is to be regarded as "masculine" and what not is primarily determined by those industrial branches which have discovered a market among young men. Whole new industrial branches, especially in the men's cosmetics field, have entered a market traditionally void of men's relationship to their bodies. According to Haug, the turnover of men's underwear and men's dress wear increased by leaps and bounds during recent years. The narcissism and exhibitionism which until recently was regarded as a specific attribute of women now is also teased in men as a new impulse to buy more and more men's fashions. Male dress increasingly acquires the character of a phallic-exhibitionist costume. Indeed, even the male nude, taboo until recently, nowadays appears as the "climax" on the commodity stage and the penis figures as the universal sex symbol which promises to equip the commodity and commodity owners with inexhaustible phallic potency. By thus peeling the patriarchal "husk" from masculinity the traditional relationship of man to man and men to women also undergoes a deep-reaching transformation. The man's appearance and the language of advertising are sexualized and, therefore, in a certain sense feminized: this relative coordination of the sexes (which also has a progressive side-effect not intended by capital) of course only affects the appearance and the forms of behavior between the sexes, not the sex-specific role distribution which continues to persist owing to the underprivileged economic and social status of women.

In its search for ever new detail markets, capital unlocks ever new "levels" of the instinctual structure. The "id" which—according to Freud—contains the biological-anthropological "instinctual dowry" of human beings can no longer withstand the psychological process of colonization through the psycho-pioneers of the commodity world. What the "id" still conceals in the form of passions, feelings, fears, and yearnings is sooner or later drawn into the light of the commodity stage and mirrored back to the buyers as the "model" of the commodity. The "archaic" symbolism of the unconscious (Freud) is deciphered more and more by the augurs of the concerns and inscribed as a particularly attractive "archaic" design into the commodity skin. Thus the archetypal sexual symbolism of dreams now populates the "dream world" of the commodity: ties, cigarettes, fenders are not only sold as material but also as sexual (say, phallic) symbolic values.

More and more segments of the instinctual structure succumb, as by-products of the capitalist process of realization, to an indigenous secondary treatment and molding whose significance increasingly supersedes the primary molding of the family socialization process. Late capitalism thus has in a certain sense relativized the Freudian primacy of the infantile formations of the personality structure of the adult, if not negated it entirely. Which "partial drives" are developed within the instinctual structure and which repressed becomes less and less a question of individual pre-genital "formations" and "fixations." Narcissism and exhibitionism in the male customer or voyeurism and fetishism in the sex and porno consumer no longer represent an individually comprehensible perversion (in the sense of classic psychoanalysis). Here it is rather a case of a socialized perversion unloosened by the pertinent capital interests (especially by the garment, cosmetics, and sex industries) as a blind side-effect of their profit strategies.

To the degree that a once-despised infantile sexuality is utilized by commodity esthetics, is it simultaneously deprived of its specific erogenous and, therefore, "character-forming" qualities. Even if the wealth of commodities—which transforms the sensuous human being's capacity to be sensuously stimulated into nothing but stimulations to buy—is constantly increasing and becomes outwardly more differentiated and refined, and tricky, the oral, anal, and phallic "partial drives" which have been satisfied or seemingly satisfied by the sexualized commodity increasingly forfeit their original quality. Curiosity pricked by commodity esthetics is no longer identical with the original curiosity of the child. The exhibitionism of the buyer who is got up according to the newest fashion no longer has anything in common with the natural self-representation of the child. Whereas the child as yet really represents his self, the consumer molded according to commodity esthetics in reality represents only how he is determined by an alien influence. Whereas the curiosity of the child still seeks to "acquire" its own body or that of the other sex, the curious sex and porno consumer only acquires his uniform standardized ideal.

Commodity-esthetically treated sexuality is therefore the exact opposite of "infantile sexuality." Whereas the latter is still interested in the sensuous use form of things, bodies, and people, the former is only interested in them as decals. According to Haug: "Esthetic abstraction, the disembodied and (because it has been released from the confines of objective reality) uninhibitedly flourishing, fruitlessly and agelessly flowering sensuousness has a retroactive effect on the structure of the perceptions and instincts of human beings."[306] The sensuous material of "infantile sexuality," too, increasingly succumbs to this "esthetic abstraction process." The original infantile instinctual material, which—according to Freud—constituted the psychosexual core of the personality, thus is pushed more and more to the periphery while "separately produced sense impressions," that is, the sensuousness determined by alien influences of the commodity world, increasingly penetrates to the deepest levels of the personality.

The Perverse "Social Partnership" Between Pleasure Principle and Reality Principle

If, according to Freud, the libido is a drive which seeks to "create ever greater units," then the "love drive" of capital has fulfilled the Freudian libido program today in perverse form: the "longing" of the buyer is confronted with more and more excessive commodity offerings which he can "love" in the sense of "buy." Sexualized commodities, those "sensuous supra-sensuous" beings, as Marx called them, offer themselves to him increasingly as "instinctual objects." The commodity landscape surrounding him becomes more and more of a sexual landscape which appears to deny him nothing anymore: every commodity segment seems to be destined for the satisfaction of a certain instinctual segment; and the "libidinous object cathexis" does not appear to have any limits, unless it be the individual's ability to pay. Haug writes:

"The living room landscape which has been melded into a proliferating family of commodities is no longer simply surrounded by individual sexual objects, individual commodities, as it used to be; now a whole complex of commodities turns it into a totally sexualized environment. Whoever owns such an apartment possesses in the reified form of this apartment the objective desire for a corresponding way of life, no matter whether or not this corresponds to his subjective desires. [. . .] This apartment is 'sexy' as, formerly, it used to be 'gemütlich.' The manifest lascivious attitude, the fluffy material and indirect lighting practically suggest to the visitor to undress like the human figures in the ads for the apartment do. The sexual instinct is invariably anticipated in this landscape, is characteristic of it. Although this sexual landscape may be the product of emancipatory urges which have been tracked down by capital as the occasion for its decorative ideas and realized in the form of commodities—once this sexual landscape has been acquired, because it promised to gratify the buyer's instinctual urges, it will in turn mold a certain instinctual structure which is no longer identical with the 'origin' of the idea [. . .]"[307]

The trend towards molding sensuousness goes so far that larger and larger segments of the social, instinctual, and need structures are churned through the meat-grinder of the capitalist realization process, so that needs other than those which have been really or seemingly satisfied by commodities soon find themselves unable to enter the buyer's consciousness. Since the buyer is confronted with things only in the form of commodities, in which parts of his dissatisfied being appear to find perfect expression and satisfaction, his instinctual and need structure too is integrated in a historically new perverse manner: since tendentiously only those needs are aroused which—from the perspective of capital realization—can be transformed into money, fewer and fewer needs present themselves to consciousness as "unfulfilled" or "frustrated."

In this sense a pathogenetic picture of "consumer society" is less and less to be characterized by classic Freudian concepts of illness. For the perfectly integrated "economic character mask" is scarcely able any longer to develop any needs and wishes of its own the unfulfillment or frustration of which (presupposing a certain ability to purchase, of course) it might "suffer." It tends only to wish for what it can buy, that is, what capital can profit on. Since its "own" authentic wishes have been deformed to the point of unrecognizability, their frustration is no longer felt as suffering. If the classic neurotic (that is, psychotic) suffered from the unfulfillment of his childhood wishes, capital has seemingly "relieved" him of his suffering by presenting him everywhere with the cliché and standardized décal of such "childhood wishes," except in purchasable form. The commodity-esthetic utilization of "childhood wishes" and their seeming fulfillment in the medium of buying thus lessens the formerly neuroticizing (that is, psychoticizing) tension between wish and frustrating reality.

The "asocial" drives of the "id," the dreams of happiness, love, and youth, are in a certain sense "resocialized" and "rehabilitated" through their functionalization for the capitalist realization process; however, with their pathogenetic character they also forfeit their subversive and rebellious character. Haug writes: "By interpreting human nature to human beings in this manner, commodity esthetics gives a twist to the progressive tendency of the drives in human beings, to their desire for gratification, joy and happiness. The driving impulses appear to have been reined in and transformed into an impulse to conform."[308] Thus the "pathogenetic cleavage" between ego and id, between reality principle and pleasure principle, appears to have been bridged too. By satisfying the "libido," the desire for pleasure, in the form of buying pleasure, it has so to speak been integrated in the capitalist reality principle. The classic potential for suffering, that is, neurosis, thus is tendentiously defused by reflecting the buyer's formerly unfulfilled wishes, if in a deformed, distorted, and abstracted form, back to him on the surface of commodities. Since even "wishing" is "bought away" from him, he cannot even "fall ill" from his wishes any longer.

The sales strategies of monopoly capital today assume an increasingly "permissive," "pleasure-accented," indeed even "lascivious" character: business capital presents itself in a certain sense as the "eternal lover" who promises to relieve its clients' sorrows with the "happiness of buying." Thus in the fall of 1971 a West Berlin department store ran the following ad: "Come relax with us! In the fascinating world of the big department store. Where you can buy lots of happiness for a little money. Even without cash! Simply with your golden customer card. And how much fun shopping at XYZ!"[309] The department store as "experience stage" becomes the house of pleasure: except not physical but sexualized commodity bodies transport the buyer into a latent state of erection of which only reaching into his pocket "relieves" him. The fascist ideology of "strength through joy," which no longer appears as openly today, has so to speak been absorbed by the commodity skin. The slogan of department store capital, instead of "strength through joy," now is "joy through buying power."

Business capital has literally inverted Freud's sentence "happiness is the subsequent fulfillment of a pre-historic wish," of a childhood wish, by propagating everywhere the "happiness" of buying as the immediate fulfillment of a long overdue (indeed, nearly once again obsolete) consumer wish. The classic conflict between ego and instinct is experienced less and less as such because the instinctual structure is determined as much by alien forces as the ego structure. The tension between the ego and the instinct lessens to the same degree that the latter appears to find its "relaxation" in the "happiness" of buying. If classic psychoanalysis understood the instinct still as an elementary biological foundation of the personality, late capitalism has long since undermined this foundation and restructured it. If human instincts and passions were largely excluded from social exchange and the traffic of commodities in the early and classic phases of capitalism, that is, repressed into the underground of the personality where they led a pathogenetic and simultaneously subversive existence, then late capitalism dredges them piece by piece out of their repression, so as to transform them into ever so many passions for buying. If human instinctuality once entered into a tendentiously pathological conflict with the reality principle of calculating and abstracting reason, today this conflict resolves itself to the same degree that the instinctual structure itself is subjected to the abstract calculations of the capitalist market. Instead of continuing to produce a "pathic cleavage" between "rational" ego and "irrational" instinct, capital today intervenes increasingly between the two poles of the psychic apparatus, so as to create a perverse harmony between them. Since the longing for pleasure functions as the trigger for the capitalist realization interest itself, the ego as representative of capitalist reality, that is, of the realization principle, perceives this longing less and less as a threat. The ego and the id become increasingly capable of "entering into a contract"; the classic antagonism is now replaced by a "social partnership" between the two "factions" of the psychic apparatus.

But this also alters the picture of the "psychopathology of everyday life." It is characteristic for the pathology of the "sphere of consumption" that—because of the increasing levelling and "disdynamicization" of the instinctual and character structures—"clinical symptoms" in the classic sense are to be found less and less (as opposed to the sphere of production where we are still dealing with the pathology of psychic dysfunctions, with manifest behavior disturbances). This pathology of the "sphere of consumption" appears less and less to take the form of classic symptoms, circumscribed within themselves, that might be immediately locatable as a defect, as dysfunction, as a "clinical" alien element within an otherwise "healthy" total personality. Rather, the total personality itself becomes a highly integrated pathogenetic entity to the degree that it becomes the total personification of the sales function. Thus what determines the pathogenetic picture of the buyer and salesman mask no longer tends to be the repression of certain specific instinctual needs, which encountered resistance and "defense" in the ego, that is, super-ego, but the tendency for the instinctual need structure to be determined by alien forces and to be molded compulsively.

If the pathology of the sphere of production still manifests itself in the form of specifically ascertainable and locatable disturbances of expression and behavior (as in psychosomatic symptoms, as "organ neurosis," as psychotic breakdown), then the pathology of the sphere of circulation is particularly characterized by the perfection, stereotyping, automatism, and abstraction of total expressive behavior in the sense of maximum functionalism for the capitalist realization process. If the classic symptom of neurosis and psychosis was still the expression of the rebellion of the pleasure principle against a frustrating reality principle, this element of protest tends to be eliminated by the new "social-partnership" integration of the pleasure principle (in the sense of buying pleasure) and reality principle (in the sense of wage labor). If the classic neurotic (that is, psychotic) was still "sincere" in the sense that his rebellious instinctual needs sought an anomalous, that is, symptomatic expression, then the "normal" anomality of the highly integrated buyer and salesman mask consists in its beginning to bear the function of a commodity-esthetic pleasure principle totally determined by alien forces. Classic symptom neurosis therefore recedes to the degree that, with the increasing subsumption of formerly autonomous work, there continues the subsumption of formerly autonomous instinctual needs under the capitalist realization process. Classic dysfunctional-symptom neurosis tends to be replaced by a kind of functional character neurosis, a commodity-esthetic compulsive character which is not so much the expression of a primarily psychosexual misdevelopment but of a secondary commodity-esthetic compulsive molding process.

This massively reproducible, symptomless, commodity-esthetic compulsive character, whose internal contradictions have been integrated in a perverse manner, of course only determines the pathogenetic picture of the sphere of circulation, that is, consumption. In contrast, in the sphere of production we find a significant increase of "functional" disturbances and pathogenetic defects. The pathogenetic picture of late capitalist society diverges, as it were, into two parts: into a commodity-esthetically molded symptomless surface picture of the total psychic functionalism which results from the totalitarian sales function of capital, and a clinical symptom picture beneath the first, a picture of the increasing psychic dysfunctionalism which results from the totalitarian production functions of capital.

Synopsis

Although Freud kept pointing out the "ultimately economic motive" in repression and instinctual renunciation, he overlooked the decisive repressive mechanism which is rooted in the very economic foundation of capitalist society, namely, the "repression" of use-value production by exchange-value production, the "repression" of particular concrete (natural-economic) work by "abstract work," or wage labor. The commodity and money structure which reproduces itself on a higher and higher level necessarily produces a social need and instinctual structure which becomes as abstract as itself. By raising itself to a general need, "abstract wealth" becomes the general motor of the "repression" of all particular, concrete, immediate needs and gratifications which it originally had to mediate. The addictive character attached to the movement of money also puts its stamp on the social instinctual structure, as Marx represented it in his portrayal of Midas and the hoarder who, "while sacrificing his carnal pleasure to the gold fetish," is the incarnation of an endless instinctual deferral and abstention—and, regarded this way, is the archetype of the capitalist neurotic.

The hoarder's abstract virtues—industriousness, continence, thriftiness, greed, and the like—finally become social and class virtues of the accumulating bourgeoisie. The "economic motive" of the accumulating bourgeoisie, which is "no longer use value and pleasure but exchange value and its increase," finds its religious guarantee in the collective compulsive neurosis of Protestantism and its characterological guarantee in the individual straightjacket of the "anal-retentive" character. The anal-reaction formation, the psychosexual capacity for instinctual control, instinctual deferral, and abstinence, become the dominant characterological qualities in the instinctual structure of the capitalizing individual; while the oral qualities, the psychosexual capacity for immediate satisfaction, for euphoria, for sensual pleasure, are correspondingly repressed. Freud's theory that civilization is created from instinctual abstinence therefore introduces the concept of the nature of capitalist accumulation —yet without analyzing its significance. Bourgeois renunciatory and anal-achievement psychology, however, only asserted itself in the proletariat when the bourgeoisie achieved power over the state and introduced a "barracks discipline" into the work process. This psychology was drilled in at an early age with the disciplining of "polymorphous perverse" childhood sexuality, that is, through the training of the (proletarian) child according to rigid conceptions of authority, cleanliness, and order. "Cultural sexual morality," which Freud made responsible for the development of neurosis, thus was the twin brother of the captalist-Protestant work morality: it had the primary function of anchoring the disposition to perform wage labor in the instinctual structure at an early age.

The dichotomy of the world as one of "abstract wealth" and the "repressed" world of sensuous-concrete wealth which develops with the commodity and money structure is also reflected in Freud's dichotomous psychology of the ego and the id. The increasing reification of social relationships reproduces itself in the subject as "pathic cleavage" between a rationally calculating ego function formed by the exchange principle and an id-function of a non-calculating and, therefore, "irrational" nature which is split off from the former. In the course of the development of the capitalist mode of production the emotionalism and immediacy of human beings came under the dictate of the hard and exact calculations of the market place; and what has remained of it was shunted off into the underground of the "personality," itself now a commodity, that is, into the "id." The central content of bourgeois socialization from then on consisted in working on the child's primary need structure until it unloosened itself from its immediate use objects and became usable for the abstract work of accumulation on the one hand and wage labor on the other. The defense mechanism of "repression," which is a specific characteristic of the bourgeois psychology of the ego, therefore, appears to be an intra-psychic continuation and elongation of the extra-psychic processes of abstraction and repression which are constantly operating in the spheres of production and circulation in capitalist commodity society.

With the increasing reification of social relationships the "libido," that is, the natural-economic use-value form of the wish, enters into a greater and greater conflict with the "reality principle" of abstracting reason. The "childhood wishes" it threatens tend to survive only in "fantasy," that is, in the form of neurotic and delusionary symptoms. "Love," "poetry," and "madness" now become synonymous with the incapacity, that is, refusal of human beings to subjugate themselves to total calculability. For the "capitalist soul" can afford "passion" and "love" only at the price of economic ruin. Therefore they look like weakness, stupidity, unhappiness, illness from the perspective of realization. Regarded in this way, neurosis would first of all be a definition, a "label," from the standpoint of the rationally calculating ego as representative of the capitalist profit principle. Regarded from the perspective of the "id," neurosis, "emotional illness" is an unconscious rebellion against the "unfeeling payment in cash" to which capital has reduced all human relationships.

The "inversion of consciousness," which is rooted in the fetish character of the commodity, reproduces itself on a higher and higher level with the development of the commodity form. Its own social conditions appear to the reified subject as "natural and thing-like" qualities. This economic mystification reproduces itself—via many mediations—on the level of the psychic apparatus whose psychology, "character," and the like also appear to the reified subject as natural and thing-like qualities, as "instinctual nature," although this is only the social sedimentation of a "second nature." Just as the material products of this second nature acquire power over their producers in the form of commodity, capital, and so forth, so do its idealistic, that is, psychic products in the form of religion, that is, of neurosis (or psychosis), acquire power over their producers once these products follow autonomous laws of their own. Regarded in this way, neurosis (that is, psychosis) would be the adequate psychological reflection of a society where, on the one hand, the autonomous means of production become a more and more threatening alien force, and, on the other hand, the anachronistic religious reflection (of this alien power) is replaced by the modern secular form of psychopathological reflex.

The "ego disturbances" Freud described should primarily be regarded against the background of the crisis of the bourgeois family which was robbed of its economic foundation by the concentration and monopolization of capital. The new historical stage of the socialization of work and capital (in the form of corporations, trusts, and so on) also drew the ground from under the feet of the bourgeois individualistic ego, of bourgeois ego autonomy. The increasing contradiction between real proletarianization and the ideal of personal autonomy finds its expression especially in the *déclassé* middle classes as "ego weakness," that is, as "neurosis." The sharpening social and political elements of crisis in the imperialist era also led to an abrupt increase of mental illnesses in all social strata. Since class contradictions, which are being ever more sharply defined, cannot be solved "progressively" via socialist revolution, they are solved "regressively," that is, interiorized as neurosis.

The incidence of mental illness, which is increasing significantly today in the era of late capitalism, especially among the working population, can be traced chiefly to the capitalist organization and division of labor. Marx has shown that manufacturing work entails an abnormal "fractionalization of the mode of work" which "seizes the individual at the root of his existence." Subsumption under the capitalist division of labor has as its consequence the fragmentation and partialization of all the individual's productive instincts and talents. His instinctual structure remains rudimentary to the degree that even the last rudiments of creativity are banned from the environment of wage labor with the increase in the division of labor. Although the work process as a whole becomes more complex, coordinated, and qualified, the work of a large number of workers becomes "simpler," more automatic, and disqualified. The increasing disqualification of work and the simultaneous "impossibility" of employing one's talents thus is a chief cause of "industrial pathology."

Today's rapid growth of functional illness and pathological defects among the working population can be chiefly traced to the structural changes in the production process and to new techniques of surplus-value exploitation. The increasing suppression of manual labor by the half-automated work process—by mental labor—has also created a displacement of organic by functional illness. The exploitation of "relative-surplus value" by the constant intensification of work, which is predominating more and more today, also has psychic impoverishment as a consequence. This increase in the incidence of mental illness is primarily the expression of a conscious or unconscious protest against new, ever more brutal forms of piece work and profit drudgery (MTM, etc).

Healthy labor power becomes "ill" because it becomes the object of ruthless capitalist realization and can be repaired only if it subjects itself to the conditions of realization of the "diseased commodity." The increasing rate of mental illness among workers has the objective function of capital infusions into the economy by supporting ever new pharmaceutical and chemical industries with the constantly growing demand for medicines and medical machinery. These are some of the industries with the highest growth and profit rate today. But doctors too are increasingly profiting from the realization of the diseased commodity; their fees increase to the same degree as the illness rate among workers.

The clinical picture of late capitalist society is further characterized by a significant increase in psychotic illness which is clearly over-represented among the proletarian population strata. The primarily "power-oriented" rigid educational practices in the working class family, the use of aggression up to and including physical violence, and the observance of externally set rules (in the production process) and norms have a more externalized form of super-ego formation as a consequence; and all of this produces a comparatively greater psychotic disposition. The primarily "love-oriented" permissive educational practices of the middle-class family and the compulsive control of instincts linked to the internalization of parental achievement norms have created, on the other hand, a comparatively higher disposition to neurosis. Workers, however, are much less able to afford manifest psycho-neurosis if only because its social consequences are much graver for them than for the upper and middle classes. For to be sick for them means being unable to guarantee the reproduction of their own labor power. A worker, therefore, "flips out" completely, that is, goes crazy, only if he wants to have the state take care of him and his family. The "loss of reality," much greater in psychosis than in neurosis, corresponds to the harshness of the social conditions of the ill individual. The proletarian psychotic regresses farther than the middle-class neurotic because the degree of instinctual frustration—as a consequence of the life-long compulsion of wage labor—is much greater for him.

The significantly higher rate of psychosis among proletarians becomes especially clear from the Freudian recognition that psychotic delusion contains simultaneously a demand for another, a new reality. Since the proletarian has to suffer most under capitalist reality, he has objectively the greatest interest in its social renewal. However, as long as he cannot change the social reality, as a consequence of political and organizational weaknesses, the isolated and impotent proletariat will instead change its conception of reality, that is, produce delusionary conceptions. The radical element contained in a delusory society has always been felt as a threat. In the madman it always persecuted the unconscious, anarchic form of revolution, as, conversely, it usually placed the revolutionary on the same level with the "psychopath." That is why it treats the "psychopathic" revolutionary, that is, the "revolutionary" psychopath, even today as if he had to be freed of the devil.

In the meantime, newer, more progressive research into psychosis and neurosis has subjected the old "custodial psychiatry" to a radical critique. The classic concept of schizophrenia as "inherited mental illness" was confronted by psychoanalytically oriented research with a genetic interpretation according to which schizophrenic "communicatory disturbances" arise from so-called "double-bind" situations, that is, from conflicts between the signal content of different levels of communication, which themselves are the result of ambivalent feelings by the parents; that is, from deep-reaching disturbances in the parental relationship. The hidden struggle between the parents is conducted in the child's psyche, which is "split." However, as progressive as psychoanalytical research of "schizophrenogene" family constellations is, it remains confined to family concepts: the "double-bind" situations characteristic of the "schizophrenogene" family are rather expression of social "double-bind" constellations, that is, of veiled class contradictions to which the proletarian child and parents are particularly exposed in school, training, and work. The "schizophrenogene" consciousness is, therefore, nothing but a destroyed, impeded class consciousness.

The more sociologically oriented research into schizophrenia was able to prove that the significantly higher rate of schizophrenia among the proletariat is primarily the consequence of "social isolation." However, this progressive sociological direction more or less neglected to consider capitalist working conditions as part of its analysis. The increase of "schizophrenic" communicatory disturbances in the final analysis must be traced to an increasing lack of communication due to a psychologically condensed and militarily organized production process where the producers are systematically isolated and atomized. If the "social isolation" within the sphere of production is doubled by the social isolation within the sphere of reproduction (living area, family), the disposition for "schizophrenic" breakdown increases as well. This—from the perspective of the wage earner—is nothing but a demonstrative refusal to "keep going on," to continue to sell his labor power under inhuman conditions. However, from the perspective of the realization process, "schizophrenia" is a "label" for defective, unprofitable labor power which is becoming rebellious; that is, it is a "defense mechanism" of the psychiatrists as the governors of the "dominant" concept of health.

In the final analysis the capitalist concepts of "health" and "illness" also provide the basis for modern sociological psychiatry's concepts of therapy and rehabilitation. The most essential instrument of this rehabilitation is "work therapy," which is supposed to put the patient back into the position of selling his labor power. Thus one hand washes the other: "clinical industry" supplies psychiatry with "psychiatric cases" by ruining labor power and thus the mental health of workers; the "industrial" hospital refurbishes labor power until it can be sold back to industry at a cut-rate price. What the "healthy" and the "ill" worker have in common is that both are determined by alien forces. In other words, the social condition under which they work, that is, become "ill" or "healthy," that is, able to work again, are totally determined by alien forces. This determination by alien forces constitutes the essence and cause of all mental illness in capitalism.

Besides psychosis of the schizophrenic type, what increasingly determines the clinical landscape of late capitalist society is drug psychosis. The consumption of psychotropic substances is also increasing in the adult working population which can endure, that is, anesthetize, its mental exhaustion in a totally rationalized work process, its increasing "functional disturbances" and "organ neurosis," frequently only by means of chemical stimulants, or so-called "happy pills." Factory owners thus have a personal interest in the "psychotropic wave." For the euphoric effect of the "happy pills" is to increase one's ability to achieve while simultaneously concealing the worst consequences of the constant intensification of work on the health of the workers. Legislators, therefore, do not so much punish drug consumption as such, which is essential for the maximum exploitation of labor power today, but only those who drop out on the "drug wave," that is, who withdraw from legal exploitation.

As becomes evident from many self-portraits, the main motive of proletarian opiate addiction is the search for recognition and status seeking. The drug scene turns out to be simply the other side of the coin of bourgeois society: not the "healthiest" and, therefore, most successful but the most "ill" and, therefore, "craziest" has the greatest market value here. In the hierarchy of the "drug scene" the opiate addict therefore stands on top. His manic-depressive psychology results largely from his class situation. The manic "high" in drug euphoria, which is usually succeeded by a phase of profound melancholy, should be regarded as an individual's unsuccessful attempt to overcome the class barriers in his imagination which he cannot overcome in reality.

Although pathological behavioral disturbances resulting from capital's function of totalitarian production manifest themselves primarily in the form of psychosomatic, psychosexual, and psychotic disturbances, the pathology resulting from the totalitarian sales function of capital manifests itself as the pathology of perfect commodity-esthetic models and behavior which cannot even be grasped anymore with Freudian concepts of illness. For the solution of its realization problems monopoly capitalism unloosens an inflationary world of "beautiful appearances," an infinite promise of happiness and value, which has as its consequence a perverse displacement of libidinous energies from the world of reified persons onto the world of personified objects. The corridors and display cases of the commodity world today become gigantic "experiential stages" which euphorize and mystify the buyer consciousness in a historically new manner. The dissolution of the commodity into artificial experiential events has the effect that the consumer tends to experience only what can be expressed in commodity categories. His "senses" are visibly transforming themselves into passive receptors of nothing but buying signals, and his relationship to the commodity world becomes more and more unreal since its "phantasmal" world of associations seeks to circumvent, more and more perfectly, the function of testing reality. Buyer behavior thus assumes more and more "projective features." The mental apparatus in a certain sense is restructured into the "projection screen" of the commodity film playing outside.

The "abstraction of sensuousness," which is immanent in the exchange principle, today also determines the sexualized appearance of the commodity body and its images which have been—as it were—peeled off from the consumer. Just as the sexual form of the commodity, so sexual needs and general behavior increasingly begin to resemble money, that is, they become unspecific. This manifests itself symptomatically in the promiscuous sexual practices of the middle-class sex and porno consumer, a behavior determined by the principle of unlimited convertibility of sexual objects. The total sexualization of the commodity world and the accompanying despecification of the sexual forms of behavior, however, means the total abstraction of the use value of sexuality. A constant promise of sexual use value drives erotic energy into a voyeuristic and exhibitionist fixation, that is, it is shunted off into subsidiary channels of the libido. The tendency towards a fragmentation of sensuousness through a progressive fragmentation of industrial labor thus is made even more potent through a commodity-esthetic "partial tease."

Firm, mature, and comprehensive object relationships occur more and more rarely as a consequence of the fragmentation of the instinctual structure. The content of the relationship with the sexual object becomes as indifferent, as fungible, as the content of work. The total levelling, draining, and abstraction of social relationships, as is typical of the commodity character, also increasingly hollows out the instinctual structure. Since the totality of the various partial functions of sensuality has been repressed by a totalitarian sense of the commodity, and all "spiritual and physical senses" by a "sense of having," the instinctual structure also remains rudimentary and underdeveloped.

The inversion of social into "natural" qualities, which is linked to the "fetish character of the commodity," today extends more and more deeply into the psychology of the "economic character mask." The appearance of entire buyer and salesman generations succumbs to a blind commodity-esthetic compulsive molding which becomes the prerequisite for "success" on the commodity stage. The face thus becomes less and less the personal expression of a human being, but rather the other-determined advertising means of the buyer, that is, sales person, who must advertise himself as "attractively" as possible in order to retain his market value. Since "youthfulness" has been seized by the capitalist sales function, everyone who does not want to succumb in the competitive struggle must undergo a kind of compulsive rejuvenation. This becomes the dominant trait of an "infantile society."

What today decides less and less about the "stamping," that is, training of the social-instinctual and character structure is less and less the fate of individual socialization, the "destiny" of primary instinctual development, but increasingly the secondary commodity-esthetic molding of the instinctual structure by the process of capitalist realization. Which sexual object is felt to be "beautiful" and "lovable," which "masculine" or "youthful," is less and less determined by the quality of infantile family object relationships and identifications but increasingly by the anonymous dicatatorship of esthetically produced commodities. Which partial drives are developed and which repressed depends primarily on the profit and sales strategies of the pertinent branches of industry. In its search for more and more partial markets capital thus opens up ever more "continents" of human sensuousness and simultaneously lets other long-discovered ones fall into disuse. The original infantile instinctual material, which constituted the psychosexual core of the "classic" personality, thus tends to be pushed to the edge while an externally determined sensuousness arising from the commodity world increasingly infiltrates the deepest layers.

That is why the pathogenetic picture of late capitalist consumer society can no longer be characterized by classic Freudian concepts. If the classic neurotic (or psychotic) suffered from the unfulfillment of his childhood wishes, business capital has tendentiously relieved him of his suffering by presenting everywhere the esthetically prepared standardized décal of his childhood wish, now in purchasable form. By satisfying libido, pleasure, in the form of buying pleasure (or the appearance thereof), it has itself been corralled by the capitalist reality principle. Since even desiring has been bought from the consumer, he can no longer "fall ill" from his desires. The classic antagonism between ego and id, the pathic cleavage between reality and pleasure principle, has been replaced by a perverse "social partnership" between both factions of the psychic apparatus. Thus it is no longer tendentiously the repression of certain particular instinctual needs which encounters the resistance of the ego, but the other-directedness and compulsive molding of the total ego *and* instinctual structure which determines the pathogenetic picture of the buyer and salesman mask.

This of course holds true only for the sphere of circulation, that is, realization, in late capitalist society. In the sphere of production, on the other hand, the increase of mental dysfunction actually signalizes a growing mental resistance to the capitalist "reality principle," the life-long compulsion to wage labor. The production sphere is therefore also the social location where symptomatic, pathogenetic resistance to the capitalist reality principle can and will switch to conscious political resistance.

Perspectives

Mass Psychic Impoverishment and the Task of a Subversive,
Materialistically Guaranteed Psychoanalysis

Probably the most popular and apparently most successful argument of
bourgeois critics of Marxism is that the "impoverishment theory" pro-
pounded by Marx has been refuted by the economic facts themselves: the
absolutely growing standard of living of the working class in highly
developed countries allegedly proves that the theory of "impoverishment" has been superseded by history. Such self-assured anti-Marxist
"proof" suppresses, of course, the fact that Marx's concept of "impoverishment" does not refer to absolute but to *relative* wages. Unfortu-
nately, even leading theoreticians and organizers of the workers' movement, such as Lasalle, have not always made that distinction. The
concept of "impoverishment" means that the wage and, thus, the living
standard of the working class does not decline absolutely, but only
relatively with regard to capital profit. In fact, not much has changed in
this respect in affluent society: the discrepancy between wages and
capital profit becomes greater and greater; that is, the working-class share
of the gross social product is steadily decreasing despite the increase of
absolute wages.

Bourgeois know-it-alls also suppress the fact that Marx's concept of
"impoverishment" does not refer to a particular national proletariat but
to the international proletariat which has been subjugated by world
capital. However, the proletariat of highly developed capitalist countries
have avoided absolute economic impoverishment (to which it was exposed in the nineteenth century and also during certain crises in the
twentieth century) only because it shared indirectly in the extra profits
which European and American capital pressed out of its colonial and
imperialist ventures in the Third World. On the basis of these immense

extra profits the leeway that monopoly capitalism had to grant the indigenous population by way of economic concessions was much greater in its imperialist than in its pre-imperialist phase. The relative affluence which the proletariat of highly developed capitalist countries has achieved, that is, fought for, therefore was paid for with the absolute impoverishment of the proletarians of African, Asian, and Latin American countries, which became poor to the same degree as wealthy imperialist countries became wealthier.

Above and beyond this, Marx's concept of "impoverishment" becomes particularly contemporaneous today if one supplements it with the psychological dimension. Although, as we said, the proletariat of the imperialist metropolises is still subjected to a relative process of economic impoverishment, a psychic impoverishment is making such striking appearance today that it deserves special attention particularly from the Marxist side. It is to the credit of SPK Heidelberg to have pointed to this shift in emphasis which is so eminently important for the theory and practice of the socialist movement: "Our society is a class society, that is, there are exploiters and exploited. However, exploitation today does not manifest itself immediately as material poverty [although this is still scandalous in outlying areas of large cities, especially in the Federal Republic; also compare *Armut in Deutschland* by Jürgen Roth[310]—author] but increasingly assumes the form of massive psychic impoverishment."[311]

The contradiction immanent in capitalist commodity production between the production of exchange values and capital on the one hand and the destruction of use values, primarily that of labor, on the other, is reaching a critical point. The technological forces of production and, thus, the productive forces of social labor develop to the degree that work for individual workers becomes more and more empty, abstract, stupid, and monotonous. And with the constant intensification, automation (under capitalist conditions), and abstraction of work the pathogenetic character also increases constantly. Today the technical possibility for the elimination of the capitalist division of labor exists as never before, but the subsumption of the human being under that division has reached its absolute high point.

The same contradiction reproduces itself on the level of consumption: the consumer stands confronted by an absolutely and quantitatively growing mass of commodities, for the "acquisition" of which, in the sense of qualitatively developing his sensuous and intellectual capacities, he becomes less and less capable. The more his sensuous life becomes a means to be utilized the more it disappears from his senses, the more "senseless" it becomes for him. Today the material forces of production have assumed a truly universal form; but the sensuous and libidinous forces behind the instincts, that is, psychosexual capacities for the "acquisition" of productive forces, have become as stupefied and atrophied as never before.

The same contradiction reproduces itself on the level of socialization: the bourgeois family organization becomes a more and more unbearable fetter of the technical, and long since possible, development of social forms of behavior and communication. R. Reiche observes: "[. . .] the psychic terror [of the family . . .] manifests itself so grandiosely today because the contradictions between the forms of behavior to which the family is bound and the forms of social intercourse between human beings that are in fact possible have increased immensely [. . .] Also the contradiction between the needs to which the family is bound, and those which press beyond it, has deepened so immensely. This contradiction presses for a forcible solution which also keeps having to be blocked off in the family time and again. That is the most secret reason why the family (besides the organization of work) becomes an additional germinal cell for so many new illnesses of civilization (psychosomatic complaints, psychosexual illnesses, depression, neuroses, schizophrenia) [. . .] The types additionally destroyed by the family must use up their remaining mental energy to dam up their illnesses and thus have no energy left for the struggle against wage labor."[312]

The shift, as Marx prophesized, of social-production forces into destructive forces reproduces itself today—within a monopolistic commodity economy—on a higher and higher level. Thus it also reproduces itself within the social-instinctual economy on a higher and higher level. The imperialist machine threatens not only the people of the Third World with immediate physical destruction but also the population of the imperialist metropolises themselves. It threatens them with gigantic mental destruction in the form of massive psychic crippling and illness. The immense destruction of social-productive forces in the form of capital destruction (economic crises, armaments production, and so on) and functional capital destruction (impeded automation in sectors which are unprofitable for capital, planned obsolescence, and the like) has its psychological complement in the unceasing destruction of mental energies in the form of "defense and repression energies" necessary to maintain the mental balance of mass neuroses and psychoses. The increasing "dead loss" of a monopolistic commodity economy corresponds to the increasing "dead loss" of instinctual energies which human beings must use to dam up their illnesses. Today the conquest of external nature has advanced as never before, but "instinctual nature" has become as denatured as never before. The U.S. provides a good example. The technically most developed nation in the world is simultaneously the mentally most crippled, brutalized, and diseased nation in the world. When Freud said that tendentially he had the "whole world as a patient," then this statement is more than ever appropriate to the capitalist world of America which meantime has become so "ill" that it requires not so much urgent therapy for its individuals as revolution in all its social foundations.

The contradiction, on the one hand, between increasing technical perfection and material wealth (of which, of course, the capitalist class garners the lion's share) and, on the other, growing mental impoverishment and illness is new in its historical convergence. The connection between the utilization of capital and mental impoverishment must, therefore, finally become the focal point of political propaganda. Besides traditional political-economic arguments, which elucidate capital's economic exploitation mechanism, political-psychological arguments elucidating the pathogenetic effects of capital domination must be given increasing importance for revolutionary mass agitation and propaganda: not only rising profits, prices, rents, taxes, armaments outlays, but also the rising rate of psychoneurotic and psychotic illnesses, functional and addictive illnesses, potency and communicatory disturbances, and the like must be made the object of political agitation and propaganda.

The mental impoverishment in all social classes and levels today assumes a form and extent as yet unheard of in Lenin's lifetime. A contemporary revolutionary theory and practice, therefore, must take particular account of it. Economic exploitation and impoverishment alone (which, as we have said, is only to be understood as relative impoverishment, as a growing discrepancy between wages and capital profit) less than ever suffices for political agitation and propaganda. A revolutionary propaganda which takes account only of the chief contradictions between wage labor and capital, without including its pathogenetic effects on the mental structure and on the consciousness of the wage-dependent masses, stops short of what is needed today. Political enlightenment about such horrendous disease among wage laborers is just as important as political education about the horrendous profits of capital.

Only when capital's "Janus-face" of increasing material affluence and mental impoverishment is seen simultaneously from both sides will capitalist exploitation be perceived not only objectively, but also subjectively as the scandal which it has always been. Only when the wage-dependent masses become aware at what economic *and* mental cost their relationship with capitalist production can be maintained—at the price of an increasing economic exhaustion *and* psychic derangement of their labor power, even of the increasing mental, intellectual, and psychic crippling of the entire Western "affluent society"—will the few shares, the personally owned home, the color television, the stereo set, the vacation lose their mystifying, that is, conciliatory effect. When the mental balance of the so-called affluent society is placed next to the profit and exploitation balance—in the Federal Republic alone there are 7,000,000 neurotics requiring treatment, roughly 2,000,000 alcoholics, 600,000 psychotics of the schizophrenic type, 250,000 youthful drug addicts, and so on (to mention only those who are statistically ascertainable)—then the ideology of affluence and consumption will become suspect once and for all.

Today one can find everywhere a historical shift in emphasis in the forms of impoverishment, that is, a displacement from (absolute) economic to mental impoverishment. Political-economic theory must therefore simultaneously imply a theory of illness and political practice with therapeutic practice. A materialistically enlightened psychoanalysis —or perhaps one should rather say, a materialistically based psychoanalytical theory of illness—acquires an important task in this respect, namely, to transform all forms of mental resistance against and refusal towards the conditions of capitalist work and socilization which express themselves as illness into a subjective instrument of politicalization. A psychoanalytically enlightened materialistic theory of illness, understood in this fashion, must demonstrate that mental disease, whatever form it takes, contains a subversive and progressive element: that it represents an unconscious form of refusal to abide by the existing conditions of exploitation and oppression in the family, or of production and consumption. Thus the beginning that Wilhelm Reich made should be actualized and simultaneously expanded, though it is no longer a question, as it was for Reich, of the demand for sexual freedom, of the fight against ''bourgeois sexual morality'' (which, in any event, has been undermined by the utilization of sexuality by commodity estheticism). Rather it is primarily a question of translating the element of passive resistance which expresses itself in mental ''illness'' into active political resistance against a diseased society. A materialistic psychoanalytical theory of illness must begin with the realization—and must propagandize this fact into public consciousness— that ''mental illness,'' whether it be neurosis or psychosis, functional or addictive, should be regarded from two contrary aspects at all times. From the perspective of ''official health,'' that is, from the viewpoint of utilization, it is a ''label'' for defective, unprofitable, even obstreperous labor power. From the viewpoint of wage labor, on the other hand, it is nothing else than unconscious mental escape, that is, an attempt to break out, from capitalist labor and socialization conditions, a symptomatic refusal ''to continue to go along.''

Although the class consciousness of a large segment of wage laborers— this holds true for the Federal Republic in particular—has been choked off, that is, repressed, by fascism and subsequently by the restoration, the workers' resistance to capitalist production relationships have by no means disappeared. At the level of psychic apparatus it has merely slipped, so to speak, one floor lower, that is, it expresses itself increasingly in the form of refusal through illness. The mass phenomena of illness therefore must today become more and more the object of public discussion and the object of political campaigns, so that the common social root of all the different mental diseases and forms of impoverishment can be recognized. Only in this way can the individual patient, who is accustomed to taking "his" illness as a "private" fate upon himself, understand its social character. Only in this way can the social loss of prestige, which is necessarily connected with illness in capitalist society, be eliminated.

If they allowed psychoanalysis any function at all, Marxists have allowed it only a limited one until now, that of a "differentiation" of the superstructure scheme, that is, as a theory of genetic socialization. And in this Marxism was justified since the psychoanalytic categories, as we have tried to show, were tied to the superstructure, that is, are blind to the extra-familial determinants of mental illnesses, of socialization- and ideology-formation processes. A materialistically and psychoanalytically versed theory of illness, as we have sketched here, begins, however, at the very "basis" by showing that psychology becomes psychopathology to the degree that it is subsumed under the utilization process of capital, that is, becomes illness. To that degree it also implies a therapeutic strategy. If psychosomatic, psychoneurotic, psychotic "reactions" are nothing but blind and unconscious "defense reactions," that is, defense mechanisms (as psychoanalysis says) against the functions of capitalist utilization under which all people are subsumed nowadays, then it becomes a question of translating these "defense reactions" into conscious political actions against a diseased society. If the social labels of "healthy" and "ill" are finally an expression of capitalist selection between intact and defective, profitable and unprofitable, adjusted and non-conforming labor power, then it is a question of mobilizing "illness" in all its forms as "resistance" against the "dominant" health.

That, of course, does not mean that—as with SPK Heidelberg—one immediately makes a revolutionary virtue out of general mental distress and proclaims "illness as the number one productive power" for revolutionizing the capitalist mode of production. "Illness, of course, contains not only a positive element, an element of resistance and refusal, which indeed can become a subjective instrument for political struggle, but also a negative element which manifests itself in "ego weakness," "regression," "loss of reality," and so forth. SPK Heidelberg's sympathy with the Red Army Faction, however, proves that the positive (tendentiously political) element of resistance in illness can engage in a highly unfortunate mixture with its negative apolitical element of "loss of reality." In political practice this has led to thinking in questionable political absolutes and anarchic impatience. If SPK Heidelberg declares the "patient" *eo ipso* into a "revolutionary class," then the "revolutionary subject" is no longer—as in Marxist revolutionary theory—derived from its objective position in the process of production. This attitude also simply ignores the class character of "illness," that is, the class differences between individual "groups of patients." Despite its absolutization of the concept of illness, it is to the credit of SPK Heidelberg to have understood the phenomenon of illness as a political problem and for the first time to have turned it into an instrument of political agitation and propaganda.

The SPK experiment primarily shows that every political and organizational model today must simultaneously contain a therapeutic model. Superannuated models of political organization, such as the Bolshevik one, should also be rethought, that is, questioned from this perspective. In view of the historically new level of mental impoverishment the structure of organizations for political struggle can no longer be determined by the sole criterion of political efficiency and organizational ability. The therapeutic viewpoint must enter and determine the structure of revolutionary organizations in the sense of creating qualitatively new, non-alienated, non-reified forms of communication. The political "self-organization" must simultaneously be a therapeutic "self-organization" in which atomized, psychically depleted, "ill" individuals, whose ability to communicate has been inhibited, acquire together with their political consciousness also a collective ego consciousness, a cooperative "ego strength." Not those forms of organization which have the "purest" political line to (in the sense of linking up with some kind of Leninist, Stalinist, or Maoist tradition) will have historical success, but that organizational form which is able to link up with historically new needs of the masses and absorb them.

One of these qualitatively new, essential mass needs is that for communication and collective life which results from "renewed atomization," the "separation of workers in the work process" (Rabehl and Heilmann), a need which—despite all economic conceptions—was also one of the impulses behind the May 1968 revolt in Paris: "The phenomenon which most surprised all observers was the extraordinary need for communication and collective life, the enthusiasm with which broad masses of people whose life had been shaped by the models of consumer society revolted against these models, were convinced of their absurdity, and—if only for the moment—were prepared to renounce them; and finally there was the ease with which the masses found their own means of communicating in this collective experience, their capacity to organize themselves and find their own discipline in their revolt" (Magri).[313]

If during the May revolt the inhabitants of certain apartment houses tore down the cement walls in their apartments not only in the metaphorical but the literal sense of the word—as Henri Lefebre recounts—then this also expresses the therapeutic demand which must be made of a revolutionary organization today: not only to overcome private property but also the pathogenetic "walls" which private property has erected between and in human beings. All purely economic strategies are necessarily shortsighted in view of the historically new level of psychic mass impoverishment. One will scarcely be able to mobilize the masses of young people who have been particularly shaped by the ideology of consumption with economic and political demands alone. The revolutionary movement must offer more today than a socialist conception of state and economy. Since the commodity character has only now, in late capitalism, fulfilled its "universal character" (Lukács), the socialist revolution too can only be conceived as a universal transformation of all social relationships which the commodity character has affected.

The historical shift of emphasis in the forms of impoverishment, the displacement from immediate economic to immediate psychic impoverishment, the revolutionary movement has to take particular account of. That is, it must provide not only a new model of the state and economy but also a new model of communication which counteracts mental mass impoverishment politically and therapeutically. In other words, it must confront late capitalist symptoms of mass impoverishment with a new communist image of man, an image of the universal development of human sensuousness as Marx sketched it in his Paris manuscripts: "Just as private property is only the sensuous expression of the fact that man becomes *objective* for himself and at the same time becomes an alien and inhuman object for himself, and just as his expression of life is his externalization of life and his realization a loss of reality, an *alien* actuality, so the positive overcoming of private property—that is, the *sensuous* appropriation of human essence and life, of objective man and of human *works* by and for man—is to be grasped not only as *immediate,* exclusive *satisfaction* or as *possession,* as *having.* Man appropriates to himself his manifold essence in an all-sided way, thus as a whole man. Every one of his *human* relationship with the world—seeing, hearing, smelling, tasting, feeling, thinking, perceiving, sensing, wishing, acting, loving—in short, all the organs of his individuality, which are immediately communal in form, are an appropriation of the object in their objective relation or their *relation to it.* [. . .] The overcoming of private property means therefore the complete *emancipation* of all human senses and aptitudes."[314]

The "Revolutionary Ferment" of a New, Emancipatory Structure of the Instincts and Consciousness

In the last part of our investigation we primarily relied on Haug's book *Zur Kritik der Warenästhetik* (Towards a Critique of Commodity Estheticism) and in part also on R. Reiche's Book *Sexuality and Class Struggle.* Haug made a very important "contribution to the social analysis of the fate of sensuousness and the development of the needs in capitalism," a contribution which, in contrast to bourgeois theoreticians of media, advertising, and manipulation, does not hoe to the surface of criticized phenomena—"superfluous needs," "consumption terror," "consumption manipulation,'' and the like. In this regard his critique of commodity estheticism is also far superior to R. Reiche's account of sexuality and class struggle, which does not trace the same phenomena, or insufficiently, back to the dynamics of the capitalist realization process. Yet Haug, too, cannot be completely acquitted of the charge that he himself levels at Reiche: that his analysis remains bound to the sphere of consumption, the sphere of commodity circulation and realization which is the actual location of "commodity esthetics." Although Haug demonstrated the "molding of the instinctual structure" within the sphere of realization much more stringently and systematically than Reiche, he too suppresses, as does Reiche, the "molding of the instinctual structure" within the sphere of production itself by means of the capitalist division and organization of labor.

Because of this deficiency Haug's analysis becomes at certain points undialectical and fatalistic. Commodity estheticism acquires an absolute importance for the molding of the instinctual structure which it has at most for the middle-class consumers who are not part of the immediate industrial process. Industrial production, however, is precisely where use values are still produced and an immediate use-value consciousness can still be formed despite real use-value depreciation. The industrial producer is not as much at the mercy of inflationary use-value promises as Haug feels, since the producer still sees them through the perspective of the producer, that is, from the viewpoint of use value. Since he, as the producer, produces not only the use value but also the use-value promise, he also has a keener, more critical view of use-value than the middle-class consumer. Since he is also a consumer with only limited buying power, he experiences the actual depreciation of use value on his own body, that is, in his pocket book. At any event, he cannot afford to buy a new car every two years, or a new television or washing machine. Consequently he is not as liable to fall prey to the seductive use-value promises which (as Haug believes) compensate for the real use-value depreciation (of his car, television, or washing machine).

Haug writes: "The corrupting effects of actual anthropological dimensions [. . .] are devastating; the people seem to have sold their consciousness. Every day they are trained in the enjoyment of what betrays them, in the enjoyment of their own defeat, in the enjoyment of identification with what dominates them [. . .]."[315] But that is to impute that industrial wage laborers, too, are tricked by the "phantasmagorical" appearance of the commodity world. "Corrupting use value," however, corrupts consciousness only in the sphere of realization, that is, consumption, before which Haug is as fixated as the rabbit before the snake. In the sphere of production, however, there is today a growing critical consciousness about the destruction of use value, primarily the use value of labor power. Here industrial wage laborers are discovering the destruction of their labor power, that is, of their most valuable use value in the form of a growing psychic impoverishment and of bodily illness. The historically new extent of the destruction of use value, including that of labor power, therefore produces rather inevitably a political conflict with a system whose destructive internal and external character becomes more and more evident.

The exhausted worker suffering from stomach ulcers or heart or circulatory illness unmasks the world of commodities and consumption more and more for what it is: as an alien world of mere appearance which he is the last to "enjoy." From the viewpoint of his own mental exhaustion and impoverishment, a commodity-esthetic heaven on earth is a cause for cynicism because he has to pay for it with piece work, overtime, and circulatory complaints. The sharpening contradiction between the inflation of use-value promise on the one hand, and the real destruction of use value on the other, therefore sets free a dynamic which is tendentiously directed against the system as such. The massive mental dysfunctions, the massive psychic misery produced by the late capitalist production process stands in crasser and crasser contradiction to the advertised happiness of the late capitalist consumer landscape. Since Haug suppresses this contradiction he no longer sees a way out of the labyrinthian hall of mirrors of the commodity esthetic; thus he no longer perceives those "revolutionary elements" which appear to begin to dissolve the fog-bound commodity-esthetic consciousness, starting with the sphere of production.

When Haug writes that "their people have allowed their consciousness to be bought," then he suppresses the structural changes which have occurred since the third industrial revolution in the economic and technical basis of the production process, and thereby also in the structure of qualification and consciousness in industrial producers. The transition from a completely mechanized mode of production to partial automation and the accompanying replacement of manual industrial by mental labor, indeed, the replacement of controlling mental labor in certain areas by self-steering and self-regulating machine systems, makes qualitatively new demands on the mental alacrity of the workers. On the one hand, highly qualified technical and scientific specialists are needed for the control and repair of partially automated machines, whose technical qualifications outdate more and more rapidly owing to a constant revolution in the technical basis of production. On the other hand, the majority of work sites demand less and less qualified factual knowledge and fewer talents. In fact, an ever greater demand is made, especially upon the unqualified worker, to be pliable to changing work conditions.

Since the modern worker is trained less to learn traditional, specialized skills but rather fungible knowledge and changing skills, that is, the learning of learning, he generally has a higher mental and intellectual mobility at his disposal than in earlier times. This mobility, however, cannot simply be confined to the narrow realm of his detail work, that is, part function, but extends itself tendentiously to recognizing and judging the totality of social contradictions and problems. The higher technical and intellectual mobility of the modern worker, therefore, simultaneously produces a higher disposition for political consciousness and emancipatory processes.

In addition, technically and scientifically qualified workers must increasingly perform work which does not correspond to their true qualifications. The contradiction between their qualified training and their disqualified work therefore tends to produce a political conflict with the capitalist organization of work. Unqualified, unskilled workers, however, are increasingly radicalized by the constant rationalization, intensification, and automation of their work and the mental and physical exhaustion owing to it. Thus during the May 1968 revolt in Paris primarily two groups of workers, highly qualified scientific and technical workers and the unqualified, developed the most radical political forms of struggle.[316] Even the most progressive demands of the Italian working class—equal wage increases for everyone, elimination of the premium, control of assembly-line speed, elimination of categories (unskilled laborer, for example)[317]—shows that the industrial wage laborer is entering into greater conflict with the principle of the capitalist organization of work despite manipulation in the sphere of consumption and despite the commodity-esthetical obfuscation to which they are subjected. Thus people are allowing themselves to be less and less "trained in the enjoyment of their own defeat, in identification with what dominates them" (Haug). The gradual reawakening of the class struggle in the West German working class also shows that it does not allow its consciousness simply to be "bought."

But the sphere of reproduction, that is, socialization also develops— through the crises and contradictions immanent within it—a "revolutionary ferment" for new emancipatory structures of instinct and consciousness. The always changing skills and knowledge necessary for the modern world of work cannot be handed down from generation to generation within the family as they used to be. Since the bourgeois family can no longer transmit the knowledge necessary for the production process it also increasingly loses its classic educational function. That is why capital evinces a growing interest in the socialization of education, especially primary socialization. This manifests itself in, among other ways, the development of "compensatory pre-school education"—favored by progressive sections of capital. This is supposed to initiate training in so-called "basic skills," that is, the ability to learn fungible skills and knowledge, which correspond to the fungible demands at the work site.

The consequence of such a step in primary education is a corresponding revolution in the psychosocial foundation of society: for the rigid type of authoritarian socialization, which the classic patriarchal family still produces, is today—again from the viewpoint of capital—more and more unprofitable. Therefore, there is a tendency for it to be replaced by a flexible type of socialization which is more pliable in regard to changing instinctual objects and objectives, and which is capable of adjusting to changing demands of the work process without overly severe "frictional losses." The classic "authoritarian personality" (Fromm) is increasingly dismantled through the socialization of education and the liberalization of childhood sexuality.

Since the bourgeois family can no longer fulfill its classic educational tasks, the classic Oedipal imagines also lose their significance for the mental development of the growing child. The Oedipal conflict with the father loses in sharpness and relevance to the degree that the fathers themselves have lost their traditional authoritarian roles. Mitscherlich describes this tendency with the concept of "the fatherless generation." More recent authors also diagnose—if only phenomenologically—the softening up, that is, elimination of the classic Oedipal conflict. Thus F. Böckelmann speaks only of a "peripherally diffuse Oedipal situation with flowing, perhaps never entirely consummated dissolution," scarcely deserving of the name. The result of this gradual shrinking of the classic Oedipal conflict is allegedly a "new form of ego weakness which no longer, as in the authoritarian sado-masochistic psyche, signifies a cornered, threatened ego but a fluid, diffuse, unbounded ego which for that very reason can focus only on its own interests, an egoistic interest identical with that of consumer society."[318]

Of course, psychoanalytical authors are blind as usual to the driving economic and social forces which prepare "the wrongful elimination of the authoritarian personality" (Böckelmann), that is, of a "fatherless society" (Mitscherlich). They are even less able to comprehend the new quality of the generation conflict, that is, the dialectic of revolution in the psychosocial foundation of society which, generally, they register only by shaking their heads. According to A. Gorz: "The acceleration of development in technical, scientific and cultural areas has among other consequences the fact that children and adolescents differentiate themselves more emphatically than before from their parents. Also they are better informed, they undergo a different training and have a different future ahead. What is already self-evident for young people and decisively influences their present and future life, is for their elders a book with seven seals. That explains why older people's frame of reference has been completely superseded."[319]

Rejecting the old "frame of reference," young people simultaneously question the social "virtues" (work discipline, industriousness, cleanliness, obedience to authority) and ideologies (of social mobility, achievement, and the like) which guarantee the psychosocial adjustment to this "frame of reference" of their elders. The capitalist morality of "work and endurance," which was also the basis of fascist ideology, increasingly loses its attraction for younger workers, especially because it becomes more and more anachronistic in view of the immense actual potential wealth of society. Traditional religious, moral, racist, and nationalist ideologies (such as "honor," "sense of duty," "heroism," racist sense of "purity," nationalist sense of "fatherland"), which fascism was still able to mobilize and hone to a fine point, can scarcely become a material force anymore. On the other hand, what assumes the function of traditional ideologies today, at least up to a point, is the immediate economic mystification of the capitalist commodity society. That "money works" or that capital and workers are "co-equal partners" is a much more effective and widely disseminated prejudice than that of the "sacredness" of the family, the people, or the fatherland. Thus, on the one hand, the revolutionary movement has it easier because it no longer needs to dismantle the mountain of traditional ideologies (with which the communist movements of the twenties and thirties still had to struggle); on the other hand, it also has a more difficult job because the economic mystification of the capitalist mode of production is fortified by an immense advertising and sales machinery.

Yet the late bourgeoisie is no longer in a position to mobilize the youthful masses with sweeping ideologies. It is also less and less able to provide ideological legitimation for economic crises, imperialist wars, and mental mass impoverishment. With the disappearance of idealism from late bourgeois ideology the view of the imperialist machine of destruction (read: bombing terror) externally, and mental destruction (read: work terror) internally is becoming less and less distorted. The waning idealism of late bourgeois ideology therefore has the consequence of a relative waning of the "super-ego" within the "fatherless generation." The super-ego of the youthful masses today becomes less and less "the bearer of tradition and all permanent values which have been passed on over the generations" (Freud[320]), since the late bourgeois generation of parents is scarcely in a position creditably to transmit "traditions" and "permanent values," be they of a political or cultural nature. The super-ego structure of the youthful masses becomes more porous and malleable to the same degree that the Oedipal conflict loses in sharpness and significance. This has the effect of the super-ego losing—and this has to be welcomed— some of its "conservative" character and mental-shackling effect.

Psychoanalytical bourgeois authors, of course, regard the waning super-ego of the "fatherless generation" and the striking lack of "valid" models, ideas, and values resulting therefrom as reason for profound concern. Behind the complaint voiced everywhere that the patriarchal generation's authority is waning is the fear that their sons and daughters indeed will take a different path and develop different political and cultural value systems for themselves. Any psychoanalytical concern about the "regressive" character of the young "ego-weak" generation only too clearly reveals their mourning over the actual disintegration of the classic bourgeois ego structure. The manifest dissolution of the classic bourgeois competitive and individual ego, however, should not be regarded a sign of impending problems but as a "historical sign": it signals the growing socialization, that is, proletarianization, of youthful instinctual and ego structures. Although this socialization occurs in a bourgeois manner, that is, is accompanied by an increasing uniformization, levelling, and "repressive desublimation" (Marcuse) of social, primarily sexual, forms of behavior, yet it simultaneously announces a new quality of communication and collective life as was completely unknown by their father's generation.

The dissolution of traditional sexual and ego structures, as formulated in such concepts as the "fatherless generation" (Mitscherlich), the "wrongful elimination of authoritarian personality" (Böckelmann), "repressive desublimation" (Marcuse), the "genital façade" (R. Reiche), has a thoroughly progressive aspect which the respective authors always overlook. One exception is Reiche who has subjected Marcuse's concept of "repressive desublimation," which was the original model for his concept of "genital façade," to a critical revision. Reiche observes: "The concept of 'repressive desublimation' has at its root a mournful attitude to the destruction of the bourgeois ego ideal. The whole concept owes its existence only to the fact that earlier forms of bourgeois instinctual molding (or more correctly its literary stylization) are being made into standards of contemporary proletarian forms of instinctual molding."[321]

In fact, the "repressively desublimated," that is, "seemingly genitally organized," youthful character, which manifests a stronger dominance of oral qualities and passive ideals, also contains a progressive dynamic: as a dissatisfied, extremely addicted forepleasure character it is more at the mercy of the anonymous commodity-esthetical seduction of "consumer society" than was the classic anal-compulsive character, that is, sadomasochistic character of the patriarchal generation, which deferred and controlled its needs compulsively; yet it puts up passive (oral) resistance to the principle of repressive achievement and competition. The youthful character's intolerance of frustration, that is, its inability to accept actual deprivation and frustration in favor of future satisfaction, so frequently bemoaned by psychoanalysis, has a thoroughly progressive side. In the concept of "instant gratification" (which has become the most popular label for the "fatherless generation") one can detect connotations of the father's outrage that his children no longer tolerate the social compulsions which he himself still internalizes. Behind the fatherless generation's inability for instinctual deferral and renunciation there indeed appears the "sunrise" of a new form of "proletarian instinctual molding" (Reiche) which must terrify bourgeois fathers.

The Marxists, therefore, must be very careful today in their use of such concepts as "regression," " repressive desublimation," "intolerance of frustration," "genital façade," and the like. The new, especially sexual, forms of youthful behavior, characterized moreover by an approximation of the sexes, seem like an ominous trend towards "regression" and "repressive desublimation" only from the perspective of the classic bourgeois competitive and individual ego, that is, the classic renunciatory character. In a reply to R. Reiche, Fernbach rightly pointed out that the "regressive" tendencies of the young also manifest something progressive, namely, a new youth culture: "This new youth culture represents at least a potentially new approximation of the sexes, not in the direction of a 'wrong solution' as Reiche described it, but in the direction of a 'strong solution' where people of both sexes are capable of loving each other (thus the traditional bourgeois man without his demand for ownership and domination) and to be loved (thus the bourgeois woman without her passivity and submissiveness)."[322] When Reiche detects only the repressive expression of manipulative advertising and commodity esthetic in the dress of the young, in their new relationship to the nakedness of the human body, he also misses the dialectic in this instance. D. Fernbach writes: "[. . .] The dress of the youth culture is on the one hand typically functional (jeans, ponchos) and on the other decorative (jewelry, headbands). It radically rejects a transformation of the body into a fetish, as Reiche believes [. . .] So this conception also rejects the novelty aspect of fashion and places value on patching old clothes and improving them. A further expression of this new sexuality is the shameless nudity *à la* Woodstock."[323]

Indeed, the Woodstock movement, which seized millions of American youth, demonstrates the contradictoriness of this new "regressive," "repressively desublimated" youthful character. The Woodstock phenomenon, usually arrogantly disregarded by the left, shows that the old capitalist consumer society is pregnant with a new youth culture which simultaneously produces the "revolutionary ferment" of a new sexual structure together with the dissolution of the traditional structure. What is interesting and typical of this phenomenon is the contradiction between the regressive form and the in many respects progressive content of the needs at the basis of this "love, music, and peace" movement. The as yet inarticulated wish for liberation from the idiocy of the eight-hour office or factory job, from the nightmare of unemployment which is victimizing increasing numbers of American youth, from the pragmatic dullness of an educational system which is divided by class and race, from the drill of military training for genocide, from the ever-present threat of police brutality—this still inarticulated progressive wish assumes the regressive form of a fidgeting and screaming Woodstock generation. The emancipatory need of the young to break through their isolation assumes the romantic form of a three-day love, peace, and music festival. The still unconscious wish to break through the naked money and exchange relationships to which capital has reduced all human relations ("Many people treat others like objects, but here it's different'') assumes the naïve form of bathing collectively in the nude. The material need to get rid of the fear of competition and existence, which the American metropolis induces in proletarian and middle-class youth, expresses itself in the idealization of country and rural life. The real need for escaping the servitude and disenfranchisement by the technically highly developed capitalist production process expresses itself in a mystical return to anarchist forms of production and life.[324]

Not that we would want to idealize the Woodstock generation, this American version of the "fatherless generation," or immediately detect revolutionary potential in it. By propagating and supporting this movement, American capital channeled this speechless, still unpolitical protest of American youth just in time, and thus defused its rebellious energies in the ritualized outbreaks of such mass spectacles. Yet the socialist movement should not simply withdraw from such mass phenomena which appear to be apolitical and regressive, but seek to understand their historically new dialectic: for, under late capitalist conditions, the initial moments of progressive needs appear to be able to manifest themselves only in regressive forms (in the sense of giving up atrophied internalizations and liberating repressed, suppressed needs). "Historical progress," Mitscherlich rightly says, "does not occur invariably in ways which should be regarded as rational in the sense of what is the dominant reason of the moment: the possibility of a new interpretation of reality may result from forms of behavior and objectives which at first frequently appear confused and abstruse."[325]

Especially does the "ridiculous" example of Woodstock show that the total levelling and uniformization of social (including sexual) relationships through the exchange and money relationship subterraneously liberates a progressive dynamic as well. Monopoly capitalism can no longer control the sexual "spirits" which it constantly implores for the solution of its problems of realization. The total sexualization of the commodity world and the simultaneous dissolution of traditional sexual taboos and moral concepts also liberates forces, contrary to the will of capital, which make the repression of sexuality, in the service of political and economic domination, at least more and more difficult. The raw and total uniformization of the youthful masses also contains—as the Woodstock example shows—the germ of conflict with all differences in social and economic status. The contradiction between the actual uniformization of the consumer and the still existing consumer and class hierarchy becomes more and more acute and, thus, more and more easily the lever for the creation of an anti-authoritarian consciousness. Such anti-authoritarian potential of the "fatherless generation" then expresses itself—if still in a romantic and individualized form—by rejecting the consumer and class hierarchy. "There's a lot of fucking here. We're living in a commune, my father thinks I'm a commie. Actually all I want to do is sit somewhere at the edge of the road. I don't want to have a career."[326] A consciousness which has been totally shaped by the logic of the equivalence exchange principle tendentiously perceives every "inequality" of possession, power, and income as a contradiction of its own rigorous uniformity and levelling. Such capitalist-coordinated consciousness thus simultaneously contains the "revolutionary ferment" of a new collective consciousness.

Moreover, the total uniformization, that is, "repressive desublimation" of the youthful structure of instinct and consciousness is an irreversible historical process. The classic bourgeois instinct and ego structure, which is based on "repressive genital primacy" and assures exclusive "ego strength" in the sense of individualistic capacity for success and competition, can no longer be saved by the "rejection of repressive desublimation" as Reiche demanded. For—according to Marx—"the higher development of individuality is bought at the price of a historical process to which individuals are sacrificed."[327] The increasing socialization and subsumption of formerly autonomous work under capital has once and for all liquidated the social conditions for "ego strength" and "autonomous," that is, "genitally" organized structures of instinct and character. That is why the attributes of the classic bourgeois character structure, such as "ego strength," "ego autonomy," "an ability to compete," as "subjective factors" can no longer be made the basis of political work. On the contrary, the socialist movement today has the task of developing forms of political organization which are no longer bound to the need of the classic bourgeois competitive and individual ego to assert itself, but enable the "weak ego," the regressively "ill" individual the opportunity for self-development within a cooperative framework. K. M. Michel says: " 'The tradition of past generations weighs like a nightmare on the consciousness of the living.' (Marx) Our nightmare bears the traits of Western individualism. Its weakness does not need to be a malady—but might even be of advantage if it makes room for new forms of thinking and acting in solidarity which are free of competition. These forms must still be developed."[328] This very dissolution, that is, weakening, of the classic bourgeois ego contains the "revolutionary ferment" of a new collective ego structure, of a kind of group ego structure based on the cooperation of numerous individual egos within the division of labor. Such "free association" of many individuals with "weak egos" thus creates the prerequisites for a new collective "ego strength," for a cooperative instinctual structure which is the psychosexual pendent for the collective acquisition of production.

APPENDIX:

The Frankfurt School, or Cooperation Between Marxism and Psychoanalysis at the Expense of Marxism

---

Adornitic "Social Psychologism"

The Frankfurt School's contribution to the Marxist-psychoanalytical controversy consists in having unmasked the theoretical and practical attempts at mediation of the German Freudo-Marxists as by turns reductions, stylizations, or revisions of the "critical theories" of the other—which, moreover, tended to result in a dangerous psychologization of social and political problems. The Frankfurt School decisively opposed any form of "psychologism" which sought to explain conflicts of social interest in terms of the instinctual conflicts of individuals. Adorno thus wrote: "The 'cult' of psychology, of which one tries to convince people and which in the meantime has made a dreary mass-consumption article of Freud in America, is the complement of the dehumanization, the illusion of the impotent that their fate depends on their individual makeup [. . .] Psychologism in any form, the unceremonious assessment of the individual, is ideology. It transfigures the individualistic form of socialization into an extra-social, natural determination of the individual. [. . .] As soon as processes, which in truth have moved away from spontaneous individual actions and are now attached to abstract subjects, are explained as coming out of the soul one consolingly humanizes the reified.''[329]

The question, however, is whether the Frankfurt School itself and its epigones are properly armed against the "psychologism" which they feel they unrelentingly oppose. While the German Freudo-Marxists sought to avert a psychoanalytical misinterpretation of social institutions and political phenomena by a fusion of historical materialism and psychoanalysis, the Frankfurt School believed that it could eliminate this danger only by categorically separating the two "critical theories." As Adorno before them (in "On Understanding Sociology and Psychology"), so today his epigones base the categorical irreconcilability of the two theories on an irreversible division of labor between sociology and psychology which supposedly reflects the real "antagonism between society and the individual." Thus Dahmer writes: "All attempts to coordinate the critical theory of the subject and that of its political economy, of letting one be absorbed by the other, are doomed to failure since the *fundamentum in re* of the existing division of labor, the contradiction of a society in which 'the higher development of the individual is only bought through a historical process in which the individual is sacrificed' (Marx), cannot be eliminated from the world through mere scientific institutions. There is no way back from the division of labor."[330]

The new "Frankfurtists" in a certain sense regard it as their life's task to keep both "critical theories" pure of reciprocal reduction, prettification, and defamation. Possessing both critical theories, they direct themselves to conduct, as it were, an eternal pendulous traffic between the two. They see the condition for cooperation between historical materialism and psychoanalysis precisely in keeping them pure of each other. Dahmer goes on to say: "Psychology and sociology, that is, their critical pendants psychoanalysis and historical materialism, investigate with divided labor the internal structure of the isolated producer of commodities and relationships determined by production [. . .] the life story of individual human beings and the history of bourgeois society."[331]

The Frankfurt School's concept of a cooperative division of labor, which makes sense on first glance, is well provided for against the crude psychoanalytical psychologism of the Laforgues, Ferenczis, and Roheims and also against the psychoanalytical naturalism of a Wilhelm

Reich. But this itself at once becomes a new "modern" psychologism which grants any critique of political economy only a purely verbal authority, so as to claim *de facto* the unlimited authority of psychoanalysis in all psychological matters. This "delimitation of authority" does not deprive psychoanalysis of its ideological-bourgeois dimension but Marx's political economy of its psychological dimension. As Dahmer observes: "Psychoanalysis and historical materialism must coexist [. . .] Social factors such as fixed value, the imperialist war, the tendential fall of the rate of profit, or the crisis of over-production cannot be traced back to the (always socially interpreted, be they legitimized or tabooified) needs of individuals. No amount of instinctual destiny or repression makes capitalism or other forms of production comprehensible in any way. Vice versa, a critique of political economy teaches us nothing about how the character masks, which those persons who are 'carriers of certain class relationships and interests' must wear, are soldered to their instincts, nothing about dreams and neuroses."[332]

Indeed, psychoanalysis cannot tell us anything about social matters, say valuation, or about the crisis of over-production; but a critique of political economy can very well make general statements about how economic development affects the social development of instincts. Thus Marx—as we showed in greater detail in Part Three—declared in principle that the process of accumulating capital has created a certain instinctual and character structure, a certain "social character" in the rising bourgeoisie, which is particularly marked by zealousness, avarice, thriftiness, and abstinence. (See also p. 130.) For lack of a genetic individual psychology he could not, of course, represent the psychosexual anchoring of these "class virtues," which should be regarded psychoanalytically as "anal-reaction formations"; and in this respect the psychoanalytic investigation of symptoms and character again comes into its limited right. The "critical critics" of the Frankfurt School, however, always suppress "Marx's revolutionary contributions to psychology, to the sociology of the psyche" (Baran), so as to transfer the monopoly of psychology to psychoanalysis, the "critical theory of the subject."

Thus these critics tirelessly seek to prove the cooperative equality in value and rank of both "critical theories" by abstract and formal contrapositions. Horn writes: "Marx's concern is the mutual cultivation of outward nature and the creation of the species as related thereto. Freud's concern is essentially the fashioning of the 'individual' inner nature, the specific problems which devolved therefrom and did not preoccupy Marx exclusively. For such a psychology did not exist at his time."[333] Such formal contrapositioning overlooks the fact that a goodly chunk of bourgeois ideology and anthropology has entered into the psychological representation of "metabolism" with its "inner nature." Not even the decisive and trickiest *"tertium comparationis"* of the "critical critics," namely, the concept of reification, can conceal this state of affairs. According to Horn: "Criticism directs itself in both instances against conditions which have petrified into things: with Marx against the commodity fetish and with psychoanalysis against cliche-mediated behavior [. . .] In both cases theoretical and practical criticism begins with the reified and criticizes commodity as well as symptom as something only apparently an immediate natural manifestation."[334] Certainly both "critical theories" are critique, here with regard to commodities, there with regard to the symptoms of reified social conditions. The qualitative difference between the categories of Marx's political economy and those of psychoanalysis, however, consists in the fact that the latter categories are themselves not free of the very reification which they are criticizing. As we have shown, almost all psychoanalytical categories, such as the concept of the ego, or aggression, or the Oedipus complex, have totally lost that historical and social-specific determination which distinguishes the concepts of political economy. It is because psychoanalysis biologizes and ontologizes opaque social determinants of the instinctual structure that it cannot simply be given equal status with "critical theory of society" as a "critical theory of the subject."

By insisting on the division of labor (namely, an equal-status cooperation between historical materialism and psychoanalysis) the "critical critics" conserve together with the "pure gold" of Freud's thought also its ideological "smut" and biological petrifications. An example is Dahmer's critique of the Reichian concept of genitality. Dahmer points out convincingly that Reich's concept of genitality naturalizes and reifies Freud's;[335] but this critique itself amounts to a vindication of Freud's concept of genitality. That Freud's concept too, as a psychological self-transfiguration of the liberal bourgeoisie, is not totally free of certain reifications, such as the priority of mental over manual labor, is suppressed by Dahmer's critique, which attacks the pupil but spares the master. The same holds true for Reich's, that is, Freud's concept of neurosis. Dahmer is correct in criticizing Reich's concept of neurosis for losing the dialectic which is what distinguished Freud's. Reich conceived of neurosis only as a disturbance, as "inhibition," as "illness," that is, as a degenerative decline of the "genital character" structure, while Freud still saw in it an element of rebelliousness against the reality principle, a progressive and subversive element. Yet when Dahmer then writes: "His [Freud's] theory of neurosis and of cultural history has been developed from the perspective of the individual whom therapy is supposed to help to become mature,"[336] he suppresses not only the fatalistic and decadent element of Freud's concept of culture (which Reich had seen very clearly), but also the contradiction between his theory of subversive neurosis and his reformistic and opportunistic therapy for neurosis. In contrast, and despite his reified concept of genitality, Reich at least sought to make the subversive element of Freud's theory of neurosis productive for therapeutic practice by advising those of his patients who had become more enlightened during therapy to engage themselves in behalf of the communist party.

In the final analysis the cooperation along the lines of a division of labor between historical materialism as a "critical theory of society" and psychoanalysis as a "critical theory of the subject," which the Frankfurt School institutionalized amounts to an inadmissible reduction of historical materialism. Dahmer has thus described the function of psychoanalysis as distinct from historical materialism: "Historical materialism speaks the truth about conditions where the individual human being, his needs, suffering, and consciousness, do *not yet* matter. Psychoanalysis speaks the truth about the human subject who is made into an object and resists this process."[337] But this statement requires a decisive qualification: psychoanalysis speaks the truth about the subject only inasmuch as this becomes the object of a familial socialization process; yet it is blind to the extra-familial determinants as well as to primary socialization and even secondary socialization, that is, to the socializing power of wage labor. On the basis of its familialistically obtuse categories psychoanalysis can grasp only the pathology of early childhood development; the actual pathology, however, which derives immediately or is mediated through the sphere of capitalist production and realization (and which was the subject of the third part of our investigation), eludes its theoretical grasp. But this very pathology constitutes its objective which the Adornitic trustees of Freud's work refuse to admit. For by doing so they would lose their most important argument for the cooperative concept of both "critical theories": the division of labor into an "ideological consciousness" whose enlightenment is the business of Marx's political economy, and into a "psychopathological consciousness" whose enlightenment is supposed to be the business of psychoanalysis. When Horn writes: "We conceive of deformations of consciousness as socially mediated sedimentations of domination,"[338] then he tacitly presupposes that deformations of consciousness are transmitted exclusively through the socialization process of the family. But precisely a critique of political economy is what can demonstrate that the socially relevant massive deformations of consciousness and instinct themselves primarily derive from the capitalist process of labor and utilization and are transmitted only secondarily through disturbances in familial socialization.

Since the "critical critics" of the Frankfurt School exclusively entrust the monopoly of psychology to psychoanalysis, they slip into a politically and economically fashioned "social psychologism"—and that despite all the lip service they pay historical materialism. This can be demonstrated, for example, in their "social psychology of German fascism." Thus they describe anti-semitism exclusively in psychoanalytic terms: as "socially mediated disturbances of consciousness'' (Horn) of the middle class to whom the Jews became projection screens for its repressed aggressive and sexual desires. Horn writes: ''The Jews became for the anti-Semites representatives of what was prohibited to themselves. Because the Jews were persecuted—ostensibly as manipulators of social misery—the real causes of the social crises remained hidden. State-organized aggressive behavior can be interpreted within the framework of this model as socialized mis-socialization whose roots are Oedipal, that is, as primarily emotionally determined conflict of interest.''[339] Horn here absolutizes the *secondary* (of course important) social-psychological components of anti-Semitism to a degree that suppresses its primary economic and political causes. It was not because the Jews were represented as the ''manipulators of social misery'' that the real causes of the social crises remained hidden but vice versa. In other words the capitalist process of production and utilization itself produces a ''mystified'' and ''irrational'' consciousness to which inflation, mass unemployment, economic crisis, and imperialist war appear ''as a fate working outside of itself'' (Marx). Thus were the Jews represented as manipulators of social misery. ''State-organized aggressive behavior'' therefore cannot be interpreted solely within the framework of this model of ''socialized mis-socialization.'' For state-organized anti-Semitism had less to do with the Oedipus complex than with an anti-capitalist and anti-bolshevik ''complex,'' that is, it had primarily a political and economic function: to divert the anti-capitalist as well as anti-bolshevik resentment of the middle class and a part of the working class onto the ''money'' Jews, that is, onto ''Bolshevik world Jewry.'' The occasion for the personalization and ''projective'' defense of social contradictions is primarily an expression of ''consciousness inversion'' which itself is immanent to the capitalist production of commodities, an expression of the reification of persons and the personalization of objects (also see pp. 154f); and it is only secondarily a consequence of ''socialized mis-socialization.'' The Frankfurt School's entire investigation of prejudice suffers from its absolutization of the components of prejudice that have been mediated by disturbances in socialization to the same degree that it suppresses the components of prejudice that derive from the capitalist process of production and utilization, the fetish character of commodities, the mere appearance of equivalence in exchange, and so on.

The true problem of the Frankfurt School is that it is so broken and disappointed by the defeat of the German workers' movement that it can grasp ''domination'' almost solely by resorting to concepts within pathology. It understands fascism only as ''socially organized psychopathology,'' as ''socialized irrationality,'' although from a capitalist viewpoint fascism was exceedingly rational. In a Sisyphean struggle with Stalinist economism, which was blind to the irrational dimension of the fascist mass movement, Adornitic and neo-Adornitic "social psychologism" for its part became blind to the profane rationality of the "irrational middle-class movement" financed by big capital, which ultimately even infected parts of the workers' movement. The Frankfurt School finally saw "psychopathology" and "irrationality" even where it was a question of simple imperialist interests. In short, the "critical critics" have always made everything more complicated than it is; to this day this constitutes the secret of their unending multiplication.

In any discussion of Marxism and psychoanalysis, however, it should not be forgotten that the Frankfurt School has always shied away from a genuine materialist critique and controversy with psychoanalysis. The division of labor which it institutionalized between psychoanalysis and historical materialism suppresses the fact that the latter in principle also provided a "critical theory of the subject." Wieser and Beyer have commented: "Those who regard this analysis of the 'subjective factor' as unconsidered by historical materialism, and consign it exclusively to the domain of psychology, run the danger of engaging in a 'second psychology' which exists independently of that which has already been initiated in socialism."[340] Adornitic theoreticians who posit a rupture between society and the individual, as well as between their respective critical pendants, Marxism and psychoanalysis, though they oppose those Freudo-Marxists who wish to steer a mediating course, join them in depriving the critique of political economy of its full psychological dimension. "Pure" political-economic categories can then, of course, no longer "cooperate" with the "pure" categories of psychoanalysis. This reduction has as a consequence, however, a reduced concept of psychology: the latter is attached solely to the processes of family socialization, which ultimately means to the sphere of consumption. The Frankfurt School and its epigones thereby reproduce the familialistic obtuseness of Freud's psychology.

Neo-Adornitic "Interaction Psychologism"

The newest attempt to provide underpinning for the Frankfurt School's concept of co-equal cooperation between Marxism and psychoanalysis is Lorenzer's version of psychoanalysis as "theory of symbolic interaction." Lorenzer writes: "What is grasped in psychoanalysis first of all are not someone's forms of behavior but simultaneously and primarily those interacting structures which are comprehended in the medium of the reporting subject. The *play*, not the actor, stands at the center [. . .] The actor—the individual—is the starting point of critical analysis. The objective of analysis is to understand the subjective refraction of the objective structures of the play [. . .] Psychoanalytic theory is one of subjective

distortion of the objective structures of interaction 'in the subject.' "[341]
In the final analysis, Lorenzer's version of psychoanalysis as a "theory
of interaction" leads to the same dead end as the structuralist view of
psychoanalysis. What are "invariable structures" for Lacan are "objective interaction structures" for Lorenzer, the "objective structures of the
play." Lorenzer reproduces the aporia of structural psychoanalysis only
in a different form. Structural psychoanalysis can no more determine
what belongs to the "invariable" biological basis of a given instinctual
structure, say the Oedipus complex, than Lorenzer is capable of determining what constitutes "objective interaction structures" and how their
"subjective refraction," that is, their social and class-specific deformations, should be regarded. But it is obvious that the "actor," depending
on what class-specific milieu he comes from, is always at the mercy of
different "rules of the game" of "interaction." Lorenzer only replaces
structuralist idealism with a new "interaction" idealism—as though there
existed "interaction structures" independent of and above and beyond all
social and class-specific forms of behavior, which should henceforth be
regarded, as it were, as the "objective spirit" of interactions.

What, incidentally, does "interaction" mean? Lorenzer has borrowed
the term from Habermas. Although he criticizes the "strict division in
principle of interaction and production" which Habermas introduced,
and emphasizes that "neither work nor interaction can be understood as
separate from production,"[342] he too seems to share Habermas's Marxian critique that the realm of "interaction," of "communicative action,"
(Habermas), falls outside Marx's concept of "work," of "instrumental
activity" (Habermas). Otherwise the theoretic effort to mediate between
the two concepts—which allegedly have fallen apart—by way of the
"symbol concept" would be superfluous. This is an instance, however,
not of a "reduced understanding" of work in Marx's sense—one which
has lost its dimension of "communicative action," as Habermas supposes
—but of a reduced understanding of Marx by Habermas and Lorenzer.
According to Marx, "man's process of self-production" is mediated
through work in the sense of "instrumental action"—which does not
mean, however, that "man's self-production" is completely identical
with "instrumental action." Work is the basis of this process, not its
exclusive content. "Interaction" in the sense of "communicative action"
and "interhuman relationships" enters into "man's self-production" as
a dimension which is mediated and structured by work. But Marx was
sufficiently Marxist not to allow such a vague concept of "interaction,"
on the basis of which entire schools of group dynamics are in the
meantime being erected, to become an analytical category within the
critique of political economy. Any attempt to assure psychoanalysis of its
own autonomous realm of authority by pointing to Marx's allegedly
limited understanding of work and production only does a poor job of

hiding its premises. If the new psychoanalytic "interaction theoreticians" cannot prove their legitimacy except by a sophisticated pointer to alleged suppressions in Marx's categories, then their legitimacy indeed appears to be somewhat dubious. What is responsible for the fact that psychoanalytic categories have not entered into historical-materialist categories is not some reduction of Marx's categories in themselves but, for one thing, the reduction of these categories by vulgar Marxists and, for another, a deepseated ideological remnant in the categories of psychoanalysis.

But let us now proceed to the heart of Lorenzer's frequently quoted "symbol theory." First of all, we should note that Lorenzer's attempt to mediate the allegedly separate realms of "work" and "interaction" by means of the formation process of linguistic symbols is by no means as original and new as it appears. E. Wulff[343] has pointed out that this attempt can already be found in Lacan who—from a structuralist viewpoint—sees the biological and social factors of the individuation process enmeshed in the universal "matrix of language," wherein "empty speech" contains the biologically pre-formed "invariable" structure and "filled speech" its social determinants. According to Lorenzer, the linguistic capacity for symbolization plays a "key role for the mediation of natural processes and social processes."[344] Simultaneously, the symbol provides another tie-in which is important for the psychoanalytic view: "The connection between consciousness and behavior. This connection the symbol accomplishes as language. Man acquires the terrain of languageness through the formation of symbols. Symbols as elements of 'language' interconnect thinking and acting by simultaneously regulating interaction as well as communication!"[345] And finally: "The two realms which chiefly characterize psychoanalysis also overlap: the realms of unconsciousness and consciousness. Those transformation processes which lead from one realm to the other run, as it were, through the symbols."[346] So as to find an adequate expression in linguistic theory for this transformation of unconsciousness and consciousness, Lorenzer created the concept of the "protosymbol." The "protosymbols" are identical with those conceptions, wishes, and thoughts which are not yet or are no longer capable of being conscious. Lorenzer writes: "The protosymbols form a circle around the accepted symbol [symbol, that is, capable of linguistic expression—author]. Inasmuch as the protosymbols have already climbed the first rungs of realization, they are constantly prepared, under certain conditions (as, for example, in dreams or certain crisis situations), to cross the threshold of consciousness."[347]

Lorenzer's symbol theory in large measure is only a clumsy paraphrase of Freud's dynamic model of the psychic apparatus. His "protosymbols" are identical with unconscious, that is, preconscious, conceptions which either cannot be or are not admitted to linguistic symbol formation at all or are excommunicated from the linguistic symbol-building process. The symbol-formation and de-symbolization processes which Lorenzer describes simply paraphrase the transformational process that Freud described from an unconscious into a conscious system and vice versa. Lorenzer advertises new conceptual constructs as new theoretical discoveries which, on closer inspection, point to matters long since known. The same holds true of the by now quite renowned concept of "linguistic destruction" which the neo-Adornites have celebrated. That every neurosis destroys the connection between word and conception and therewith also the connection between language and acting, communication and interaction, is sufficiently well known to us since Freud. But the terminological neologisms of the "destruction of language," the "linguistic game," that is, the concept of de-symbolization, adds nothing to Freud's perceptions. The objective of analytical therapy, for Freud "the making conscious of the unconscious," Lorenzer calls "the recreation of the fissured language game."[348]

The symbolic concept becomes for Lorenzer a *passe-partout* which accomplishes true marvels wherever Marxism does not appear to have the key for an understanding of psychoanalysis. The chief function of this concept is that it allows one to conduct a Janus-like, or better, a "social partnership-like" politic in the relationship of historical materialism and psychoanalysis. For "work" and "interaction" appear like cooperative, tandem values before the "highness" of the symbol concept. Lorenzer states: "Symbols as elements of language and language as discourse and action point to communication and work in the same manner. The symbol here is not only the Platonic precursor of work but is that self-created means of production [!] of the subject of the species [. . .] Symbol is synthesis analogous to material production because always rooted in inner nature, from which the symbol as product [!] has been wrested, as well as in conflict with outer nature from which the concrete tangible product goes forth."[349]

Lorenzer's concept of the symbol—that is his whole secret—simply becomes part of an artificial alloy with the corresponding Marxist concepts, so as to participate in their solidarity, a process in which the "pure" gold of those Marxist concepts is, of course, lost. The symbols as "self-created means of production of the object of the species" is a poor conceptual hybrid which explains nothing. That the symbol has to be "wrested from inner nature" does not by a long shot bring the symbol-building process into plausible material connection with the process of material production. It makes no sense for of all things the concept of symbol, which plays a central role neither in psychoanalysis nor in the critique of political economy, to function as a universal clothes pin between the two—as, say, in the following modus: "The intervention into symbol formation is at all times attached to three 'realities,' namely, biophysiological physical acts, 'real' interaction, and 'material' production: the symbol as 'means of production' is part of all three levels of human activity. Such a determination of psychoanalysis allows for an analysis of the objective conditions in the organization of domination *and* in the organization of work."[350] The conceptual trinity which has been pinned together by the symbol concept—"biological-physiological physical acts," "real interaction," and "material production"—thus withdraws; and this constitutes its secret ideological mission, even in its beginnings from a clear Marxist positing of priorities: the priority of "material production" over "real interaction" which is decisively shaped by the organization of work and cannot be specified without it at all.

Lorenzer does have a fairly clear notion of the dilemma of psychoanalysis when he writes that although "the repression established by domination in infantile relationships with objects can be concretely discerned, the connection between the organization of domination and force and the organization of work remains outside psychoanalytic critique [. . .] Its critical perception appears to reach only as far as a derived contradiction without being able to think as far as a concrete connection with relationships in production [. . .]"[351] Yet his version of psychoanalysis as a "theory of symbolic interaction" likewise does not find a way out of this dilemma. This is so particularly because—as Lorenzer correctly remarks —"the relative invariability of the biological basis stands confronted by the historical situation as a construct of changeable factors."[352] An analysis of historical changeability should receive absolute primacy. Precisely because a "theory of psychoanalytic interaction" always runs the danger of considering the social and cultural-specific determinants of "interaction" as "objective" and "invariable" does a critique of political economy, that is, of specific social and cultural forms of behavior (within and without the process of familial socialization) have to be given absolute priority. Lorenzer says that "Psychoanalysis [. . .] has to avoid isolated observation of a familial field just as much as it must not prevent discussion about 'domination' from extending into the next area of discussion [. . .] the deformation of subjects under the yoke of relationships within production [. . .]"[353] Yet at another place a "critique of deformed interaction" again becomes the exclusive task of psychoanalysis, although, as we have noted, deformations of consciousness and instinct which result from the process of production are completely inaccessible to psychoanalysis.

Lorenzer assumed the legacy of the Frankfurt School not only in the following sense: "Doubtless the investigation of the dialectic of individual and society which the Frankfurt School has already placed at the center of things will have to be further developed [. . .]."[354] But he faithfully carries on this legacy in the sense of the Frankfurt School's reduction of the Marxist "legacy," namely, the critique of political economy. The concepts of commodity, money, capital, class, and so forth are more or less swallowed up by Lorenzer's centrally mediating category, that of the concept of symbol. Even such verbal lip service as "the connection between the organization of work and the individual"[355] are of little avail. The category of "work" leads for Lorenzer just as abstract and formal an existence as the concept of "domination" does among his Adornitic precursors. But particularly in a "mediating" theory which seeks to make visible the connection between "domination"-established repression in an infantile relationship with objects and the "organization of work" must the category of "capital" occupy the center of things! But towards this category Lorenzer appears to have what one can only call a phobia. To assign psychoanalysis a selective and limited significance within the framework of historical materialism, and under its control, does not sit well with this former student of Mitscherlich. "Psychoanalysis as a 'critique of the subject' confronts the critique of a political-economic situation neither as rival nor as assistant science to critical theory but as its other half."[356] The fact that the psychoanalytic in contrast to the political-economic "half" has been largely sullied by the bourgeois ideology and anthropology of Freud and therefore might enter into a "misalliance" with the latter is something Lorenzer refuses to admit. One has the impression that psychoanalysts who have only the merest acquaintance with Marx's political economy are fighting rather for their own slightly tainted legitimacy as psychoanalysts instead of for a truly responsible clarification of the relationship of Marxism and psychoanalysis.

Translator's Note

Because of the highly specialized nature of the section on the Frankfurt School, I decided to shift it to the Appendix. Otherwise, it might have posed a barrier between Parts Two and Three.

In a few instances, quotes had to be re-translated from German to English because the German anthologies from which they derive were not readily available. The quotes from the work of Sigmund Freud use the text of the *Standard Edition* except, occasionally, where the quote is very brief. For the quotes from the work of Karl Marx I relied, respectively, on the International Publishers' editions of *Capital* and *A Contribution to the Critique of Political Economy;* on the Vintage Books edition of *Grundrisse;* and on the Anchor Books edition of *The Writings of the Young Marx on Philosophy and Society.* I did not discover until after the translation had been type-set that R. Reiche's *Sexuality and Class Struggle,* from which Schneider quotes extensively, had been published by F. Praeger in the United States and by New Left Books in England. In a few instances I relied on Lee Baxendall's edition of Wilhelm Reich's Sex-Pol essays (Vintage Books). The other Wilhelm Reich titles Schneider refers to are all published by Farrar, Straus & Giroux. The quotes from Lukács' *History and Class Consciousness* were taken from the M.I.T. Press edition. The Brecht quotes from *St. Joan of the Stockyards* were adapted from Frank Jones' translation published by Indiana University Press. Grateful acknowledgment is made to all the above.

Thanks for assistance with the translation go to Stanley Aronowitz, Eike Gebhardt, and Robert S. Stewart. Any inconsistency in usage, particularly in Marxian and psychoanalytic terminology, is entirely my fault.

Michael Roloff
June, 1975

NOTES:

Part One: With Freud Against Vulgar Marxism

1. V. Jurinec, "Psychoanalyse und Marxismus," in *Psychoanalyse und Marxismus, Dokumentation einer Kontroverse,* Frankfurt/Main 1970, pp. 69 ff.
2. K. Wells, "Weder materialistisch noch dialektisch," in *Psychoanalyse, Marxismus und Sozialwissenschaften,* Rotdruck, '-Gravenhage 1971, p. 155.
3. S. Freud, *Gesammelte Werke,* vol. 5, Frankfurt/Main 1967, pp. 67 ff.
4. R. Brun, "Über die Vereinbarkeit der Psychoanalyse, mit dem dialektischen Materialismus," in *"Psychoanalyse, Marxismus und Sozialwissenschaften, op. cit.,* p. 148.
5. V. Jurinec, *op. cit.,* p. 90.
6. V. Jurinec, *op. cit.,* p. 89.
7. V. Jurinec, *op. cit.,* p. 78.
8. A. Stoljarov, "Der Freudismus and die Freudo-Marxisten," in *Psychoanalyse und Marxismus, Dokumentation einer Kontroverse, op. cit.,* p. 303.
9. L. Rosenkötter, "Über Kriterien der Wissenschaftlichkeit der Psychoanalyse," in *Psychoanalyse, Marxismus und Socialwissenschaften, op. cit.,* p. 90
10. S. Freud: *G.W.,* vol. 13, p. 247.
11. I. Althusser, "Freud und Lacan," *Internationale marxistische Diskussion* 10, Berlin 1970. p. 8.
12. V. Jurinec, *op. cit.,* p. 101.
13. V. Jurinec, *ibid.*
14. S. Freud, *G.W.,* vol. 2/3
15. V. Jurinec, *op. cit.,* p. 102.
16. J. Gabel, *"Ideologie und Schizophrenie—Formen der Entfremdung,"* Frankfurt/Main 1967.
17. V. Jurinec, *op. cit.,* p. 104.
18. M. Foucault, *Psychologie und Geisteskrankheit,* Frankfurt/Main 1968, pp. 64 ff.

19. W. Reich, "Dialektischer Materialismus und Psychoanalyse," in *Psychoanalyse und Marxismus, Dokumentation einer Kontroverse, op. cit.*, p. 171.
20. W. Reich, *ibid.*, p. 162 ff.
21. S. Freud, *G.W.*, vol. 13, p. 53.
22. K. Wells, *op. cit.*, p. 159.
23. I. Caruso, "Die Psychoanalytische Situation als mikrosoziales Modell, in *Psychoanalyse, Marxismus und Socialwissenschaften, op. cit.*, p. 22.
24. S. Freud, *G.W.*, vol. 11, p. 181.
25. R. Osborn, *Marxismus und Psychoanalyse*, Frankfurt/Main 1970, p. 160.
26. S. Freud, *G.W.*, vol. 11, p. 389.
27. A. Thalheimer, "Die Auflösung des Austromarxismus," in *Unter dem Banner des Marxismus* 1, 1926, p. 517.
28. S. Freud, *G.W.*, vol. 10, p. 97.
29. Th. Adorno, "Zum Verhältnis von Soziologie und Psychologie," in *Soziologica, Aufsätze, Max Horkheimer zum 60. Geburtstag gewidmet*, Frankfurt/Main 1955, p. 25.
30. W. Reich, *op. cit.*, p. 153.
31. V. Jurinec, *op. cit.*, p. 87.
32. H. Dahmer, "W. Reich—Seine Stellung zu Marx und Freud," in *Marxismus, Psychoanalyse, Sexpol*, vol. 2, Frankfurt/Main 1972, p. 94.
33. S. Bernfeld, Sozialismus und Psychoanalyse," in *Psychoanalyse und Marxismus, Dokumentation einer Kontroverse, op. cit.*, pp. 47–48.
34. S. Freud, *G.W.*, vol. 13, p. 365.
35. W. Reich, *op. cit.*, p. 139.
36. R. Laforgue, "Schuldgefühl und Nationalcharakter. Über die Erotisierung der sozialen Beziehungen des Menschen," in *Die Psychoanalytische Bewegung* 3, 1931, pp. 407–431.
37. S. Ferenczi, "Zur Ontogenese des Geldinteresses," in *Bausteine zur Psychoanalyse*, vol. 1, Stuttgart/Bern 1964, pp. 109–119.
38. Kolnai, *Psychoanalyse und Soziologie*, Rotdruck 1970.
39. V. Jurinec, *op. cit.*, pp. 105 ff.
40. S. Bernfeld, "Die kommunistische Diskussion um die Psychoanalyse und Reichs 'Wiederlegung der Todestriebhypothese,' " in *Marxismus und Psychoanalyse, Dokumentation einer Kontroverse, op. cit.*, p. 274.
41. S. Bernfeld, *ibid.*, p. 268.
42. Th. Adorno, "Die revidierte Psychoanalyse," in *Gesammelte Schriften* 8, Frankfurt/Main 1972, p. 35.
43. J. Habermas, *Erkenntnis und Interesse*, Frankfurt/Main 1965.
44. K. Marx, *Grundrisse der Kritik der Politischen Ökonomie*, Berlin 1953, p. 6.
45. Th. Adorno, "Zum Verhältnis von soziologie und Psychologie," *op. cit.*, p. 21.
46. S. Freud, *G.W.*, vol. 8, p. 111.
47. S. Freud, *G.W.*, vol. 15, p. 160.
48. S. Freud, *G.W.*, vol. 11, pp. 322 ff.
49. S. Freud, *G.W.*, vol. 7.
50. S. Freud, *G.W.*, vol. 15, p. 185.
51. S. Freud, *G.W.*, vol. 11, pp. 450–451.
52. W. Jurinec, *op. cit.*, p. 112.

53. S. Freud, *G.W.*, vol. 14, p. 331.
54. S. Freud, *G.W.*, vol. 14, p. 333.
55. S. Freud, *G.W.*, vol. 14, pp. 463–464.
56. S. Freud, *G.W.*, vol. 14, pp. 326 ff.
57. F. Gantheret, "Freud und die gesellschaftlich-politische Fragestellung," in *Marxismus, Psychoanalyse, Sexpol*, vol. 2, *op. cit.*, p. 59.
58. F. Engels, "Ludwig Feuerbach und der Ausgang der klassischen deutschen Philosophie," MEW, vol. 21, pp. 282 and 297.
59. F. Engels, *ibid.*, pp. 281 ff.
60. I. Sapir, "Freudismus, Soziologie, Psychologie," in *Psychoanalyse und Marxismus, Dokumentation einer Kontroverse, op. cit.*, p. 164.
61. Max Eastman, quoted from J. C. Mariategui, "Freudismus und Marxismus," in *Psychoanalyse, Marxismus und Socialwissenschaften, op. cit.*, p. 164.
62. See note 58 above.
63. S. Bernfeld, *Socialismus und Psychoanalyse, op. cit.*, p. 50.
64. V. I. Lenin, *Über die Religion*, Berlin 1972, pp. 6 ff.
65. S. Freud, *G.W.*, vol. 15, pp. 175 ff.
66. H. J. Sandkühler, "Psychoanalyse und Marxismus," in *Psychoanalyse und Marxismus, Dokumentation einer Kontroverse, op. cit.*, p. 23.
67. H. Dahmer, "Psychoanalyse und Historischer Materialismus," in *Psychoanalyse als Sozialwissenschaft*, Frankfurt/Main 1971, p. 66.
68. C. Zetkin, *Ausgewählte Reden und Schriften*, vol. 3, Berlin 1960, p. 134. See also *Erinnerungen an Lenin*, Berlin 1967, pp. 62 ff.
69. P. Brückner, "Marx, Freud," in *Marxismus, Psychoanalyse, Sexpol*, vol. 2, *op. cit.*, p. 380.
70. A. Stoljarov, *op. cit.*, p. 308.
71. Also compare W. Reich, *Die sexuelle Revolution*, Frankfurt/Main 1966, part 2.
72. L. Trotsky, *Die verratene Revolution*, Frankfurt/Main 1966, pp. 150 ff.
73. H. J. Sandkühler, *op. cit.*, pp. 29–30.
74. Also compare E. Mandel, *Marxistische Wirtschaftstheorie*, Frankfurt/Main 1968, chapter 15: "Die Sovjetwirtschaft."
75. P. Brückner, *op. cit.*, pp. 380–381.
76. A. Stoljarov, *op. cit.*, p. 308.
77. H. J. Sandkühler, *op. cit.*, p. 30.
78. S. Freud, *G.W.*, vol. 15, p. 195.
79. K. Marx, *Das Kapital*, vol. 1, p. 514.
80. S. Freud, *G.W.*, vol. 14.
81. K. Marx, *Das Kapital*, vol. 1, p. 16.
82. I. Stalin, "Ökonomische Prozesse des Sozialismus in der UdSSR," quoted in O. Negt, Einleitung zu A. Deborin and N. Bucharin, *Kontroverse über dialektischen und mechanischen Materialismus*, Frankfurt/Main 1969, p. 42.
83. K. Marx and F. Engels, *Die Deutsche Ideologie*, MEW, vol. 3. p. 38.
84. Has been cut.
85. G. Lukács, *Geschichte und Klassenbewusstein*, Berlin 1923, p. 86.
86. G. Lukács, *ibid.*, p. 58.
87. G. Lukács, *ibid.*, p. 271.
88. G. Lukács, *ibid.*, p. 312.

89. G. Lukács, *ibid.*, p. 54.
90. G. Lukács, *ibid.*, p. 53.
91. G. Lukács, *ibid.*, p. 62.
92. H. Schnädelbach, "Was ist Ideologie?" in *Das Argument*, Nr. 50, Berlin 1970, Sonderband pp. 71 ff.
93. K. Horn, "Psychoanalyse—Anpassungslehre oder Kritische Theorie des Subjekts?" in *Marxismus, Psychoanalyse, Sexpol*, vol. 2, *op. cit.*, p. 137.
94. W. Reich, *Massenpsychologie des Faschismus*, Berlin 1968, second edition, Raubdruck.
95. L. Trotsky, *Literatur und Revolution*, Berlin 1968.
96. L. Trotsky, *Mein Leben*, Frankfurt/Main 1961, Kap.: "Die 2. Emigration und der deutsche Sozialismus."
97. L. Trotsky, *Der einzige Weg*, Berlin 1932, Raubdruck.
98. H. Lange, "Trotzki in Coyoacan," in *Theaterstücke 1960–72*, Reinbek 1973, p. 291.
99. Kollektiv Hispano Suiza, *Arbeiter und Apparate*, Berlin 1972, p. 158.
100. Anna Freud, *Das Ich und die Abwehrmechanismen*, München, no year.
101. G. Leistikov, "Ein Rufer in der Wüste und sein Ruf," in *Marxismus, Psychoanalyse, Sexpol, op. cit.*, vol. 1, p. 189.
102. W. Reich, *Massenpsychologie des Faschismus, op. cit.*, p. 32.
103. W. Pieck, quoted in R. Reiche, *Sexualität und Klassenkampf*, Frankfurt/Main 1971, p. 25 (footnote).
104. E. Fromm, "Über Methode und Aufgabe einer analytischen Sozialpsychologie," in *Analytische Sozialpsychologie und Gesellschaftstheorie*, Frankfurt/Main 1970.
105. S. Freud, *G.W.*, vol. 15, p. 73.
106. J. M. Brohm, "Psychoanalyse und Revolution," in *Marxismus, Psychoanalyse, Sexpol, op. cit.*, vol. 2, pp. 274 ff.
107. S. Freud, *G.W.*, vol. 15, pp. 73–74.
108. P. Brückner, *op. cit.*, pp. 388–389.
109. Also compare A. Rosenberg, *Die Geschichte der Weimarer Republik*, Frankfurt/Main 1961.
110. W. Reich (Parell), *Was ist Klassenbewusstsein*, Amsterdam 1968, p. 14.
111. E. Bloch, *Erbschaft dieser Zeit*, Frankfurt/Main 1962, pp. 149 and 153.
112. W. Reich, "Dialektischer Materialismus und Psychoanalyse," Anhang zu *Zur Anwendung der psychoanalyse in der Geschichtsforschung*, Berlin 1968, pp. 53–54.
113. W. Reich, *Der Einbruch der Sexualmoral*, Kopenhagen 1935.
114. W. Reich, *Charakteranalyse*, Köln 1970, p. 566.
115. W. Reich, *Die sexuelle Revolution*, Frankfurt/Main 1966, p. 26.
116. W. Reich, *Charaketeranalyse*, Kap.: "Die Widerlegung von Freuds Todestriebhypothese."
117. W. Reich, "Das Urgesetz des vegetativen Lebens," in *Zeitschrift für politische Psychologie und Sexualökonomie*, vol. 1, Kopenhagen 1934, p. 126.
118. W. Reich, *Die Funktion des Orgasmus*, Köln 1968, p. 202.

119. E. Ruebsam, "Der heilige W. Reich und sein Fetisch Genitalität," in *Das Argument*, Nr. 60, pp. 180 ff.
120. W. Reich, "Weitere Anmerkungen über die therapeutische Anwendung der Genitallibido," in *Internazionale Zeitschrift für Psychoanalyse, 1925,* p. 307.
121. H. Marcuse, *Triebstruktur und Gesellschaft,* Frankfurt/Main 1965, pp. 53–55.
122. H. Dahmer, *W. Reich—Seine Stellung zu Marx und Freud, op. cit.*, p. 95.
123. H. Dahmer, *ibid.*, p. 97.
124. W. Reich, *Die Funktion des Orgasmus, op. cit.*, p. 19.
125. H. Dahmer, *ibid.*, p. 87.
126. H. Dahmer, *Psychoanalyse und Historischer Materialismus, op. cit.*, p. 85.
127. W. Reich, *Massenpsychologie des Faschismus,* Köln 1971, pp. 23 and 30.
128. W. Reich, *ibid.*, p. 281.
129. E. Fromm, *Über Methode und Aufgabe einer analytischen Sozialpsychologie, op. cit.*, p. 34.
130. W. Reich, *Dialektischer Materialismus und Psychoanalyse, op. cit.*, p. 176.
131. W. Reich, *Massenpsychologie des Faschismus, op. cit.*, p. 22.
132. W. Reich, *Dialektischer Materialismus und Psychoanalyse, op. cit.*, p. 158.
133. W. Reich, *Anhang zu Dialektischer Materialismus und Psychoanalyse, op. cit.*, p. 46.
134. W. Reich, *ibid.*, p. 48.
135. H. Wieser and J. Beyer, *Kapitalmystifikation, Psychoanalyse und Ideologie, op. cit.*, p. 130.
136. Also compare M. Schneider, "Gegen den linken Dogmatismus, eine Alterskrankheit des Kommunismus," in *Kursbuch 25*, Berlin 1971.
137. Dante, *Divina Comedia,* Canto 7.
138. J. M. Brohm, *Psychoanalyse und Revolution, op. cit.*, p. 261.

Part Two: With Marx Against the Bourgeois Ideology of Psychoanalysis

1. K. Marx, MEW, *Erganzungsband,* First Part, pp. 542–543.
2. P. Brückner, *Marx, Freud* (see note 69, Part I), pp. 367 ff.
3. H. Dahmer, *Psychoanalyse und Historischer Materialismus* (see note 66, Part I), p. 87.
4. E. Wulf, "Psychoanalytische Herrschaftswissenschaft," in *Kursbuch* 29, Berlin 1972, p. 12.
5. R. Reiche, "Ist der Ödipuskomplex universell?" in *Kursbuch* 29, Berlin 1972, pp. 163–164.
6. D. Wyss, *Die tiefenpsychologischen Schulen von den Anfängen bis zur Gegenwart,* Göttingen 1970, third edition.
7. F. Nietzsche, *Werke in drei Bänden,* vol. 2, München 1954, p. 834.
8. S. Freud, *G.W.,* vol. 14, p. 493.
9. K. M. Michel, "Wer wann warum politisch wird—und wozu. Ein Beispiel für die Unwissenheit der Wissenschaft," in *Kursbuch 25*, Berlin 1971, p. 31.
10. H. Kurnitzky, *Versuch über Gebrauchswert,* Berlin 1970, p. 31.
11. S. Freud, *G.W.,* vol. 14, p. 473.

12. S. Freud, *ibid.*
13. H. Kurnitzky, *op. cit.*, p. 55.
14. I. Deutscher, "Die sozialistische Konzeption vom Menschen," in *Internationale Sozialistische Publikation*, p. 6.
15. H. Haseloff, "Zur Bedeutung soziologischer Denkweisen für die Psychoanalyse," in *Marxismus, Psychoanalyse und Sozialwissenshaften*, p. 244.
16. H. Haseloff, "Zur Soziologie psychoanalytischen Wissens," in *ibid.*, p. 47.
17. P. Brückner, *Marx, Freud, op. cit.*, p. 369.
18. H. Haseloff, *op. cit.*, p. 57.
19. A. Sohn-Rethel, *Geistige und körperliche Arbeit*, Frankfurt/Main 1970.
20. P. Brückner, *op. cit.*, p. 370.
21. G. Lukács, *op. cit.*, p. 110.
22. I. Althusser, *Freud und Lacan*, Berlin 1970.
23. K. Marx, *Das Kapital*, vol. 1, pp. 167 ff.
24. F. Engels, *Das Kapital von Marx*, MEW, vol. 16, p. 239.
25. E. Wulf, "Grundfragen transkultureller Psychiatrie," in *Das Argument*, Nr. 50, 1969, p. 245.
26. H. Ibsen, *Peer Gynt.*
27. B. Brecht, *Herr Puntila und sein Knecht Matti, G. W.*, vol. 4, Frankfurt/Main 1967, pp. 1676 ff.
28. I. Deutscher, "Die sozialistische Konzeption vom Menschen," *op. cit.*
29. Also compare W. Schöne, *Uber die Psychoanalyse in der Ethnologie*, Dortmund 1966.
30. S. Ferenczi, *Zur Ontologie des Geldinteresses*, pp. 109–119.
31. G. Rohheim, "La Psychologie racial et le capitalisme," in *PPsA*, Paris 1929, 1, pp. 122–149.
32. Also compare R. Reiche, "Ist der Öedipuskomplex universell?" *op. cit.* "*The controversy between Jones and Malinovsky*," p. 166.
33. S. Nacht, "Psychoanalyse und Ethnologie," in *Psychoanalyse, Marxismus und Sozialwissenschaften, op. cit.*, p. 375.
34. G. Eisermann, "Die soziologischen Beziehungen der Tiefenpsychologie," in *ibid.*, pp. 222–223.
35. K. Horney, *The Neurotic in Our Time*, 1937.
36. H. Marcuse, "Der Revisionismus in der Psychoanalyse," Anhang zu *Triebstruktur und Gesellschaft* (compare note 121, Part I).
37. R. Steigerwald, "Eine Kritik an H. Marcuses Schrift: Triebstruktur und Gesellschaft," in *Marxismus, Psychoanalyse, Sexpol, op. cit.*, vol. 2.
38. M. Foucault, *Psychologie und Geisteskrankheit*, Frankfurt/Main 1968, p. 46.
39. M. Foucault, *ibid.*, p. 45–46.
40. M. Foucault, *ibid.*, p. 35.
41. M. Foucault, *ibid.*, pp. 47–48.
42. M. Foucault, *ibid.*, p. 59.
43. M. Foucault, *ibid.*, p. 70.
44. I. Althusser, *Freud und Lacan, op. cit.*, p. 23.
45. I. Althusser, *ibid.*, p. 23.
46. I. Althusser, *ibid.*, p. 26.
47. I. Althusser, *ibid.*, p. 25–26.
48. I. Althusser, *ibid.*, p. 26.

49. I. Althusser, *ibid.*, p. 30.
50. A. Parsons, "Is the Oedipus Complex Universal? The Jones-Malinovski Debate Revised," in Anne Parsons, *Belief, Magic and Anomie*, New York 1969, p. 8.
51. R. Reiche, "Ist der Öedipuskomplex universell?" *op. cit.*, pp. 147 ff.
52. Parin, "Der Ausgang des ödipalen Konflikts in drei verscheidenen Kulturen," in *Kursbuch* 29, Berlin 1972, p. 186.
53. Parin, *ibid.*, p. 198.
54. Parin, *ibid.*, p. 183.
55. G. Lukács, *op. cit.*, p. 112.
56. *Balle, Malle, Hupe und Arthur, Berliner Reichskabarett* (Record), Verlag Wagenbach, Berlin 1972.
57. R. Reiche, *Was heisst proletarische Familie?*, unpublished manuscript, Frankfurt/Main 1971. pp. 8f.
58. Parin, *op. cit.*, p. 199.
59. I. Caruso, "Die psychoanalytische Situation als mikrosoziales Modell," in *Marxismus, Psychoanalyse und Sozialwissenschaften, op. cit.*, p. 20.
60. E. Hörnle, *Grundfragen proletarischer Erziehung*, Darmstadt 1969, p. 58.
61. S. Freud, *G.W.*, vol. 8, pp. 49–50.
62. W. Reich, *Dialektischer Materialismus und Psychoanalyse*, p. 158.
63. K. Marx, MEW, *Ergänzungsband*, First Part, p. 518.
64. E. Hörnle, *op. cit.*, p. 115.
65. E. Hörnle, *op. cit.*, p. 125 and p. 53.
66. Th. Adorno, "Zum Verhältnis von Soziologie und Psychologie," pp. 25–26 (compare note 29, Part I).
67. S. Freud, *G.W.*, vol. 15, p. 162.
68. S. Freud, *ibid.*
69. S. Freud, *G.W.*, vol. 14, p. 247.
70. K. Hartung and R. Wolff, "Psychische Verelendung und die Politik der Psychiatrie," in *Kursbuch* 28, Berlin 1972, p. 77.
71. F. Riemann, "Die Struktur des Analytikers und ihr Einfluss auf den Behandlungsverlauf," in *Fortschritte der Psychoanalyse*, vol. 1, Göttingen 1964, p. 160.
72. J. M. Brohm (compare note 106, Part I), *op. cit.*, p. 251.
73. J. M. Brohm, *op. cit.*, p. 252.
74. K. Hartung and R. Wolff, *op. cit.*, p. 71.
75. S. Freud, *G.W.*, vol. 16, p. 94.
76. S. Freud, *G.W.*, vol. 10, p. 319.
77. Thomas L., in "Auf der Couch (und dahinter)," *Kursbuch* 29, *op. cit.*, p. 92.
78. S. Freud, *G.W.*, vol. 5, p. 20.
79. K. Hartung and R. Wolff, *op. cit.*, p. 71.
80. K. M. Michel, "Auf der Couch (und dahinter)," *op. cit.*, p. 41.
81. S. Freud, *G.W.*, vol. 8, p. 464.
82. Thomas L., *op. cit.*, p. 94.
83. S. Freud, *G.W.*, vol. 12, p. 188.
84. S. Freud, as quoted in E. Jones, *Das Leben und Werk von Sigmund Freud*, vol. 3, p. 197.
85. K. Hartung and R. Wolff, *op. cit.*, p. 73.

86. K. Hartung and R. Wolff, *op. cit.*, p. 76.
87. I. Caruso, "Die psychoanalytische Situation als mikrosoziales Modell," *op. cit.*, p. 24.
88. K. Hartung and R. Wolff, *op. cit.*, p. 76.
89. R. Spitz, "Übertragung und Gegenübertragung," in *Psyche* 10, pp. 67 ff.
90. S. Freud, *G.W.*, vol. 8, p. 384.
91. Wolf D., in "Auf der Couch (und dahinter)," *op. cit.*, p. 80.
92. P. Watzlawick and others, *Menschliche Kommunikation*, Bern 1972, pp. 299 f.; quoted in K. M. Michel, "Auf der Couch (und dahinter)", *op. cit.*, pp. 59. ff.
93. J.-P. Sartre, "Der Narr mit dem Tonband oder die psychoanalysierte Psychoanalyse," in *Neues Forum*, Heft 192, 1969, pp. 705 ff.
94. S. Freud, *G.W.*, vol. 17, p. 103.
95. I. Caruso, "Psychoanalyse, Ideologie und Ideologiekritik," in *Marxismus, Psychoanalyse, Sexpol*, vol. 1, *op. cit.*, p. 62.
96. Elke L., in "Auf der Couch (und dahinter)," *op. cit.*, p. 84.
97. Elke L., *ibid.*, p. 87.
98. Elke L. *ibid.*, pp. 87–88.
99. S. Freud, *G.W.*, vol. 15, p. 101.
100. C. Lévi-Strauss, *Strukturale Anthropologie*, Frankfurt/Main 1967, pp. 222 ff.
101. N. O. Brown, "Psychoanalytische Therapie und Kultur," in *Psychoanalyse, Marxismus und Sozialwissenschaften, op. cit.*, pp. 38–39.
102. Elke L., *op. cit.*, p. 88.
103. N. O. Brown, *op. cit.*, pp. 41 and 43.
104. S. Freud, *G.W.*, vol. 17, p. 98.
105. N. O. Brown, *op. cit.*, p. 39.
106. Thomas L., *op. cit.*, p. 96.
107. Thomas L., *op. cit.*, p. 93.
108. K. M. Michel, "Auf der Couch (und dahinter)," *op. cit.*, p. 56.
109. Elke L., *op. cit.*, p. 86.
110. Ingrid B., in "Auf der Couch (und dahinter)," *op. cit.*
111. Thomas L., *op. cit.*, 91.
112. Thomas L., *op. cit.*, p. 89.
113. Thomas L., *op. cit.*, p. 93.
114. Wolf D., *op. cit.*, p. 78.
115. Thomas L., *op. cit.*, p. 94.
116. D. Rappaport, *Struktur der psychoanalytischen Theorie*, Stuttgart 1970.

Part Three: The Utilization of Capital and Psychic Impoverishment, or Society as Illness

1. P. Brückner, *Marx, Freud, op. cit.*, p. 362.
2. K. Marx, MEW, *Ergänzungsband*, First Part, pp. 541 ff.
3. P. Baran, "Persönlichkeit und Gesellschaft," in *Psychoanalyse, Marxismus und Sozialwissenschaften, op. cit.*, pp. 191 and 199.
4. S. Freud, *G.W.*, vol. 14, p. 505.
5. K. M. Michel, "Auf der Couch (und dahinter)," *op. cit.*, p. 99.

6. S. Freud, *G.W.*, vol. 14, p. 322.
7. K. Marx, *Das Kapital*, vol. 1, pp. 123–124.
8. K. Marx, *ibid.*, p. 52.
9. K. Marx, *ibid.*, p. 147.
10. W. F. Haug, *Zur Kritik der Warenästhetik*, Frankfurt/Main 1971, p. 148.
11. G. Lukács, *Geschichte und Klassenbewusstsein*, *op. cit.*, p. 105.
12. A. Sohn-Rethel, *Geistige und Körperliche Arbeit*, *op. cit.*
13. K. Marx, *Das Kapital*, vol. 1, p. 88.
14. K. Marx, *Grundrisse zur Kritik der Politischen Ökonomie*, *op. cit.*, p. 67.
15. K. Marx, *Das Kapital*, vol. 1, p. 164.
16. K. Marx, *ibid.*, pp. 91–92.
17. K. Marx, *Grundrisse . . .*, *op. cit.*, p. 135.
18. B. Brecht, *Die heilige Johanna der Schlachthöfe*, *G.W.*, Stücke vol. 2, p. 680.
19. Ovid, *Metamorphoses*, lib. 11, verses 102–163.
20. H. Kurnitzky, *Versuch über den Gebrauchswert*, *op. cit.*, p. 56.
21. K. Marx, *Grundrisse . . .*, *op. cit.*, p. 144.
22. *Die Erzählungen aus den Tausendun deine Nächten*, vol. 4, Wiesbaden 1953.
23. Dante, *Divina Comedia*, Canto 30.
24. K. Marx, *Das Kapital*, vol. 1, p. 147.
25. K. Marx, *Grundrisse . . .*, *op. cit.*, 134.
26. Dante, *Divina Comedia*, Canto 7.
27. S. Freud, *G.W.*, vol. 13, pp. 44–45.
28. H. Kurnitzky, *op. cit.*, p. 28.
29. B. Brecht, "Die Sieben Todsünden der Kleinbürger," in *Gedichte* 3, Frankfurt/Main 1961, p. 151.
30. R. Bastide, "Marxismus und Psychoanalyse," in *Marxisimus, Psychoanalyse und Sozialwissenschaften*, *op. cit.*, 166.
31. K. Marx, *Das Kapital*, vol. 1, p. 146.
32. G. Lukács, *op. cit.*, p. 107–108.
33. K. Marx, *Das Kapital*, vol. 1, p. 618.
34. K. Marx, MEW, *Ergänzungsband*, First Part, p. 556.
35. W. F. Haug, *op. cit.*, pp. 21–22.
36. K. Marx, *ibid.*, p. 555.
37. K. Marx, *Das Kapital*, vol. 1, p. 618.
38. Quoted in K. Marx, *ibid.*, p. 623.
39. K. Marx, *ibid.*, p. 93.
40. K. Marx, *ibid.*, p. 292. footnote 124.
41. R. Reiche, "Sexualität und Klassenkampf," Neue Kritik, 1968, p. 34.
42. M. Weber, *Die protestantische Ethik*, München und Hamburg 1965.
43. R. Reiche, "Ist der Ödipuskomplex universell?" *op. cit.*, pp. 169–170.
44. K. Marx, *Das Kapital*, vol. 1, p. 620.
45. K. Marx, *ibid.*, p. 618–620.
46. K. Marx, *ibid.*, p. 620.
47. H. M. Plato, *Das Subjekt und seine Bedürfnisse: Zur Problematik der Entfremdung und des Fetischismus bei Marx*, Diplomarbeit am Psychologischen Institut Berlin 1971, p. 67.

48. Quoted in K. Marx, *Das Kapital,* vol. 1, p. 291.
49. K. Marx, *Das Kapital,* vol. 1, p. 365.
50. K. Marx, *ibid.,* p. 447.
51. R. Reiche, *Sexualität und Klassenkampf, op. cit.,* p. 36.
52. B. Brecht, *Die heilige Johanna der Schlachthöfe, op. cit.,* p. 757.
53. S. Freud, *G.W.,* vol. 13, pp. 251 and 253.
54. Th. Adorno, "Zum Verhältnis von Soziologie und Psychologie," *op. cit.,* p. 17.
55. A. Sohn-Rethel, *op. cit.*
56. K. Marx, *Grundrisse . . . , op. cit.,* p. 74.
57. G. Lukács, *op. cit.,* p. 116.
58. F. Engels, quoted in W. Benjamin, *Charles Baudelaire—Ein Lyriker im Zeitalter des Hochkapitalismus,* Frankfurt/Main 1969, p. 127.
59. K. Marx, *Das Kapital,* vol. 1, p. 248.
60. Th. Adorno, *op. cit.,* p. 25.
61. G. Lukács, *op. cit.,* pp. 99–100.
62. G. Lukács, *ibid.,* p. 100.
63. Th. Adorno, *op. cit.,* pp. 20 and 25.
64. P. Baran, "Persönlichkeit und Gesellschaft," *op. cit.,* p. 197.
65. Quoted in D. Forte, *Martin Luther und Thomas Münzer: oder Die Einführung der Buchhaltung,* Berlin 1971, p. 25.
66. G. Lukács, *op. cit.,* p. 111.
67. SPK, *Aus der Krankheit eine Waffe machen,* Trikont 1972, p. 85.
68. R. Reiche, "Ist der Ödipuskomplex universell?" *op. cit.,* pp. 171–172.
69. S. Freud, *Traumdeutung,* Frankfurt/Main 1961, p. 491.
70. G. Lukács, *op. cit.,* p. 105.
71. S. Freud, quoted in H. Kurnitzky, *op. cit.,* p. 3.
72. Quoted in D. Forte, *op. cit.,* p. 25.
73. R. Reiche, "Was heisst proletarische Familie?" *op. cit.,* p. 26.
74. D. Cooper, *Psychiatrie und Antipsychiatrie,* Frankfurt/Main 1971, p. 11.
75. S. Freud, *G.W.,* vol. 13, p. 365.
76. W. Shakespeare, *A Midsummer Night's Dream.*
77. H. Lange, *Dramen über die Entstehung der Grundrente,* Rowohlt Verlag (to be published).
78. H. Lange, *ibid.*
79. H. Lange, *ibid.*
80. B. Brecht, *Herr Puntila und sein Knecht Matti, G.W.,* vol. 4, *op. cit.,* p. 1616.
81. B. Brecht, *Die heilige Johanna der Schlachthöfe, op. cit.,* p. 785.
82. K. Marx, MEW, vol. 4. p. 464.
83. R. Rosdolsky, *Zur Entstehungsgeschichte des Marxschens Kapitals, der Rohentwurf des Kapitals 1857/1858,* especially Parts 1–4, Frankfurt/Main 1969, p. 147.
84. K. Marx, MEW, vol. 13, pp. 34–35.
85. K. Marx, MEW, vol. 13, p. 22.
86. K. Marx, *Das Kapital,* vol. 1, pp. 107–108.
87. K. Marx, *ibid.,* vol. 2, p. 835.

88. K. Marx, *ibid.*, vol. 1, p. 562.
89. K. Marx, *Resultate des unmittelbaren Produktionsprozesses,* Frankfurt 1969, p. 47.
90. K. Marx, *Das Kapital,* vol. 3, p. 405.
91. K. Marx, *ibid.*, pp. 838–839.
92. Th. Adorno and M. Horkheimer, *Dialektik der Aufklärung,* Amsterdam 1947, p. 247.
93. K. Marx, *Das Kapital,* vol. 1, p. 247.
94. K. Marx and F. Engels quoting Feuerbach, in *Deutsche Ideologie,* Berlin 1960, p. 590.
95. P. Brückner, *Marx, Freud, op. cit.,* p. 363.
96. K. Marx. *Das Kapital,* vol. 1, p. 86.
97. V. I. Lenin, *Über die Religion, op. cit.*
98. K. Marx, *Das Kapital,* vol. 1, p. 89.
99. V. I. Lenin, *op. cit.*
100. S. Freud, *G.W.,* vol. 8, p. 54.
101. E Hörnle, *Grundfragen proletarischer Erziehung, op. cit.,* p. 42.
102. K. Marx and F. Engels, MEW, vol. 4, p. 478.
103. E. Wulf, *Grundfragen transkultureller Psychiatrie, op. cit.,* p. 250.
104. I. Sapir, "Freudismus, Soziologie, Psychologie," *op. cit.,* pp. 218–219.
105. R. Osborn, *op. cit.* p. 29.
106. *Marxismus, Psychoanalyse, Sexpol,* vol. 1, *op. cit.* p. 166.
107. Quoted in F. Engels, "Die Lage der arbeitenden Klasse in England," MEW, vol. 2, p. 389.
108. E. Bornemann, "Zur Analyse der Bandarbeit," in *Arbeitsphysiologie,* vol. 2, 1967, p. 31
109. E. Borneman, *ibid.,* p. 122.
110. T. Parsons, "Definition von Gesundheit und Krankheit im Lichte der Wertbegriff und der sozialen Struktur Amerikas," in A. Mitscherlich and others, *Der Kranke in der modernen Gesellschaft,* Köln/Berlin 1967, p. 59.
111. A. Mitscherlich, *Krankheit als Konflikt,* vol. 1, Frankfurt/Main 1966, p. 46.
112. A. Mitscherlich, *ibid.,* p. 9.
113. R. T. Collins in A Q. Maisel, *The Health of the People Who Work,* New York 1960, p. 125.
114. S. G. Rogg and C. A. D'Alonzo, *Emotions and the Job,* Springfield 1965, p. 72.
115. H. Levinson, *Men, Management and Mental Health,* Cambridge, Mass. 1962, p. 47.
116. A. de Veer, *Success and Failure in Industry: A Psychomedical Study,* Assen, The Netherlands 1955.
117. J. Gadourek, *Absences and Well-Being of Workers,* Assen, The Netherlands 1965.
118. A. Kornhauser, *Mental Health of the Industrial Worker,* New York 1965.
119. M. Planz, *Krankheit und sozialer Wandel,* Stuttgart, p. 165.
120. J. Roth, *Armut in der BRD,* Darmstadt 1971, p. 99.
121. K. Marx, MEW, *Ergänzungsband,* First Part, p. 514.
122. K. Marx, *Grundrisse . . . , op. cit.,* pp. 366 ff.

123. K. Marx, *ibid.*, p. 358.
124. K. Marx, *ibid.*, p. 387.
125. K. Marx, MEW, *Ergänzungsband*, First Part, p. 513.
126. K. Marx, *ibid.*, p. 514.
127. K. Marx, *ibid.*
128. K. Marx, *Das Kapital*, vol. 1, p. 328 ff.
129. G. Lukács, *op. cit.*, p. 110.
130. K. Marx, MEW, *Ergänzungsband*, First Part, p. 515.
131. K. Marx, *Das Kapital*, vol. 1, p. 382.
132. K. Marx, *ibid.*, p. 384.
133. K. Marx, *ibid.*, p. 38 .
134. G Lukács, *op. cit.*, p. 114.
135. G. Lukács, *ibid.*, p. 110.
136. K. Marx, *Das Kapital*, vol. 1, p. 383.
137. M. Foucault, *Psychologie und Geisteskrankheit*, *op. cit.*, p. 34.
138. J.-P. Sartre, *Kritik der Dialektischen Vernunft*, Reinbek 1967, p. 248.
139. P. Hülsmann, *Die berufstätige Frau, Arbeitsmedizinische Leitsätze*, Stuttgart 1962, p. 35.
140. P. Hülsmann, *ibid.*, p. 37.
141. Dr. Buckup in *Automation, Risiko und Chance*, vol. 1, p. 474.
142. J.-P. Sartre, *ibid.*, pp. 248 ff.
143. K. Marx, *Das Kapital*, vol. 1, p. 445.
144. P. Schneider, "Die Frauen bei Bosch," *Kursbuch* 21, Berlin 1970, p. 100.
145. G. Wallraff, quoted in E. Brechstein, *Die Sozialisation des Arbeiterkindes in Familie und Schule*, Freiburg 1971, Raubdruck, p. 30.
146. A. Mitscherlich, *Krankheit als Konflikt*, vol. 1, *op. cit.*, p. 95.
147. *Gesundheitsbericht der Bundesregierung vom 18. 12. 1970*, p. 85, quoted in J. Scholmer, *Die Krankheit der Medizin*, Neuwied 1971, p. 11.
148. J. Scholmer, *ibid.*, p. 13.
149. K. Marx, *Das Kapital*, vol. 1, pp. 445 ff.
150. Quoted in R. W. Charles, "Life in the Automatic Factory," in HBR, Jan./Feb. 1958, p. 112.
151. W. Rieland, *Fiatstriks, Massenkampf und Organisationsfrage*, München 1970, p. 9.
152. W. Rieland, *ibid.*, p. 12.
153. Kern und Schumann, quoted in Autorenkollektiv, Marxistische Arbeitsgruppe Historiker: *Schulungstext zur Kritik der Politischen Ökonomie*, West Berlin, pp. 158 ff.
154. Quoted in *Zentralblatt für Arbeitswissenschaaft und soziale Betriebspraxis*, Heft 1, 1960, pp. 1–4.
155. R. Reiche, *Sexualität und Klassenkampf*, Trikont, p. 71.
156. F. Vilmar and Symanowski, *Die Welt des Arbeiters: Junge Pfarrer berichten aus der Fabrik*, Frankfurt/Main 1963, pp. 52 ff.
157. F. Vilmar and Symanowski, *ibid.*, p. 53.
158. A. Brock and others, "Theorie und Praxis der Gewerkschaften, Themenkreis Betrieb 4." *Die Würde des Menschen in der Arbeitswelt*, Stuttgart 1969, p. 87.
159. M. Foucault, *op. cit.*, p. 81.

160. G. Wallraff, *Industriereportagen: Als Arbeiter in deutschen Grossbetrieben,* Reinbek 1970, p. 91.
161. M. Foucault, *op. cit.,* p. 81.
162. P. Schneider, "Die Frauen bei Bosch," *op. cit.,* p. 96.
163. P. Schneider, *ibid.,* p. 98.
164. Quoted in Autorenkollektiv, *op. cit.,* pp. 152 ff.
165. Quoted in *Sozialistisch Politik,* 1969, vol. 3, p. 27.
166. Quoted in A. Hell and H. Prine, *Wo lebt man besser?* Berlin, 1970, p. 30.
167. W. Gerns, "Bemerkungen zur Marxschen Theorie der Lage der Arbeiterklasse," in *Marxistische Blätter,* Sonderheft 2, 1967, p. 61.
168. T. Kieselbach and others, *Krankheit—ihre Beziehungen zur gesellschaftlichen Organisation der Arbeit und Klassenstruktur im Spätkapitalismus,* Psychologisches Institute der Universität Münster, p. 59.
169. T. Kieselbach, *op. cit.,* p. 59.
170. M. Pflanz, *Krankheit und sozialer Wandel, op. cit.*
171. J. Gadourek, *op. cit.*
172. A. Kornhauser, *op. cit.*
173. P. Schneider, "Die Frauen bei Bosch," *op. cit.,* p. 99.
174. Quoted in H. H. Abholz, "Die Rolle des industriellen Arbeitsplatzes für die Äetiologie psychicher Erkrankung," in *Das Argument,* Nr. 60, Sonderband, p. 145.
175. T. Ripke, "Warenproduktion, Kapitalismus und Gesundheitswesen," in *Das Argument,* Nr. 60, Sonderband, p. 48.
176. IZRU, "Zum Problem Widerstände, Die Sich Der Praktischen Kritik Entgegenstellen . . .," in *Kursbuch* 28, 1972, p. 122.
177. In Deutsche Bank, *Anlagestudie, Schweizer, Pharmazeutika,* 8, 1971.
178. SPK, *op. cit.,* p. 76.
179. F. C. Delius, *Unsere Siemens-Welt,* Berlin, *op. cit.,* p. 76.
180. E. Wulf, "Der Arzt und sein Geld," in *Das Argument,* Nr. 69, p. 960.
181. E. Wulf, *ibid.,* p. 961, footnote 9.
182. *Welt der Arbeit* of September 26, 1969.
183. IZRU, *op. cit.,* p. 123.
184. A. Castellina, *Norditalien I, Region im Umbruch,* WDR, 3, Program of February 9, 1971, quoted in Kieselbach, *op. cit.*
185. R. Reiche, "Was heisst proletarische Familie?" *op. cit.,* p. 6.
186. Ziff 1 in B. Brecht, *Flüchtlingsgespräche, G.W.,* vol. 14, p. 1504.
187. Ziffel, *ibid.,* p. 1502.
188. S. Freud, *G.W.,* vol. 13, p. 388.
189. S. Freud, *ibid.,* pp. 389–390.
190. Langner and Michael, *Life Stress and Mental Health: The Midtown Manhattan Study,* Glencoe 1963.
191. A. D. Hollinghead and F. C. Redlich, *Social Class and Mental Illness,* New York 1958.
192. W. Gottschalch, "Krankheit, Neurose, Psychose," in W. Gottschalch and others, *Sozialisationsforschung,* Frankfurt/Main 1971, p. 148.
193. M. N. Schönwetter, *Zur Schichtspezifischen Sozialisationsforschung,* in W. T. Gottschalch, *op. cit.,* p. 90.
194. M. N. Schönwetter, *ibid.,* p. 88.

195. M. N. Schönwetter, *ibid.*, p. 85.
196. E. Hörnle, *op. cit.*, p. 62.
197. M. N. Schönwetter, op. cit., p. 98.
198. E. L. Koos, "Krankheit in Regionville," in Mitscherlich and others, *Der Kranke in der modernen Gesellschaft, op. cit.*, pp. 304 ff.
199. E. L. Koos, *ibid.*, pp. 305 ff.
200. E. L. Koos, *ibid.*, p. 306.
201. E. L. Koos, *ibid.*, p. 307.
202. K. Hartung and R. Wolff, "Psychische Verelendung und die Politik der Psychiatrie," *op. cit.*, p. 29.
203. H. Berndt, "Zur Soziogenese psychiatrischer Krankheiten," in A. Mitscherlich and others, *Der Kranke in der Modernen Gesellschaft, op. cit.*, pp. 454–482.
204. K. Hartung and R. Wolff, *op. cit.*, p. 21.
205. K. Marx, MEW, vol. 1, p. 381.
206. S. Freud, *G.W.*, vol. 13, pp. 367–368.
207. K. Hartung and R. Wolff, *op. cit.*, p. 2.
208. K. Hartung and R. Wolff, *op. cit.*, p. 4.
209. K. Hartung and R. Wolff, *op. cit.*, p. 18.
210. K. Hartung and R. Wolff, *op. cit.*, p. 45.
211. T. Moser, *Repressive Kriminalpsychiatrie*, Frankfurt/Main 1971, p. 181.
212. K. Hartung and R. Wolff, *op. cit.*, p. 5.
213. K. Hartung and R. Wolff, *op. cit.*, p. 55.
214. K. Hartung and R. Wolff, *op. cit.*, p. 39.
215. K. Hartung and R. Wolff, *op. cit.*, p. 37.
216. D. Cooper, *op. cit.*, p. 36.
217. R. D. Laing, *Phänomenologie der Erfahrung*, Frankfurt/Main 1971, p. 110.
218. G. Vinnai, "Identitätszerstörung im Erziehungsprozess," in *Ästhetik und Kommunikation*, vol. 4, Reinbek, p. 31.
219. Quoted in J. Roth, *Armut in der BRD, op. cit.*, p. 104.
220. Faris and Dunham, *Mental Disorders in Urban Areas*, Chicago 1967, p. 98.
221. Leighton and others, *My Name Is Legion: Foundations for a Theory of Man in Relation to Culture*, New York 1959.
222. H. Häfner and others in *Sozialpsychiatrie*, Nr. 3, 1969, pp. 134 f.
223. K. Hartung and R. Wolff, *op. cit.*, p. 27.
224. H. J. Weitbrecht, *Psychiatrie im Grundriss*, Berlin 1963, p. 342.
225. K. Hartung and R. Wolff, *op. cit.*, p. 15.
226. K. Marx, *Das Kapital*, vol. 1, p. 361.
227. Quoted in A. Gorz, "Zur Lage der angelernten Arbeiter," in *Politikon*, 1972.
228. B. Rabehl and Heilmann, *Die Legende von der Bolschewisierung der KPD*, Berlin 1970, p. 74.
229. K. S. Weinberg (ed.), *The Sociology of Mental Disorders*, Chicago 1967, p. 98.
230. S. Leavy and L. Freedman, "Psychoneurosis and Economic Life," in S. Weinberg, *op. cit.*, p. 112.
231. S. Leavy and L. Freedman, *ibid.* p. 112.
232. K. Hartung and R. Wolff, *op. cit.*, p. 46.
233. S. Leavy and L. Freedman, *op. cit.*, p. 112.

234. Quoted in K. Hartung and R. Wolff, *op. cit.*, p. 61.

235. J. Roth, "Patientenselbstorganisation und Staatsapparat," in *Kursbuch* 29, Berlin 1972, p. 109.

236. T. Kieselbach, *op. cit.*, p. 71.

237. Clements and others, quoted in M. Bauer and M. Richartz, "Angepasste Psychiatrie als Psychiatrie der Anpassung," in *Das Argument*, Nr. 60, 1970, p. 153.

238. H. Paul "Psychische Gesundheit in der Industrie," Bericht von der 3. Jahrestagung der World Federation for Mental Health vom 31. 8—7. 9. 1950 in Paris, *Soziale Welt*, 1950/1951, vol. 2, pp. 100 ff.

239. IZRU, *op. cit.*, p. 153.

240. Quoted in J. Roth, *op. cit.*, p. 109.

241. Quoted in J. Roth, *ibid.*, p. 109.

242. Quoted in F. C. Delkus, *op. cit.*, p. 87.

243. F. Basaglia, *Die negierte Institution*, Frankfurt/Main 1971.

244. F. Basaglia, *ibid.*, p. 29.

245. Quoted in K. Hartung and R. Wolff, *op. cit.*, pp. 88–90.

246. Hamburger *Sonntagsblatt* of February 19, 1971.

247. According to *report* (ARD) of April 24, 1972.

248. Quoted in J. Neye, "Einige Gesichtspunkte zum Drogenkonsum und Kapitalismus unter besonderer Berücksichtigung psychotroper Substanzen," in *Arbeitspapiere zum Anti-Drogen-Kongress*, Hamburg March 18–19, 1972, *Konkret*-Sonderbroschüre, p. D-8.

249. B. Horisberger, "Untersuchungen über den Medikamentenmissbrauch in einem Grossbetrieb der Schweizerischen Uhrenindustrie," in *Schweiz. Med. Wschar.*, 1958, 88, pp. 920–926.

250. E. Parow, "Das Release-Konzept," Hamburg, in *Arbeitspapiere zum Anti-Drogen-Kongress, op. cit.*, p. C-22.

251. Protokoll der Arbeitsgemeinschaft für Wohlfahrtspflege in Berlin e. V. vom 3. 6. 1970.

252. M. Herzog, "Akkordarbeiterinnen bei AEG/Telefunken," in *Kursbuch* 21, Berlin 1970, pp. 115 ff.

253. J. Neye, *op. cit.*, p. D-6.

254. Quoted in J. Neye, *op. cit.*, p. D-17.

255. Quoted in J. Neye, *op. cit.*, p. D-15.

256. U. Ehebald, "Psychische und soziale Motivation zum Drogenkonsum," in *Arbeitspapiere zum Anti-Drogen-Kongress, op. cit.*, p. C-44.

257. U. Ehebald, *ibid.*, p. C-42.

258. W. F. Haug, *Kritk der Warenästhetik, op. cit.*

259. W. F. Haug, *ibid.*, p. 16.

260. W. F. Haug, *ibid.*, p. 27.

261. K. Marx, *Das Kapital*, vol. 1, p. 91.

262. W. F. Haug, *op. cit.*

263. R. Barthes, *Mythen des Alltags*, Frankfurt/Main 1964, p. 76.

264. O. Münzberg, unpublished manuscript, Berlin 1969.

265. W. F. Haug, *op. cit.*, p. 87.

266. H. M. Enzensberger, "Eine Theorie des Tourismus," in *Einzelheiten I*, Frankfurt/Main 1966, p. 203.

267. W. F. Haug, *op. cit.*, p. 127.

268. W. Alf, *Der Begriff des Faschismus und andere Aufsätze zur Zeitge-schichte*, Frankfurt/Main 1971, p. 23, footnote 17.
269. K. Marx, MEW, *Ergänzungband*, First Part, p. 547.
270. R. Reiche, *op. cit.*, p. 41.
271. R. Reiche, *ibid.*, p. 91.
272. S. Freud, *G.W.*, vol. 14, pp. 431 ff.
273. W. Benjamin, *Charles Baudelaire—ein Lyriker im Zeitalter des Hochkapital-ismus*, Frankfurt/Main 1969, p. 59.
274. W. Benjamin, *ibid.*, p. 58.
275. V. Packard, *Die Geheimen Verführer*, Düsseldorf, no year.
276. B. Brecht, quoted by R. Heuer, *Konkret*, September 1972.
277. R. Heuer, *ibid.*
278. R. Osborn, *op. cit.*, p. 161.
279. Mao Tse-tung, *Über den Widerspruch*, Verlag für fremdsprachige Literatur, Peking, *Ausgewählte Werke*, vol. 1, pp. 365 ff.
280. K. Marx, MEW, *Ergänzungsband*, First Part pp. 546 ff.
281. W. F. Haug, *op. cit.*, p. 157.
282. W. F. Haug, *ibid.*
283. R. Reiche, *Sexualität und Klassenkampf*, *op. cit.*, p. 104.
284. R. Reiche, *ibid.*, p. 107.
285. H. M. Plato, *op. cit.*, pp. 55 ff.
286. W. Benjamin, *Charles Baudelaire . . .*, *op. cit.*
287. Quoted in Walter Benjamin, *op. cit.*, p. 127.
288. B. Brecht, "Liebesunterricht," *G.W.*, vol. 10, p. 890.
289. W. F. Haug, *op. cit.*, p. 80.
290. K. Marx, MEW, *Ergänzungsband*, First Part, p. 540.
291. K. Marx, *ibid.*, p. 549.
292. R. Reiche, *op. cit.*, p. 91.
293. P. Schneider, "Die Kulturrevolution und das Schicksal der Phantasie im Spätkapitalismus," in *Kursbuch* 19, 1969, p. 14.
294. U. Ehebald, *op. cit.*, p. C-43.
295. W. F. Haug, *op. cit.*, p. 28.
296. S. Krakauer, *Die Angestellten*, Schriften, vol. 1., Frankfurt/Main 1971, pp. 222–224.
297. W. Reich, *Charakteranalyse*, *op. cit.* (Chapter: "Zür Erschütterung des narzisstischen Schutzpanzers."
298. W. F. Haug, *op. cit.*, p. 85.
299. W. F. Haug, *ibid.* p. 92.
300. Harriet Hubbard Ayer, quoted in Haug, *ibid.*, p. 95.
301. W. F. Haug, *ibid.*, p. 96.
302. R. Reiche, *op. cit.*, p. 95.
303. W. F. Haug, *op. cit.*, pp. 117–118.
304. Ray Bradbury, *Das Böse kommut auf leisen Sohlen*, 1969.
305. W. F. Haug, *op. cit.*, p. 98.
306. W. F. Haug, *op. cit.*, p. 150.
307. W. F. Haug, *op. cit.*, p. 121.
308. W. F. Haug, *ibid.*, p. 65.
309. Kadewe advertisement in *Tagesspeigel* of October 17, 1971.

Perspectives

310. J. Roth, *op. cit.*
311. *Dokumentation zum Sozialistischen Patientenkollektiv Heidelberg,* First Part, p. 1, Heidelberg 1972.
312. R. Reiche, Was heisste proletarische Familie?'' *op. cit.*
313. L. Magri, ''Der französische Mai und die Revolution im Westen,'' in *Sozialistisches Jahrbuch* 2, Berlin 1970, p. 53.
314. K. Marx, MEW, *Ergänzungsband,* First Part, pp. 539–540.
315. W. F. Haug, *op. cit.*, p. 66.
316. Compare also L. Magri, *op cit.*
317. Compare also ''Klassenkämpf · in Italien,'' in *Kursbuch* 26, Berlin 1972.
318. F. Böckelmann's *Die schlechte Aufhebung der autoritären Persönlichkeit,* Frankfurt/Main 1971, pp. 49 and 51.
319. A. Gorz, ''Revolutionäre Lehren aus dem Mai,'' in *Revolution in Frankreich,* Frankfurt/Main 1968, pp. 106 ff.
320. S. Freud (compare note 105, Part I).
321. R. Reiche, Vorwort für die Taschenbuchausgabe von *Sexualität und Klassenkampf,* Frankfurt/Main 1968, pp. 106 ff.
322. D. Fernbach, ''Sexualität und Revolution,'' in *Marxismus, Psychoanalyse, Sexpol,* vol. 2, Frankfurt/Main 1972, p. 299.
323. D. Fernbach, *ibid.*, p. 299.
324. Also compare M. Schneider, ''Die Woodstockgeneration,'' in *Konkret,* October 1971.
325. A. Mitscherlich, ''Protest und Revolution,'' in *Psyche* 7, 1970, p. 510.
326. M. Schneider, *op. cit.*
327. K. Marx, MEW, vol. 26, p. 111.
328. K. M. Michel, ''Wer wann warum politisch wird—und wozu. Ein Beispiel für die Unwissenheit der Wissenschaft,'' in *Kurbuch* 25, Berlin 1972, p. 32.

Appendix: The Frankfurt School

329. Th. Adorno, ''Zum Verhältnis von Soziologie und Psycholgie,'' *op. cit.*, pp. 20 and 22.
330. H. Dahmer, *Psychoanalyse und Historischer Materialismus, op. cit.*, p. 64.
331. H. Dahmer, *op. cit.*, p. 63.
332. H. Dahmer, *op. cit.*, p. 64.
333. K. Horn, *Psychoanalyse—Anpassungslehre oder Kritische Theorie des Subjekts, op. cit.*, p. 135.
334. K. Horn, *op. cit.*
335. H. Dahmer, *Wilhelm Reich—Seine Stellung zu Marx und Freud, op. cit.*
336. H. Dahmer, *Psychoanalyse und Historischer Materialismus, op. cit.*, p. 86.
337. H. Dahmer, *ibid.*, p. 70.
338. K. Horn, *op. cit.*, p. 144.
339. K. Horn, *op. cit.*, p. 135.
340. H. Wieser and J. Beyer (compare Part I), *op. cit.*
341. A. Lorenzer, ''Symbol, Interaktion und Praxis,'' in *Psychoanalyse als Sozialwissenschaft* (compare Part 1), *op. cit.*, pp. 43–44.
342. A. Lorenzer, *ibid.* p. 51.
343. E. Wulf, *Psychoanalyse als Herrschaftswissenschaft, op. cit.*, p. 5.

344. A. Lorenzer, *op. cit.*, p. 38.
345. A. Lorenzer, *ibid.*
346. A. Lorenzer, *op. cit.* p. 39.
347. A. Lorenzer, *op. cit.*, p. 40.
348. A. Lorenzer, *op. cit.*, p. 43.
349. A. Lorenzer, *op. cit.*, pp. 50–51.
350. A. Lorenzer, *op. cit.*, pp. 53–54.
351. A. Lorenzer, *op. cit.*, pp. 44–45.
352. A. Lorenzer, *op. cit.*, p. 54.
353. A. Lorenzer, *op. cit.*, p. 33.
354. A. Lorenzer, *op. cit.*, p. 32.
355. A. Lorenzer, *op. cit.*, p. 34.
356. A. Lorenzer, *op. cit.*, p. 55.